T0361107

The People Make the Place

Dynamic Linkages Between
Individuals and Organizations

LEA'S ORGANIZATION AND MANAGEMENT SERIES

Series Editors

Arthur P. Brief
University of Utah
James P. Walsh
University of Michigan

Associate Series Editor

Sara L. Rynes
University of Iowa

Ashforth (Au.) • Role Transitions in Organizational Life: An Identity-Based Perspective.

Bartel/Blader/Wrzesniewski (Ed.) • Identity and the Modern Organization.

Bartunek (Au.) • Organizational and Educational Change: The Life and Role of a Change Agent Group.

Beach (Ed.) • Image Theory: Theoretical and Empirical Foundations.

Brett/Drasgow (Eds.) • The Psychology of Work: Theoretically Based Empirical Research.

Chhokar/Brodbeck/House (Eds.) • Culture and Leadership Across the World: The GLOBE Book of In-Depth Studies of 25 Societies.

Darley/Messick/Tyler (Eds.) • Social Influences on Ethical Behavior in Organizations.

Denison (Ed.) • Managing Organizational Change in Transition Economies.

Dutton/Ragins (Ed.) • Exploring Positive Relationships at Work: Building a Theoretical and Research Foundation.

Earley/Gibson (Aus.) • Multinational Work Teams: A New Perspective.

Elsbach (Au.) • Organizational Perception Management.

Garud/Karnoe (Eds.) • Path Dependence and Creation.

Harris (Ed.) • Handbook of Research in International Human Resource Management.

Jacoby (Au.) • Employing Bureaucracy: Managers, Unions, and the Transformation of Work in the 20th Century, Revised Edition.

Kossek/Lambert (Eds.) • Work and Life Integration: Organizational, Cultural and Individual Perspectives.

Lampel/Shamsie/Lant (Eds.) • The Business of Culture: Strategic Perspectives on Entertainment and Media.

Lant/Shapira (Eds.) • Organizational Cognition: Computation and Interpretation.

Lord/Brown (Aus.) • Leadership Processes and Follower Self-Identity.

Margolis/Walsh (Aus.) • People and Profits? The Search Between a Company's Social and Financial Performance.

Messick/Kramer (Eds.) • The Psychology of Leadership: Some New Approaches.

Pearce (Au.) • Organization and Management in the Embrace of the Government.

Peterson/Mannix (Eds.) • Leading and Managing People in the Dynamic Organization.

Rafaeli/Pratt (Eds.) • Artifacts and Organizations: Beyond Mere Symbolism.

Riggio/Murphy/Pirozzolo (Eds.) • Multiple Intelligences and Leadership.

Schneider/Smith (Eds.) • Personality and Organizations.

Smith (Ed.) • The People Make the Place: Dynamic Linkages Between Individuals and Organizations.

Thompson/Choi (Eds.) • Creativity and Innovation in Organizational Teams.

Thompson/Levine/Messick (Eds.) • Shared Cognition in Organizations: The Management of Knowledge.

The People Make the Place

Dynamic Linkages Between
Individuals and Organizations

Edited by

D. Brent Smith

Psychology Press
Taylor & Francis Group
NEW YORK AND HOVE

Psychology Press
Taylor & Francis Group
711 Third Avenue
New York, NY 10017

Psychology Press
Taylor & Francis Group
27 Church Road
Hove
East Sussex BN3 2FA

Psychology Press is an imprint of the Taylor & Francis Group, an informa business

First issued in paperback 2012

© 2008 by Taylor & Francis Group, LLC
International Standard Book Number-13: 978-0-8058-5300-1 (Hardcover)
International Standard Book Number-13: 978-0-415-65254-4 (Paperback)

Except as permitted under U.S. Copyright Law, no part of this book may be reprinted, reproduced, transmitted, or utilized in any form by any electronic, mechanical, or other means, now known or hereafter invented, including photocopying, microfilming, and recording, or in any information storage or retrieval system, without written permission from the publishers.

Trademark Notice: Product or corporate names may be trademarks or registered trademarks, and are used only for identification and explanation without intent to infringe.

Library of Congress Cataloging-in-Publication Data

The people make the place : dynamic linkages between individuals and
    organizations / [edited by] D. Brent Smith.
       p. cm. -- (LEA's organization and management series)
    Includes bibliographical references and index.
    ISBN 978-0-8058-5300-1 (alk. paper)
    1. Schneider, Benjamin, 1938- 2. Corporate culture. 3. Organizational behavior. 4.
Personnel management. I. Smith, D. Brent.

HD58.7.P462 2008
302.3'5--dc22   2007044865

Visit the Taylor & Francis Web site at
http://www.taylorandfrancis.com

and the Psychology Press Web site at
http://www.psypress.com

To Ben

Contents

Series Preface

This book is a celebration of an intellectual life, that of Ben Schneider. We can think of no other industrial organizational psychologist who has helped us better understand how organizations tick. For example, Ben's attraction-selection-attrition theory and his extensive body of work on organizational climate are novel, provocative, compelling, and thus, have been tremendously influential.

The breadth of that influence is evident in this volume. Building upon Ben's scholarship, the authors of the chapters address such topics as: friendship clusters and climate schemas in organizations, the meaning of cognitive similarity in teams, the climate of the morally good corporation, and the conditions under which people do make the place. If you have not been a fan of Ben's work prior to reading this collection, you will be after. You're in for a treat! Correspondingly, we obviously are proud to have this book in honor of Ben in our series.

Arthur P. Brief
University of Utah

James P. Walsh
University of Michigan

1

The Person and the Situation

D. BRENT SMITH
London Business School

On May 29, 2004, friends, students, and colleagues of Ben Schneider gathered at the University of Maryland to pay tribute to his remarkable career (a career that is far from over). This book is the outcome of that gathering and the work of those impacted by both Ben's friendship and his scholarship. The chapters in this book represent updates to some of Ben's seminal work (e.g., on climate and the attraction-selection–attrition [ASA] model), extensions of his thinking into new areas (like ethics), and the occasional challenge to some of his original ideas (e.g., the role of situations as behavioral determinants). The chapters stand alone as significant contributions to our understanding of the psychology of work. At the same time, they reveal the substantial impact Ben has had on the field. My role has simply been to organize the papers into a book—a task made quite simple by the quality of the authors' work.

Before I provide a quick outline of the book, I feel it necessary to comment on my experiences with Ben. Ben has had a significant and lasting impression on my life. I am certain much deeper than he is aware.

In 1992, I had the good fortune to be admitted to the doctoral program in psychology at the University of Maryland, where I would spend the next five or so years of my life. I have often told students that I would have remained a doctoral student forever had it not been for two things: Ben Schneider and the meager pay (well, it seems meager now). We all know that pay is not a motivator; so, it certainly must have been Ben. In fact, I have no doubt it was. Where I am today is without question a debt I owe to Ben. His guidance and thoughtful mentorship steered me in directions I never intended to go. And I remain to this day ever grateful that he did.

I will forever remember my first meeting with Ben. I had just arrived at Maryland. Ben, unfortunately, was about to leave for a sabbatical in France and had asked to meet the new students prior to his departure.

During our brief conversation, he asked me what I wanted to do when I finished the program. I told him, with the assurance of someone who really had no idea what he wanted to do when he grew up, that I wanted to be a consultant specializing in assessment and selection. This was, after all, what I knew; I had worked for a consulting firm that did just this. Fortunately, Ben called me on the carpet and told me that, in fact, this was not what I wanted to do—I wanted to become an academic. In all honesty, I had really never considered that option (as I have never been particularly thoughtful about major life decisions—well, other than marriage). Nonetheless, I was struck by his quick reply. In retrospect, I am not sure if Ben was being sagacious or just indicating a preference for students to prepare themselves for an academic role even if they ultimately chose not to pursue it. After all, this perspective is one of the lasting impression's Ben made on me—you cannot divorce science from practice and you should never try. In the end, this initial interaction and my subsequent years with Ben led me to pursue an academic career, one that led me from Cornell to Rice and now to the London Business School. I cannot imagine any other career and have often wondered what might have happened had he not made that comment in our initial meeting.

Of course, steering me in the right direction also meant preparing me for the role. I had more than a few rough edges and a healthy dose of counterdependence, and on a couple of very important dimensions, I was Ben's complete antithesis (particularly when it comes to detail orientation and conscientiousness). The research might suggest that because of these differences, Ben would give me less time and attention than some of his other students. This was never the case, and although I occasionally drove Ben to his wit's end, he was (and is) endlessly gracious and willing to put in the time and effort necessary to nudge me in the needed direction. I have heard this sentiment from so many past students and junior faculty who have been impacted by Ben's encouragement. Of course, it should be noted that Ben is also quite capable of finding just the right moment to deliver an appropriate reprimand for misbehavior—and I put him in the position of doing this on more than one occasion. But the reprimand was always appropriate for the situation (and the person) and helped me understand the importance of accountability. Ben does not know this, but now that my time in the classroom is spent primarily with executives, he very frequently serves as the basis of the examples I use in corporate programs. Yes, I change the names and the context, but the examples of good management practice, particularly my examples of effective coaching and mentoring, often reflect my experiences with Ben. For me, he demonstrated himself to be the consummate mentor.

I mentioned in the beginning of this that I would have stayed a graduate student forever were in not for Ben. In fact, Ben was largely the reason I *would* have stayed a graduate student forever. The atmosphere (dare I say climate) he created at Maryland was very difficult to leave (and even harder for me to try to replicate). Of course, Ben will likely say that he inherited a terrific program from Jack Bartlett and Irv Goldstein, and no doubt this is true. But day to day it was Ben's influence (and the behaviors he rewarded, supported, and expected) that maintained the standards and norms of the group and made us all feel like colleagues with an important contribution to make. Ben certainly made the place. So, in the end, Ben was the reason I wanted to stay and the reason I left. For both, I am extremely grateful. I do hope, someday, to learn to be the kind of mentor Ben was for me. Fortunately, I have a great model to follow.

I should also mention that this book and, in particular, the list of authors were keenly influenced by Ben's colleagues at Maryland—Paul Hanges, Katherine Klein, and Michelle Gelfand. Appropriately representing Ben's work is no easy task. He has made such significant contributions to so many areas (human resources selection, service marketing, organizational climate) that we were concerned the book might appear somewhat fragmented. This turned out to be far from the case. In fact, the chapters here appropriately represent Ben's theme: It is the people in a situation that largely determine behavior in that setting and, subsequently, shape structure, climate, and culture.

The book is loosely organized in three sections. The first section updates and extends Ben's seminal work on the attraction–selection–attrition (ASA) model. Dickson, Resick, and Goldstein provide a review of recent literature supporting the original propositions in Ben's 1985 presidential address to the Society for Industrial and Organizational Psychology (SIOP) and offer guidance on yet to be explored areas. Jackson and Chung explore the contributions of ASA thinking to diversity research. Chatman, Wong, and Joyce focus their attention on the interactional underpinnings of the ASA model and occasionally challenge some of Ben's initial propositions regarding the role of people in creating the situation. Finally, Ployhart and Schmitt discuss the implications of the ASA model for staffing organizations. The second section examines the climate construct. Newman, Hanges, Duan, and Ramesh offer a network model of the origins of climates in organizations, while Rentsch, Small, and Hanges examine the role of cognitions and cognitive similarity in a climate. And finally, the third section offers applications of Ben's thinking to a variety of areas, some old and some new, including service (by Bowen), the "good" corporation (by Bradely, Brief, and Smith-Crowe), strategic human resources management (by Nishii and Wright), and a very creative chapter examining the impact of changing structures without changing people (by Wanous and Reichers). Lastly, Ben has graciously provided an integrative review to conclude the book. His chapter provides an outstanding overview of the themes in the book. It could be read as either an introduction or a conclusion.

2

Seeking Explanations in People, Not in the Results of Their Behavior
Twenty-Plus Years of the Attraction-Selection-Attrition Model

MARCUS W. DICKSON
Wayne State University

CHRISTIAN J. RESICK
Drexel University

HAROLD W. GOLDSTEIN
Baruch College, CUNY

> Enough is enough. We are psychologists and behavioral scientists; let us seek explanations in people, not in the results of their behavior. The people make the place.
>
> —*Ben Schneider, presidential address to SIOP, August 24, 1985*

Ben Schneider's presidential address to the Society for Industrial and Organizational Psychology (SIOP) in 1985 was not the first time that he had presented the attraction–selection–attrition (ASA) framework—he had previously published articles presenting the model and had described it at some length (e.g., Schneider, 1983). But the presidential address, and especially the classic 1987 article that grew from that address, is often described as the starting point for ASA research, probably because of the clarity with which the model was presented, the wide industrial and organizational (I–O) audience it reached, and the passion that Ben showed in presenting his argument that "the people make the place."

We are pleased to have the honor of writing the overview chapter for this festschrift book celebrating Ben Schneider's work and the contributions of ASA to the fields of industrial/organizational psychology and organizational behavior. We do not intend here to provide an exhaustive literature review related to ASA; as of this writing, Web of Science reports that "The People Make the Place" has been cited in more than 500 published articles and chapters, and an exhaustive review is well beyond the scope of this chapter (however, see Kristof-Brown, Zimmerman, & Johnson, 2005, for an excellent meta-analysis of the related person–environment [P–E] fit literature). Instead, we will review the components of the ASA model and briefly discuss research supporting each component of the model separately, and then as a whole. We will discuss areas beyond the workplace where the "homogeneity hypothesis"—the idea that over time organizations come to comprise increasingly homogeneous groups of people—has taken root. Finally, we will discuss some potential boundary conditions to ASA and highlight some future research opportunities related to the model.

THE ASA MODEL

ASA as it was originally proposed was generally referred to as a model rather than a theory. Over time, and especially after the 1995 update article by Schneider, Goldstein, and Smith, ASA was more often referred to as a theory. Clearly, ASA is better developed and understood today—and is more complex today—than when it was first proposed. This can be seen more clearly in a review of each of the components of the ASA model and of recent research related to those components.

The ASA model begins with a simple but important observation about how organizations differ from more artificial research settings like social–psychological laboratories. Simply put, and as we have often heard Ben say, people are not randomly assigned to organizations. They go through a variety of processes on the way to organizational membership, and these processes have some predictable influences on the type of people who ultimately end up as members of any given organization. Further, organizations are significantly affected by the characteristics of the organizational founder and other organizational leaders, who create organizations in their own images through the people they seek out and the structures they enact, thus leading to the creation of a culture that appeals to certain types of people.

Schneider was certainly not the first to discuss the fact that people tend to seek out environments where there are similar others. The Hebrew writer Jesus the son of Sirach of Jerusalem wrote in about 200 B.C.E. that "birds resort unto their like: so truth will return to them that practice her" (Ecclesiasticus 27:10)—the earliest known phrasing of the aphorism "Birds of a feather flock together." Schneider was also not the first to focus on the importance to the organization of selecting individuals who will fit into their assigned positions—Plato discussed this aspect of fit in *The Republic* (Tinsley, 2000), and the Chinese imperial government had established civil service examinations to match people with jobs almost 2,000 years ago (Binning, Adorno, & LeBreton, in press). Schneider was not even the first to talk about this process in a psychological or organizational framework—Parsons' (1909) discussion of vocational choice focused on individuals finding appropriate professions for themselves (professions that would suit their personal characteristics), and the question of how individuals' seek environments help or hinder them in fulfilling their physical and psychological needs (e.g., jobs where they will fit) can be traced at least back to Murray's (1938) need–press theory (Kristof, 1996).

What Schneider *did* do was recognize the organizational implications of lots of individuals all seeking organizations where they would fit, and of lots of organizations seeking employees who would fit, and of people who decide they do not fit, leaving in order to find better fit elsewhere—over time, organizations would come to be filled with increasingly similar, or homogeneous, employees. Schneider then talked about the importance of the founder and other leaders in establishing what type of homogeneity would be in their organization and the human resource systems and processes put in place that would facilitate this move toward homogeneity. Schneider was generally operating in descriptive, rather than prescriptive, mode. He never said that the tendency to homogeneity was a morally good or bad thing; he simply said that homogeneity occurs, that it can have differential impact in different organizational environments, that organizations need to be aware of it, and that they perhaps can manage it.

In this chapter, we will discuss each of the three components of the ASA model in turn, along with a brief discussion of organizational socialization, which helps to smooth the rough edges of fit. We start with a discussion of what Schneider refers to as attraction—the process by which certain individuals are drawn to seek out employment at certain organizations.

Attraction

Out of the total range of possible organizations from which people could seek employment, each individual selects only certain organizations to which to apply. Clearly, people apply to those organizations that offer employment within their chosen field—psychologists do not typically apply for positions with particle physics laboratories, for example. Holland's work on vocational choice and the RIASEC model (e.g., Holland, 1973, 1997) addresses this process, and it clearly implies that people who share certain work values and interests are likely to be congregated in certain professions. Research by others has supported Holland's model, and thus the attraction proposition of ASA. For example, Boone, van Olffen, and Roijakkers (2004) recently demonstrated that people of similar personality types were likely to be congregated in specific areas of study in school. Thus, the people who would be professionally qualified to apply for a job within a specific job class or industry are likely to share at least some characteristics. Along these same lines, Allen (1998) assessed the extent to which differences between graduate students in library science and in organizational behavior could be explained by ASA theory, and concluded that the values of these two groups of preprofessionals differed significantly, with the future librarians much more likely to value reflectiveness, information sharing, and having a clear guiding philosophy, and the future business professionals much more likely to value aggressiveness, competitiveness, and achievement orientation.

Beyond broad fit with one's chosen profession, Schneider argues, people will seek out employment opportunities in organizations that they believe hold values similar to their own. Applicants base these decisions on a variety of factors, including their perceptions of the organization based on ads announcing vacancies, advertisements for the organization's products or services, and their own experience with the organization during the hiring and interviewing process (e.g., Boswell, Roehling, LePine, & Moynihan, 2003).

Though fit perceptions could be based on a wide variety of factors, a great deal of the research conducted to date has focused on applicant personality and personal values, with less research on other types of individual difference characteristics. This is at least partly due to the emphasis on values in theoretical work on person–organization (P–O) fit. Kristof-Brown et al. (2005, p. 285) note: "Chatman's (1989) seminal theory of PO fit focused attention primarily on values. With the subsequent validation of the Organizational Culture Profile (O'Reilly, Chatman, & Caldwell, 1991), a values-based instrument, value congruence became widely accepted as the defining operationalization of PO fit." Indeed, there are a great many studies that have focused on values congruence as predictors of person–organization fit (e.g., Cable & Edwards, 2004; Chatman, 1991; Judge & Cable, 1997; O'Reilly et al., 1991), though the majority of these have addressed in-job fit, as opposed to a priori assessments by job applicants about the degree of values congruence that exists with a potential employer. Nonetheless, it is clear that during the application and interview process, candidates are seeking fit on a variety of dimensions.

Other research has shown that organizational attraction is driven not only by values similarity, but also by factors related to personality. For example, Judge and Cable (1997) surveyed students who were actively seeking employment in their preferred fields (business, engineering, or industrial relations). Their survey focused on personality, as well as characteristics of organizational cultures that the respondents most preferred. Results showed that the Big 5 personality dimensions (conscientiousness, agreeableness, neuroticism, openness to experience, and extraversion) predicted preferences for aspects of organizational cultures in ways that made conceptual sense. For example, they hypothesized and found that respondents who were high on the personality dimension of agreeableness preferred organizations that were supportive or team oriented, and did not prefer organizations that were aggressive, outcome oriented, or decisive. However, the authors do note that overall, the relationships were somewhat weaker than expected.

Similarly, Lievens, Decaesteker, Coetsier, and Geirnaert (2001) found that individual personality characteristics were valid predictors of the type of organization to which the individual was most attracted. As one example of this finding, participants in the Lievens et al. study (who were upper-level undergraduates presented with hypothetical scenarios about prospective employers) who were high on *openness to experience* showed a stronger attraction toward multinational organizations than did their low-openness colleagues.

Other individual differences besides the Big 5 personality traits and personal values can also influence the perceived attractiveness of an organization. As with the Big 5 personality results, these findings are generally conceptually clear and not difficult to interpret. For example, Turban and Keon (1993) found that participants with high levels of need for achievement preferred organizations that rewarded performance, while those lower on this dimension were more attracted to organizations rewarding seniority. In the same study, these authors found that those with high self-esteem were more attracted to firms that were smaller and less centralized than were their low self-esteem counterparts.

Turban, Lau, Ngo, Chow, and Si (2001) assessed the workplace preferences of employees in the People's Republic of China and found that while most employees had a preference for foreign-owned rather than state-owned firms, that preference was reversed for respondents who were high on risk aversion, and also for respondents who had a lower need for pay. This raises an interesting question, of course, regarding the potential for values and other characteristics to conflict—foreign-owned firms almost always pay more than state-owned firms in the People's Republic of China, but those people who had less need for pay preferred state-owned firms. Though we will focus on boundary conditions of ASA later in this chapter, this situation perhaps implies a boundary condition—those people who have the luxury of adhering to their values when seeking employment do so (i.e., those who did not need the higher pay provided by foreign-owned firms could choose to work for state-owned firms), while others with greater immediate need do not (i.e., those needing higher pay will seek it, despite potential values misfits with the organization—a point we return to later in this chapter when discussing economic conditions as a boundary condition of ASA). Of course, this is speculation, as no data on the participants' belief in communism or in the state were collected (and in all likelihood, such data could not have been collected). Nonetheless, it raises interesting questions about which individuals' behaviors are most likely to be described accurately by the ASA model and its propositions.

The studies described above bring to light the issues as to what matters more—congruence between individual and organization in terms of values (what several researchers [e.g., Caplan, 1987; Edwards, 1991; Kristof, 1996] refer to as needs–supplies fit) or the degree to which a person receives what he or she needs psychologically from the organization (referred to as supplementary fit [e.g., Chatman, 1989]). The relative influence of personality, values, and other individual differences remains a point of much investigation in the P–E fit and organizational attractiveness literatures, though Kristof-Brown et al. (2005) and Cable and Edwards (2004) both find that work attitudes (including desire to remain with the organization) are affected to roughly equal degrees by the degree of values congruence between employee and organization, and by the degree of psychological need fulfillment provided by the employment situation.

Finally, this process of organizational attraction also occurs across organization types; it is not limited only to the traditional for-profit sector. One interesting example comes from Burnett, Vaughan, and Moody (1997), who matched the values profiles of nine sororities (based on member survey responses) to the values preferences of sorority pledges and found that the pledges were most attracted to—and if given a bid, joined—sororities whose values matched their own.

All of this research paints a similar picture—the range of possible human variation that could exist in a given organization's potential applicant pool is restricted based on personal values, personality, and other individual characteristics of the people who choose to enter a profession and apply or not to apply for a specific job opening. As Schneider has noted, this is the first decision point in a process leading to increasing organizational homogeneity.

Selection

Just as individuals seek out organizations in which they will fit, organizations seek employees who will fit with the existing culture and other employees, as well as employees who will fit the organization in terms of providing the knowledge, skills, abilities, certifications, and so forth, that the organization needs. Thus, Schneider argues (1983, 1987a; Schneider, Goldstein, & Smith, 1995), selection is a second decision point at which the possible range of variability in employee characteristics narrows.[1]

One of the questions that is central to the selection aspect of ASA is whether organizations are actually capable of assessing fit a priori. In other words, if organizations hire based on their expectation of employees' fit with the organization, but those expectations are inaccurate, then the whole homogeneity hypothesis and reduction in variation process has to be reconsidered. However, Parsons, Cable, and Wilkerson (1999) found that recruiters using a standard question-and-answer interview format were able to accurately assess candidates' personal values as reported in their completion of the Organizational Culture Profile. Additionally, Cable and Judge (1997) found that recruiters were accurate in assessing the values congruence of applicants with their respective organizations' values. Further, they found that the recruiters' assessments of candidate values congruence carried significant weight in the ultimate hiring decisions made by their organizations. Likewise, Kristof-Brown (2000) also found that recruiters' perceptions of an applicant's fit with the organization were related to hiring recommendations. Thus, the evidence suggests that organizations can accurately assess the personal values of applicants, can accurately assess the degree to which applicants' values are congruent with those of the hiring organization, and do use this information in making hiring decisions.

Using a somewhat less direct assessment of the selection component of ASA, Giberson, Resick, and Dickson (2005) surveyed CEOs of 32 organizations, along with up to 30 subordinates in each organization for whom the CEO played a role in their hiring. The researchers found consistent congruence between leaders' and subordinates' personality and values characteristics. Moreover, they found that the exact characteristics upon which leaders and members were similar differed across organizations. In other words, different organizations had different perceptions of the "right type" and seemingly sought people who fit that type. This result echoes that of Van Vianen and Kmieciak's (1998) study of organizational recruiters, in which they found that recruiters clearly have in mind and pursue what they think of as right types, but only for certain dimensions of personality, and that these dimensions are not consistent across recruiters from different organizations.

Indeed, the literature is clear that both vocational interests/values (most often assessed by Holland's RIASEC model) and personality (most often assessed in a Big 5 framework) play a role in the employment decisions made by applicants and employers. Research by De Fruyt and Miervielde (1999) led them to conclude that "both models can be easily tied into Schneider's ASA framework, with the RIASEC model describing the attraction side and the FFM the selection component" (p. 724). In their study, 934 senior college graduates in various subjects completed both the NEO a measure of the Big 5 personality traits) and the Holland Self-Directed Search (a measure of personal career type preferences). One year later, the respondents described their labor market position and jobs, using the Position Classification Inventory. Not surprisingly, respondent personality traits of extraversion and conscientiousness predicted whether the person was employed. However, respondent vocational interests and values predicted the *nature* of their employment, above and beyond what could be predicted by the various personality dimensions.

Thus, both applicant personality and personal values, interests, and motives play a role in determining the positions to which applicants are attracted, and the candidates that employers select into the selection system. Interestingly, however (and somewhat ironically), it appears that when the sort of formal job analytic model typically employed by I–O psychologists is used, there is less opportunity for personality traits, values, interests, and motives that are not explicitly job relevant to come into play in selection. This would likely reduce the influence of the selection aspect of ASA in creating homogeneity. On the other hand, many competencies captured in a job analysis could arguably be considered as reflecting aspects of personality and values (e.g., personal integrity, valuing diversity), and thus the selection systems designed to measure such competencies could facilitate the selection proposition of ASA. This question remains ripe for future research.

Attraction and Selection as Overlapping and Simultaneous Processes.   As we mentioned at the outset of describing the ASA model, the delineation among the attraction, selection, and attrition stages is not nearly as clear-cut as the model implies. This is particularly true of the attraction and selection phases. Attraction manifests with the initial decision to apply for a position, continues through a hiring process that could include multiple interviews and assessments, and concludes with a decision to accept or reject a job offer if one is received. Overlapping this attraction phase is selection, in which the organization first selects an applicant as a potential candidate for the position, and then continues to select (or not select) the applicant through the series of interviews and assessments. At any point in what could be a lengthy process, the candidate could opt out and no longer pursue the organization, or the organization could opt out and no longer pursue the applicant. The former would be attributed to attraction, and the latter to selection, even though they can occur simultaneously (see Figure 2.1). In addition, the two processes are also arguably interactive. For example, interviews of candidates, ostensibly for the purpose of selection, often become at least in part recruiting efforts, and thus would be more related to the attraction phase. Additionally, during the selection process, if members of an organization feel a strong desire to hire an individual that they feel fits the organization, they may exhibit behaviors and take actions that attempt to further attract the individual. Similarly, if during the selection process, the individual feels more attraction to the organization based on the staffing experience, the individual may engage in more active impression management and increase efforts to display relevant skills and competencies so that the organization will select him or her. Better clarity about the iterative nature of attraction and selection would be beneficial for understanding the homogenization process.

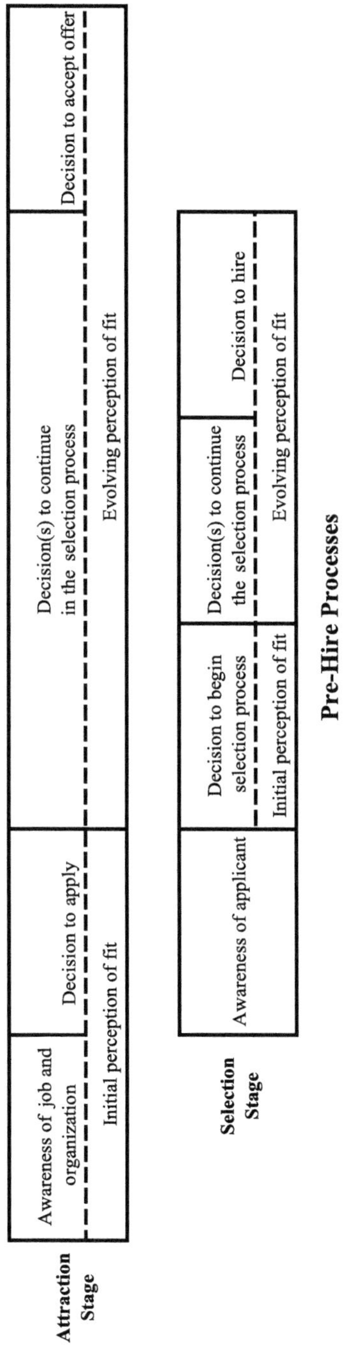

Pre-Hire Processes

FIGURE 2.1

Attrition

ASA suggests that there are many reasons why employees would want to look for new employment opportunities, but emphasizes that employee perception of poor fit with the organization is one of those reasons. Schneider has pointed out many times that when employees leave an organization because of bad fit, they do not simply go into limbo—they leave in order to seek out better fit elsewhere.

The amount of research on actual employee turnover (i.e., attrition) is relatively small compared to the volume of research on employee attraction and organizational selection. One reason for this is that it is quite difficult to acquire accurate data from people who have actually left an organization—exit interviews and surveys have been shown for years to have questionable validity, at best (e.g., Giacalone, Knouse, & Montagliani, 1997; Lefkowitz & Katz, 1969), and post-termination follow-up interviews are notoriously difficult to carry out. Thus, much of the research related to the attrition stage of the ASA model has been based on employees' reported intention to quit, rather than on actual turnover.

Lauver and Kristof-Brown (2001) examined two specific aspects of fit and how they related to turnover intentions. Specifically, they examined person–organization fit and person–job fit, and concluded that both sets of fit perceptions accounted for unique variance in the prediction of turnover intentions, with person–organization fit accounting for more variance than person–job fit. This highlights the multifaceted nature of fit perceptions, and the differing roles that various facets of fit can have in the ASA process.

As noted earlier, Holland's work on vocational preferences focused on personality and values as predictors of the profession for which an individual would be best suited. Schneider has argued that sometimes people find they have "made a mistake" in their choice of job or profession, and thus leave in search of better fit elsewhere. Thomas, Benne, Marr, Thomas, and Hume (2000) examined this aspect of attrition from (along with attraction to) coursework required for a career in engineering based on personality type, and found that certain personality types were likely to remain in the field, while others who had started professional training were likely to abandon their training. Using the Myers-Briggs Type Indicator (MBTI) as the personality measure, Thomas and colleagues found that Introverted Judgers (IJs) and Introverted Intuitives (INs) are most likely to persist in engineering, while Sensing Perceivers (SPs) and Extroversion, Intuition, Thinking, Perceiving (ENTP) and Extroversion, Intuition, Feeling, Perceiving (ENFP) types are most likely to leave their engineering education. Interestingly, MBTI type did not predict performance in the course, which is explained by the authors as resulting from the restriction of range occurring as a result of ASA processes.

In one of the earlier studies to explicitly incorporate ASA into its hypotheses, Jackson et al. (1991) examined the importance of "interpersonal context," which they operationalized at the individual level as dissimilarity from the mean and at the group level as group heterogeneity, on seven variables: age, tenure, education level, curriculum, alma mater, military service, and career experiences. Analyzing a 4-year data set of 93 top management teams in bank holding companies, they found that it was possible to predict which individuals would turn over based on their dissimilarity with the other members of their team. Further, the team turnover rate was predictable based on the level of heterogeneity on the seven variables within the top management team. Finally, they showed that holding companies that primarily recruited internally ended up with higher levels of homogeneity in the top management team later on, lending further support to ASA predictions about fit and the homogeneity hypothesis.

Agius, Arfken, Dickson, Mitchelson, and Anderson (2005) looked at issues of attraction and attrition in a sample of substance abuse treatment clinics (an industry noted for its typically high levels of turnover; e.g., McLellan, Carise, & Kleber, 2003). Clinicians in 15 substance abuse treatment clinics were surveyed over a period of 3 years, recording which clinicians were consistent in the sample, which were new in the sample, and which left the sample. At the organization level, Agius et al.'s results showed that there was little consistency in the demographic characteristics of new clinicians, but that there was moderate consistency in the substance abuse treatment-related values. Further, the values of the new clinicians were similar to those held by the clinicians who remained in the sample. Finally, those leaving their respective organizations shared little in common other than their dissimilarity to both the clinicians remaining in the respective organizations and the clinicians joining those organizations.

Finally, it is important to recognize that of course not all attrition is due to poor fit. In fact, the ASA model would suggest that of attraction, selection, and attrition, attrition due to fit issues should have the smallest effect on the level of homogeneity in the organization because attrition due to poor fit should only occur if both the employee and the organization had made errors in assessing the potential fit in the first place, if the organization's circumstances had changed leading to a change of fit, or if the person changed in some way leading to a change in the level of fit. In addition, it is important to realize that attrition is also a two-way street. That is, not only can an individual choose to leave because of poor fit, but also an organization can choose to fire an individual for poor fit, not just poor performance. There is to date very little research on all of these issues.

Tests of Multiple Aspects of the Model

One of the potential criticisms of the ASA model and theory is that it is difficult to test all of the components of the model in one study; indeed, most of the ASA research to date has focused on one or at most two of the components of attraction, selection, and attrition. Further, in the majority of cases, the research has been cross-sectional rather than longitudinal, as is really required in order to test the model's hypotheses about increasing homogeneity over time.

The only study we are aware in which all three of the components of ASA were tested longitudinally was conducted by Jonathan Ziegert (under the supervision of Ben Schneider) as his master's thesis research at the University of Maryland. Ziegert and Schneider (2001) examined the sorority rush process, gathering personality and values data from the women rushing sororities and from the sisters who were already members of the various sororities. They found that personality congruence played the major role in sororities' early identification of rushees to consider and in rushees' early identification of sororities to consider. However, later in the rush cycle, when final offers of membership were made and accepted, values congruence played a greater role than did personality congruence. Finally, in a 2-year follow-up, they found that of the women who did pledge a sorority, those with the greatest values discrepancy compared to the other sorority sisters were most likely to have dropped out of the sorority, lending further support to the attrition aspect of the ASA model.

Does the Proposed Homogeneity Occur?

The research discussed to this point has focused on the various processes included within the ASA model, particularly addressing the implications of P–O fit. However, Schneider (1987a) proposed the ASA model to understand and predict the behavior of organizations, not individuals. These processes were presented to explain how organizational cultures, climates, styles, and effectiveness are a reflection of the people who work there. As such, the ASA framework research supporting the individual processes is really all moot if the homogeneity proposed by the ASA model cannot be demonstrated to actually occur. Fortunately, research has begun to focus explicitly on that question.

Ostroff and Rothausen (1997) were among the first to address the notion of organizational homogeneity by examining employee tenure in 29 secondary schools. Among a sample of teachers they found that organizational tenure had a moderating effect on the relationship between personal characteristics and environmental characteristics, such that the teachers who were newer (i.e., had lower tenure) fit the schools' climates less well than did those teachers who had been there longer (i.e., had higher tenure). One possible explanation is that those with higher tenure had changed over time to become more congruent with the school climate. Conversely, those teachers with higher tenure may have always fit the school climate and decided not to move on because of their fit. Either way, homogeneity increased as tenure increased, and thus the results provide indirect support for the homogeneity hypothesis. However, the underlying causal processes are uncertain.

Schaubroeck, Ganster, and Jones (1998) also provide indirect support for the development of organizational homogeneity. In a multiorganization study, they found that personality characteristics of the organization members could be predicted by the respondents' organizational membership and the characteristics of the occupations they held. Finally, Denton's (1999) test of the homogeneity hypothesis focused on the question of whether personality of group members becomes more homogeneous as organizational tenure increases. The sample included managers of retail stores. The results showed that, in fact, variance on personality measures decreased as organizational tenure increased, though the results (based on an n of 87) were not statistically significant. At the store level of analysis, however, the homogeneity hypothesis was clearly supported.

The first direct test of the homogeneity hypothesis was conducted by Schneider, Smith, Taylor, and Fleenor (1998). Among a sample of approximately 13,000 managers representing 142 U.S. organizations, Schneider et al. examined whether within-organization variability was sufficiently small enough to reliably differentiate organizations based on member MBTI profiles. Using multivariate analysis of variance (MANOVA), they found that organizations could be distinguished based on managers' MBTI profiles, suggesting that managers within these organizations have similar personality profiles. Their study, however, only addressed the management layer. Giberson et al. (2005) replicated and extended Schneider et al.'s (1998) work by examining homogeneity across organizational levels and using a Big 5 measure of personality along with a measure of 10 personal values. Also using MANOVA analytical procedures, Giberson et al. found that organizations could be distinguished based on three of the Big 5 traits along with all 10 personal values.

The findings from these studies provide empirical support for Schneider's proposition that over time, the variability in the types of people in an organization decreases and employee pools tend to become more homogeneous. Later in this chapter, however, we will discuss several boundary conditions that could limit or eliminate the tendency toward homogeneity.

DEVELOPMENTS IN ASA RESEARCH

Since the 1995 ASA model update (Schneider et al., 1995), there have been at least two notable developments in explaining how homogeneity develops and in approaches to examining ASA processes. These developments include an increased recognition of the important role of socialization in the homogenization process, along with the recognition that perceptions of fit, in addition to objective fit, play a key role in attraction, selection, and attrition decisions.

Socialization

Schneider (1987a; Schneider et al., 1995) has been very clear throughout his writing on ASA that organizational socialization plays a critical role in establishing and enhancing fit. Socialization is not explicitly included in the model, however, because it is not a specific decision point in the organizational staffing process, as the decisions to apply, offer a job, accept a job offer, dismiss an employee, and leave an organization voluntarily are all specific decision points. Nonetheless, there is substantial evidence that organizational socialization plays a role in enhancing individual fit with the organization.

The socialization literature is voluminous, and we will only briefly touch upon it here. One interesting example relating to the homogeneity hypothesis comes from Thomas and Anderson (1999), who longitudinally examined changes in the perceptions of new recruits to the British Army, in terms of values and acceptability of specific practices within the Army. As these new recruits became more experienced soldiers, they showed considerable shifts on almost every measured dimension, and these shifts were almost uniformly in the direction of the perceptions of those held by more senior soldiers.

Of course, socialization pressures in the armed forces are typically quite strong. Outside of a military context, several additional studies have also found that socialization processes affect both objective and perceived fit. Cable and Parsons (2001), for one, found that individuals who joined organizations that use formal socialization processes had greater levels of perceived fit with their organization after a year and a half. Moreover, these same individuals also experienced a shift in their work-related values to be more congruent with the cultural values of the organization.

Interestingly, only certain types of socialization activities appear to be associated with increased P–O fit. Socially oriented aspects of socialization, which address the opportunity for social interactions with mentors, roles models, and co-workers, appear to have the strongest relationship to increased fit. For example, Cooper-Thomas, Van Vianen, and Anderson (2004) and Shantz, Baltes, Randall, and Resick (2005) found that socially oriented aspects of socialization were associated with changes in perceptions of fit with the organization in the direction of viewing the organization as compatible with their personality and values.

Attraction and selection forces would suggest that a certain degree of similarity is likely to exist among individuals at entry; nonetheless, these studies have demonstrated that perceptions and values likely shift over time in the direction of the commonly held beliefs in the organization. Perhaps given strong socialization processes, homogeneity will increase over time because the characteristics and goals of organization members change. Conversely, though, it may also be that early organizational efforts at socialization provide a new employee with more accurate and detailed information about the organization and job, leading to a relatively quick decision to leave the organization based on poor fit. There is, however, little research addressing issues of changing perceptions of fit due to changes in either the organization or the person.

Increased Focus on Perceived Fit in ASA Research

Researchers are also increasingly focusing on the role of perceived P–O fit in relation to each of the attraction, selection, and attrition stages. From a methodological perspective, analyses of objective fit gather separate information regarding (1) personal values, preferences, and so forth, and (2) the values, norms, and so forth, that are characteristic of organizations and their members (i.e., aggregates of the values/norms measures), and then assess the degree of congruence between the two entities using polynomial regression or difference scores (e.g., Cable & Edwards, 2004; Cable & Parson, 2001; Chatman, 1991; Judge & Cable, 1997; O'Reilly et al., 1991). In contrast, research focusing on perceived P–O fit involves asking people to indicate the degree to which they believe they are a good fit with an organization and its members (e.g., Cable & DeRue, 2002; Cable & Judge, 1996; Lauver & Kristof-Brown, 2001; Resick, Baltes, & Shantz, 2007; Saks & Ashforth, 1997). While both objective fit and perceived fit with an organization's environment are important for individual-level outcomes, objective reality is filtered through individual perceptions (Kristof-Brown et al., 2005). As a result, the perceptions that people form about their organizations—and those of employers about their employees—are likely to be more cognitively accessible (Judge & Cable, 1997), and therefore a more proximal indicator (Cable & DeRue, 2002) of attraction and attrition decisions.

Across studies, Kristof-Brown et al. (2005) found substantial effect sizes for the relationship between P–O fit and organizational attraction ($\rho = .46$); however, larger effect sizes were found for perceived fit measures ($\rho = .62$) than indirect (studies where person and organization attributes are measured separately) fit measures ($\rho = .22$). Similarly, P–O fit was negatively associated with intentions to quit ($\rho = -.35$), and these relationships were stronger for perceived fit ($\rho = -.52$) than indirect, objective fit measures ($\rho = -.19$). Regarding the ASA cycle, this suggests that perceptions have a key role in the organizational homogenization process.

Carrying this same logic to the selection stage, managers' and recruiters' perceptions of a candidate's fit with the organization should also be most cognitively accessible, and thus most proximally related to their selection decisions. A few studies provide evidence that fit perceptions play a role in the recruiting process. For example, Kristof-Brown (2000) found that recruiters' perceptions of a candidate's fit with both the job and the organization were related to their hiring recommendations. Moreover, Chuang and Sackett (2005) examined the relative importance of recruiters' perceptions of a candidate's job fit and organization fit during multistage interviews. They found that recruiters weighed the importance of a candidate's fit with a job more heavily in early interview stages and fit with the organization more heavily during later stages.

EVOLUTION OF THE ASA CONSTRUCT

As we have reviewed thus far, since the original publication of "The People Make the Place," a substantial body of work has emerged that provides empirical support for many of the ASA model's propositions, as well as theoretical clarification of the model's assertions and implications. But how can we assess the theory's level of maturity? Fortunately, Schneider, in work produced with colleague Arnon Reichers (1990), developed a model of construct evolution. Reichers and Schneider argued that theories typically mature through three phases:

- *Introduction and elaboration*, in which the construct is conceived of (or adapted from another field), and researchers define the concept, identify approaches to operationalize the concept, and demonstrate its usefulness
- *Evaluation and augmentation*, in which early research and critical reviews appear that attempt to clarify the concept and its usefulness, and conflicting results appear and are addressed
- *Consolidation and accommodation*, in which controversies surrounding the construct begin to diminish, and antecedents, consequences, and boundary conditions become well established

We estimate that ASA theory is currently somewhere between the second and third phases of construct evolution. The elements of the construct are well defined, and the usefulness of ASA as an explanatory tool for organizational homogeneity seems well established, moving the theory out of the first stage. Further, ASA now generally appears in I–O and Organizational Behavior (OB) textbooks as an established and accepted model, rather than as some hot new idea in need of verification. Research findings about ASA are typically presented as supporting or not supporting the model, and the recent literature on P–O fit has largely taken ASA as a given. Additionally, there has been debate and question about the soundness of ASA, and a substantial amount of research on the topic, suggesting development into the second stage of construct evolution. However, we would argue that ASA is not yet in the consolidation and accommodation stage, for several reasons. First, Reichers and Schneider (1990) describe the third stage by saying:

> It is at this point in concept development that many researchers move on to "younger" concepts, and the overall quantity of research devoted to the topic declines. A few persistent individuals, however, continue to chip away

at the remaining mysteries inherent in the mature concept. Occasionally, some aspect of the concept's history will be revived and recycled by a particular researcher, leading to further explication and retort. (p. 7)

We would certainly argue that the overall quality of research on ASA processes is not declining. In fact, as numerous articles and books have been devoted to refining the conceptual clarity of multilevel constructs and providing consistent guidelines for conducting multilevel research (e.g., Chan, 1998; House, Rousseau, & Thomas-Hunt, 1995; Klein & Kozlowski, 2000), we suggest that research on ASA processes is becoming increasingly sophisticated. Second, boundary conditions of ASA are not yet clear, and it is obviously important to understand when and under what conditions to expect the tendency toward homogeneity to be active. In the next sections, we discuss several likely boundary conditions and present a number of emerging questions that need to be addressed regarding ASA theory.

BOUNDARY CONDITIONS OF THE MODEL

To date, research has not examined the conditions that may affect ASA processes and resulting homogeneity. We now examine some potential boundary conditions to the ASA model's propositions, addressing characteristics of organizations (organizational age and size) as well as characteristics of the external operating environment (societal culture and economic conditions).

Organizational Age and Life Cycle Stage

Schneider (1987a) cautions that the homogeneity arising from ASA processes is detrimental to organizational survival because organizations become stagnant, myopic, and less able to adapt to changes in the competitive environment. If this prognosis is correct, then those organizations that have been able to survive over time have somehow been able to avoid stagnation and have found ways to break the cycle of homogeneity. Perhaps, then, ASA processes are likely to be more apparent and have a more pronounced effect in organizations in their early years of operation.

Initial evidence for age as a boundary condition on the ASA model comes from Resick, Giberson, and Dickson's (2002) study of organizational cultures and modal personalities. Among 30 small to mid-sized organizations, they found that the cultural values shared among organizational respondents were predictive of several organizational-level average personality traits or personal work values. However, these relationships were predominantly found in younger organizations (in existence for less than 21 years), while there were virtually no relationships in older organizations. Similar support is provided by Schminke, Ambrose, and Neubaum's

(2005) study of leader moral development and climates regarding ethics. In line with Schein's (2004) speculation that founders embed their personal characteristics into the culture and climates of the organizations they lead, as well as Schneider's (1987a) speculation that the homogenization processes begins with founders, Schminke et al. (2005) found that the moral development level of CEOs based on scores from the Defining Issues Test (DIT; Rest, 1986) was associated with climates regarding ethics in their organization, and this relationship was stronger in younger as opposed to older organizations. Finally, Giberson, Resick, and Dickson (2002) found that homogeneity of personality and values had a nonlinear, inverted U-shaped relationship with aggregate levels of satisfaction and commitment in younger, but not older, organizations. For younger organizations, moderate levels of similarity among members were related to higher levels of satisfaction and commitment, while low levels or high levels of similarity were related to lower levels of satisfaction or commitment. In older organizations there was virtually no relationship between satisfaction or commitment levels and homogeneity.

Together these studies provide some evidence that ASA phenomena are bounded, at least to some extent, by organizational age and more likely to occur during earlier stages of development. As organizations mature and are forced to adapt to changes in the external environment, they are perhaps also forced to change organizational leadership, membership, and cultures and climates. This, in turn, would disrupt the component processes of attraction, selection, and attrition and ultimately result in a weaker relationship among cultures, climates, modal personality, and leader's personality for older organizations.

While age is a meaningful indicator of human development, it is perhaps not the best indicator of organizational development. Organizational life cycle stage is perhaps a more useful mechanism through which to examine boundaries on ASA processes. Quinn and Cameron's (1983) integrative model of four organizational life cycle stages (entrepreneurial, collectivity, formalization and control, and elaboration) may provide some guidance here. Perhaps selection is most active in the entrepreneurial stage, where the founder is still active in hiring specific individuals, and there may be little organizational reputation or structure to which potential employees could be attracted. By the collectivity stage, when the organization is characterized by informal communication and structure, members are likely to have a sense of cohesion, cooperation, and commitment. It is at this stage that the attraction–selection–attrition cycle is likely in full force and homogeneity begins to emerge. Similarity among members on characteristics such as personality and attitudes enhances the quality of interpersonal experiences with one another, building cooperation and cohesion (Byrne, 1969, 1971). Organizations that reach the formalization and control stage are likely dealing with policies, practices, and structures becoming formalized, and the organization is focused on efficiency of operations. Homogeneity is likely strongest at this stage and has its greatest implications for organizational adaptation. Those organizations that are able to adapt in some way enter the fourth life cycle stage, elaboration, where they acknowledge the need to adapt to the environment and change. Those organizations that have been able to successfully elaborate likely experienced changes that shift away from attracting, selecting, and retaining similar types of people, and thus breaking the cycle of homogeneity. Once an organization reaches and works through this stage, ASA processes quite likely have a weaker effect.

Organizational Size

Schneider et al. (1995) noted that smaller organizations are particularly susceptible to becoming homogeneous. As organizations grow and become increasingly complex, subunits become more differentiated to address the myriad issues facing the organization (Lawrence & Lorsch, 1967), and as a result, people tend to interact more with their immediate co-workers than they do with individuals in others areas of the company. These social interactions help people to make sense of their work environment (Rentsch, 1990) and are also likely to be more proximally related to selection decisions, attrition decisions, and formation of subcultures and climates. It seems likely that ASA processes have more organization-wide effects in smaller organizations and more unit-level effects in larger organizations. Some initial evidence for this boundary condition comes from Haudek's (2001) study of the variability in organizational culture perceptions across time. Haudek (2001) measured culture perceptions at two points in time ranging from 12 to 48 months apart, and found that smaller organizations experienced a decrease in variability in culture perceptions from time 1 to time 2, while larger organizations experienced little change or even an increase in variability across time.

Turning to the unit-level of analysis, several studies have found that agreement among members' perceptions of their work environments is greatest among members who interact regularly with one another (Klein, Conn, Smith, & Sorra, 2001; Rentsch, 1990). It follows, then, that members of these units will develop norms, expectations, and assumptions that are similar to those held throughout the organization, yet somewhat distinct to that particular unit (conceptually similar, for example, to regional cultural differences found within a single country). These unit-level expectations have implications for ASA decision points. In larger organizations, actual selection decisions are likely to be made by management at the unit level, and attrition may be a function of manager–employee relations. Indeed, Buckingham and Coffman (1999) have argued based on their extensive Gallup survey data that the relationship a person has with his "immediate manager determines how long he stays and how productive he is" (p. 235).

The impact of homogeneity at the unit level, then, needs to be examined. Perhaps homogeneity helps to improve unit-level operations up to a point, at which it leads to complacency. Alternatively, the relationship between unit-level homogeneity and performance may depend on the nature of the work in the department. Perhaps more boundary spanning departments need to have a diversity of personalities as they need to be competitive with the external environment. In contrast, homogeneity may help in more stable support functions. Second, research could examine homogeneity within units, along with homogeneity and heterogeneity across units in relation to overall firm performance. This approach ties in with the previous discussion about organizational age, in that organizational age and size are generally correlated. It is perhaps likely that as organizations grow older and larger, the consistency throughout the organization diminishes as specialization takes hold, and ASA processes occur at the division, department, or unit level of analysis, rather than at the organization level. In such a case, the effects would be no less pronounced, and no less serious, but would be more difficult to identify.

Societal Culture

Organizations increasingly compete in a global marketplace not only for their goods and services, but also in recruiting talented workers. Researchers have responded by examining the differences in values and practices that exist across cultures and how these cultural differences impact functions such as internal operations, workplace values, and recruiting and retention efforts (see Hofstede, 1980; House & Javidan, 2004). While findings indicate that societal-level forces affect generally accepted practices at the organization level (Dickson, BeShears, & Gupta, 2004), research has yet to explore how ASA processes unfold and impact organizations across cultures.

One aspect of societal culture, individualism-collectivism, may have a particularly important impact on the nature of ASA processes. Individualism–collectivism has been considered a fundamental distinguishing characteristic of societal cultures (e.g., Hofstede, 1980). Individualistic cultures emphasize personal interests over group interests and stress personal rights and freedoms over collective well-being (Hofstede, 1980). Moreover, employer–employee relationships in individualistic cultures are more calculative, and tasks are given a greater priority than relationships (Parkes, Bochner, & Schneider, 2001). In contrast, group interests and well-being take precedence over individual interests, rights, and freedoms in collectivistic cultures (Hofstede, 1980). Moreover, in collectivist cultures, relationships are given a greater priority than tasks (Parkes et al., 2001), people emphasize relatedness to their social groups, and duty and obligation are important determinants of behavior (Gelfand, Bhawuk, Nishii, & Bechtold, 2004). This natural tendency toward conformity that is fundamental to collectivistic cultures likely results in individuals being less concerned about their personal fit with the organization, and in homogeneity developing more quickly and pervasively than in individualistic cultures.

This then raises the question of how homogeneity is related to organizational adaptation in collectivistic societies. One possibility is that homogeneity is less of a hindrance to organizations' adaptation efforts. Perhaps members are generally committed to the organization's goals and strategic initiatives. It would follow then that when the strategic direction or operating goals change, people would naturally commit to the new direction. Alternatively, organizations in collectivistic cultures may have a more difficult time adapting to changes in the environment. The greater focus on relationships over task accomplishments may translate into top management being reluctant to change strategic initiatives or operating goals, so as not to disrupt the lives of employees. Further, organizations may face a laborious process of gaining commitment to revised goals when changes must be implemented. These are questions that need to be examined to more fully understand the nature of the ASA model across cultures.

Economic Conditions

Like societal culture, economic conditions are another aspect of the extraorganizational environment that likely impacts ASA processes. Prior research has demonstrated a relationship between both the perceptions of economic opportunities, such as scarcity of alternative employment opportunities (e.g., Hui, 1988), and actual labor market conditions (e.g., Steel, 1996) with job search and turnover intentions. A weak economy and fewer available job opportunities will likely have a considerable impact on job search and job choice decisions. For example, people are likely to be less concerned about their fit with an organization when applying for jobs and be more likely to accept job offers regardless of their perceived fit with an organization if there are fewer opportunities available, as the only alternative may be unemployment. Further, when people perceive that they have few viable work opportunities other than their present one (rather than objectively have few opportunities; Hui, 1988), the relationship between dissatisfaction in various forms and intention to quit (Doran, Stone, Brief, & George, 1991), job search intent (Shaw & Gupta, 2001), and voluntary turnover (Hui, 1988) is attenuated. When employment opportunities are scarce, organizational fit is of less importance to a person's commitment to his or her organization or satisfaction with the job (Schneider, 2001). In general, people do not try to leave their organizations when they think there is nowhere else to go to, even if they are highly dissatisfied and believe that the organization is not a good fit.

As such, we suggest that economic conditions are a boundary condition on the ASA model's predictions. During a weak economy, conditions in the labor market are likely to restrict attraction–selection–attrition processes, resulting in a lessoning of a tendency for organizations to move toward homogeneity. During stable or prosperous economic times, people have more job opportunities available and are likely to be more willing to seek out new employment and be more selective in the organizations they chose to apply to and join.

Emerging Questions About ASA

We have also identified several emerging questions about ASA theory addressing both macro, organization-level issues as well as micro, individual-level issues. From an organizational operations perspective, questions address three areas: (1) the operationalization of homogeneity, and the nature of the relationship between homogeneity and organizational effectiveness, (2) the optimal balance between homogeneity and heterogeneity, and (3) mechanisms for reducing extreme homogeneity. Questions aimed at microlevel processes focus on fit with the organization as a dependent variable. We elaborate on these questions below.

One major question concerns how to operationalize homogeneity in organizations. Among the few studies in this area, there has been little consistency with regard to the operationalization of homogeneity. For example, both Schneider et al. (1998) and Giberson et al. (2005) tested the homogeneity hypothesis using multivariate analysis of variance (MANOVA) procedures to compare within-organization variability of personality characteristics to between-organization variability. In contrast, Denton (1999) tested for group homogeneity by computing Levene's tests for homogeneity of variance. Ostroff and Rothausen (1997) used still another method to understand homogeneity by using hierarchical regression with organizational climate as the dependent variable and personal characteristics and tenure as independent variables. The effect of this lack of consistency may result in researchers from different groups literally speaking a different language regarding organizational homogeneity and prevent researchers from building on one another's research findings. Researchers need to achieve a common understanding regarding how to operationally examine homogeneity to continue to advance ASA propositions.

This leads to perhaps the most salient question regarding ASA theory that still needs to be addressed: the positive and negative consequences of homogeneity. The social psychology literature suggests that similarity among people in terms of characteristics such as attitudes or personality is associated with better interactions among people (Byrne, 1969, 1971). Further, similarity among people likely helps a newly formed organization to operate in a coordinated manner, and facilitates the emergences of climates and culture (Schein, 2004). Yet, Schneider and colleagues (1987a, 1995) have cautioned that homogenous organizations are in danger of becoming myopic and unable to adapt to changes in their operating environment. (Cox and Blake [1991] make similar arguments specifically regarding ethnic and gender diversity.) Research is needed that explicitly examines the positive and negative effects of homogeneity on organizational operations, along with whether these effects vary across organizational life cycle stages. Perhaps homogeneity negatively affects some indicators of effectiveness and not others (strategic decision processes but not stakeholder relations, for example). Examination of these questions, in particular, will provide a better understanding of the impact of ASA processes, further enhancing its utility for both organizational development efforts and scientific inquiry.

Another set of emerging questions focuses on how to break up the ASA cycle and reduce extreme homogeneity. The naturally occurring tendency toward homogeneity (and accompanying resistance to change) is likely to be broken only through conscious intervention or response to some form of crisis situation. What, then, are the mechanisms by which organizations are able to quickly and effectively disrupt the ASA cycle (Goldstein, Ruminson, & Yusko, 2002)? In the short term, perhaps organizations benefit from the efforts of key individual contributors (e.g., situational engineers) responsible for investigating alternatives or ensuring diverse perspectives. Additionally, formal training and development programs might help to promote divergent or creative thinking. For longer-term efforts, perhaps organizations can use human resources systems to reduce homogeneity, for example, consciously selecting or promoting individuals who demonstrate competency in their knowledge, skill, and abilities (KSAs) yet have values that differ from the organization's members. In addition, perhaps socialization may be used to play a role in reducing homogeneity as well as creating homogeneity.

Despite the fact that the ASA model was developed to explain organizational homogeneity, rather than individual-level fit (Schneider et al., 1995), many authors continue to rely on the ASA model as a guiding framework for P–O fit investigations. We turn now to emerging questions addressing the microfocused aspects of the ASA model. These questions focus on fit as a dependent variable. The first set of questions focuses on the stages of organizational attraction. How do organizational attraction and perceptions of fit or misfit with an organization evolve over time? Here, it seems that a critical gap in the understanding of the attraction processes relates to the cues that people use to form a perception of fit or misfit. What information do people focus on, and does the type and amount of information change over time? These same issues are faced in both the attraction stage and the selection stage, but the focus of information is likely different. During the attraction stage, applicants are processing cues about the organization from brief interactions with members as well as limited exposure to the organization's structure and procedures. At the same time, managers and recruiters are likely focusing on cues about the applicant from brief interactions and the presentation of credentials.

Second, longitudinal investigations of what prompts changes in individuals' levels of fit over time, from prehire to turnover, are needed to expand on Schneider's theory at the individual level. One set of studies that does address fit as an outcome are those that examine how socialization practices influence subsequent levels of fit (Adkins, 1995; Cable & Parsons, 2001; Chatman, 1991; Riordan, Weatherly, Vandenberg, & Self, 2001). As shown in Figure 2.2, a person's perceptions of fit with an organization develop over multiple stages both pre- and posthire. What is lacking in this line of research is a comprehensive theory regarding how individual actions and organizational practices prior to, during, and immediately following entry impact both perceived and actual levels of fit. Without a good theory to explain this process, it is difficult to predict when individuals will become more like their co-workers and organizations, when jobs will change to reflect individuals' characteristics, when cognitive distortion will be used to change perceived but not actual fit, or when attrition will be the primary means by which greater levels of fit will be achieved.

IMPLICATIONS OF ASA THEORY AND RESEARCH: ASA IN UNEXPECTED SETTINGS

Thus far in this chapter, we have addressed studies on ASA and fit that focused on top management teams in bank holding companies, interns at a large manufacturing firm, job-seeking undergraduate and graduate students, employees across industries and organizations in the People's Republic of China, pledges and sisters in college sororities, organizational recruiters, engineering students staying or leaving the field of engineering, soldiers in the British Army, and retail store managers, among others. Clearly, ASA has been investigated in a wide range of settings, and ASA processes have been used to explain outcomes in a wide range of organizational contexts. However, ASA has found its way into some unexpected places as well. We mention here two brief examples.

Houston, Carter, and Smither (1997) examined professional tennis players across the range of their careers. Their argument was that if talented young tennis players developed a greater sense of competitiveness during their time on the professional tennis tour, then that would imply that competitiveness has a situational origin in the tour itself. Instead, however, they found that competitiveness as a trait of professional tennis players is consistent across the career, suggesting a person rather than a situation origin. They tied this outcome to ASA, suggesting that those without the necessary competitive trait would not fit in with the constant competitive demands of the life of a professional tennis player, and would sooner or later find that the tour was not really a good fit for them, and they would leave professional tennis.

Kahana, Lovegreen, Kahana, and Kahana (2003) looked into an entirely different setting—retirement communities for older adults. Again relying on ASA, they suggest that different communities of older adults will come

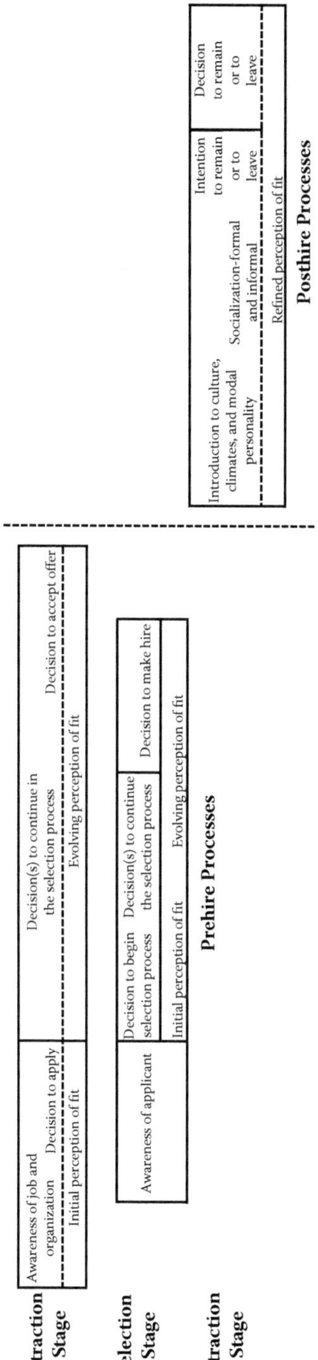

FIGURE 2.2

to have similar people within a community, with differences in the types of people found in different communities. These differences, they argue, emerge from the nature of the community (e.g., whether there are front porches on the homes, thus facilitating interaction between residents) and the rules for the facilities (e.g., whether there are rules promoting social interaction), which will attract some people (e.g., extroverts would be attracted to the types of communities with front porches and lots of social interaction) and repel others.

Clearly, the idea of organizational homogeneity emerging through the forces of attraction, selection, and attrition is intuitively appealing to researchers in a variety of fields, and we note ASA's emergence in an ever-wider range of outlets. This is not to say, however, that the focus on the person in the organization—a focus that Schneider has called for since at least 1983—is always heeded. The focus on structure as an explanation for behavior remains strong, even when a person-oriented approach seems to be the more likely explanation. At the conference from which this festschrift book emerged, we provided two recent examples of structural approaches to problems that seemed to us to have—at least to some degree —origins in personal characteristics. One was the explanation of workplace bullying as being caused by such structural characteristics as reward systems, power imbalances, and organizational changes (Salin, 2003). We wondered whether it was possible that bullying occurs in the workplace because the people in the workplace are bullies. Could it be that characteristics of individuals that are associated with bullying are among the characteristics relied upon in the selection process, and that people who are not bullies and do not intend to be bullied leave for another organization where bullying is less prevalent?

Similarly, we considered Dyck and Starke's (1999) analysis of "break-away" religious congregations, which focused primarily on structural and macro environmental processes. But they also found that breaks occurred along fault lines based on incongruent goals held by congregation members—clearly in keeping with Schneider's assertion that it is primarily goals that attract and keep group members (Schneider, 1983, 1987a). Is this one of potentially many cases where outcomes only appear to originate in structures? Though the person orientation has regained a great deal of strength in the last couple of decades, it seems that we need to reemphasize Schneider's (1987b) assertion that $E = f(P, B)$. These two studies are simply two examples reminding us that there is still a need to persuade researchers to consider "seek[ing] explanations in people not in the results of their behavior" (Schneider, 1987a, p. 451).

CONCLUSIONS

In writing this chapter, we have each thought about why we became involved in research on ASA in the first place. We have generally concluded we became enthralled with the ASA model because (1) it made so much sense, (2) we could explain it to our family members in a way that they could understand, and (3) it really resonated with people in the working world. It seemed to us that if this model had strong theory, research support, and face validity, it was something that we wanted to be working with.

Finally, let us mention one brief story. We wrote to the Society for I–O Psychology's main office in order to check on the exact date of Ben's presidential address to SIOP in 1985. We described briefly why we needed the information, and Lee Hakel, then the executive director of SIOP, wrote back to us about her impressions of the importance of ASA (Lee Hakel, personal communication, 2004). She wrote: "I–Os don't [usually] talk to business people in language they understand. I always thought that Ben's statement was near perfect in communicating with everyone. Who knew there was all that science behind it?"

There is a lot of science behind it, as there is behind all of Ben Schneider's work. We look forward to seeing that science grow over the coming years as researchers continue to explore the impact of organizational homogeneity, and to better understand the processes and implications of attraction, selection, and attrition.

ENDNOTES

1. There is, of course, a vast literature on personnel selection (c.f. Hough & Oswald, 2000). A great deal of the literature on P–E fit and P–O fit would fall into this category, as would a great deal of the literature on the relationships between personal values/personality and job performance, turnover, and other organizational outcomes. However, much of this research is only tangentially relevant to ASA, and so we will not address it here.
2. A wealth of literature at the team level of analysis deals with analogous issues. See Guzzo and Dickson (1996) for a review of the team literature on diversity.

REFERENCES

Adkins, C. L. (1995). Previous work experience and organizational socialization: A longitudinal examination. *Academy of Management Journal, 38,* 839–854.

Agius, E., Arfken, C. L., Dickson, M. W., Mitchelson, J. K., & Anderson, H. L. (2004, October). *Impact of turnover on organizational climate of substance abuse treatment clinics.* Paper presented at the Meeting of the Addiction Health Services Research Conference, Philadelphia.

Allen, G. (1998). Work values in librarianship. *Library & Information Science Research, 20,* 415–424.

Binning, J. F., Adorno, A. J., & LeBreton, J. M. (in press). Person–environment fit and performance. In D. L. Segal & J. C. Thomas (Eds.), *Comprehensive handbook of personality and psychopathology: Personality and everyday functioning* (Vol. 1). New York: Wiley.

Boone, C., van Olffen, W., & Roijakkers, N. (2004). Selection on the road to a career: Evidence of personality sorting in educational choice. *Journal of Career Development, 31*, 61–78.

Boswell, W. R., Roehling, M. V., LePine, M. A., & Moynihan, L. M. (2003). Individual job-choice decisions and the impact of job attributes and recruitment practices: A longitudinal field study. *Human Resource Management, 42*, 23–37.

Buckingham, M., & Coffman, C. (1999). *First break all the rules: What the world's greatest managers do differently.* New York: Simon & Schuster.

Burnett, J., Vaughan, M., & Moody, D. (1997). The importance of person–organization value congruence for female students joining college sororities. *Journal of College Student Development, 38*, 297–300.

Byrne, D. (1969). Attitude and attraction. In Berkowitz L. (Ed.), *Advances in experimental social psychology* (Vol. 4, pp. 35–90). New York: Academic Press.

Byrne, D. (1971). *The attraction paradigm.* New York: Academic Press.

Cable, D. M., & DeRue, D. S. (2002). The convergent and discriminant validity of subjective fit perceptions. *Journal of Applied Psychology, 87*, 875–884.

Cable, D. M., & Edwards, J. R. (2004). Complementary and supplementary fit: A theoretical and empirical integration. *Journal of Applied Psychology, 89*, 822–834.

Cable, D. M., & Judge, T. A. (1996). Person–organization fit, job choice decisions, and organizational entry. *Organizational Behavior and Human Decision Processes, 67*, 294–311.

Cable, D. M., & Judge, T. A. (1997). Interviewers' perceptions of person–organization fit and organizational selection decisions. *Journal of Applied Psychology, 82*, 546–561.

Cable, D. M., & Parsons, C. K. (2001). Socialization tactics and person–organization fit. *Personnel Psychology, 54*, 1–23.

Caplan, R. D. (1987). Person–environment fit theory and organizations: Commensurate dimensions, time perspectives, and mechanisms. *Journal of Vocational Behavior, 31*, 248–267.

Chan, D. (1998). Functional relations among constructs in the same content domain at different levels of analysis: A typology of composition models. *Journal of Applied Psychology, 83*, 234–246.

Chatman J. (1989). Improving interactional organizational research: A model of person–organization fit. *Academy of Management Review, 14*, 333–349.

Chatman, J. A. (1991). Matching people and organizations: Selection and socialization in public accounting firms. *Administrative Science Quarterly, 36*, 459–484.

Chuang, A., & Sackett, P. R. (2005). The perceived importance of person-job fit and personal-organization fit between and within interview stages. *Social Behavior & Personality, 33*, 209–226.

Cooper-Thomas, H. D., Van Vianen, A., & Anderson, N. (2004). Changes in person–organization fit: The impact of socialization tactics on perceived and actual P–O fit. *European Journal of Work and Organizational Psychology, 13*, 52–78.

Cox, T. H., Jr., & Blake, S. (1991). Managing cultural diversity: Implications for organizational competitiveness. *Academy of Management Executive, 5*, 45–57.

De Fruyt, F., & Mervielde, I. (1999). RIASEC types and big five traits as predictors of employment status and nature of employment. *Personnel Psychology, 52*, 701–727.

Denton, D. W. (1999). The attraction–selection–attrition model of organizational behavior and the homogeneity of managerial personality. *Current Research in Social Psychology, 4*, 146–159.

Dickson, M. W., BeShears, R. S., & Gupta, V. (2004). The impact of societal culture and industry on organizational culture: Theoretical explanations. In R. J. House, P. J. Hanges, M. Javidan, P. W. Dorfman, & V. Gupta (Eds.), *Culture, leadership, and organizations: The GLOBE study of 62 societies* (pp. 74–86). Thousand Oaks, CA: Sage.

Doran, L. I., Stone, V. K., Brief, A. P., & George, J. M. (1991). Behavioral intentions as predictors of job attitudes: The role of economic choice. *Journal of Applied Psychology, 76*, 40–45.

Dyck, B., & Starke, F. A. (1999). The formation of breakaway organizations: Observations and a process model. *Administrative Science Quarterly, 44*, 792–822.

Gelfand, M. J., Bhawuk, D. P. S., Nishii, L. H., & Bechtold, D. J. (2004). Individualism and collectivism. In R. J. House, P. J. Hanges, M. Javidan, P. W. Dorfman, & V. Gupta (Eds.), *Culture, leadership, and organizations: The GLOBE study of 62 societies* (pp. 438–513). Thousand Oaks, CA: Sage.

Giacalone, R. A., Knouse, S. B., & Montagliani, A. (1997). Motivation for and prevention of honest responding in exit interviews and surveys. *Journal of Psychology, 131*, 438–448.

Giberson, T. R., Resick, C. J., & Dickson, M. W. (2002, August). Examining the relationship between organizational homogeneity and organizational outcomes. In C. J. Resick & M. W. Dickson (Chairs), *Person–organization fit: Balancing its constructive and destructive forces.* Paper presented at the 2002 Annual Meetings of the Academy of Management, Denver.

Giberson, T. R., Resick, C. J., & Dickson, M. W. (2005). Embedding leader characteristics: An examination of homogeneity of personality and values in organizations. *Journal of Applied Psychology, 90*, 1002–1010.

Goldstein, H. W., Ruminson, K. C., & Yusko, K. P. (2002). Breaking homogeneity in work organizations. In C. J. Resick & M. W. Dickson (Chairs), *Person–organization fit: Balancing its constructive and destructive forces.* Paper presented at the 2002 Annual Meetings of the Academy of Management, Denver.

Guzzo, R. A., & Dickson, M. W. (1996). Teams in organizations: Recent research on performance and effectiveness. *Annual Review of Psychology, 47*, 307–338.

Haudek, G. (2001, April). A culture variance test of the ASA homogeneity hypothesis. In M. W. Dickson (Chair), *The attraction–selection–attrition model: Current research and theory.* Paper presented at the 2001 Conference of the Society for Industrial and Organizational Psychology, San Diego.

Hofstede, G. (1980). *Culture's consequences.* Beverly Hills: Sage.

Holland, J. L. (1973). *Making vocational choices: A theory of careers.* Englewood Cliffs, NJ: Prentice Hall.

Holland, J. L. (1997). *Making vocational choices: A theory of careers* (3rd ed.). Odessa, FL: Psychological Assessment Resources.

Hough, L. M., & Oswald, F. L. (2000). Personnel selection: Looking toward the future—remembering the past. *Annual Review of Psychology, 51,* 631–664.

House, R. J. & Javidan, M. (2004). Overview of GLOBE. In R. J. House, P. J. Hanges, M. Javidan, P. W. Dorfman, & V. Gupta (Eds.), *Culture, leadership, and organizations: The GLOBE study of 62 societies* (pp. 9–26). Thousand Oaks, CA: Sage.

House, R., Rousseau, D. M., & Thomas-Hunt, M. (1995). The meso paradigm: A framework for the integration of micro and macro organizational behavior. *Research in Organizational Behavior, 17,* 71–114.

Houston, J. M., Carter, D., & Smither, R. (1997). Competitiveness in elite professional athletes. *Perceptual and Motor Skills, 84,* 1447–1454.

Hui, C. H. (1988). Impacts of objective and subjective labour market conditions on employee turnover. *Journal of Occupational Psychology, 61,* 211–219.

Jackson, S. E., Brett, J. F., Sessa, V. I., Cooper, D. M., Julin, J. A., & Peyronnin, K. (1991). Some differences make a difference: Individual dissimilarity and group heterogeneity as correlates of recruitment, promotions, and turnover. *Journal of Applied Psychology, 76,* 675–689.

Judge, T. A., & Cable, D. M. (1997). Applicant personality, organizational culture, and organizational attraction. *Personnel Psychology, 50,* 359–393.

Kahana, E., Lovegreen, L., Kahana, B., & Kahana, M. (2003). Person, environment, and person–environment fit as influences on residential satisfaction of elders. *Environment and Behavior, 35,* 434–453.

Klein, K. J., Conn, A. B., Smith, D. B., & Sorra, J. S. (2001). Is everyone in agreement? An exploration of within-group agreement in employee perceptions of the work environment. *Journal of Applied Psychology, 86,* 3–16.

Klein, K. J., & Kozlowski, S. W. J. (2000). From micro to meso: Critical steps in conceptualizing and conducting multilevel research. *Organizational Research Methods, 3,* 211–236.

Kristof, A. L. (1996). Person–organization fit: An integrative review of its conceptualizations, measurement, and implications. *Personnel Psychology, 49,* 1–49.

Kristof-Brown, A. L. (2000). Perceived applicant fit: Distinguishing between recruiters' perceptions of person-job and person–organization fit. *Personnel Psychology, 53,* 643–671.

Kristof-Brown, A. L., Zimmerman, R. D., & Johnson, E. C. (2005). Consequences of individuals' fit at work: A meta-analysis of person-job, person–organization, person-group, and person-supervisor fit. *Personnel Psychology, 58,* 281–342.

Lauver, K. J., & Kristof-Brown, A. (2001). Distinguishing between employees' perceptions of person-job and person–organization fit. *Journal of Vocational Behavior, 59,* 454–470.

Lawrence, P. R., & Lorsch, J. W. (1967). Differentiation and integration in complex organizations. *Administrative Science Quarterly, 12,* 1–47.

Lefkowitz, J., & Katz, M. L. (1969). Validity of exit interviews. *Personnel Psychology, 22,* 445–454.

Lievens, F., Decaesteker, C., Coetsier, P., & Geirnaert, J. (2001). Organizational attractiveness for prospective applicants: A person–organization fit perspective. *Applied Psychology: An International Review, 50,* 30–51.

McLellan, A. T., Carise, D., & Kleber, H. D. (2003). Can the national addiction treatment infrastructure support the public's demand for quality care? *Journal of Substance Abuse Treatment, 25*, 117–121.

Murray, A. H. (1938). *Explorations in personality*. Boston: Houghton-Mifflin.

O'Reilly, C. A., Chatman, J., & Caldwell, D. F. (1991). People and organizational culture: A profile comparison approach to assessing person–organization fit. *Academy of Management Journal, 34*, 487–516.

Ostroff, C., & Rothausen, T. J. (1997). The moderating effect of tenure in person–environment fit: A field study in educational organizations. *Journal of Occupational and Organizational Psychology, 70*, 173–188.

Parkes, L. P., Bochner, S., & Schneider, S. K. (2001). Person–organization fit across cultures: An empirical investigation of individualism and collectivism. *Applied Psychology: An International Review, 50*, 81–108.

Parsons, C. K., Cable, D. M., & Wilkerson, J. M. (1999). Assessment of applicant work values through interviews: The impact of focus and functional relevance. *Journal of Occupational and Organizational Psychology, 72*, 561–566.

Parsons, F. (1909). *Choosing a vocation*. Boston: Houghton-Mifflin.

Quinn, R. E., & Cameron, K. (1983). Organizational life cycles and shifting criteria of effectiveness: Some preliminary evidence. *Management Science, 29*, 33–51.

Reichers, A. E., & Schneider, B. (1990). Climate and culture: An evolution of constructs. In B. Schneider (Ed.), *Organizational climate and culture* (pp. 5–39). San Francisco: Jossey-Bass.

Rentsch, J. R. (1990). Climate and culture: Interaction and qualitative differences in organizational meaning. *Journal of Applied Psychology, 75*, 668–681.

Resick, C. J., Giberson, T. R., & Dickson, M. W. (2002). *Linking shared personality and values to organizational culture*. Paper presented at the Society for Industrial and Organizational Psychology, Toronto.

Resick, C. J., Baltes, B. B., & Shantz, C. A. (2007). Person–organization fit and work-related attitudes and decisions: Examining interactive effects with job fit and conscientiousness. *Journal of Applied Psychology, 92*(5), 1446–1455.

Rest, J. R. (1986). *Moral development: Advances in theory and research*. New York: Praeger.

Riordan, C. M., Weatherly, E. W., Vandenberg, R. J., & Self, R. M. (2001). The effects of pre-entry experiences and socialization tactics on newcomer attitudes and turnover. *Journal of Managerial Issues, 13*, 159–176.

Saks, A. M., & Ashforth, B. E. (1997). A longitudinal investigation of the relationships between job information sources, applicant perceptions of fit, and work outcomes. *Personnel Psychology, 50*, 395–426.

Salin, D. (2003). Ways of explaining workplace bullying: A review of enabling, motivating and precipitating structures and processes in the work environment. *Human Relations, 56*, 1213–1232.

Schaubroeck, J., Ganster, D. C., & Jones, J. R. (1998). Organization and occupation influences in the attraction–selection–attrition process. *Journal of Applied Psychology, 83*, 869–891.

Schein, E. H. (2004). *Organizational culture and leadership* (3rd ed.). San Francisco: Jossey-Bass.

Schminke, M., Ambrose, M. L., & Neubaum, D. O. (2005). The effect of leader moral development on ethical climate and employee attitudes. *Organizational Behavior and Human Decision Processes, 97*, 135–151.

Schneider, B. (1983). An interactionist perspective on organizational effectiveness. In K. S. Cameron & D. S. Whetten (Eds.), *Organizational effectiveness: A comparison of multiple models* (pp. 27–54). New York: Academic Press.

Schneider, B. (1987a). The people make the place. *Personnel Psychology, 40,* 437–453.

Schneider, B. (1987b). E = *f*(P,B): The road to a radical approach to person–environment fit. *Journal of Vocational Behavior, 31,* 353–361.

Schneider, B. (2001). Fits about fit. *Applied Psychology: An International Review, 50,* 141–152.

Schneider B., Goldstein, H. W., & Smith, D. B. (1995). The ASA framework: An update. *Personnel Psychology, 48,* 747–773.

Schneider, B., Smith, D. B., Taylor, S., & Fleenor, J. (1998). Personality and organizations: A test of the homogeneity of personality hypothesis. *Journal of Applied Psychology, 83,* 462–470.

Shantz, C. A., Baltes, B. B., Randall, K. R., & Resick, C. J. (2005). *Socialization, satisfaction, and person–environment fit.* Working paper, Wayne State University, Detroit, MI.

Shaw, J. D., & Gupta, N. (2001). Pay fairness and employee outcomes: Exacerbation and attenuation effects of financial need. *Journal of Occupational & Organizational Psychology, 74,* 299–320.

Steel, R. P. (1996). Labor market dimensions as predictors of the reenlistment decisions of military personnel. *Journal of Applied Psychology, 81,* 421–428.

Thomas, A., Benne, M. R., Marr, M. J., Thomas, E. W., & Hume, R. M. (2000). The evidence remains stable: MBTI predicts attraction and attrition in engineering program. *Journal of Psychological Type, 55,* 35–42.

Thomas, H. D. C., & Anderson, N. R. (1999). Changes in newcomer psychological contracts during organization socialization: A study of recruits into the British Army. *Journal of Organizational Behavior, 19,* 745–767.

Tinsley, H. E. A. (2000). The congruence myth: An analysis of the efficacy of the person–environment fit model. *Journal of Vocational Behavior, 56,* 147–179.

Turban, D. B., & Keon, T. L. (1993). Organizational attractiveness: An interactionist perspective. *Journal of Applied Psychology, 78,* 184–193.

Turban, D. B., Lau, C. M., Ngo, H. Y., Chow, I., & Si, S. X. (2001). Organizational attractiveness of firms in the People's Republic of China: A P–O fit perspective. *Journal of Applied Psychology, 86,* 194–206.

Van Vianen, A., & Kmieciak, Y. M. (1998). The match between recruiters' perceptions of organizational climate and personality of the ideal applicant for a management position. *International Journal of Selection and Assessment, 6,* 153–163.

Ziegert, J., & Schneider, B. (2001). *Do women make the sorority? An analysis of the attraction–selection–attrition model applied to sorority recruitment.* Paper presented at the Annual Meeting of the Society for Industrial and Organizational Psychology, San Diego.

3

The People Make the Place Complicated

SUSAN E. JACKSON
Rutgers University and GSBA Zürich

YUNHYUNG CHUNG
Rutgers University of Idaho

When Ben Schneider gave his presidential address to the Society for Industrial and Organizational Psychology two decades ago, he argued that "the attributes of people … are the fundamental determinants of organizational behavior" (1987, p. 437). Using the dynamic cycle of like people being attracted to organizations, selection into organizations of similar others, and attrition of misfits from organizations (the ASA model), Schneider explained how organizations evolve toward psychological homogeneity. In his presidential address and elsewhere, Schneider has consistently emphasized the importance of people's psychological attributes (e.g., personality, interests) as the primary characteristics driving ASA dynamics. That is, his work assumes that people primarily attend to and are attracted or repelled by the psychological attributes of others.

A long history of psychological research on person perception and stereotyping shows that people also attend to and are attracted or repelled by the social characteristics of others—their ethnicity, age, educational background, and so on. Indeed, people often rely on social cues such as these to draw inferences about a person's psychological attributes. This reality stimulated Congress to create legislation promoting equal employment opportunities for qualified job applicants, regardless of their race, color, sex, religion, or national origin. Due partly to such legislation, workforce diversity is a challenging reality in most U.S. organizations today.

Increasingly, it is recognized as a significant management challenge in other countries as well (Mangaliso & Nkomo, 2001).

For legal, social, and economic reasons, effectively managing a diverse workforce is necessary for organizations that seek to gain a sustainable competitive advantage. Yet, while some executives proclaim the virtues of a diverse workforce, the empirical evidence reveals that few employers have fully succeeded in leveraging workforce diversity to achieve positive outcomes (Kochan et al., 2003).

The difficulty that organizations encounter as they attempt to effectively manage diversity is reflected in the investments employers make in diversity initiatives to improve morale, commitment, and productivity. Almost all large U.S. companies have implemented diversity initiatives to address racial and gender diversity (Grensing-Pophal, 2002), yet employees' complaints and legal claims alleging unfair discrimination and harassment at work have increased steadily. In the year 2000, the total value of monetary awards won by the Equal Employment Opportunity Commission was approximately $300 million—a threefold increase from 1990.

Like employers, organizational scholars have struggled to understand how demographic diversity shapes organizational life. Research on workplace diversity has mushroomed during the past two decades, and today the diversity umbrella covers research of many types (for an overview of the debates and history associated with the diversity research, see Ashkanasy, Hartel, & Daus, 2002). Some of this work is rooted in Schneider's ASA model, but most is not.

Numerous empirical studies of workplace diversity confirm what employers already know—diversity (that is, heterogeneity) can be disruptive. The evidence clearly shows that workplace diversity can increase conflict, reduce social cohesion, and increase turnover. Yet, as suggested in Schneider's description of how "the people make the place," there also is evidence showing that diversity is associated with greater innovation, improved strategic decision making, and improved organizational performance (for comprehensive reviews, see Jackson, Joshi, & Erhardt, 2003; Milliken & Martins, 1996; Webber & Donahue, 2001; Williams & O'Reilly, 1998).

The human composition of organizations is pretty complicated, it seems. Competing forces operate to drive organizations toward homogeneity *and* heterogeneity. To be effective, organizations need to find a balance or a mix of these two extremes. A major challenge for scholars, then, is to understand the dynamics of organizational composition well enough to offer practical advice about how to manage it.

A solid base of empirical evidence from studies conducted during the past 20 years can serve as a foundation for the next decade of research on organizational composition, but advances in our understanding are likely to be slow if we merely accumulate incrementally findings from studies of ASA dynamics and workforce diversity. Each stream of work focuses on issues that are relatively simplistic when compared to the complexity of organizational life. A more fruitful approach going forward may be to integrate research on the attraction–selection–attrition (ASA) processes described by Schneider (1987) with research on the dynamics of workforce diversity. With this view of the future as our guide, in this chapter we describe recent developments in research on workplace diversity and comment on their implications for research on ASA dynamics. The chapter is organized around four features of research on workplace diversity: its far-reaching theoretical roots, the broad range of attributes used as indicators of diversity, the many units of analysis that have been studied, and consideration of the role of context.

For the purposes of this discussion, we consider the defining features of ASA research to be the assessment of the psychological composition of organizations (business units) and empirical results that are directly relevant to the attraction–selection–attrition process. In comparison, the defining feature of research on workplace diversity is assessment of the demographic composition of work units, which can range in size from at least three people (e.g., work team diversity) to everyone in a large organization (organizational diversity).

THEORETICAL PERSPECTIVES FOR UNDERSTANDING WORKPLACE DIVERSITY

This chapter is written as if there are two different and easily identified streams of research to be integrated—one on workplace diversity and another on the ASA model. In fact, these two categories are quite fuzzy and some integration is already apparent—that is, a few studies of workplace diversity are grounded in the logic of the ASA perspective. In addition, studies of workplace diversity are grounded in the logic of organizational demography (Pfeffer, 1983), the social identity perspective, and the upper echelon perspective (Hambrick & Mason, 1984).

ASA Model

Although the ASA model was not formulated to explain the dynamics of demographic composition, Schneider and his colleagues have been open to using the model as an explanation for the effects of workplace diversity, stating: "Of course, there has been increasing interest in demographic diversity in organizations …, but B. Schneider's writings have studiously ignored this issue. We … believe that these [ASA] predictions apply equally well to demographic and personality diversity in organizations" (Schneider, Goldstein, & Smith, 1995, p. 760).

Consistent with this view, some diversity researchers have argued that the dynamics of attraction–selection–attrition may explain the impact of diversity on turnover and the long-term demographic homogenization observed in top management teams (Boone, van Olffen, van Witteloostuijn, & De Brabander, 2004; Jackson et al., 1991). Even when the ASA model is not explicitly cited in a study of workplace diversity, it often is clear that the research shares the same ancestors in that it is grounded in psychological studies of similarity and attraction (e.g., Byrne, 1971).

Organizational Demography

Diversity researchers also embrace the more sociological logic of Pfeffer's (1983) discussion of organizational demography. Pfeffer argued that the demographic composition of organizations (i.e., organizational demography) influences the behavioral patterns that occur there, including communications, job transfers, promotions, and turnover. Among the demographic attributes that Pfeffer identified as important were age, tenure, sex, race, socioeconomic background, and religion. Sociological studies and marketing research have both shown that differences in people's attitudes and values are reliably associated with differences in their standing on demographic characteristics such as these. The similarity effect provides a rationale for why demographic compositions of organizations are likely to be related to organizational phenomena, such as cohesiveness, communication networks, and employee flows.

Social Identity Perspective

Several studies of workplace diversity have been grounded in the social identity perspective, which encompasses self-categorization theory and social identity theory (Reynolds, Turner, & Haslam, 2003). The social identity perspective asserts that individuals classify themselves and others based on overt demographic attributes, including ethnicity and gender (Ashforth & Mael, 1989; Tajfel & Turner, 1979). Demographically similar individuals classify themselves as members of the "in-group"; those who are demographically dissimilar are classified as the "out-group."

Whereas the ASA perspective assumes that actual psychological similarity is of primary importance, the social identity perspective assumes that perceptions of similarity drive behavior. People bring many attributes to each situation, but only some of these become salient. Salient attributes become the basis for categorizing in-groups and out-groups. Furthermore, the social identity perspective assumes that the mix of people in a situation determines which differences make a difference.

Several decades of research demonstrate that people favor members of their in-group and discriminate against out-group members (for a review, see Hewstone, Rubin, & Willis, 2002). These dynamics arise even when group membership is randomly assigned on the basis of meaningless cues. In addition, the degree of in-group favoring and out-group harming behaviors appears to be contingent on the relative size and implicit status of the subgroups involved (Chattopadhyay, Tluchowska, & George, 2004;

Hewstone et al., 2002). Thus, the social identity perspective combines an understanding of individual-level processes with an appreciation of how social context influences individual-level processes.

Upper Echelon Perspective

Finally, many studies under the diversity umbrella draw their logic from the upper echelon perspective, which argues that the composition of top management teams (TMTs) has important consequences for strategic decision-making processes and organizational performance (see Hambrick & Mason, 1984). The distinctive features of upper echelon research are its focus on executive team decision making and the implications of team composition for organizational effectiveness (for a review, see Carpenter, Geletkanycz, & Sanders, 2004). Like Schneider, Hambrick and Mason assumed that cognitive and psychological attributes were the most important determinants of how people behave; they also assumed that psychological attributes are correlated with demographic attributes. Accepting the need to balance rigor against practical considerations, research on the composition of upper echelons typically focuses on demographic attributes.

Toward Theoretical Integration

As in so much of life, scholars who study differences seem to be attracted to perceived similarities and avoid discussing differences. Thus, when scholars draw on more than one of the four theoretical approaches described above, they often presume that different perspectives are grounded in a common foundational logic. All four perspectives do assume that the personal attributes and the interpersonal context created by the mix of personal attributes represented in the workforce are key determinants of individual behavior and organizational outcomes. And the four perspectives all acknowledge that similarity is an important determinant of interpersonal attraction. Nevertheless, there also are important differences among the four perspectives. Research that addresses these conceptual differences may help advance our understanding of how the many types of diversity present in organizations affect the lives of employees.

Despite its popularity, the similarity–attraction logic does not fully account for the effects of team composition and organizational demography. Nor does it easily explain why team diversity is sometimes beneficial to performance. And neither the ASA model nor the social identity perspective accounts for studies that find significant effects of team composition but no corresponding effects for individual-level differences (e.g., Boone et al., 2004; Jackson et al., 1991).

As a first step toward integrating these various streams of research, we recommend differentiating between personal and social identities. A personal identity is formed by the individual's particular personality, physical attributes, psychological traits, values, and so on, whereas a social identity is formed by social categorization of groups (Ashforth & Mael, 1989; Brown, 2000). Substantial evidence shows that people use social identities to categorize themselves and others into in-groups and out-groups, and these social categorizations have important consequences for interpersonal and intergroup relations. Social categorization effects occur even when employees have little direct interaction with one another (e.g., Tsui, Egan, & O'Reilly, 1992). We know of no studies that have examined whether personal identities serve as the basis for in-group/out-group categorization. Nor do we know of research that demonstrates that personal identities influence intergroup conflict or cooperation. If in-group/out-group categorization and its consequences are elicited by personal identities, which personal characteristics are most likely to stimulate such categorization and under what conditions?

Theoretical integration of the perspectives described also requires attending more carefully to the three issues we address next: the specific dimensions of diversity, the units of analysis under investigation, and organizational context.

INDIVIDUAL ATTRIBUTES AND DIMENSIONS OF DIVERSITY

For the purpose of this chapter, we have argued that the inclusion of readily detected attributes is a defining characteristic of research on workplace diversity. In their review of recent studies of team and organizational composition, Jackson et al. (2003) found that readily detected attributes accounted for 89% of the compositional effects reported in recent studies. The most frequently studied dimensions of diversity were age, sex, education, functional background, tenure, and ethnicity. From a legal perspective, readily detectable attributes such as age, sex, and ethnicity are of interest because they represent protected categories. These dimensions of diversity are of interest to organizations aiming to comply with Title VII law. Use of these demographic attributes in diversity research links the work directly to managers' concerns.

Demographics as Proxies for Psychological Characteristics

Consistent with the assumptions made by many psychologists, some diversity researchers use readily detectable demographic attributes as proxies for individual values or work-related knowledge. For some demographic attributes, there is direct empirical evidence of associations with psychological characteristics. For example, age is negatively correlated with risk-taking propensity (Vroom & Pahl, 1971) and the cognitive processes adults use for problem solving (Datan, Rodeheaver, & Hughes, 1987). The societal conditions (e.g., economic depressions vs. booms and periods of war vs. peace) experienced by different age cohorts seem to influence attitudes and values (see Elder, 1974, 1975; Thernstrom, 1973). For executives, the accrual of tenure is associated with commitment to the status quo (Finkelstein & Hambrick, 1990; Hambrick, Geletkanycz, & Fredrickson, 1993). Educational curriculum choices are associated with personality, attitudes, and cognitive styles (Holland, 1973). And while there is little evidence relating personality or cognitive styles to gender or ethnicity, it is apparent that these characteristics are associated with experiences that are likely to influence the perspectives of men versus women and people from different ethnic backgrounds.

Investigating Psychological and Demographic Attributes

A psychological perspective on diversity dynamics might imply that personality, values, and attitudes are the dimensions of difference that explain diversity effects. If so, studies that assess only demographic attributes would be of little value because psychological attributes are only weakly correlated with demographic attributes. But as we have already noted, it is a mistake to assume that people attend only to psychological differences. Demographic differences also are important, for they are the basis of categorizations into in-groups and out-groups (Turner & Haslam, 2001). In-group and out-group categorizations are formed on the basis of minimal information. Simply knowing that another person is similar (e.g., knowing that the person belongs to one's own demographic group) is sufficient to trigger in-group categorization and cooperation (Oakes, Haslam, & Turner, 1994). People need not interact with one another in order to perceive that they share common interests.

Could failure to include both demographic and psychological characteristics in ASA research increase the risk of drawing inaccurate conclusions about which interpersonal dissimilarities are most likely to generate ASA dynamics? Could failure to include demographic attributes in the ASA model increase the risk of concluding that psychological attributes matter most, when in fact the observed effects are due to demographic diversity? Although not widely recognized, the potential for such errors of inference seems apparent.

Consider the following: Personality and values correlate with choice of occupations, and thus the functional units that eventually employ members of different occupations (see Jordan, Herriot, & Chalmers, 1991; Schaubroeck, Ganster, & Jones, 1998). In many organizations, conflicts occur among occupational groups arising from competition for resources as well as competition for status and prestige. Arguably, occupational differences among employees are more salient than personality differences—especially for employees who are not in direct daily contact with one another, which is true for most employees who are members of a business unit or organization (vs. a small group or work team). According to the social identity perspective, the salience of occupations means that in-group/out-group categorizations and their negative consequences are more likely to be based on occupational membership than personality. Suppose a study of several business units found that people within each business unit had relatively similar personalities, and that units with more personality heterogeneity were less cohesive. Such a result might occur due to conflicts among occupational groups rather than personality differences. If occupational heterogeneity was not assessed, an incorrect inference would be made about the importance of personality heterogeneity.

Including measures of underlying (psychological) diversity as well as readily detected (social) diversity presents an opportunity for gaining new insights about the effects of composition in organizations. The potential value of this approach was demonstrated in a study that assessed both gender and attitudinal diversity (Harrison, Price, Gavin, & Florey, 2002). The study found that readily detected diversity influenced team functioning when teams had little experience together, but over time underlying diversity was more influential. Although the number of studies considering underlying diversity is still small, including measures of both demographic and psychological attributes appears to be a promising direction for the future.

Considering Attribute Profiles

Clearly, studies that assess only one aspect of diversity fail to capture the full spectrum of diversity found in organizations. People are more complicated than that. By failing to control for the possible correlations among attributes, scholars risk drawing inappropriate inferences about which dimensions of diversity account for observed effects. But a more serious flaw in the diversity literature is that most researchers attempt to identify the unique and independent effects of various dimensions of diversity (e.g., sex, racio-ethnicity, age); very few studies (less than 5%) have addressed the question of whether the effect of one particular dimension of diversity depends on the presence or absence of other dimensions of diversity. This is true even when multiple dimensions of diversity are included in a study (see Jackson et al., 2003).

A few studies that have examined multidimensional diversity illustrate the potential value of this approach. Jehn, Northcraft, and Neale (1999) found that informational (education and function) diversity was negatively related to group efficiency when social category diversity (sex and age) was high, but not when it was low. Pelled, Eisenhardt, and Xin (1999) found that the consequences of diversity for team conflict were best understood by taking into account interactive effects for specific dimensions of diversity. In a study of sales team performance, Jackson and Joshi (2004) found that the effects on team performance of any one type of diversity—gender, ethnic, or tenure—depended on the other types of diversity present in the team. Specifically, team performance was lowest for teams with a combination of relatively high tenure diversity *and* high gender diversity *and* high ethnic diversity.

Recent theoretical contributions to the field call for a multidimensional approach to assessing diversity (e.g., Jackson & Joshi, 2001; Lau & Murnighan, 1998; Ofori-Dankwa & Julian, 2002). It seems likely that social processes and their outcomes are influenced by the confluence of diversity dimensions. An R&D team member may identify herself as well as her team members using multiple attributes (e.g., "White female engineer" or "Asian male scientist"). The team's outcomes may be determined by the configuration of team members' demographic or identity profiles (cf. Frable, 1997). Conceptually, it makes sense that the diversity of *attribute profiles* found within teams is likely to influence individual and team outcomes. Unfortunately, diversity researchers (ourselves included) have not yet succeeded in tackling the challenge of empirically assessing multidimensional diversity. Personality researchers interested in understanding the structure of personality systems face a similar challenge (see Mischel, 2004). By recognizing the parallel concerns of scholars working in these two fields, we may be able to make more rapid advances in each.

The Contours of Composition

As we have already noted, most research on workplace diversity has focused on one or perhaps two attributes. Empirical work has proceeded as if the effects of individual attributes are independent of one another, and as if the combined effects across several attributes are additive. In an additive model, the effects of each dimension of diversity are assessed independently of other dimensions of diversity. An alternative is to consider whether an individual's many attributes combine to create unique, multidimensional profiles that capture people as whole persons. Conclusions drawn from studies that considered only additive effects will be inaccurate if the effects of diversity depend on particular attribute combinations or configurations.

For individuals, it is well known that race and gender jointly influence the returns employees receive on their human capital investments (Friedman & Krackhardt, 1997; Smith & Elliott, 1997): White males gain the maximum returns on investment in human capital in comparison to White females or Black males. Other studies have shown that the experiences of Black women differ in a number of ways from those of White women (e.g., Bell & Nkomo, 2001; Frable, 1997). In the diversity literature, the potential value of considering the joint effects of multiple dimensions of team diversity is widely recognized (e.g., see Joshi & Jackson, 2003; Lau & Murnighan, 1998; Webber & Donahue, 2001). Despite awareness of this issue, only about 5% of recent studies of diversity addressed the question of whether the effect of a particular dimension of diversity depends on the presence or absence of other dimensions of diversity (Jackson et al., 2003). The need for large samples, an abundance of technical problems associated with data analysis and interpretation, and a lack of consensus about how to measure and test multidimensional effects are all likely reasons for the dearth of empirical evidence.

In a relatively new approach to addressing this issue, Lau and Murnighan (1998) developed predictions about the dynamics created by team fault lines, which they define as "hypothetical dividing lines that may split a group into subgroups based on one or more attributes" (p. 328). Fault lines—that is, clear bifurcation of a group into two subgroups—may stimulate team members' awareness of subgroups and their affiliation with a subgroup (Lau & Murnighan, 1998). When fault lines are present, team members may find it more difficult to identify with the team as a whole.

Since Lau and Murnighan (1998) developed the concept of fault lines, a few scholars have created fault line propensity measures and investigated their relationships with team processes and team performance. Thatcher, Jehn, and Zanutto (2002) created fault line scores that capture the interactions between (1) fault line strength (*Fau*), the percent of total variation in overall group characteristics accounted for by a strongest group split, and (2) the Euclidean distance between two subgroups identified by the group split procedure. Bezrukova, Thatcher, and Jehn (2000) compared team heterogeneity measures (Blau's index) with *Fau* fault line scores and found that fault lines were better predictors of task and relationship conflicts and performance. In a study of factional groups, Li and Hambrick (2005) used a modified *d*-statistic to assess the strength of fault lines in teams that included people from two different organizations; they found that fault lines were associated with more task and emotional conflicts and lower team performance. Finally, Shaw (2004) developed a measure of fault line strength that takes into account both subgroup internal alignment and cross-subgroup differences. Drawing on Shaw's (2004) approach, Chung, Jackson, and Shaw (2005) found that fault line strength was negatively associated with team performance, recognition, and monetary rewards. The studies cited above indicate that strong fault lines create conflicts that interfere with team performance. In contrast, when fault lines are weak, group learning may occur (Lau & Murnighan, in press).

Whether the concept of fault lines can be fruitfully applied to compositional studies of personality and values remains to be seen. It is not clear, for example, whether certain constellations or clusterings of personalities, values, and abilities lead employees to experience psychologically defined fault lines. The possibility is an interesting one, however, and is worthy of investigation. If psychological fault lines are present in organizations, they may accentuate the selection and attrition processes that are central to the ASA model.

Differences Are Not Symmetrical

To date, research on the ASA model has approached the issue of differences among individuals as if all differences were created equal. Many studies of workplace diversity have taken this same approach. Yet the accumulating evidence shows that differences are not created equal. For diversity researchers, it is increasingly clear that the status of one's identity group shapes one's responses to being different. In most American organizations, men and Whites enjoy higher status than women and Blacks (Baron & Newman, 1990). Status, in turn, is associated with responses to team and organizational composition. People with high-status social identities tend to maintain identification with their demographic in-groups even when they are in the numerical minority, which may bolster their self-esteem and insulate them from the negative effects of their minority position (Hewstone et al., 2002; Tajfel & Turner, 1985). Members of low-status groups tend to accept their "inferior" position and are less likely to display discriminatory behavior against higher-status out-group members even when the size of their in-group is relatively large (Sachdev & Bourhis, 1985, 1987, 1991).

In organizations, high-status members appear to be more sensitive to the degree to which they are in the majority. A study of 834 employees in 151 work units in 3 organizations found that men who worked in situations where men were in the majority reported significantly stronger commitment and lower turnover intentions than men who worked in situations where they were in a smaller majority. In contrast, women's commitment and turnover intentions were unaffected by the size of their identity group. Whites who were different in race from the majority perceived lower organizational attachment (commitment, absences, and intention to stay) than did Whites who were similar in race to the majority. However, for non-Whites, racial dissimilarity was not significantly related to organizational attachment (Tsui et al., 1992).

In a laboratory study of attitude similarity, Chen and Kenrick (2002) found that people responded more strongly to undesirable attributes of people who belonged to their in-group rather than their out-group. Although dissimilarity was clearly less attractive, it was apparently more repulsive among people who were otherwise similar.

To date, studies of personality fit have not considered the question of whether employees respond asymmetrically to psychological differences. Since agreeable team members are friendly, trusting, and tolerant, agreeableness may improve interpersonal cooperation and long-term team viability (Barrick, Stewart, Neubert, & Mount, 1998). Furthermore, we might hypothesize that people who score high on agreeableness are more tolerant of the different personalities of others. As another possibility, perhaps sensitivity to differences on a particular dimension of personality is greater among people who score either quite high or quite low on that dimension. In other words, in addition to personality attributes being the basis of perceived differences, they may predict to whom differences make a difference.

THE VALUE OF MULTILEVEL RESEARCH

As we have already described, the body of theory in which diversity research is grounded reflects the complicated, multilevel nature of diversity phenomena (e.g., see Jackson, May, & Whitney, 1995; Triandis, 1992; Tsui, Xin, & Egan, 1995). As a whole, the empirical research on workplace diversity includes work conducted at the levels of individuals, dyads, small groups and teams, social networks, business units, and organizations. Pfeffer's (1983) landmark treatise on organizational demography focused on organizations, business units, and departments as the units of analysis. Subsequently, the concept of relational demography spurred studies that combined the individual and group or business unit levels of analysis (see Riordan, 2000; Tsui & Gutek, 1999). The social identity perspective emphasizes the team level of analysis, although it also has been applied to social networks (e.g., Ibarra, 1992). Hambrick and Mason's (1984) seminal article on upper echelons focused on top management teams and organizations as the units of analysis.

As we draw on these perspectives to guide research on workplace diversity, many of us assume that theoretical constructs are portable across different levels of analysis, despite cogent warnings against such a foolhardy approach (Klein, Dansereau, & Hall, 1994; Rousseau, 1985, 2000). In addition, until very recently, most studies have focused on phenomena at only one level of analysis, ignoring multilevel complications.

The lack of strong theoretical frameworks that specify cross-level or multilevel diversity dynamics is one reason for the lack of cross-level and multilevel research. No theoretical perspective offers parsimonious predictions about the role of individual demographics and demographic composition at the levels of dyads, teams, business units, and so on. If no extant theories make predictions about related phenomena at other levels of analysis, researchers may not look for the phenomenon. Alternatively, they may look for and discover multilevel effects, but then find that it is difficult to gain acceptance for work that is more exploratory and less clearly theory driven. These same problems may explain why there have been so few multilevel studies of the ASA model (for a recent example of such a study, see Klein, Lim, Saltz, & Mayer, 2004).

The ASA model argues that the cumulative effects of individual-level decisions create organizational-level phenomena such as homogeneity (Schneider, 1987); it typically is used to explain the causes and consequences of a person's attraction to and fit with an organization

(Schneider, Smith, & Goldstein, 2000). The predictions of the ASA model are consistent with the results of numerous studies of group relational demography, which show that being dissimilar to one's immediate work group is associated with a variety of employment outcomes, including increased turnover (Kirchmeyer, 1995; O'Reilly, Caldwell, & Barnett, 1989; Tsui et al., 1992; Wagner, Pfeffer, & O'Reilly, 1984; Wiersema & Bird, 1993). But do individual-level decisions and behavior completely account for the positive relationship found between team-level diversity and team turnover rates? Or might these results be due in part to phenomena that are better understood at higher levels of analysis?

In a study of TMTs in the U.S. financial services industry, Jackson et al. (1991) predicted that individual-level similarity would account for a positive relationship between team demographic diversity and team turnover rates. As expected, the authors found that more diverse teams experienced higher turnover during a 4-year period. However, contrary to predictions they made based on the ASA model, executives' similarity to their teammates was unrelated to their propensity to leave. Jackson et al. speculated that the association between group heterogeneity and group turnover rates created discomfort for all group members, resulting in elevated turnover propensity for everyone. Apparently, the observed homogeneity among teams was due to a similarity effect in the selection and promotion process, but not to a dissimilarity effect for exit decisions.

More recent work by Jackson and colleagues provides other examples of the value of multilevel analyses. In a study of sales teams, Jackson and Joshi (2004) modeled diversity effects at three levels of analysis: individual managers, teams, and business units (districts). Looking at performance as the outcome, their results revealed significant interactions between individual- and team-level predictors as well as additional effects at the district level. In an investigation of pay equity, Joshi, Liao, and Jackson (2006) found that pay equity was unrelated to team-level diversity, but it was significantly related to district-level diversity. In both studies, differential effects at the team and district levels were unexpected. The theoretical perspectives used provided no rationale for arguing that the effects of diversity should be different for small work teams and larger work units.

Looking ahead, increased use of multilevel analytic techniques may prove useful as diversity researchers strive to understand the growing body of inconsistent results. Likewise, multilevel tests of the ASA model may be needed to fully understand how the forces that create the mix of personalities and values present in complex organizations with complicated formal structures that cluster people into teams, departments, levels, and so on.

Organizational Networks

For employees who work in medium to large organizations, much of daily life is lived in the context of teams, departments, and the other social units that comprise an organization, but just as individuals seldom work in isolation, work teams and departments rely on others for the resources and support needed to function effectively (Hackman, 1999). As organizations become flatter and more interconnected, employees spend more and more of their time working on tasks that require interteam and even interorganizational cooperation. Team members often engage in boundary spanning to seek out new ideas, gather information, and coordinate on technical or design issues (Ancona & Caldwell, 1992). As they cross formal boundaries, they share and obtain tacit knowledge as well as tangible resources (Anand, Glick, & Manz, 2002; Tsai, 2002; Tsai & Ghoshal, 1998). Through these and other activities, employees become embedded in organizational networks, which act like glue binding together units of the organization.

Demographic similarity seems to facilitate communication among members of informal organizational networks (Brass, 1995; Ibarra, 1992; Oh, Chung, & Labianca, 2004; Reagans & Zuckerman, 2001; Reagans, Zuckerman, & McEvily, 2004), perhaps because it heightens feelings of interpersonal attraction and trust. As a consequence, organizational networks tend to be homophilous rather than heterogeneous (McPherson, Smith-Lovin, & Cook, 2001; Ruff, Aldrich, & Carter, 2003).

Gender, ethnicity, and age all provide a basis for the development of relationships outside of one's work group. A study of male and female managers in an advertising firm found that men formed same-gender networks, which served both social and instrumental goals (Ibarra, 1992). A study of friendship networks of MBA students (Mehra, Kilduff, & Brass, 1998) found that students formed friendships with others from similar ethnic backgrounds. A study of project groups found that engineers tended to communicate with others outside the project group based on age similarity (Zenger & Lawrence, 1989).

Just as team members can serve as conduits for interteam cooperation, homophilous networks are likely to develop among team leaders and department managers. Demographic similarity among team leaders or members of management may explain workflow and decision-making networks (Bunderson, 2003). If demographic similarity of team leaders facilitates interteam cooperation, the teams working under similar leaders may achieve higher performance (e.g., see Joshi et al., 2006).

Likewise, psychological similarity may play a role in shaping social networks. For example, a study of teams working for a national service program found that demographic similarity had little consequence for the formation of advice and friendship networks (Klein et al., 2004). The authors concluded that "surface" (demographic) similarity is less important than "deep" similarity of values and attitudes (cf. Harrison et al., 2002).

Going forward, it seems likely that studies of both workplace diversity and the ASA model will increasingly emphasize the informal social structures that hold organizational units together. When such networks are leveraged by teams or departments to gain access to knowledge and resources, or to improve coordination with other units, they are likely to enhance organizational effectiveness, as well as team effectiveness. The challenge for organizations, then, is to facilitate the development of cohesiveness within social units while also encouraging employees to build relationships beyond the boundaries of their primary realm of activity.

Research that sheds light on the combined effects of demographic and psychological network composition may provide insights into how to better manage organizational networks. For example, it is interesting to speculate about whether affinity networks—such as those intended to promote the development of women and minorities—might benefit organizations by strengthening the organizational glue. Are organizational networks characterized by homogeneity of psychological characteristics also? Does an employee's psychological similarity to other members of a network predict whether he or she is likely to remain in the network over time? Future research that uses the ASA model to investigate organizational networks is needed to answer questions such as these.

CONTEXT AS A MODERATOR OF SIMILARITY EFFECTS

As Johns (2001) observed: "There are several reasons why scholars should consider, study, and report organizational context. Perhaps the most central, if mundane, reason is that, like Everest, it is there" (p. 34). And it is clear that context matters. Yet, as Schneider (2001) observed, even those who study person–environment fit and its consequences usually do not consider how the environment (context) influences person-fit dynamics.

In their continuing attempts to understand the complex pattern of findings regarding how diversity influences organizations, some scholars have begun to examine context as a potential moderator of diversity effects. This line of research views organizational context as a factor that may influence whether diversity has positive or negative consequences.

Demography as Context

In the diversity literature, one newly emerging approach to examining context is closely associated with the emergence of multilevel research. Consistent with Schneider's (1987) argument that "the people make the place," the social composition of higher-level aggregates (e.g., business units) can be treated as demographic contexts that shape the effects of diversity in lower-level aggregates (e.g., teams). Using this approach, Joshi et al. (2005) found that the gender and ethnic composition of business units moderated the effects of individual dissimilarity on performance and pay. In a study of retail stores, however, Leonard, Levine, and Joshi (2004) found no support for the hypothesis that community demographics moderate the effects of store demographics. Perhaps most relevant for research on the ASA model is a study of turnover among employees of a Fortune 500 service firm, which found that the effect on turnover of being in a demographic minority was stronger for minority groups with smaller proportions of similar others employed in the same job. In addition, the authors reported a marginally significant effect for the demographic composition of jobs at higher levels than the target employee (Zatzick, Elvira, & Cohen, 2003).

Recently, Joshi (2006) identified three forms of organizational composition and discussed how they are likely to moderate the effects of workplace diversity. Briefly, she argued that the negative consequences of diversity are more likely to be found in monolithic organizations (which are characterized by demographic homogeneous, stratification, and segregation), while the benefits of diversity should be more visible in pluralistic and multicultural organizations (which are less stratified and segregated).

Temporal Context

Several studies indicate that the effects of workplace diversity are moderated by temporal factors. We have already mentioned the finding of Harrison et al. (2003) concerning the shifting importance of surface- and deep-level attributes. Likewise, another study found that the negative effects of racio-ethnicity, functional background, and organizational tenure diversity were weaker in longer tenured work teams (Pelled et al., 1999). A study of top management teams found that the effects of TMT demographic diversity were stronger for teams that had spent less time working together (Carpenter, 2002). More recently, in a study of turnover among restaurant employees, demographic misfit was found to be more predictive of turnover during the initial weeks of employment compared to later, for adult workers (Sacco & Schmitt, 2005).

Time is central to the ASA model's description of how organizations evolve. To date, ASA studies have treated time as a predictor of homogeneity. For example, Denton (1999) found that retail store managers with longer tenure in an organization had more similar personalities than those with shorter tenure. Ostroff and Rothhausen (1997) found a similar pattern among school teachers. Given that tenure cohorts are characterized by differing degrees of homogeneity, it seems natural to wonder whether this matters—for individuals as well as their employing organizations.

Task Type

In research on team diversity, the work itself is perhaps the most frequently cited contextual factor mentioned as a potential moderator of diversity dynamics. The generally accepted assumption is that the potential benefits of diversity for performance are greater when the task requires creativity and innovation. When the task is routine, or when speed is the goal, diversity may interfere with performance (e.g., see Jackson, 1992; Williams & O'Reilly, 1998). Although several laboratory experiments seem to support this proposition, clear evidence is not yet available from field studies. Studies of the ASA model could contribute to the accumulating evidence on the role of tasks simply by including good descriptions of the tasks engaged in by the employees studied.

Cultures and Climates

Several authors have argued that organizational cultures shape diversity dynamics. Cox (1993) and Cox and Tung (1997) argued that the consequences of diversity depend on the degree of structure and informal integration present in the organization. Ely and Thomas (2001) argued that diversity is more likely to lead to positive outcomes when the organizational culture emphasizes "integration-and-learning." Empirical studies that examine the effects of dissimilarity (relational demography) in organizations with differing cultures seem to support this general line of reasoning (Chatman, Polzer, Barsade, & Neale, 1998; Dass & Parker, 1999; Gilbert & Ivancevich, 2000).

Just as organizational culture may moderate the effects of organizational diversity, team climates and internal team processes may moderate the effect of team diversity. West (2002) argued that several aspects of team climate must be present in order for teams to effectively use their knowledge for innovation, including shared team objectives, feelings of safety, and effective conflict management, among others.

Many organizations that adopt initiatives to improve employees' tolerance of diversity and their ability to leverage differences to achieve better performance take a broad approach to the topic of diversity. For example, training sessions often discuss how differences in personalities and cognitive styles (as well as demographic differences) can influence the way employees treat one another and the way teams function. Training for managers often emphasizes the importance of focusing on performance-related characteristics of employees rather than allowing personality characteristics that have little job relevance to influence managers' evaluations. Through such training and other means, it seems likely that some organizations develop cultures that truly embrace personality differences. Schneider (1987) observed that "unless organizations consciously fight restriction in the range of the kinds of people they contain, when the environment changes they will (1) not be aware that it has changed, and (2) probably not be capable of changing.... In fact, the ASA model is quite grim with respect to how organizations will cope with the requirements of change" (p. 446). From this it follows that long-lived organizations have found ways to fight range restriction in their workforce. How have they done this? When it comes to increasing tolerance for personality differences, what works and what does not work? Managers may need answers to questions like these in order to ensure their organizations survive.

Business Strategy

Two decades of research on the performance-related effects of top management team diversity has produced an accumulation of conflicting evidence. One explanation for the inconsistent results is that the strategic context of firms moderates the relationship. Yet the specific role of strategic context remains unclear. One line of reasoning suggests that TMT diversity should be more beneficial under conditions of greater strategic complexity because diversity helps the team deal with the demands of complexity (Richard, 2000). Another line of reasoning suggests that TMT diversity will be more detrimental under conditions of greater strategic complexity because diversity makes the necessary coordination among team members more difficult (Boone et al., 2004; Carpenter, 2002).

The logic of the ASA model also suggests that an organization's strategy might moderate the firm-level (and perhaps individual-level) consequences of similarity-based attraction and attrition. ASA dynamics should be most detrimental to firms pursuing strategies that emphasize responsiveness to rapidly changing markets. ASA dynamics may be less detrimental, and even beneficial, to organizations that depend on strong and stable internal cultures for their success. Studies conducted within a single organization usually are not able to empirically evaluate the role of the strategic context in shaping ASA dynamics or observing their consequences. Nevertheless, it would be helpful to provide descriptions of the strategic context of research sites when publishing future ASA research. As studies accumulate, the role of strategic context may eventually be discerned.

CONCLUSION

We have argued that the places people make are complicated—a bit more complicated than suggested by Schneider's original formulation of the ASA model. Research on workplace diversity has begun to recognize and confront these complications, which creates an opportunity for ASA scholars to learn from their successes and failures.

It seems appropriate to end a chapter about diversity with a call for greater integration. In this case, the integration that we look forward to is among researchers interested in the wide range of phenomena now being investigated through the double-sided lens of similarity and difference. We began this chapter by describing four of the most often cited perspectives on difference: the ASA model (Schneider, 1983, 1987), organizational demography (Pfeffer, 1983), the social identity perspective (Turner & Haslam, 2001), and the upper echelon perspective (Hambrick & Mason,

1984). We also acknowledged the growing body of relevant research on social networks (Burt, 1982). As scholars working in each of these theoretical domains have become increasingly aware of research in other related domains, theoretical and empirical cross-fertilization has quickened. We believe this trend is healthy and hope that this chapter stimulates even greater integration among these areas.

Clearly, Schneider's ASA model has been well received by management scholars, who have used it to gain new insights into the functioning of top management teams, business units, and smaller work teams. It is unfortunate that management scholars seldom assess the personalities or styles of the employees in their studies. More often they apply the logic of the ASA model to studies of demographic composition. On the other hand, psychologists interested in testing the ASA model have largely ignored the demographic characteristics of employees and organizations, except perhaps to treat them as nuisance variables.

It is unlikely that management scholars interested in top management team demography will adopt the practice of regularly including measures of psychological attributes as additional ingredients in their studies. But it seems quite feasible for psychologists to include demographic measures as legitimate components in the profile of person characteristics that are assumed to be primary influences on the thoughts, feelings, and behaviors of employees. We hope to see research on the ASA model move in this direction.

The development of the ASA model and our understanding of organizational composition may also be enhanced by imitating some of the recent trends in workplace diversity research. As we have suggested, the most notable trends worthy of imitation are nonadditive approaches to modeling the effects of personal attributes and social composition, multilevel research, and investigations of context as a potential moderator of compositional effects.

Finally, we encourage ASA scholars to closely examine the theoretical logic of related (competing?) models of organizational composition, and contribute to the process of developing more comprehensive—and more complicated—frameworks. For example, the evidence suggests that attraction and attrition processes are not symmetrical or mirror images. The evidence also suggests that the dynamics of composition do not operate identically at all possible levels of analysis. The evidence suggests that context matters. These empirical developments provide opportunities for theoretical integration and development. Perhaps Ben Schneider is already working on this challenge. If not, we hope this chapter stimulates the next generation of scholars to carry on this important work.

REFERENCES

Anand, V., Glick, W. H., & Manz, C. C. (2002). Thriving on the knowledge of outsiders: Tapping organizational social capital. *Academy of Management Executive, 16,* 87–101.

Ancona, D. G., & Caldwell, D. F. (1992). Bridging the boundary: External activity and performance in organizational teams. *Administrative Science Quarterly, 37,* 634–665.

Ashforth, B. E., & Mael, F. (1989). Social identity theory and the organization. *Academy of Management Review, 14,* 20–39.

Ashkanasy, N. M., Hartel, C., & Daus, C. (2002). Diversity and emotion: The new frontiers in organizational behavior research. *Journal of Management, 28,* 307–338.

Baron, J. N., & Newman, A. E. (1990). For what it's worth: Organizations, occupations, and the value of work done by women and nonwhites. *American Sociological Review, 55,* 155–175.

Barrick, M. R., Stewart, G. L., Neubert, M., & Mount, M. K. (1998). Relating member ability and personality to work team processes and team effectiveness. *Journal of Applied Psychology, 83,* 377–391.

Bell, E. L. J., & Nkomo, S. M. (2001). *Our separate ways: Black and White women and the struggle for professional identity.* Boston: Harvard Business School Press.

Bezrukova, K., Thatcher, S. M. B., & Jehn, K. A. (2004). *Comparing the effects of group heterogeneity and faultlines on conflict and performance: An empirical assessment of contrasting models.* Unpublished manuscript.

Boone, C., van Olffen, W., van Witteloostuijn, A., & De Brabander, B. (2004). The genesis of top management team diversity: Selective turnover among top management teams in Dutch newspaper publishing, 1970–94. *Academy of Management Journal, 47,* 633–757.

Brass, D. J. (1995). A social network perspective on human resources management. In G. R. Ferris (Ed.), *Research in personnel and human resources management* (Vol. 13, pp. 39–79). Greenwich, CT: JAI Press.

Brown, R. (2000). Social identity theory: Past achievements, current problems and future challenges. *European Journal of Social Psychology, 30,* 745–778.

Bunderson, J. S. (2003). Team member functional background and involvement in management teams: Direct effects and the moderating role of power centralization. *Academy of Management Journal, 46,* 458–474.

Burt, R. S. (1982). *Toward a structural theory of action: Network models of social structure, perception, and action: Quantitative studies in social relations.* New York: Academic Press.

Byrne, D. (1971). *The attraction paradigm.* New York: Academic Press.

Carpenter, M. (2002). The implications of strategy and social context for the relationship between top management team heterogeneity and firm performance. *Strategic Management Journal, 23,* 275–284.

Carpenter, M. A., Geletkanycz, M. A., & Sanders, W. G. (2004). Upper echelons research revisited: Antecedents, elements, and consequences of top management team composition. *Journal of Management, 30,* 749–779.

Chatman, J. A., Polzer, J. T., Barsade, S. G., & Neale, M. A. (1998). Being different yet feeling similar: The influence of demographic composition and organizational culture on work processes and outcomes. *Administrative Science Quarterly, 43,* 749–783.

Chattopadhyay, P., Tluchowska, M., & George, E. (2004). Identifying the in-group: A closer look at the influence of demographic dissimilarity on employee social identity. *Academy of Management Review, 29,* 180–202.

Chen, F., & Kenrick, D. T. (2002). Repulsion or attraction: Group membership and assumed attitude similarity. *Journal of Personality & Social Psychology, 83,* 111–125.

Chung, Y., Jackson, S. E., & Shaw, J. B. (2005). *Multi-level effects of demographic faultlines on team performance and rewards.* Paper presented at the meeting of the Academy of Management, Honolulu, HI.

Cox, T., Jr. (1993). *Cultural diversity in organizations: Theory, research & practice.* San Francisco: Berrett-Koehler.

Cox, T., Jr., & Tung, R. L. (1997). The multicultural organization revisited. In C. L. Cooper & S. E. Jackson (Eds.), *Creating tomorrow's organizations.* New York: Wiley.

Dass, P., & Parker, B. (1999). Strategies for managing human resource diversity: From resistance to learning. *Academy of Management Executive, 13,* 68–79.

Denton, D. W. (1999). The attraction–selection–attrition model of organizational behavior and the homogeneity of managerial personality. *Current Research in Social Psychology, 4,* 1–9.

Datan, N., Rodeheaver, D., & Hughes, F. (1987). Adult development and aging. *Annual Review of Psychology, 38,* 153–180.

Elder, G. H., Jr. (1974). *Children of the Great Depression.* Chicago: University of Illinois Press.

Elder, G. H., Jr. (1975). Age differentiation and the life course. *Annual Review of Sociology, 1,* 165–190.

Ely, R. J., & Thomas, D. A. (2001). Cultural diversity at work: The effects of diversity perspectives on work group processes and outcomes. *Administrative Science Quarterly, 46,* 229–273.

Finkelstein, S., & Hambrick, D. C. (1990). Top-management-team tenure and organizational outcomes: The moderating role of managerial discretion. *Administrative Science Quarterly, 35,* 484–503.

Frable, D. E. S. (1997). Gender, racial, ethnic, sexual, and class identities. *Annual Review of Psychology, 48,* 139–162.

Friedman, R., & Krackhardt, D. (1997). Social capital and career mobility: A structural theory of lower returns to education for Asian employees. *Journal of Applied Behavioral Science, 33,* 316–334.

Gilbert, J. A., & Ivancevich, J. M. (2000). Valuing diversity: A tale of two organizations. *Academy of Management Executive, 14,* 93–105.

Grensing-Pophal, L. (2002, May). Reaching for diversity. *HR Magazine,* 53–56.

Hackman, J. R. (1999). Thinking differently about context. In R. Wageman (Ed.), *Research on managing groups and teams: Groups in context* (pp. 233–247). Stamford, CT: JAI Press.

Hambrick, D. C., & Mason, P. A. (1984). Upper echelons: The organization as a reflection of its top managers. *Academy of Management Review, 9,* 193–206.

Hambrick, R. C., Geletkanycz, M. A., & Fredrickson, J. W. (1993). Top executive commitment to the status quo: Some tests of its determinants. *Strategic Management Journal, 14,* 401–418.

Harrison, D. A., Price, K. H., Gavin, G. H., & Florey, A. (2002). Time, teams, and task performance: A longitudinal study of the changing effects of diversity on group performance. *Academy of Management Journal, 45,* 1029–1045.

Hewstone, M., Rubin, M., & Willis, H. (2002). Intergroup bias. *Annual Review of Psychology, 53,* 575–604.

Holland, J. L. (1973). *Making vocational choices: A theory of careers.* Englewood Cliffs, NJ: Prentice Hall.

Ibarra, H. (1992). Homophily and differential returns: Sex differences in network structure and access in an advertising firm. *Administrative Science Quarterly, 37,* 422–447.

Jackson, S. E. (1992). Team composition in organizational settings: Issues in managing an increasingly diverse workforce. In Worchel, S., Wood, W., & Simpson, J. (Eds.), *Group Process and Productivity,* pp. 138–173. Newbury Park, CA: Sage.

Jackson, S. E., Brett, J. F., Sessa, V. I., Cooper, D. M., Julin, J. A., & Peyronnin, K. (1991). Some differences make a difference: Individual dissimilarity and group heterogeneity as correlates of recruitment, promotions, and turnover. *Journal of Applied Psychology, 76,* 675–689.

Jackson, S. E., & Joshi, A. (2001). Research on domestic and international diversity in organizations: A merger that works? In N. Anderson, D. S. Ones, H. K. Sinangil, & C. Viswesvaran (Eds.), *Handbook of work, industrial and organizational psychology* (pp. 206–231). Thousand Oaks, CA: Sage.

Jackson, S. E., & Joshi, A. (2004). Diversity in social context: A multi-attribute, multi-level analysis of team diversity and performance. *Journal of Organizational Behavior, 25,* 675–702.

Jackson, S. E., Joshi, A., & Erhardt, N. L. (2003). Recent research on team and organizational diversity: SWOT analysis and implications. *Journal of Management, 29,* 801–830.

Jackson, S. E., May K. E., & Whitney, K. (1995). Under the dynamics of diversity in decision-making teams. In R. A. Guzzo & E. Salas (Eds.), *Team effectiveness and decision making in organizations* (pp. 204–261). San Francisco: Jossey-Bass.

Jehn, K. A., Northcraft, G. B., & Neale, M. A. (1999). Why differences make a difference: A field study in diversity, conflict, and performance in workgroups. *Administrative Science Quarterly, 44,* 741–763.

Johns, G. (2001). In praise of context. *Journal of Organizational Behavior, 22,* 31–42.

Jordan, M., Herriot, P., & Chalmers, C. (1991). Testing Schneider's ASA theory. *Applied Psychology: An International Review, 40,* 47–53.

Joshi, A. (2006). The influence of organizational demography on the external networking behavior of teams. *Academy of Management Review, 31:* 459–481.

Joshi, A., & Jackson, S. E. (2003). Managing workforce diversity to enhance cooperation in organizations. In M. A. West, D. Tjosvold, & K. Smith (Eds.), *International handbook of organizational teamwork and cooperative working* (pp. 277–296). New York: Wiley.

Joshi, A., Liao, H., & Jackson, S. E. (2006). Cross-level effects of workplace diversity on sales performance and pay. *Academy of Management Journal, 49,* 459–481.

Kirchmeyer, C. (1995). Demographic similarity to the work group. *Journal of Organizational Behavior, 16*, 67–83.

Klein, K. J., Dansereau, F., & Hall, R. J. (1994). Levels issues in theory development, data collection, and analysis. *Academy of Management Review, 19*, 195–229.

Klein, K. J., Lim, B. C., Saltz, J. L., & Mayer, D. M. (2004). How do they get there? An examination of the antecedents of network centrality in team networks. *Academy of Management Journal, 47*, 952–963.

Kochan, T., Bezrukova, K., Ely, R., Jackson, S., Joshi, A., Jehn, K., Leonard, J., Levine, D., & Thomas, D. (2003). The effects of diversity on business performance: Report of a feasibility study of the diversity research network. *Human Resource Management Journal, 42*, 3–21.

Lau, D. C., & Murnighan, J. K. (1998). Demographic diversity and faultlines: The compositional dynamics of organizational groups. *Academy of Management Review, 23*, 325–340.

Lau, D. C., & Murnighan, J. K. (2005). Interactions within groups and subgroups: The dynamic effects of demographic faultlines. *Academy of Management Journal, 48*, 645–660.

Leonard, J. S., Levine, D. I., & Joshi, A. (2004). Do birds of a feather shop together? The effects on performance of employees' similarity with one another and with customers. *Journal of Organizational Behavior, 25*, 731–755.

Li, J. T., & Hambrick, D. C. (2005). Factional groups: A new vantage on demographic faultlines, conflict and disintegration in work teams. *Academy of Management Journal, 48*, 794–813.

Mangaliso, M. P., & Nkomo, S. M. (2001). Eskom's Chairman Reuel Khoza on the transformation of South African business. *Academy of Management Executive, 5*, 8–15.

McPherson, J. M., Smith-Lovin, L., & Cook, J. (2001). Birds of a feather: Homophily in social networks. *Annual Review of Sociology, 27*, 415–444.

Mehra, A., Kilduff, M., & Brass, D. J. (1998). At the margins: A distinctiveness approach to the social identity and social networks of underrepresented groups. *Academy of Management Journal, 41*, 441–452.

Milliken, F. J., & Martins, L. L. (1996). Searching for common threads: Understanding the multiple effects of diversity in organizational groups. *Academy of Management Review, 21*, 402–434.

Mischel, W. (2004). Toward an integrative science of the person. *Annual Review of Psychology, 55*, 1–22.

Oakes, P. J., Haslam, S. A., & Turner, J. C. (1994). *Stereotyping and social reality.* Oxford: Blackwell.

Ofori-Dankwa, J. C., & Julian, S. D. (2002). Toward diversity and similarity curves: Implications for theory. *Human Relations, 55*, 199–224.

Oh, H., Chung, M., & Labianca, G. (2004). Group social capital and group effectiveness: The role of informal socializing ties. *Academy of Management Journal, 47*, 860–875.

O'Reilly, C. A., Caldwell, D. F., & Barnett, W. P. (1989). Work group demography, social integration, and turnover. *Administrative Science Quarterly, 34*, 21–37.

Ostroff, C., & Rothausen, T. J. (1997). The moderating effect of tenure in person–environment fit: A field study in educational organizations. *Journal of Occupational and Organizational Psychology, 70*, 173–188.

Pelled, L. H., Eisenhardt, K. M., & Xin, K. R. (1999). Exploring the Black box: An analysis of work group diversity, conflict and performance. *Administrative Science Quarterly, 44*, 1–28.

Pfeffer, J. (1983). Organizational demography. In B. Staw & L. Cummings (Eds.), *Research in organizational behavior* (Vol. 5, pp. 299–357). Greenwich, CT: JAI Press.

Reagans, R., & Zuckerman, E. (2001). Networks, diversity, and productivity: The social capital of corporate R&D teams. *Organization Science, 12*, 502–517.

Reagans, R., Zuckerman, E., & McEvily, B. (2004). How to make the team: Social networks vs. demography as criteria for designing effective projects in a contract R&D firm. *Administrative Science Quarterly, 49*, 101–133.

Reynolds, K. J., Turner, J. C., & Haslam, S. A. (2003). Social identity and self-categorization theories' contribution to understanding identification, salience and diversity in teams and organizations. In J. Polzer (Ed.), *Identity issues in groups: Research on managing groups and teams* (Vol. 5, pp. 279–304). Oxford: JAI Elsevier Science.

Richard, O. C. (2000). Racial diversity, business strategy, and firm performance: A resource-based view. *Academy of Management Journal, 43*, 164–177.

Riordan, C. M. (2000). Relational demography within groups: Past developments, contradictions, and new directions. In G. R. Ferris (Ed.), *Research in personnel and human resource management* (Vol. 19, pp. 131–173). Oxford: Elsevier Science.

Rousseau, D. M. (1985). Issues of level in organizational research: Multi-level and cross-level perspectives. In L. L. Cummings & B. Staw (Eds.), *Research in organizational behavior* (Vol. 7, pp. 1–37). Greenwich, CT: JAI Press.

Rousseau, D. M. (2000). Multilevel competencies and missing linkages. In K. J. Klein & S. W. J. Kozlowski (Eds.), *Mutilevel theory, research, and methods in organizations* (pp. 572–582). San Francisco: Jossey-Bass.

Ruff, M., Aldrich, H. E., & Carter, N. M. (2003). The structure of founding teams: Homophily, strong ties, and isolation among U.S. entrepreneurs. *American Sociological Review, 68*, 195–222.

Sacco, J. M., & Schmitt, N. (2005). A dynamic multilevel model of demographic diversity and misfit effects. *Journal of Applied Psychology, 90*, 203–231.

Sachdev, I., & Bourhis, R. Y. (1985). Social categorization and power differentials in group relations. *European Journal of Social Psychology, 15*, 415–434.

Sachdev, I., & Bourhis, R. Y. (1987). Status differentials and intergroup relations. *European Journal of Social Psychology, 17*, 277–293.

Sachdev, I., & Bourhis, R. Y. (1991). Power and status differentials in minority and majority group relations. *European Journal of Social Psychology, 21*, 1–24.

Schaubroeck, J., Ganster, D. C., & Jones, J. R. (1998). Organization and occupation influences in the attraction–selection–attrition process. *Journal of Applied Psychology, 83*, 869–891.

Schneider, B. (1983). Interactional psychology and organizational behavior. In L. L. Cummings & B. M. Staw (Eds.), *Research in organizational behavior* (Vol. 5, pp. 1–31). Greenwich, CT: JAI Press.

Schneider, B. (1987). The people make the place. *Personnel Psychology, 40*, 437–453.

Schneider, B. (2001). Fits about fit. *International Review of Applied Psychology, 50*, 141–152.

Schneider, B., Goldstein, H. W., & Smith, D. B. (1995). The ASA framework: An update. *Personnel Psychology, 48*, 747–779.

Schneider, B., Smith, D. B., & Goldstein, H. W. (2000). Attraction–selection–attrition: Toward a person–environment psychology of organizations. In W. W. Bruce & K. H. Craik (Eds.), *Person–environment psychology: New directions and perspectives* (2nd ed., pp. 61–85). Mahwah, NJ: Lawrence Erlbaum Associates.

Shaw, J. B. (2004). The development and analysis of a measure of group faultlines. *Organizational Research Methods, 7,* 66–100.

Smith, R. A., & Elliott, J. (2000). *Does ethnic concentration influence access to authority? An examination of contemporary urban labor markets.* Paper presented at the annual meeting of the Southern Sociological Society, New Orleans.

Tajfel, H., & Turner, J. C. (1979). An intergrative theory of intergroup conflict. In W. G. Austin & S. Worchel (Eds.), *The social psychology of intergroup relations.* Monterey, CA: Brooks/Cole.

Tajfel, H., & Turner, J. C. (1985). The social identity theory of intergroup behavior. In S. Worchel & W. Austin (Eds.), *Psychology of intergroup relations* (Vol. 2, pp. 7–24). Chicago: Nelson-Hall.

Thatcher, S. M. B., Jehn, K. A., & Zanutto, E. (2002). Cracks in diversity research: The effects of faultlines on conflict and performance. *Group Decision and Negotiation, 12,* 217–241.

Thernstrom, S. (1973). *The other Bostonians: Poverty and progress in the American metropolis, 1880–1970.* Cambridge, MA: Harvard University Press.

Triandis, H. C. (1992). The importance of contexts in studies of diversity. In S. E. Jackson (Ed.), *Diversity in the workplace: Human resources initiatives* (pp. 225–233). New York: Guilford Press.

Tsai, W. (2002). Social structure of "coopetition" within a multiunit organization: Coordination, competition, and intra-organizational knowledge sharing, *Organizational Science, 13,* 179–190.

Tsai, W., & Ghoshal, S. (1998). Social capital and value creation: The role of intrafirm networks. *Academy of Management Journal, 41,* 464–476.

Tsui, A., Xin, K., & Egan, T. D. (1995). Relational demography: The missing link in vertical dyadic linkage. In S. E. Jackson & M. N. Ruderman (Eds.), *Diversity in work teams: Research paradigms for a changing workplace* (pp. 97–129). Washington, DC: American Psychological Association.

Tsui, A. S., Egan, T. D., & O'Reilly, C. A., III. (1992). Being different: Relational demography and organizational attachment. *Administrative Science Quarterly, 4,* 549–580.

Tsui, A. S., & Gutek, B. A. (1999). *Demographic differences in organizations: Current research and future directions.* Lanham, MD: Lexington Books.

Turner, J. C., & Haslam, S. A. (2001). Social identity, organizations and leadership. In M. E. Turner (Ed.), *Groups at work: Theory and research* (pp. 25–65). Mahwah, NJ: Lawrence Erlbaum Associates.

Vroom, V. H., & Pahl, B. (1971). Relationship between age & risk taking among managers. *Journal of Applied Psychology, 55,* 399–405.

Wagner, W. G., Pfeffer, J., & O'Reilly, C. A., III. (1984). Organizational demography and turnover in top-management groups. *Administrative Science Quarterly, 29,* 74–92.

Webber, S. S., & Donahue, L. M. (2001). Impact of highly and less job-related diversity on work group cohesion and performance: A meta-analysis. *Journal of Management, 27,* 141–162.

West, M. A. (2002). Sparkling fountains or stagnant ponds: An integrative model of creativity and innovation implementation in work groups. *Applied Psychology: An International Review, 51,* 355–387.

Wiersema, M. F., & Bird, A. (1993). Organizational demography in Japanese firms: Group heterogeneity, individual dissimilarity, and top management team turnover. *Academy of Management Journal, 36,* 996–1025.

Williams, K. Y., & O'Reilly, C. A. (1998). Demography and diversity in organizations: A review of 40 years of research. In B. M. Staw & L. L. Cummings (Eds.), *Research in organizational behavior* (Vol. 20, pp. 77–140). Greenwich, CT: JAI Press.

Zatzick, C. D., Elvira, M. M., & Cohen, L. E. (2003). When is more better? The effects of racial composition on voluntary turnover. *Organization Science, 14,* 483–496.

Zenger, T. R., & Lawrence, B. S. (1989). Organizational demography: The differential effects of age and tenure distribution on technical communication. *Academy of Management Journal, 32,* 353–376.

4

When Do People Make the Place?
Considering the Interactionist Foundations
of the Attraction–Selection–Attrition Model

JENNIFER A. CHATMAN
University of California

ELAINE M. WONG
Northwestern University

CANEEL K. JOYCE
University of California

Without question, one of Ben Schneider's most important contributions has been to formulate and test the attraction–selection–attrition (ASA) model (e.g., Schneider, 1987). One can view his 1987 seminal paper in the context of research and debates that preceded it, particularly through the theoretical lens of the person–situation debate. Though psychologists had long struggled to answer the nature–nurture question of whether stable person characteristics or situational attributes account for more variation in behavior, the debate became most heated after Walter Mischel wrote a treatise on the primacy of situations in 1968. Many, such as Block (1978) and Bowers (1973), argued against Mischel's initial position. Most researchers in organizational psychology now accept that behavior is a function of characteristics of the person and the environment (Magnusson & Endler, 1977). The challenge, however, as Schneider (1987) astutely noted, has been to develop concepts and methods that determine not only *if* person and situation attributes are valid predictors of behavior, but also, more importantly, *when* and *to what extent* they predict behavior.

Schneider's (1987) model began with the view that people are not randomly assigned to most situations in life, and particularly not to work organizations. Instead, people and human settings are inseparable; people are attracted to and select into situations that they think they will fit. In Schneider's view, this explains why even organizations that have very similar goals and are of comparable size and structure look and feel different from one another. The ASA cycle starts as people are differentially attracted to an organization based on its modal personality, or the typical personality of members. Organizations then select those who are most compatible. Because a lack of congruence is aversive, "misfits" are unlikely to remain with that organization (e.g., Vandenberghe, 1999).

A key prediction from this process is that organizations quickly become homogeneous with respect to the personality characteristics of the people in them (Schneider, Smith, Fleenor, & Taylor, 1998). At its extreme, the ASA framework suggests that situations are not independent of the people within them; the situation is a construction of the people there behaving as they do, such that "structure, process, and culture are the *outcome* of the people in an organization, not the cause of the behavior of the organization" (Schneider, 1978; Schneider, Goldstein, & Smith, 1995, p. 751, italics added). Thus, from Schneider's perspective, organizations are functions of the kinds of people they contain.

When Schneider introduced the ASA model, he revitalized the then waning focus in organizational psychology on person–situation congruence. Researchers began considering recruiting processes from this perspective (e.g., Bretz, Asch, & Dreher, 1989; Judge & Bretz, 1992; Pervin, 1989; Rynes & Gerhart, 1990; Vancouver & Schmitt, 1991), especially focusing on identifying which potential recruits were likely to be successful within an organization (e.g., Caldwell & O'Reilly, 1990). This focus provided insight into some of the consequences of fit, demonstrating the rather commonsense prediction that people who have personal characteristics that are aligned with the modal personality of the organization are more likely to adjust to that organization than are those who do not fit. As such, the congruence approach provides a predictive lens that specifies who will fit into certain organizations as well as pragmatic value regarding whom an organization should hire.

As the above discussion illustrates, a congruence approach to the ASA model is helpful in generating global predictions about person–situation behaviors. However, congruence as typically conceptualized is too broad a concept to generate insight about the nature of person–situation interactions and predict specific behaviors. Further, the outcomes of congruence are typically conceptualized as adjustment or effectiveness, and typically operationalized in terms of satisfaction, commitment, and longevity in the organization, these are global behaviors arising from many factors; tracking them is not necessarily informative, nor is achieving fit necessarily desirable for organizations or individuals. It would be more useful to decouple *stated adjustment* from *actual behavior* to determine what behaviors emerge and whether the behaviors associated with stated adjustment are actually functional and adaptive. For example, people could adjust to dysfunctional organizations and end up contributing to continued dysfunction rather than to changing the organization in positive ways (e.g., Felps & Mitchell, 2003). Further, from a developmental perspective, it is not always good to be well adjusted. People may grow and learn more in situations that challenge their assumptions or capabilities (e.g., Wrzeniewski & Dutton, 2001). Further, groups that are less homogeneous, a form of congruence, are more likely to be innovative (e.g., Bantel & Jackson, 1989; Chatman, Polzer, Barsade, & Neale, 1998). Thus, we need to more closely scrutinize the actual behaviors that arise from various person–situation combinations.

What we are suggesting is not new, but rather is reminiscent of the initial foundation of the ASA model in interactional psychology; Schneider introduced the ASA model in a 1983 paper as deeply rooted in the context of interactionism:

> People select themselves into and out of situations based on the general fit of themselves to the situation. Self selection ... results in relatively homogeneous settings ... [and] it is the interactions of people with similar others that defines work settings.... Thus, the oft' made observation that people appear more stable than Mischel's (1968) conclusions would suggest is probably true because we typically observe people in a relatively narrow range of situations and, then, over many observational periods. (Schneider, 1983, pp. 13–14)

Embracing the interactional roots of the ASA model to focus on more specific behaviors, such as cooperative behavior, extroversion, or honesty, rather than simply who is likely to be successful in the sense of being well adjusted or acting similarly to others in a situation, requires knowledge of an individual's propensity to behave in a particular way, derived from personal characteristics such as personality, the situational inducements to behave in that way, and how they combine. Consequently, an interactional approach clarifies the conditions under which we should and should not expect to predict behavior from personal characteristics and to increase our understanding of the sources of behavior in organizations. It also is a more robust way to assess behavioral coherence across time and situations; congruence approaches offer few specifics in this regard.

The purpose of this chapter is to consider the value of viewing the ASA model through its roots in person–situation interaction rather than through a congruence lens. We argue that the ASA model is underutilized if only considered with respect to person–organization congruence, and that an interactionist lens provides greater insight into the fundamental, often reciprocal relationship between people and situations, and how the complexities of this relationship influence behavior. In particular, through the application of an interactionist approach to the ASA model, we can better understand when and how some people make the place.

We begin by considering the limits of a congruence approach and illustrate the value of an interactional model in terms of understanding and predicting ASA-relevant behaviors. We do so by focusing on two variants on the person-situation relationship: how some people are affected differently by a situation than are others, and how people influence situations. In both cases, we begin by discussing a study designed to address each type of person-situation relationship, and then consider other relevant research that, though not necessarily intended as a focus, has implications for the ASA model. Through the chapter, we focus on how people and situations interact in fine-grained, behaviorally explicit terms. We believe that behaviorally specific predictions are critical to establishing the boundary conditions of attraction, selection, and attrition processes. Most importantly, this more fine-grained approach will enable us to understand the myriad processes that underlie how and when people make the place.

WHY FOCUSING ON CONGRUENCE IS NOT ENOUGH: MISFIT AS A PATH TO DISCOVERY

People and organizations can be compared based on their values, and a well-substantiated body of research has shown that the fit (congruence or match) between people and their organizations is more influential than either individuals' or organizational values alone (e.g., Chatman, 1989; O'Reilly, Chatman, & Caldwell, 1991). Fit is developed through selection (e.g., Cable & Judge, 1996) and socialization (e.g., Morrison, 1993). Beyond negatively influencing a person's commitment, performance, and satisfaction, having low fit or being a misfit can lead a person to leave an organization (Chatman, 1991). Alternatively, individuals with low fit can also try to change their organization's values, which is still somewhat consistent with the ASA model. Despite these occurrences, yet another solution to low fit or misfit is for the individual to adapt his or her behavior to fit that of the situation. We seek to extend the ASA model by focusing on misfits.

Researchers have long observed the impact that situations can have on people's behavior. Among the most well known example is Asch's (1956) pioneering research on conformity, which demonstrated startling effects of social influence in which subjects were likely to yield to the majority point of view even if it was obviously incorrect. Or Milgram's (1963) obedience studies that showed that, while subjects expressed anxiety over administering shocks to a confederate for incorrect answers, they obeyed the researcher's rules to continue administering them. And, of course, the infamous prisoner study (Haney, Banks, & Zimbardo, 1973), which elicited such dramatic and potentially dangerous behavior in response to random assignments to being a guard or a prisoner that the experiment had to be terminated early.

These examples illustrate how situations can dramatically influence people's behavior. In each case, individual differences were overwhelmed by situational circumstances as people behaved in convergent ways that were often highly atypical for them as individuals. For skeptics of the laboratory approach who believe that experiments are strong situations that preclude our ability to detect coherence in individual behavior (e.g., Kenrick & Funder, 1988), there is persuasive evidence from the vast socialization literature showing that genuinely internalized and lasting value changes occur as a result of organizational membership (e.g., Alwin, Cohen, & Newcomb, 1991; Jones, 1986; Van Maanen, 1975), with one study showing that socialization experiences have over three times more influence on recruit adjustment than does their initial personality upon entering the organization (Chatman, 1991). Thus, while not a revelation, it is important to remember that sometimes people make the place, in terms of influencing organizational values, but at many other times people adapt their behavior and even their fundamental values to match the setting; that is, sometimes the place makes the person (e.g., Greenwald, 1992). We therefore pose the question, "When do people make the place?"

This question is especially pertinent in organizational settings because organizations can be conceptualized as strong situations (e.g., Davis-Blake & Pfeffer, 1989) that influence members' values and behavior, in some cases regardless of how similar or different a person is from an organization when he initially joins. As Schneider has acknowledged, organizations vary in what he calls climate strength (Schneider, Salvaggio, & Subirats, 2002), defined in terms of within-organization variability in climate perceptions, such that less variability implies a stronger climate. Weaker, compared to stronger, climates have less influence on people's behavior. This reasoning does not, however, consider the possibility that organizational membership may include processes other than attraction, selection, and attrition. Specifically, some people who do not fit may adjust their perceptions, values, and behavior rather than leave.

Figure 4.1 helps to summarize this discussion, using integrity as an example (though, of course, many other examples that compare person and situational attributes could be used, such as creativity or extroversion). Specifically, congruence models would focus on the matching quadrants (1 and 4). Regarding the mismatch quadrants (2 and 3), a congruence approach would presume that they are equivalent—an additive interaction. An interactive approach would consider a number of possible patterns for the mismatch quadrants. In Option 1, a cross-situational consistency perspective, personal dispositions, in this case, integrity, transcend the context. People behave in accordance with their personal disposition (honest) regardless of the organization's culture (honest or dishonest). Honest people act with high integrity regardless of whether

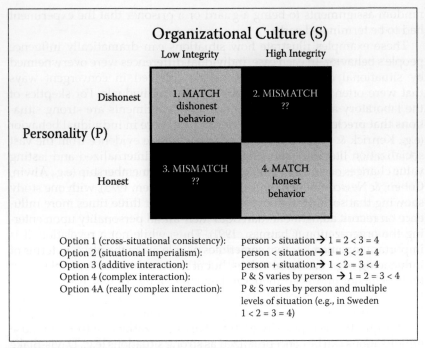

Option 1 (cross-situational consistency):   person > situation→ 1 = 2 < 3 = 4
Option 2 (situational imperialism):   person < situation→ 1 = 3 < 2 = 4
Option 3 (additive interaction):   person + situation→ 1 < 2 = 3 < 4
Option 4 (complex interaction):   P & S varies by person → 1 = 2 = 3 < 4
Option 4A (really complex interaction):   P & S varies by person and multiple
                                            levels of situation (e.g., in Sweden
                                            1 < 2 = 3 = 4)

FIGURE 4.1 Person X situation mismatches.

their organizational culture emphasizes integrity, while dishonest people are dishonest regardless of their organization's cultural emphasis.

Option 2 proposes a scenario in which situations dominate such that, regardless of their personal disposition, people adapt behaviorally to their organization's cultural orientation. When the culture emphasizes integrity, both honest and dishonest people exhibit honesty, such as complying with rules and whistle-blowing; when it emphasizes low integrity, both types of people would be expected to behave dishonestly, perhaps by participating in attempts to misrepresent (overstate) the organization's financial status. Options 1 and 2 represent the extreme views of the person–situation debate and, as past research has shown (e.g., Funder & Ozer, 1983), are typically unlikely to withstand theoretical and empirical evaluation.

Option 3 presents the typical congruence model, based on an additive interaction. In this case, people and situation characteristics "add up" to determine behavior. Mismatches between personality and organizational culture come out equivalently such that honest or dishonest people in mismatched cultures (high and low integrity) are equivalently moderately honest—not as honest as when they are in high-integrity cultures and not as dishonest as dishonest people in low-integrity cultures. For instance, people may comply with rules, precluding them from lying or stealing with respect to organizational activities, but fail to blow the whistle if others fail to comply.

It is only Options 4 and 4A that represent genuine interactional thinking. In these cases, the interaction between the person and situation depends on the particular combination of person–situation attributes. For instance, Option 4 calls into question whether honest or dishonest people might demonstrate greater cross-situational consistency in some situations rather than in others. Perhaps honest people are more likely to succumb to organizational pressure to be dishonest than dishonest people are to behave honestly as a member of a high-integrity organization.

Option 4A is an even more complex variant suggesting that person and situation characteristics vary by person and multiple levels of the situation, including, in this hypothetical example, organizational culture and societal culture. Whether dishonest people succumb to organizational pressure to behave honestly or honest people succumb to pressure to behave dishonestly can be influenced by the norms for honesty and integrity that exist at the societal level. For example, business operations in Japan are more uniformly ethical than in, for example, the United States and Canada (Vitell, Nwachukwu, & Barnes, 1993).

The behaviorally specific predictions engendered by an interactional, rather than congruence, perspective can lead to interesting, subtle, and sometimes counterintuitive findings. Next we consider ways in which the ASA model is informed by considering when some people are more affected than others by some types of situations.

DO SOME SITUATIONS INFLUENCE SOME PEOPLE MORE THAN OTHER PEOPLE?

The Case for Cooperation

In contrasting the congruence and interactionist perspectives, consider cooperative behavior. A congruence perspective would focus on matches, predicting that a cooperative person would likely thrive in an organization that values teams, while an individualist would thrive in one that values individual achievement. For example, Chatman and Barsade (1995) showed that cooperative people behaved most cooperatively when they were members of organizations that emphasized collectivism rather than individualism, and likewise, individualistic people behaved most individualistically when they were members of organizations that emphasized individualism. The congruence perspective would typically stop with that somewhat obvious finding—when people have the requisite skills, knowledge, and inclination to behave in accordance with situational demands, they will do so.

An interactionist perspective, however, pushes the insight further. Specifically, it adds to our understanding of the behavioral expression of personality by showing that people who tend to behave individualistically behave more consistently, even in situations emphasizing cooperation, while those who have more cooperative personalities behave more inconsistently. In other words, cooperators will cooperate when situational norms warrant, but behave individualistically when situational norms emphasize individual achievement. Framed in another way, cooperative people may be viewed as more responsive to the organization's culture, since they exhibited greater variance in their level of cooperative behavior across the two cultures than did individualistic people. Figure 4.2 presents data from Chatman and Barsade's (1995) study and from a field replication by Chatman and Spataro (2005) in a financial services organization. It shows the consistency in this finding across contexts—an MBA sample and a sample of senior executives in a financial services organization—and, more importantly, across a variety of cooperative behaviors. In each case, cooperators adjusted while individualists did not.

In sum, individuals' values interact with those of the organization to influence the extent of cooperative behavior. Moreover, it is only through this interactionist lens that we can come to understand and predict how individual differences are likely to interact with organizational characteristics, that is, that cooperative people will be more responsive to the organizational culture and that individualistic people will be more behaviorally consistent across situations.

Examining behaviorally specific interactions in this way may enable predictions about group and organization changes as a function of member characteristics. Returning to the case of cooperation, organizations, in Western cultures at least, may be prone to move toward individualism since individualistic people maintain their individualistic behavior even in the face of situational norms to cooperate, while cooperative people adjust their behavior to fit with situational demands, whether individualistic or cooperative, even if it means going against their personality. If dispositionally cooperative people are more likely to adjust to their organizational or business unit culture, individualism will spread (unless no individualists are ever hired) and that culture is therefore likely to become more individualistic over time. "Individualistic people may have a limited ability to play cooperative roles" (Chatman & Barsade, 1995, p. 426), and therefore could contribute to a decreasingly collectivistic culture. By understanding the ways in which specific person characteristics and situation characteristics interact, we can anticipate when people are likely to affect situations and when situations are likely to affect people. We can even begin to substantiate, in finer detail, Schneider's claim about people influencing organizational behavior through the ASA process discussed more fully in the second section of this chapter.

Additional Evidence for Differential Situational Influence

To develop greater insight into how and when people make the place, we recommend that researchers focus more on misfit and fine-grained behavioral outcomes rather than on the broad outcomes, like adjustment,

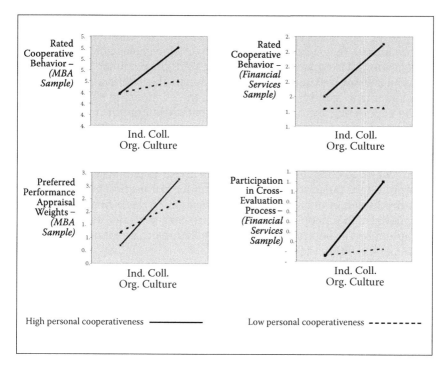

FIGURE 4.2 Complex interaction in which person and situation both vary by person: the case of cooperative behavior.

that are typically assessed in congruence research. Below we review additional research that enables us to better understand the microbehavioral changes or stability that people exhibit in the face of various organizational situations. We found relevant research that covered a number of person–side domains and chose to focus on three: personality, dispositional affect, and demographic characteristics. We focus on personality and the closely related domain of dispositional affect because it harkens to the interactional roots of the ASA model. We consider group and organizational demography because it influences behavior, but also because individuals have distinct demographic attributes that influence their behavior; in the aggregate. Therefore demography can also be considered a situational attribute (e.g., O'Reilly, Caldwell, & Barnett, 1989). This review is not meant to be exhaustive, but rather illustrates how viewing person–side attributes from an interactionist perspective adds to our understanding of each component of the ASA model.

Personality and the ASA Model.   Researchers have examined numerous personality characteristics from congruence and interactionist perspectives. For example, Molleman, Nauta, and Jehn (2004) investigated the moderating role of team task autonomy on the relationship between group-level personality traits (conscientiousness, emotional stability, and openness to experience) and team effectiveness (job satisfaction and learning). Using survey data from 133 undergraduate groups, they found that team task autonomy strengthened the relationship between conscientiousness and learning as well as the relationship between openness to experience and satisfaction, but that it did not affect the relationship between emotional stability and team effectiveness. Thus, situation characteristics, in this case task autonomy, differentially influenced the relationship between various team personality characteristics and team effectiveness. A congruence approach to these personality characteristics would have failed to uncover the situational variation by which they influenced team effectiveness. The implication of these findings for the ASA model is that people who not only are conscientious, but also prefer task autonomy, are more likely to be attracted to organizations with such modal personalities and structures.

Kilduff and Day's (1994) study of how self-monitoring influences job performance adds to our understanding of the selection component in the ASA model. They found that high self-monitors were more likely to change employers, move locations, and attain cross-company promotions than were low self-monitors. Additionally, for those who remained with the same employer, high self-monitors achieved more internal promotions than did low self-monitors. Two points are relevant to the ASA model. First, beyond the congruence between individuals' personalities and the organization, individuals had to read the organizational situation and adapt their personalities to organizational needs to be successful. Second, this finding suggests that, like the cooperators in Chatman and Barsade's (1995) study, high self-monitors were more aware of and responsive to their organizational context than were low self-monitors. To the extent that organizations continually select existing members into various positions (e.g., for promotion), this finding also implies that high self-monitors will be better at adjusting their behaviors to meet organizational needs, and therefore be more actively selected for promotion.

Dispositional Affect and the ASA Model.   An interactionist examination of dispositional affect also provides a fine-grained understanding of the ASA model. Staw and Barsade proposed competing hypotheses for the influence of positive affect (PA) and negative affect (NA) on performance, arguing that, on the one hand, high PA individuals may exhibit higher levels of performance since they are more energized, flexible, creative, and persistent. On the other hand, high NA people may do better since they process information more accurately. Staw and Barsade (1993) provided results from a business simulation that supported the happier but smarter hypothesis; positive affect was positively associated with performance. Beyond how closely dispositional affect is aligned with an organization, under stressful, time-constrained situations, high PA people may fare better than high NA individuals. Should the performance differences between high PA and NA individuals become widespread within an organization, fast-paced, time-constrained organizations are likely to attract and select people who are high on PA.

Similarly, Lyubomirsky and Ross (1997) examined how characteristically happy and unhappy people differed in their responsiveness to social comparison information. They hypothesized and found support for the notion that happy individuals are less sensitive to unsolicited social comparison information and less vulnerable to unfavorable social comparison information than are unhappy individuals. Given the different responses of happy and unhappy people to social comparisons, attrition would likely be higher among unhappy rather than happy individuals generally, and particularly in organizations that regularly compare and publicize employee behaviors and effectiveness. In sum, understanding the way in which dispositional affect interacts with specific organizational aspects sheds light on the complexity of the ASA model.

Demographic Characteristics and the ASA Model.   A preponderance of demography research suggests that the ways in which demographic characteristics interact with those of the organization has implications for the ASA model. For example, Jackson, Stone, and Alvarez (1993) reviewed research on socialization and demography, noting that individuals who are in the minority with respect to their gender, ethnicity, age, and status, and who are less behaviorally flexible, are less susceptible to organizational socialization than are those who are more demographically similar to their colleagues. Moreover, they proposed that, depending on an organization's demographic composition, socialization patterns may differ such that those who are similar to current members will be socialized more intensively; that is, they will be more responsive to the organization's socialization efforts. Given that socialization processes are negatively related to turnover, organizations will, over time, retain members who are similar across a broad range of demographic characteristics. These members will, in turn, attract and select similar others and reject those who are different.

Karakowsky and Siegel (1999) examined the effects of work groups' sex composition and gender orientation of the group's task on group members' patterns of emergent leadership behavior. Using an experimental design they found that incongruence of a group member's sex with the gender orientation of the task resulted in lower levels of exhibited leader behaviors. They also found that members working on gender-incongruent tasks displayed significantly less leadership behavior when they were also in the numerical minority with respect to sex than those who were in the numerical majority. This finding suggests that knowing who will rise to leadership roles and be selected into leadership positions within an organization requires understanding much more than just congruence. Rather, an interactionist lens that considers the different outcomes of combinations of the person's sex, his sex relative to the sex composition of his work group, and the gender orientation of the work he is doing is needed to predict emergent leadership. Even though this study focused on emergent leadership, one implication is that as patterns of successful leadership develop, the interaction of these person and situation characteristics is likely to influence who is selected for leadership positions.

Research by Chatman and O'Reilly (2004) and Tsui, Egan, and O'Reilly (1992) uncovered several asymmetrical effects of being demographically different on attrition. Chatman and O'Reilly found an interaction between sex and group sex composition, indicating that men and women differed in their reports of the likelihood that they would transfer out of work groups with varying sex composition. Specifically, men in the study were more eager to leave their work groups as the proportions of women in their work groups increased, while women indicated the greatest likelihood of leaving homogeneous groups of women and groups that had an equal number of men and women. These results imply that rather than the congruence of demographic characteristics with those of the organization, it is the interaction of sex in specific work groups that affects attrition. In other words, attrition due to sex cannot be uniformly determined without considering the specific combination of the individuals' sex and their work group's sex composition.

Likewise, Tsui et al. (1992) examined the effects of increasing diversity in age, tenure, education, sex, and race on three forms of attachment (psychological commitment, absences, and intention to stay) for majority members. Their findings indicated asymmetrical effects for being different such that Whites and men showed larger negative effects for increased unit heterogeneity than did women or non-Whites. As such, Whites and men may be more likely to leave an organization that is increasingly heterogeneous than women or non-Whites. Note that, again, this pattern could not be predicted by the congruence approach. Only when an interactionist lens was applied were departures accurately predicted.

Our brief review of three person–side constructs—personality, dispositional affect, and demography—shows that the relationship between people and situation characteristics, particularly with regard to organizational membership and tasks, is complex. Specifically, in each case, a congruence lens would limit insight into the ASA model because of its global focus on aggregate behaviors and general focus on fit rather than misfit. A congruence lens would also make it difficult to identify the source of comparable attributes of person and situation. In contrast, an interactionist lens deepens our understanding of the ASA model and, as such, our ability to predict who will be affected by which situations by drawing attention to the unique and complex ways in which person characteristics combine with organizational attributes. Next we consider when and how people will have lasting impact on organizations.

WHEN WILL PEOPLE AFFECT SITUATIONS?

Historically, social and organizational psychologists have been more concerned with how people are influenced by situations than with how individuals shape situations (e.g., Aronson, 1984). Thus, one of the more provocative claims of the ASA model is that people create structures and processes in organizations that reflect the aggregated or modal organizational personality (e.g., Schneider et al., 1998). Because the ASA research to date has focused exclusively on aggregate personality, substantiation for the claim has remained broad and leaves much of the underlying mechanisms by which structures and processes are formed to the imagination. Below we discuss research that offers clues about the specific mechanisms by which people, individually and in the aggregate, may have lasting impact on their organizations.

Considering a Network-Based Approach to Understanding Culture Transmission

Recently, Chatman, Lee, Harrison, and Carroll (2007) attempted to identify the underlying processes by which people 'make' their organizational culture, that is, their system of shared values and norms that defines what is important and how members ought to feel and behave. In a study of high-level professionals working in 11 business units of a large financial services organization, they sought to determine how network peer relationships (friendship ties) and work-based relationships (instrumental ties) served as conduits of culture and influenced levels of enculturation, or how closely members' values corresponded to their organization's values.

Chatman et al. (2007) defined peer enculturation as the similarity between an individual's perception of his or her business unit's culture and his or her peers' perceptions of that same culture, respectively. They considered how network partners and network position influenced veteran employees' understanding of their organizational culture. Starting from the well-known finding that people who are more demographically similar to one another are more likely to form relationships (e.g., McPherson, Smith-Lovin, & Cook, 2001), they found that focal individuals' peer enculturation could be predicted from the perceptions of their primary network peers, but that focal individuals' work-based relationships had no effect on peer enculturation.

This study revealed a number of ASA-relevant implications. First, though understanding one's business unit culture is relevant to work effectiveness and is instrumentally important, such cultural understanding does not appear to be transmitted across the instrumental network. This finding suggests that adopting others' views may require a level of intimacy and trust that primary relationships afford. It also supports the notion that different tasks and aspects of organizational life are supported and conveyed through different types of ties, through a social structure created informally by organizational members (e.g., Hansen, 1999). The research also begins to identify the mechanisms that support culture transmission within organizations, noting that demographic homogeneity among peers is at least one potent source of cultural influence. Thus, demographic homophily is a basis for tie formation within organizations and serves as a mechanism for cultural transmission. Certain types of network ties, particularly among homophilous pairs, are the underlying mechanism by which people transmit the place, and likely sustain and reproduce it.

Second, the reflected enculturation of one's peers was a powerful determinant of one's own level of enculturation. This reflected enculturation, or socialization as a function of whom a person is friends with, must be considered along with other known sources of cultural influence, including formal and intentional socialization (e.g., Morrison, 1994) and personality traits or individual differences that contribute to personal susceptibility to socialization tactics (e.g., Chatman, 1991). It also suggests that person and situation attributes have reciprocal influence on one another; people make the place while the place, defined in terms of those whom they have chosen as friends, is making them.

Additional Evidence of People Influencing Situations

Other evidence points to the specific mechanisms by which people influence organizational structures and processes. In the following sections we discuss how personality, dispositional affect, and demography interact with organizational attributes to determine how people influence organizations.

Personality and the ASA Model.   Researchers have been particularly interested in prominent organization figures, such as founders and CEOs, and how their personalities might affect organizational structures and processes. In a longitudinal study of high-technology start-up firms, Baron and Hannan (2002) showed that a founder's "blueprint" for his organization, his mental model of how the organization would "look and feel," had a pervasive and long-lasting influence over how the organization developed, who was hired, and how effectively it executed it's stated strategy (see also Baron, Burton, & Hannan, 1999). Founding blueprints tended to be extremely robust, often lasting through all stages of organizational growth and decline. Further, attempted changes in organizational blueprints were highly destabilizing to young technology start-ups, causing employee turnover, reducing bottom-line financial performance, and even threatening the firm's survival. Though the concept of a blueprint is not a personality characteristic per se, it reflects a founder's fundamental values and mental models regarding organizational membership, including how employees are selected, the basis of their attachment, and how their efforts are coordinated and controlled. This research is therefore relevant to the ASA model as it specifies a cognitive factor that leads founders to develop their organizations in particular ways, providing insight into, for example, the origination of founders' goals (e.g., Schneider et al., 1995), and how the interaction of these goals with the organization and its environmental context affects attraction, selection, and attrition processes.

Similarly, Schein (1983) argued that the founder plays an instrumental role in creating organizational culture by rigorously screening employees to identify those who support his or her ideals and values. Once selected, founders continue to socialize their employees into their way of thinking and serve as a role model, encouraging employees to internalize these values. While this discussion might appear to suggest that it is merely important for employees' values to be congruent with those of the organization, if we look deeper and take an interactionist view, Schein's research implies that employee fit is particularly important during periods of organizational creation and change, and during these periods those who hold and promote the founder's values will have greater impact on the organization than they will during stable periods.

Even senior executives who are not founders can have an inordinate influence on organizations under certain circumstances. For example, Miller and Droge (1986) examined the CEO's need for achievement in relation to organizational structure and found that the relationships between need for achievement and structure were highest in samples of small and young firms, indicating that the CEO's personality influenced structure, rather than the reverse. As such, senior leaders' personality was highly influential in small firms in which the impact of the leader can be direct and pervasive. Moreover, their results suggested that leaders who have a high need for achievement but who work for large or old firms may be more likely to leave as they become frustrated with their limited ability to influence the organization's outcomes. In sum, this discussion of leader and founder individual differences underscores the importance of taking an interactionist approach to the ASA model. One common thread to these studies is that personality factors such as charisma or need for achievement are not sufficient for leaders to have a lasting impact on their organizations. Instead, leadership effectiveness also depends on such situational factors as need for change and firm size or age.

Dispositional Affect and the ASA Model.   By applying an interactionist approach to the ASA model, we can also better understand when individuals' dispositional affect influences the situation. Grandey, Fisk, Mattila, Jansen, and Sideman (2005) examined the use of service providers to engage in emotion management through the use of authentic smiles. They found that authentic smiles enhanced customers' impressions of service provider friendliness, which, in turn, had a positive relationship with customer satisfaction. Given that customer satisfaction depends on the congruence of employees' values with those of the organization, but also with the actual service or the product, this study suggests that it is the interaction of these person factors with those of the service encounter that attract repeat business as well as future job candidates.

Other research on emotional convergence (Anderson, Keltner, & John, 2003) and emotional contagion (Barsade, 2002) lends further insight to the ASA model from an interactionist perspective. Anderson et al. (2003) studied dating partners and college roommates and found that they became more similar in their emotional responses over the course of a year. Interestingly, lower-status partners shifted their emotional responses more in order to converge with their higher-status counterparts. The benefits of this emotional convergence or similarity were that these relationships exhibited greater cohesion and were less likely to dissolve. One implication of these findings is that relationship success or maintenance does not depend on the mere alignment of partner emotions, but the degree of emotional similarity that was achieved, and the degree of emotional similarity depended on the extent to which the less powerful partner altered his or her emotions. In short, relationship success depends on selecting individuals who share common feelings as well as a willingness to adjust their emotional responses. If lower-status individuals are unwilling to adjust their responses, they or their partners may feel dissatisfied with the relationship and leave in search of one that offers greater emotional similarity.

Similarly, Barsade (2002) examined the transfer of emotion between individuals, termed emotional contagion, and its influence on work group outcomes, including cooperation, conflict, and performance. Group members in a simulated organizational meeting experienced positive emotional contagion, benefiting groups by improving cooperation, decreasing conflict, and increasing perceptions of task performance. In this way, Barsade argued that emotional contagion is a form of social influence and notes that its effect depends on the emotion valence. Given that people typically desire to maintain positive moods (Isen & Baron, 1991), it is likely that those who promote positive emotional contagion, that is, individuals high on positive affect, may be more likely to be selected into organizations, while those who are high on negative affect will be more likely to leave. It also suggests that one member can have an inordinate influence on co-workers, creating a context in which members are highly engaged and productive, or dysfunctional (e.g., Felps & Mitchell, 2003).

Demographic Characteristics and the ASA Model. Research on the effects of demographic diversity also illustrates the value in taking an interactionist approach to the ASA model in considering the conditions under which people are most likely to influence their context. For example, Chatman, Berdahl, Boisnier, Spataro, and Anderson (2006) found that numerical distinctiveness and historical atypicality interacted such that those in the numerical minority but for whom their sex was historically congruent with the task (e.g., men and math tasks) had a disproportionate influence on their group's performance, regardless of their actual level of expertise on the task. This implies that people whose gender is typical for the task make the place some of the time, that is, when they are in the numerical minority.

Examining group composition is also relevant to selection. In a study assessing the impact of cultural diversity on group process and performance, Watson, Kumar, and Michaelsen (1993) found that homogeneous groups initially scored higher on both process and performance effectiveness, but that over time, both groups showed improvements, and heterogeneous groups even came to score higher on two performance measures. They concluded that capitalizing on diversity might be time dependent such that when people get to know each other better and learn and draw upon each others skills, they will be able to achieve higher levels of performance. Whereas Chatman et al.'s (2006) study highlights the importance of the interaction between gender atypicality and the task, Watson et al.'s (1993) study draws attention to the interaction between diversity and time. Thus, while at first glance the results might suggest that selecting diverse workers may be disadvantageous to group processes and performance, organizations must make selection decisions by considering the combined impact of the groups to which individuals will be assigned as well as the length of their project.

Thomas (1990) examined the influence of race on protégés' experiences of forming developmental relationships among Black and White managers. Whites had almost no developmental relationships with persons of another race, while Blacks formed developmental relationships with people of other races and were more likely to form relationships outside the formal lines of authority and outside their departments, creating new social networks within their organizations.

Finally, Harrison and Carroll (1991, 2006) have used computer simulation technology to develop formal models that identify the influence of members' demographic attributes on the stability of organizational culture. Though many of their findings are consistent with what the ASA model would predict, some reveal new insights derived from understanding the simultaneous influence of person and organizational components. For example, Harrison and Carroll (1991) found that rapid growth and high turnover contributed to greater cultural stability, rather than instability as is typically predicted because new employees are likely more susceptible to socialization while those who leave (the attrition component) are likely more resistant to being socialized into the culture. Further, their simulations revealed that culture may actually get stronger in declining organizations because employees with shorter tenure are the most likely to leave (Harrison & Carroll, 1991, p. 577). This simulation approach is valuable in that it provides a fine-grained understanding of how people influence and change culture, in this case as a result of their demographic makeup, their network ties, and their entry and exit behavior.

SUMMARY AND CONCLUSION

Our first and foremost objective in this chapter was to honor Ben Schneider's enormous contribution to organizational psychology: the ASA model. The ASA model revitalized interest in understanding person–situation fit and helped to pinpoint who is likely to be well adjusted, effective, and successful within particular organizations. Our second objective was to offer a course correction to the form that subsequent research in this domain has taken by challenging researchers to move from studying congruence and adjustment to focusing on incongruence between people and situations and the specific resulting behaviors. A person's success in an organization may not depend on mere congruence of personal and situational factors, but rather on their interaction. That is, the various person and situation combinations—some of which are congruence based and some of which are explicitly incongruent—determine when some people will be more responsive to some organizational attributes and when some people will have greater influence on emerging structures and processes.

We have argued that viewing the ASA model through a person–situation interaction lens rather than the more typical congruence lens is advantageous for three reasons. First, an interactionist approach focuses on how people who do not fit an organization influence it or are influenced by it. This provides more information about the different ways that people's attributes combine and interact with contextual attributes than does a congruence approach, which typically predicts a simple additive influence of the two. Second, an interactive focus enables us to understand the fine-grained behavioral outcomes of various combinations of person and organizational characteristics. In so doing, and third, an interactive lens generates insight to the underlying processes by which people come to make the place.

Focus on Misfits

We believe that researchers should focus on complex interactions as suggested in Options 3, 4, and 4A in Figure 4.1. Our review of research on personality, dispositional affect, and demographic characteristics revealed how people differentially respond to the organizational context, influencing the modal personality that develops in the organization, as well as determining who will be attracted to, selected into, and leave the organization. For example, men and non-Whites may be more inclined to leave their groups when they are in the numerical minority, whereas women are more likely to leave their groups when they are balanced or homogeneously comprised of women. And cooperators and high self-monitors are more likely to adjust their behavior to suit the situation, while individualists and low self-monitors are more behaviorally consistent across organizational contexts. This review, therefore, offered evidence of how certain types of misfits between people and organizations affect behavior.

Though a marked increase in research that highlights misfits has begun to emerge, it may still not go far enough. For instance, Jansen and Kristof-Brown's (2005) study of misfit between individual and work group pace illustrated that the effects of misfit differentially affected those who outpaced or were slower than their group, with those who were slower experiencing more strain. The study makes an important contribution by beginning to examine how misfit occurs due to specific combinations of individual and organizational characteristics. But the next step would be to examine the specific behavioral reactions to this misfit. For example, slower individuals might be more likely to leave the organization, try to increase their pace so that they can reduce the strain of being slower than their group, or could try to convince their group members to take a slower approach to work.

Similarly, Kristof-Brown, Barrick, and Stevens (2005) argued that misfit serves a complementary purpose for work groups. Specifically, they argued that groups with some introverts and some extroverts are more effective because these two personality types complement each other, which increases attraction to their teams, and in turn their willingness to contribute to their teams. Again, the focus on misfit is refreshing, and the study raises several questions that future research may seek to address. First, would equivalent adjustment arise from extroverted people joining an introverted team, or from introverted people joining an extroverted team? Second, what is the source of behavioral variation—is it situation or person driven? And third, what might be the specific behavioral manifestations of introverts joining extroverts, and how might these differ from extroverts joining introverts? Future research should therefore examine how specific combinations of person and organization factors influence misfit and identify the implications for ASA processes.

Focus on Specific Behaviors: Disaggregate Adjustment

An interactionist approach to ASA moves from examining stated adjustment or effectiveness to studying specific behaviors. Examining these specific behaviors can provide a clear window into a person's adjustment, but simply focusing on stated adjustment does not provide insight into how, in behavioral terms, a person has adjusted or not to an organizational setting. Closely related, an interactionist focus enables an understanding of the source and consequences of adjustment, decoupling adjustment as typically operationalized from actual behavior. Thus, we encourage researchers to consider how person–situation interactions affect specific adaptive or effective behaviors.

Identify Processes Underlying People's Influence on Organizations

Our final argument for applying an interactionist lens to the ASA model is that it provides insight into the underlying processes that determine when and how people are able to influence situations, and we again reviewed research on personality, dispositional affect, and demography that illustrates this point. As evidence, we suggested that exploring the actual source of the structure or process, such as social networks, group and organizational demography, or founders' blueprints, may provide more explicit insight into how people have lasting impact on their organizations. In particular, founders and leaders, through their mental models and personality-relevant behaviors, may have lasting influence on organizational structures and whether processes emerge and change or stagnate over time. And in a highly reciprocal interaction, patterns of demographic distribution in organizations may enable certain people to have substantial influence in particular situations (e.g., minority members with expertise on the task), while constraining behavior in other ways by limiting opportunities to access mentors and resources.

Our goal was to illustrate the value of viewing the ASA model through its roots in person–situation interaction rather than through a congruence lens. In doing so, we suggested that such an approach provides an increased understanding of misfits, insight to sources and consequences of variation in specific person–situation behaviors, and greater understanding of the underlying processes by which the ASA model operates. We attempted to illustrate the ways in which an interactionist approach allows us to predict how and when people will make, or be made, by the place.

REFERENCES

Alwin, D. F., Cohen, R. L., & Newcomb, T. M. (1991). *Political attitudes over the life span: The Bennington women after fifty years.* Madison: University of Wisconsin Press.

Anderson, C., Keltner, D., & John, O. (2003). Emotional convergence between people over time. *Journal of Personality and Social Psychology, 8,* 1054–1068.

Aronson, E. (1984). Experimentation in social psychology. In G. Lindzey & E. Aronson (Eds.), *Handbook of social psychology* (Vol. 1, pp. 441–446). New York: Random House.

Asch, S. E. (1956). Studies of independence and conformity. 1. A minority of one against a unanimous majority. *Psychological Monographs, 70,* 1–70.

Bantel, K., & Jackson, S. (1989). Top management and innovations in banking: Does the composition of the team make a difference? *Strategic Management Journal, 10,* 107–124.

Baron, J., Burton, M. D., & Hannan, M. (1999). Engineering bureaucracy: The genesis of formal policies, positions, and structures in high-technology firms. *Journal of Law, Economics, and Organization, 15,* 1–41.

Baron, J., & Hannan, M. (2002, Spring). Organizational blueprints for success in high-tech start ups: Lessons from the Stanford Project on Emerging Companies. *California Management Review,* 3–32.

Barsade, S. (2002). The ripple effect: Emotional contagion and its influence on group behavior. *Administrative Science Quarterly, 47,* 644–675.

Block, J. (1978). *The Q-sort method in personality assessment and psychiatric research.* Palo Alto, CA: Consulting Psychologists Press.

Bowers, K. S. (1973). Situationism in psychology: An analysis and a critique. *Psychological Review, 80,* 307–336.

Bretz, R. D., Jr., Asch, R. A., & Dreher, G. F. (1989). Do people make the place? An examination of the attraction–selection–attrition hypothesis. *Personnel Psychology, 42,* 561–581.

Cable, D. M., & Judge, T. A. (1996). Person–organization fit, job choice decisions and organizational entry. *Organizational Behavior Human Decision Processes, 67,* 294–312.

Caldwell, D., & O'Reilly, C. (1990). Measuring person-job fit using a profile comparison process. *Journal of Applied Psychology, 75,* 648–657.

Chatman, J. A. (1989). Improving interactional organizational research: A model of person–organization fit. *Academy of Management Review, 14,* 333.

Chatman, J. A. (1991). Matching people and organizations: Selection and socialization in public accounting firms. *Administrative Science Quarterly, 36,* 459.

Chatman, J. A., & Barsade, S. G. (1995). Personality, organizational culture, and cooperation: Evidence from a business simulation. *Administrative Science Quarterly, 40,* 423–443.

Chatman, J. A., Boisnier, A., Berdahl, J., Spataro, S., & Anderson, C. (2006). *The typical, the rare, and the outnumbered: Disentangling the effects of numerical distinctiveness and sex-stereotyped tasks on individuals' perceptions of category salience and performance in groups.* Working paper, Haas School of Business, University of California, Berkeley.

Chatman, J. A., Lee, G., Harrison, J. R., & Carroll, G. (2006). *The influence of social networks on cultural transmission and enculturation: An empirical investigation.* Working paper, Haas School of Business, University of California, Berkeley.

Chatman, J. A., & O'Reilly, C. A. (2004). Asymmetric reactions to work group sex diversity among men and women. *Academy of Management Journal, 47,* 193–208.

Chatman, J. A., Polzer, J. T., Barsade, S. G., & Neale, M. A. (1998). Being different yet feeling similar: The influence of demographic composition and organizational culture on work processes and outcomes. *Administrative Science Quarterly, 43,* 749–780.

Chatman, J. A., & Spataro, S. (2005). Getting people to cooperate: Understanding relational demography-based variations in people's responsiveness to organizational inducements. *Academy of Management Journal, 48,* 321–331.

Davis-Blake, A., & Pfeffer, J. (1989). Just a mirage: The search for dispositional effects in organizational research. *Academy of Management Review, 14,* 385.

Felps, W., & Mitchell, T. R. (2003). *When do bad apples spoil the barrel: A theory of destructive group members and dysfunctional groups.* Working paper, School of Business, University of Washington, Seattle.

Funder, D. C., & Ozer, D. J. (1983). Behavior as a function of the situation. *Journal of Personality and Social Psychology, 44,* 107–112.

Grandey, A. A., Fisk, G. M., Mattila, A. S., Jansen, K. J., & Sideman, L. A. (2005). Is "service with a smile" enough? Authenticity of positive displays during service encounters. *Organizational Behavior and Human Decision Processes, 96,* 38–55.

Greenwald, A. G. (1992). Dissonance theory and self theory: Fifteen more years. *Psychological Inquiry, 3,* 329–331.

Haney, C., Banks, W. C., & Zimbardo, P. G. (1973). Interpersonal dynamics in a simulated prison. *International Journal of Criminology and Penology, 1,* 69–97.

Hansen, M. T. (1999). The search-transfer problem: The role of weak ties in sharing knowledge across organization subunits. *Administrative Science Quarterly, 44,* 82–111.

Harrison, J. R., & Carroll, G. R. (1991). Keeping the faith: A model of cultural transmission in formal organizations. *Administrative Science Quarterly, 36,* 552–582.

Harrison, J. R., & Carroll, G. R. (2006). *Culture and demography in organizations.* Princeton, NJ: Princeton University Press.

Isen, A. M., & Baron, R. A. (1991). Positive affect as a factor in organizational behavior. In B. M. Staw & L. L. Cummings (Eds.), *Research in organizational behavior* (Vol. 13, pp. 1–54). Greenwich, CT: JAI Press.

Jackson, S. E., Stone, V. K., & Alvarez, E. D. (1993). Socialization amidst diversity: Impact of demographics on work team old-timers and newcomers. In L. L. Cummings & B. M. Staw (Eds.), *Research in organizational behavior* (Vol. 15, pp. 45–109). Greenwich, CT: JAI Press.

Jansen, K. J., & Kristof-Brown, A. L. (2005). Marching to the beat of a different drummer: Examining the impact of pacing congruence. *Organizational Behavior and Human Decision Processes, 97*(2), 93–105.

Jones, G. R. (1986). Socialization tactics, self-efficacy, and newcomers' adjustments to organizations. *Academy of Management Journal, 29,* 262–279.

Judge, T. A., & Bretz, R. D. (1992). Effects of work values on job choice decisions. *Journal of Applied Psychology, 77,* 261.

Karakowsky, L., & Siegel, J. P. (1999). The effects of proportional representation and gender orientation of the task on emergent leadership behavior in mixed-gender work groups. *Journal of Applied Psychology, 84,* 620–631.

Kenrick, D. T., & Funder, D. C. (1988). Profiting from controversy: Lessons from the person–situation debate. *American Psychologist, 43,* 23–35.

Kilduff, M. & Day, D. V. (1994). Do chameleons get ahead? The effects of self-monitoring on managerial careers. *Academy of Management Journal, 37:* 1047.

Kristof-Brown, A., Barrick, M. R., & Stevens, C. K. (2005). When opposites attract: A multi-sample demonstration of complementary person–team fit on extraversion. *Journal of Personality, 73*(4), 935–957.

Lyubomirsky, S., & Ross, L. (1997). Hedonic consequences of social comparison: A contrast of happy and unhappy people. *Journal of Personality and Social Psychology, 73,* 1141–1157.

Magnusson, D., & Endler, N. (1977). Interactional psychology: Present status and future prospects. In D. Magnusson & N. Endler (Eds.), *Personality at the crossroads: Current issues in interactional psychology* (pp. 3–35). Hillsdale, NJ: Erlbaum.

McPherson, M., Smith-Lovin, L., & Cook, J. M. (2001). Birds of a feather: Homophily in social networks. *Annual Review of Sociology, 27,* 415–444.

Milgram, S. (1963). Behavioral study of obedience. *Journal of Abnormal Psychology, 67*, 371.

Miller, D., & Droge, C. (1986). Psychological and traditional determinants of structure. *Administrative Science Quarterly, 31*, 539–560.

Mischel, W. (1968). *Personality and assessment.* New York: Wiley & Sons.

Molleman, E., Nauta, A., & Jehn, K. E. (2004) Person-job fit applied to teamwork: A multi-level approach. *Small Group Research, 36*, 515–539.

Morrison, E. W. (1993). Newcomer information seeking: Exploring types, modes, sources, and outcomes. *Academy of Management Journal, 36*, 557–589.

Morrison, E. W. (1994). Role definitions and organizational citizenship behavior: The importance of the employee's perspective. *Academy of Management Journal, 37*, 1543–1567.

O'Reilly, C., Caldwell, D., & Barnett, W. (1989). Work group demography, social integration, and turnover. *Administrative Science Quarterly, 34*, 21–37.

O'Reilly, C., Chatman, J. A., & Caldwell, D. (1991). People and organizational culture: A profile comparison approach to assessing person–organization fit. *Academy of Management Journal, 34*, 487–516.

Pervin, L. A. (1989). *Personality: Theory and research* (5th ed.). New York: Wiley.

Rynes, S. L., & Gerhart, B. (1990). Interviewer assessment of applicant "fit": An exploratory investigation. *Personnel Psychology, 43*, 13–22.

Schein, E. H. (1983). The role of the founder in creating organizational culture. *Organizational Dynamics, 12*, 13–28.

Schneider, B. (1978). Person–situation selection: A review of some ability-situation interaction research. *Personnel Psychology, 31*, 281–297.

Schneider, B. (1983). Interactional psychology and organizational behavior. In B. M. Staw & L. L. Cummings (Eds.), *Research in organizational behavior* (Vol. 5, pp. 1–31). Greenwich, CT: JAI Press.

Schneider, B. (1987). The people make the place. *Personnel Psychology, 40*, 437–453.

Schneider, B., Goldstein, H. W., & Smith, D. B. (1995). The ASA framework: An update. *Personnel Psychology, 48*, 747–773.

Schneider, B., Salvaggio, A. N., & Subirats, M. (2002). Climate strength: A new direction for climate research. *Journal of Applied Psychology, 87*, 220–229.

Schneider, B., Smith, D. B., Fleenor, J., & Taylor, S. (1998). Personality and organizations: A test of the homogeneity hypothesis. *Journal of Applied Psychology, 83*, 462–470.

Staw, B. M., & Barsade, S. G. (1993). Affect and managerial performance: A test of the sadder-but-wiser vs. happier-and-smarter hypothesis. *Administrative Science Quarterly, 38*, 304.

Thomas, D. A. (1990). The impact of race on managers' experiences of developmental relationships (mentoring and sponsorship): An intra-organizational study. *Journal of Organizational Behavior, 11*, 479–492.

Tsui, A. S., Egan, T. D., & O'Reilly, C. A. (1992). Being different: Relational demography and organizational attachment. *Administrative Science Quarterly, 37*, 549–579.

Vancouver, J., & Schmitt, N. (1991). An exploratory examination of person–organization fit: Organizational goal congruence. *Personnel Psychology, 44*, 333–352.

Vandenberghe, C. (1999). Organizational culture, person-culture fit, and turnover: A replication in the health care industry. *Journal of Organizational Behavior, 20,* 175–184.

Van Maanen, J. (1975). Police organization: A longitudinal examination of job attitudes in an urban police department. *Administrative Science Quarterly, 20,* 207–228.

Vitell, S. J., Nwachukwu, S. N., & Barnes, J. H. (1993). The effects of culture on ethical decision-making: An application of Hofstede's typology. *Journal of Business Ethics, 12,* 753–760.

Watson, W. E., Kumar, K., & Michaelsen, L. (1993). Cultural diversity's impact on interaction processes and performance: Comparing homogeneous and diverse task groups. *Academy of Management Journal, 36,* 590–602.

Wrzeniewski, A., & Dutton, J. E. (2001). Crafting a job: Revisioning employees as active crafters of their work. *Academy of Management Review, 26,* 179–201.

5

The Attraction–Selection–Attrition Model and Staffing
Some Multilevel Implications

ROBERT E. PLOYHART
University of South Carolina

NEAL SCHMITT
Michigan State University

The attraction–selection–attrition (ASA; Schneider, 1987) model fundamentally influenced staffing research and practice. It remains one of the most highly cited articles of all time. Although it was published nearly 20 years ago, it remains relevant and continues to be cited frequently. In this chapter we first briefly review two key implications of the ASA model for staffing and describe some representative research on these topics. But our plan with this chapter is not to provide a review; such work has already been done (e.g., Schneider, Goldstein, & Smith, 1995). Instead, we will spend more time speculating on the future of the ASA model for staffing. We believe, and will hopefully convince readers, that the ASA model offers much more than a description of how "the people make the place." We argue the ASA model offers a unique perspective on staffing that spans multiple levels and offers the possibility of uniting micro and macro staffing. As such, it may be even more relevant and useful today than when it was originally published.

TWO KEY PREDICTIONS OF THE ASA FOR STAFFING

There are many interesting predictions the ASA model makes, but for our purposes perhaps the two most important are about fit and homogeneity.

The Importance of Fit

In the ASA, fit generally refers to person–environment (P–E) fit, and the environment is typically operationalized as various job or organizational characteristics. Fit is essentially a match between an individual's and an organization's values, interests, and personality (Kristof, 1996). We all know fit from personal experience; we have left or joined organizations because of our perceived fit with them, and organizations have offered or refused jobs to us for similar reasons. Fit is hypothesized to produce a number of favorable outcomes, such as increased satisfaction, performance, and organizational attraction. Schneider's ASA model led to an increased recognition that fit is an important aspect of recruitment and selection. In general, applicants and organizations are attracted to, select, and remain with each other when there is strong fit.

Research on fit has occurred primarily in the recruiting area, where the basic question is how the match between applicant characteristics and job/organizational characteristics influences various recruiting outcomes like organizational attraction and job choice (e.g., Bretz & Judge, 1994; Cable & Judge, 1994, 1996, 1997; Chatman, 1989, 1991; Ryan, Sacco, McFarland, & Kriska, 2000). Applicant characteristics that are usually considered include personality, interests, and values. Job/organizational characteristics often include pay, compensation structure, values, culture, and climate. Sometimes the organizational characteristics are provided by a survey of a key informant (e.g., manager); other times they are based on a survey of employees within the organization. In the recruitment literature, we typically focus on *supplementary fit* because what the applicant brings to the organization (in terms of personality, interests, and values) supplements or is similar to the organization's existing culture and climate, and vice versa (Kristof, 1996; Muchinsky & Monahan, 1987).

Selection researchers also consider fit, but from a different perspective. Here, the goal is to identify which applicants have the necessary knowledge, skills, abilities, and other characteristics (KSAOs) to perform effectively on the job. This is known as *complementary fit* because the applicant brings KSAOs that are currently lacking in the organization, and the organization provides compensation and other resources that the applicant requires (Kristof, 1996; Muchinsky & Monahan, 1987). Of course, the way we identify the missing KSAOs is from a job analysis.

There are two ways of operationalizing fit. One is an objective operationalization such as the statistical interaction between an individual's

characteristics (e.g., personality, values) and a job/organization's characteristics (e.g., pay, location). A second is a subjective operationalization where
individuals give a self-report assessment of their fit perceptions. It is also
important to note that fit may occur with more than a job or organization;
it may also occur with a work group (Kristof-Brown, Jansen, & Colbert,
2002). We return to this point shortly because we believe it has important
implications that have not fully been realized in staffing or the ASA.

The Homogeneity Hypothesis

A second critical prediction in the ASA model is that of homogeneity.
The hypothesis is that over time, through attraction–selection–attrition
processes (which are really ways of producing fit), organizations become
composed of individuals who are increasingly homogeneous in terms of
their personalities, values, interests, and related characteristics. It is interesting to note that the ASA model was not the first to make such predictions.
Holland's Realistic, Investigative, Artistic, Social, Enterprising, Conventional (RIASEC) model of occupational types made similar predictions as
far back as the 1960s (see Holland, 1997). But the ASA model was unique in
describing how individuals, when similar enough to one another, could *in
the aggregate* produce different-looking organizations. That is, one reason
organizations differ in terms of their processes, cultures, and structures
is because of the dominant characteristics of the people in them. That is a
powerful idea because it is a person-centered approach for understanding
organizations and organizational consequences. It also suggests that the
research and practice of applied psychologists and human resource spe-
cialists should have organizational-level consequences.

Despite the power of this hypothesis, there is little research examining
it (probably because of the difficulty in getting the data). However, the
research that has been conducted is supportive (Jordan, Herriot, & Chalmers, 1991; Ployhart, Weekley, & Baughman, 2004; Schaubroeck, Ganster, &
Jones, 1998; Schneider, Smith, Taylor, & Fleenor, 1998). Across these studies, personality homogeneity was found within jobs, occupations, and
organizations. This means we can distinguish and compare these units in
terms of their personalities and values. Stated differently, unit members
are sufficiently similar in their personalities relative to other units that a
unit mean personality value sufficiently summarizes the personalities of
the individuals within the unit. This means organizations manifest personalities that represent the dominant personalities of their employees.

We should point out that the ASA model does not predict that homogeneity is always a good thing. The prediction is that early in a group's
or an organization's formation, homogeneity is typically positive because
it contributes to better coordination and cohesion. However, over time,
homogeneity may become negative because it contributes to faulty thinking (e.g., groupthink) and an inability to change and adapt.

THE ASA MODEL IS A MULTILEVEL MODEL

The mutually reinforcing concepts of fit and homogeneity are critical parts of the ASA model. They have stimulated considerable research and increased our understanding of the science and practice of recruitment/ selection. But we see some interesting theoretical possibilities that to our knowledge have not been explored. In particular, we argue that the ASA model is really a multilevel model.

In fact, Schneider's writing on the ASA model suggests he was most interested in discovering how individuals create organizational differences. The target for his theory, emphasized consistently and clearly, was on organizational-level outcomes. This was an important attempt to link individual and organizational levels of analysis, and for Schneider, the linking mechanism was homogeneity. We can see this in Figure 5.1. We start with a heterogeneous mix of KSAOs among potential applicants. However, through the recruitment (attraction) and selection filters, we winnow this heterogeneous mix into a more homogeneous set of KSAOs. Further, over time and through the process of differential attrition, this individual-level mix of KSAOs becomes increasingly homogeneous, contributing to the emergence of an organizational-level personality.

Although the ASA model predicts this consequence, it leaves unspecified precisely how we define, conceptualize, and study the homogeneity process (e.g., Schneider et al., 1995). This is hardly any fault of the man or the model; at the time it was written, multilevel thinking was still uncommon in organizational psychology. But in the years since his 1987 article, and thanks partly to Schneider, we have seen many advancements in multilevel theories and methods (for an excellent overview, see Kozlowski & Klein, 2000). Based on these advancements, we are in a better position to conceptualize homogeneity and what it really means.

In multilevel language (Kozlowski & Klein, 2000), homogeneity is really a process of *emergence*, whereby higher-level contextual forces

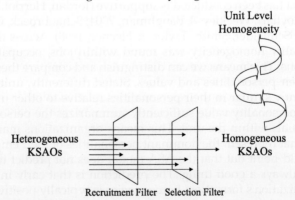

FIGURE 5.1 The attraction–selection–attrition process. As organizations attract, select, and retain individuals with similar knowledge, skills, abilities, and other characteristics (KSAOs), the unit becomes homogeneous on those KSAOs.

shape lower-level constructs to create and form higher-level constructs. For example, climate represents the shared perceptions of unit members. Even though climate may be measured at the individual level, its level of theory is at the unit level. In staffing, we know the contextual forces consist of the fit-invoking filters of recruitment and selection (not to mention applicant self-selection and withdrawal; Ryan et al., 2000). Through attraction–selection–attrition processes, the organization becomes increasingly composed of similar individuals. Thus, homogeneity is an emergent process.

If one buys this argument, then we can apply the many principles of emergence (Chan, 1998; Kozlowski & Klein, 2000) to better understand homogeneity creation and formation across levels. The primary question is whether homogeneity is best conceptualized as a composition model or compilation model. A *composition model* operationalizes the unit construct as a unit mean and justifies this based on the agreement (or similarity) of within-unit observations. For example, the agreement of within-unit (job, occupation, organization) personality is assessed, and if sufficiently high, one aggregates the within-unit scores to the unit level (Bliese, 2000, 2002). In this model, the unit average personality traits summarize or describe the members' personality traits.

On the other hand, multilevel theory teaches us that composition models are just one form of emergence. Another form is known as the *compilation model*, which emphasizes dispersion, dissensus, or dissimilarity. Just as means and standard deviations capture different forms of a distribution, compilation captures something distinct from composition. Because compilation models conceptualize the unit-level construct as one of dispersion, there is no need to justify agreement as a precursor to aggregation (Bliese, 2000). Instead, one operationalizes the unit-level construct using the within-group standard deviation, variance, or average deviation indices (Bliese, 2000; Burke & Dunlap, 2002).

If the ASA concept of homogeneity is an emergent process, then we need to clarify which form of emergence is relevant or whether both forms are relevant simultaneously. Continuing to leave this point unspecified will not contribute to better theory building and testing. In his original description of the ASA model, Schneider (1987) frequently made reference to sharedness and similarity. Therefore, homogeneity has frequently been framed in terms of a composition model because the idea is that people within a unit become similar over time, and most tests of the homogeneity hypothesis have used this conceptualization. Indeed, the very definition of homogeneity is one of similarity.

But is it not possible that compilation processes could also be relevant within the ASA model? We have seen examples in groups and teams research that show the consequences of heterogeneity, or what in multilevel language is called a compilation model (for reviews, see Moynihan & Peterson, 2004; Stewart, 2003). In fact, this research suggests composition and compilation may both be relevant simultaneously because they predict different outcomes (e.g., Barrick, Stewart, Neubert, & Mount, 1998). Ployhart et al. (2004) recently argued that what the ASA model calls homogeneity may simultaneously refer to both similarity and dispersion, and suggested it would be better for us to reframe the term *homogeneity* with the term *emergence*. For example, Schneider (1987) argued that the long-term consequences of homogeneity would be negative. But it is hard to imagine how an organization composed of members higher on conscientiousness and agreeableness could produce negative consequences (interestingly, we would not predict this based on individual-level data). Rather, we may think of negative consequences of homogeneity coming from a lack of dispersion present in organizational-level conscientiousness and agreeableness. So, we may want high mean levels of a trait like conscientiousness (composition), but a reasonable amount of dispersion (compilation) within the unit to ensure ideas do not become rigid and entrenched.

By the way, Schneider, Salvaggio, and Subirats (2002) showed the consequences of such variability. When examining the effect of branch climate on various outcomes, they found branch mean climate perceptions interacted with the branch variance in climate perceptions. They called this variance climate strength and showed that branches with stronger climates (low variance) exhibited stronger relations between aggregate perceptions and organizational outcomes.

We speculate the negative consequences of homogeneity Schneider was referring to in the ASA model are not caused as much by the unit mean, as homogeneity has typically been conceptualized, but by a lack of dispersion or variance in the unit-level construct. This does not mean the ASA model is wrong, but it does mean the ASA model may have misattributed the consequences of homogeneity. We suggest it is heterogeneity, as conceptualized in a compilation model, that may most contribute to negative consequences. When there is little variability among a unit, we may see the types of negative consequences predicted by the ASA model. But homogeneity, as conceptualized in a composition model, may or may not have negative consequences, depending on the nature of the unit-level construct. For example, high mean levels of conscientiousness will usually be a good thing, while high mean levels of neuroticism will usually be a bad thing.

IMPLICATIONS OF A MULTILEVEL ASA MODEL

If the ASA model is really a multilevel model, and the process through which individual-level KSAOs contribute to organizational differences is one of emergence, then we have some potentially exciting new directions for ASA theory and research.

New Implications for Homogeneity

We redefined homogeneity as a process of emergence, and therefore have both composition and compilation models describing unit-level phenomena. We can now determine whether it is unit means, unit variances, or possibly their interaction that influences organizational processes, structure, and culture. For example, do organizations that show more variance in aggregate personality and values apply HR practices more inconsistently than organizations that have less variance? Is it unit means or unit variances that most cause the negative consequences of similarity predicted in the ASA model? Relatedly, we wonder for what kinds of tasks or structures will homogeneity/heterogeneity be good or bad? What kinds of recruitment and staffing practices contribute to different forms of composition and compilation? Do procedures with higher validity produce higher means and lower variances on those characteristics at the unit level? The prediction is that they do. What, then, does staffing do if a lack of dispersion at the unit level is contributing to negative outcomes? Hire to create more dispersion? This would require hiring people very different from those already employed. This is inconsistent with the notion of fit and is certainly at odds with the way we normally think of selection (not to mention the way the legal system is structured).

Perhaps one means to resolve these questions is to again consider multilevel theory. We should expect there to be a clustering or nesting of emergence, such that lower levels show stronger agreement and less dispersion than we find at higher levels. To the extent these different intermediate units (e.g., work groups, departments) are relatively autonomous, we might find sufficient dispersion at higher levels to thwart the negative consequences predicted from the ASA model. For example, we would expect people within a work group to be more similar to each other than to those from the entire organization. Therefore, any negative consequences for a lack of dispersion would be noticed first and most strongly at these lower levels, and appropriate interventions could then be taken to break this upward trend toward low dispersion. (By the way, this process is nearly identical to that predicted by Darwin's theory of evolution and the process of natural selection. Lizards from one island are more similar to each other than lizards of the same species from different, isolated islands. Over time, different species adapt to their local environments just as people adapt to organizations.)

Our point here is that there are a lot of predictions based on multilevel theories that could go a long way toward refining predictions in the ASA model. Multilevel theory could help clarify some inconsistencies and contradictions within the ASA model, and it could generate several new questions not previously considered.

New Implications for Fit

A multilevel ASA model may also refine our thinking about the concept of fit. Kristof-Brown et al. (2002) showed how there are different levels of fit, including job, work group, and organization. This is an important finding and suggests that fit may also benefit from a refined multilevel perspective. For example, what level of fit most impacts applicants' decision making? Does person–organization fit matter most in early stages, but person–job fit matter most in later stages? Do they predict different outcomes? We are just starting to consider such questions.

Another implication is how we might go about modeling objective fit, typically operationalized as the statistical interaction between person and environment characteristics. We may need to adopt methods such as hierarchical linear modeling (HLM) because we have applicants/employees nested within environments. This is important because when observations (employees or applicants) are not independent of each other (due to a contextual influence like an organization's influence), interpretation of statistical significance tests in traditional models like regression become potentially biased (Bliese, 2000, 2002). Perhaps there is a way to use HLM to model the polynomial approach offered by Edwards (1991, 2002). Relatedly, the way in which we conceptualize the environment should be based on composition or compilation models, or both. In such a model, the environment would be the unit average or unit standard deviation of employees' scores on some attribute. In fact, maybe the very meaning of a compilation model—an index of dispersion—can be used as an index of fit, just like compilation models are used to index diversity (Bliese, 2000). It is unclear whether fit can occur unless there is a sufficient degree of similarity within a unit; hence, unit dispersion may moderate the relationship between fit and various outcomes.

New Implications for Staffing

The ASA model continues to be rare in its ability to link *organizational-level* consequences to the hiring of *individuals*. A multilevel ASA model helps articulate how this happens, and Figure 5.2 and Figure 5.3 illustrate what an important change in thinking this creates. In Figure 5.2, we illustrate the traditional and still dominant individual-level staffing model. In this model, all relevant constructs, processes, and relationships occur within this single level. Higher-level constructs and processes, like diversity, are not present. Contrast this to Figure 5.3, which shows a simple multilevel staffing model. In this model we see how hiring particular kinds of employees leads to composition/compilation

FIGURE 5.2 Traditional individual level personnel selection model.

processes that ultimately produce unit-level KSAO composition. And notice how it is this aggregate-level KSAO composition that relates to unit-level outcomes—not the individual differences at the individual level.

In more recent work, Schneider, Smith, and Sipe (2000) argued that this aggregate KSAO composition may also have consequences that cross levels of analysis. They noted how meta-analyses have typically

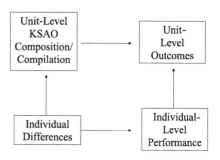

FIGURE 5.3 Multilevel staffing model.

not found moderators of individual-level predictor–criterion relationships. While generally true, this does not mean the organizational level exerts no influence on the individual staffing model. Rather, the effect of the organization and aggregate KSAOs may have direct effects on the individual-level criterion. This is shown in Figure 5.4, where there is a direct effect for the organization on the individual-level criterion, but no moderating effect on the individual-level relationship. For example, why is it that two people with equal KSAOs do not perform equally on the same job in two organizations? Schneider and colleagues argue this occurs because organizational differences affect individual differences (Schneider et al., 2000).

We should not be so quick to ignore contextual influence in staffing even when there are no moderators of validity. If our real interest is in performance (after all, predictors only help us identify top performers), then to borrow the language of Schneider et al. (2000), this "organizational direct effect" is also of relevance to staffing. An example of this was recently found in Ployhart et al. (2004), where individual-level personality and job/organizational aggregate personality both explained significant incremental variance in individual-level satisfaction and performance. Even though there was no moderator of the individual-level relationships,

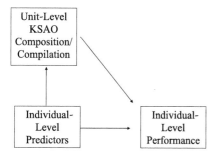

FIGURE 5.4 Multilevel staffing model.

the organizational direct effect was present and helped explain criterion variance. Quite simply, some individuals were more satisfied and performed better because of job/ organizational personality differences. This thinking opens staffing to a host of interesting possibilities that are discussed in detail by Schneider and colleagues (Ployhart & Schneider, 2002, in press; Schneider et al., 2000). The key point is that aggregate KSAOs may have important consequences not identified in the individual-level staffing model, even though individual-level staffing is what helped create them.

It is interesting to note that while in the selection literature we are just starting to recognize the importance of these aggregate KSAOs, the macro HR/HR strategy literature has recognized their importance for some time. In today's language, we may jazz up this talk of aggregate KSAOs with the term *human capital*, which for all intents and purposes refers to the same thing. And by doing so, we now have a link to a large and growing literature that discusses the firm-level importance of human capital (e.g., Barney, 1991; Becker, 1964). So we see the ASA model, by focusing on organizational-level outcomes, helps link our micro and macro literatures together. These literatures have largely proceeded in isolation, yet should have consequences for each other. The ASA model helps identify these mutual consequences. For example, an important contribution of a multilevel ASA model to macro HR is its ability to conceptualize and explain human capital emergence, something that the macro/strategic literature has not fully considered. We may be able to show how different HR practices and policies, the domain of macro HR, influence human capital emergence through attraction–selection–attrition.

New Challenges for Testing the ASA

A multilevel ASA model was present in Schneider's (1987) original writing—it just took us time to recognize this, and we now must struggle with operationalizing it. This task will not be easy. In staffing, our dominant way of thinking has been at the individual level. The legal system we try to comply with is set up to protect the individual. HR practices and policies are usually focused on individuals. Our methodologies, such as job analysis, are individual-level methods. For example, as noted by Schmitt (2002), how will one generate task and KSAO statements for teams and what will be the relevant dimensions upon which to make ratings? Is this approach even feasible? We are faced with some serious challenges in operationalizing a multilevel ASA model. Another similar problem that we have grappled with in the traditional selection research paradigm for decades (Schmidt & Kaplan, 1971) involves how we combine criteria to provide a single value representing individual effectiveness. With multiple levels of analysis, we will have the same problem at the unit or organizational level. The complexity of multiple levels adds yet another perplexing but important dimension to the composite criterion problem.

Another important element that must be built into future tests of the ASA model is time. ASA processes unfold over time, and yet there is practically no research that has adopted a longitudinal methodology. We need to study recruitment processes longitudinally to understand how fit perceptions are formed and change across stages of recruitment. We need to follow individuals through selection processes to understand how fit contributes to withdrawal. And it is certainly going to take time, perhaps a long time, for human capital to emerge from individual-level recruitment and staffing. This is not the typical approach for staffing, but must be done if we are going to test the ASA as it was intended.

Thus, we are going to need to adopt research methods that are multilevel and longitudinal to accurately test propositions of the ASA model. These designs must sample multiple units. However, this does not mean we have to study multiple organizations because a multilevel ASA model recognizes that even within a single organization, there will be a nesting of KSAOs within different lower-level units. But we must adopt such a between-unit approach to study the ASA in staffing, and that is something staffing researchers rarely do outside of meta-analysis.

One potential solution to the problems with obtaining this kind of data is to use computational modeling. Computational models are becoming a dominant methodology in cognitive science, but their application to the applied world has been limited (see Ilgen & Hulin, 2000). Computational models are mathematical/statistical simulations of theories. They involve writing a series of "if … then" kinds of statements that specify how changes occur in dependent variables as a function of changes among independent variables. The difficulty with applying computational models to the real world is the large number of potential variables that need to be considered and a frequent lack of specificity in our theories that seek to describe relationships among these variables. However, the ASA model prescribes a clear set of processes that unfold over time. The tools and theory are sufficiently precise so that one could model a variety of ASA processes on the computer, identify the most interesting of these findings, and try to replicate only these interesting findings in the real world. This would be a more economical way to test the ASA model and could lead to a number of important innovations in a much shorter period of time.

CONCLUSION

Schneider's (1987) ASA model changed staffing forever. It continues to be a dominant and important part of the selection literature. We believe an integration of multilevel theory with the ASA will lead to exciting new challenges and developments, and continue to make the ASA an important model for years to come. But the road will not be easy. The problems raised about the nature of multilevel phenomena in staffing have not been addressed, but they must be if we are to seriously realize the full implications of the ASA model. A colleague of one of the authors has harassed him for years about the "boring" nature of selection research. We like to think it is just because he does not engage in such research, but the problems raised above are anything but boring. They are challenging and interesting and have important implications.

REFERENCES

Barney, J. (1991). Firm resources and sustained competitive advantage. *Journal of Management, 17*, 99–120.

Barrick, M. R., Stewart, G. L., Neubert, M. J., & Mount, M. K. (1998). Relating member ability and personality to work-team processes and team effectiveness. *Journal of Applied Psychology, 83*, 377–391.

Becker, G. S. (1964). *Human capital.* New York: Columbia University Press.

Bliese, P. D. 2000. Within-group agreement, non-independence, and reliability: Implications for data aggregation and analysis. In K. J. Klein & S. W. J. Kozlowski (Eds.), *Multilevel theory, research, and methods in organizations: Foundations, extensions, and new directions* (pp. 349–381). San Francisco: Jossey-Bass.

Bliese, P. D. (2002). Multilevel random coefficient modeling in organizational research: Examples using SAS and S-PLUS. In F. Drasgow & N. Schmitt (Eds.), *Measuring and analyzing behavior in organizations: Advances in measurement and data analysis* (pp. 401–445). San Francisco: Jossey-Bass.

Bretz, R., & Judge, T. (1994). The role of human resource systems in job applicant decision processes. *Journal of Management, 20*, 531–551.

Burke, M. J., & Dunlap, W. P. (2002). Estimating interrater agreement with the average deviation index: A user's guide. *Organizational Research Methods, 5*, 159–172.

Cable, D., & Judge, T. (1994). Pay preferences and job search decisions: A person–organization fit perspective. *Personnel Psychology, 47*, 317–348.

Cable, D., & Judge, T. (1996). Person–organization fit, job choice decisions, and organizational entry. *Organizational Behavior and Human Decision Processes, 67*, 294–311.

Cable, D., & Judge, T. (1997). Interviewers' perceptions of person–organization fit and organizational selection decisions. *Journal of Applied Psychology, 82*, 546–561.

Chan, D. (1998). Functional relations among constructs in the same content domain at different levels of analysis: A typology of composition models. *Journal of Applied Psychology, 83*, 234–246.

Chatman, J. A. (1989). Improving interactional organizational research: A model of person–organization fit. *Academy of Management Review, 14*, 333–349.

Chatman, J. A. (1991). Matching people and organizations: Selection and socialization in public accounting firms. *Administrative Science Quarterly, 36*, 459–484.

Edwards, J. R. (1991). Person-job fit: A conceptual integration, literature review and methodological critique. In C. L. Cooper & I. T. Robertson (Eds.), *International review of industrial/organizational psychology* (Vol. 6, pp. 283–357). New York: Wiley.

Edwards, J. R. (2002). Alternatives to difference scores: Polynomial regression analysis and response surface methodology. In F. Drasgow & N. Schmitt (Eds.), *Measuring and analyzing behavior in organizations: Advances in measurement and data analysis* (pp. 350–400). San Francisco: Jossey-Bass.

Holland, J. L. (1997). *Making vocational choices: A theory of vocational personalities and work environments* (3rd ed.). Odessa, FL: PAR.

Ilgen, D. R., & Hulin, C. L. (2000). *Computational modeling of behavior in organizations: The third scientific discipline.* Washington, DC: American Psychological Association.

Jordan, M., Herriot, P., & Chalmers, C. (1991). Testing Schneider's ASA theory. *Applied Psychology, 40*, 47–53.

Kozlowski, S. W. J., & Klein, K. J. (2000). A multilevel approach to theory and research in organizations: Contextual, temporal, and emergent processes. In K. J. Klein & S. W. J. Kozlowski (Eds.), *Multilevel theory, research, and methods in organizations: Foundations, extensions, and new directions* (pp. 3–90). San Francisco: Jossey-Bass.

Kristof, A. L. (1996). Person–organization fit: An integrative review of its conceptualizations, measurement, and implications. *Personnel Psychology, 49*, 1–49.

Kristof-Brown, A. L, Jansen, K. J., & Colbert, A. E. (2002). A policy-capturing study of the simultaneous effects of fit with jobs, groups, and organizations. *Journal of Applied Psychology, 87*, 985–993.

Moynihan, L. M., & Peterson, R. S. (2004). The role of personality in group processes. In B. Schneider & D. B. Smith (Eds.), *Personality and organizations* (pp. 317–345). Mahwah, NJ: Lawrence Erlbaum Associates.

Muchinsky, P. M., & Monahan, C. J. (1987). What is person–environment congruence? Supplementary versus complementary models of fit. *Journal of Vocational Behavior, 31*, 268–277.

Ployhart, R. E., & Schneider, B. (2005). Multilevel selection and prediction: Theories, methods, and models. In A. Evers, O. Smit-Voskuyl, & N. Anderson (Eds.), *Handbook of personnel selection*: 495–516. Oxford, UK: Basil Blackwell.

Ployhart, R. E., & Schneider, B. (2002). A multilevel perspective on personnel selection: Implications for selection system design, assessment, and construct validation. In F. J. Dansereau & F. Yammarino (Eds.), *Research in multi-level issues: The many faces of multi-level issues* (Vol. 1, pp. 95–140). Oxford: Elsevier Science.

Ployhart, R. E., Weekley, J. A., & Baughman, K. (2006). The structure and function of human capital emergence: A multilevel examination of the Attraction–Selection–Attrition model. *Academy of Management Journal, 49*, 661–677.

Ryan, A. M., Sacco, J., McFarland, L., & Kriska, D. (2000). Applicant self-selection: Correlates of withdrawal from a multiple hurdle process. *Journal of Applied Psychology, 85*, 163–179.

Schaubroeck, J., Ganster, D. C., & Jones, J. R. (1998). Organization and occupation influences in the attraction–selection–attrition process. *Journal of Applied Psychology, 83*, 869–891.

Schmidt, F. L., & Kaplan, L. B. (1971). Composite vs. multiple criteria: A review and resolution of the controversy. *Personnel Psychology, 24*, 419–434.

Schmitt, N. (2002). A multi-level perspective on personnel selection: Are we ready? In F. J. Dansereau & F. Yamarino (Eds.), *Research in multi-level issues: The many faces of multi-level issues* (Vol. 1, pp. 155–164). Oxford: Elsevier Science Ltd.

Schneider, B. (1987). The people make the place. *Personnel Psychology, 40*, 437–453.

Schneider, B., Goldstein, H. W., & Smith, D. B. (1995). The ASA framework: An update. *Personnel Psychology, 48*, 747–773.

Schneider, B., Salvaggio, A. N., & Subirats, M. (2002). Climate strength: A new direction for climate research. *Journal of Applied Psychology, 87*, 220–229.

Schneider, B., Smith, D., & Sipe, W. P. (2000). Personnel selection psychology: Multilevel considerations. In K. J. Klein & S. W. J. Kozlowski (Eds.), *Multilevel theory, research, and methods in organizations: Foundations, extensions, and new directions* (pp. 3–90). San Francisco: Jossey-Bass.

Schneider, B., Smith, D. B., Taylor, S., & Fleenor, J. (1998). Personality and organizations: A test of the homogeneity of personality hypothesis. *Journal of Applied Psychology, 83,* 462–470.

Stewart, G. L. (2003). Toward an understanding of the multilevel role of personality in teams. In M. Barrick & A. M. Ryan (Eds.), *Personality and work* (pp. 183–204). San Francisco: Jossey-Bass.

6

A Network Model of Organizational Climate
Friendship Clusters, Subgroup Agreement, and Climate Schemas

DANIEL A. NEWMAN
Texas A&M University

PAUL J. HANGES
University of Maryland

LILI DUAN
University of Maryland

ANURADHA RAMESH
University of Maryland

The symbolic interactionist approach maintains that people in communicative interactions with each other, respond to, define, and interpret elements of the situation in particular ways. These characteristic modes of interpretation and definition form distinct subgroup climates within organizations.

—*Ben Schneider and Arnon Reichers, "On the Etiology of Climates," 1983, p. 33*

OVERVIEW

Organizational climate has been defined as shared individual perceptions of what is rewarded, supported, and expected. We extend this
notion by integrating it with the literature on social networks and neural
network models of cognition. First, we introduce "subgroup climate" as
a social construct similar to organizational climate, for which the membership boundary of climate sharedness is determined by social network
clustering, rather than by formal group affiliation. Second, we reconcep-
tualize climate perceptions as a pattern of activation weights in a neural network schema, linking possible behaviors to valued outcomes. We
argue that neural network (connectionist) theories of cognition can be
integrated with social network (balance and contagion) approaches to
yield new propositions regarding the nature and measurement of organizational climate. Using this perspective, we further propose that climate
is not only a perceptual outcome of managerial practices, but is also a
driving force behind informal employee organizing.

Organizational climate has been of interest to researchers since the construct was first brought into the organizational literature in the 1960s (see
Ostroff, Kinicki, & Tamkins, 2003). In general, climate refers to the meanings that people collectively place on the intraorganizational environment
(Schneider, 2000). The biggest contention among early climate researchers
involved the use of individual-level perceptions to characterize organization-level phenomena (Glick, 1985; James, Joyce, & Slocum, 1988). Over
the years, researchers have decided that even though the roots of climate
are in the cognitions, emotions, and expectations of individuals, organizational climate is limited to those perceptions held in common by a group.
Indeed, in their definition of organizational climate, Reichers & Schneider
(1990) emphasized that climate is the *shared* perceptions of both formal
and informal organizational practices, policies, and procedures. With the
aid of co-workers, supervisors, and even customers, employees develop a
coherent interpretation of their organizational environment. In particular,
information is consolidated into a gestalt for what behavior is expected,
rewarded, and supported in the organization (Reichers & Schneider, 1990).
Climate impressions vary from nonspecific or attitudinal (e.g., a warm and
inviting climate) to those more focused on some specific goal or outcome
(e.g., climate for safety, climate for service, climate for achievement; Schneider & Reichers, 1983; Schneider, Salvaggio, & Subirats, 2002).

The early literature made a distinction between psychological and organizational climate (James & Jones, 1974). *Psychological climate* is the perception that an individual has about the organization. *Organizational climate*,
on the other hand, refers to the *shared or common* aspects of psychological
climate held by a group of people. Because people interact with their environment based upon their perceptions of that environment, it is expected
that a group of people will behave in similar ways the more similar their
psychological climates. Scientific interest has probably remained high

with the climate construct because of empirical evidence demonstrating its utility for predicting important organizational outcomes. For example, service climate has been found to predict customer satisfaction (Schneider et al., 2002); safety climate has been found to predict the frequency of safe behavior in a work setting (Zohar, 1980); organizational climate perceptions predict positive attitudes (e.g., Carr, Schmidt, Ford, & DeShon, 2003; Glisson & James, 2002), as well as absenteeism and turnover (Steel, Shane, & Kennedy, 1990) and performance (Lawler, Hall, & Oldham, 1974). Clearly, when organizational climate is strong (i.e., the variance in psychological climate is minimized), the range of behavior exhibited within that organization is restricted. Behaviors consistent with the organizational climate should be more frequently displayed than behaviors inconsistent with that climate.

In the present chapter, we attempt to make two distinct contributions—both based on emerging network paradigms. First, we advance the idea that climate perceptions need not be shared at the level of the formal organizational unit. Instead, informal social networks define cohesive interpersonal subgroups within which strong, local climates can be found. Second, we suggest that a different sort of network—a cognitive schema or neural network—leads to a reconceptualization of how individuals and groups perceive what is rewarded, supported, and expected. From this view, climate is defined as a stable activation pattern among intrapsychic concepts. These two (social and neural network) perspectives are then integrated, suggesting (1) a nested relationship through which cognitive schemas come to be shared within local social network subgroups, and (2) both types of networks are subject to the balance principle, which creates segregation and local regions of homogeneity, for both people and mental concepts.

SOCIAL NETWORK PERSPECTIVE

A *social network* is a pattern of relations or ties (e.g., friendship, workflow, communication, advice) among individuals. Figure 6.1 shows an example of a friendship network diagram. Social networks are typically conceptualized as creating a structure of interdependence among autonomous individual actors, forming channels for the flow of resources and information, and imposing both opportunities and constraints on individual action (Wasserman & Faust, 1994). The network paradigm is a truly interdisciplinary product, whose roots have been traced to gestalt interpersonal psychotherapy (Moreno, 1934; Moreno & Jennings, 1938), mathematical graph theory (Harary, Norman, & Cartwright, 1965), sociology (Homans, 1951; Simmel, 1908), social psychology (Festinger, 1949; Heider, 1946), and anthropology (Barnes, 1954; Mayo, 1933; Warner & Lunt, 1941), among other fields (see Scott, 2000). The theory and method have enjoyed

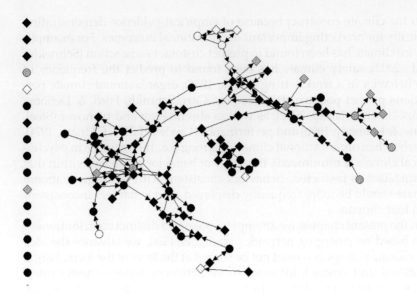

FIGURE 6.1   Friendship network; Gray node = African American, White node = Asian American, Black node = Caucasian American; Diamond = Female, Circle = Male.

growing popularity in organizational science (Borgatti & Foster, 2003; Brass, Galaskiewicz, Greve, & Tsai, 2004).

In Figure 6.1, the network nodes represent individual actors in the social system, while the lines connecting these nodes represent ties between the actors. The data depicted are from a single organizational unit (Ramesh & Newman, 2005), where paths between actors are friendship nominations. The nodes appearing along the left margin are called *isolates*, or members of the organization who did not identify any friends in the organizational unit and were not identified by any of the other unit members as a friend (i.e., those who neither gave nor received a friendship tie).

What becomes apparent upon inspection of Figure 6.1 is that this particular organization comprises network clusters, or informal friendship groups. There are many ways of mathematically defining network subgroups, which we will review later. Initially, however, it is useful to note that apparent clusters exist. We have subjectively identified three such subgroups. The two, more sparse clusters on the northeast and southwest regions of Figure 6.1 are labeled Group 1 and Group 3, while the dense, central cluster is labeled Group 2.

Balance Theory

Heider's (1946, 1958) balance theory, along with its descendant structural balance theory (see Doreian, 2002), provides a useful explanatory

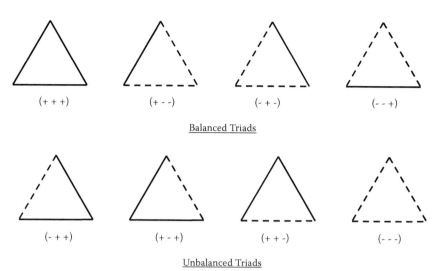

FIGURE 6.2 Heider's balanced and unbalanced triads; dotted line = negative relation; triangle vertices could be labeled *p*, *o*, and *x*, respectively.

framework for the development and maintenance of shared perceptions and network patterns. In Heider's (1946) formulation, a triad consisting of person *p*, person *o*, and [person or] object *x* is considered *balanced* under four conditions: (1) *p* likes *o*, and *p* and *o* both like *x* (all three relations are positive; + + +); (2) *p* likes *o*, and *p* and *o* both dislike *x* (+ – –); (3) *p* dislikes *o*, *p* likes *x*, and *o* dislikes *x* (– + –); or (4) *p* dislikes *o*, *p* dislikes *x*, and *o* likes *x* (– – +). These balanced triads are shown in Figure 6.2. In the converse, a triad is considered *unbalanced* if there is only one dislike relation (Figure 6.2), or if there are three dislike relations. In summary, a triad is balanced if there are exactly zero negative relations (e.g., "My friend and I like the same object" and "The friend of my friend is my friend") or if there are exactly two negative relations (e.g., "My friend and I dislike the same object" and "The enemy of my enemy is my friend"). Otherwise, the triad is imbalanced. According to Heider (1946), "If no balanced state exists, then forces towards this state will arise. Either the dynamic characters will change, or the unit relations will be changed through action or through cognitive reorganization" (pp. 107–108). To restate, if one is in a state of imbalance, either her attitude toward the object will change or her friendship status with the other actor will change, in order to restore balance.

Traditionally, only the narrow notion of *cognitive balance within an individual's perceptions* is ascribed to Heider (e.g., Krackhardt & Kilduff,

1999), while balance in patterns of *actual relationship choices* within groups is ascribed to other theorists (see Harary et al., 1965; Kilduff & Tsai, 2003; Scott, 2000). Also, there may exist some important logical exceptions to the balanced triads hypothesis. Heider (1946) notes, for instance, that when the relation involves either ownership of x or romantic love of x, this creates jealousy and competition between p and o, leading to mutual dislike. Another possible exception to the balance principle relates to the idea that an all-negative triad can be balanced (i.e., when the triad members occupy distinct social groups; Davis, 1967).

An important extension of Heider's (1946, 1958) theory came when Cartwright and Harary mathematically formalized the notion of balance for large networks. Noting that a signed network (consisting entirely of positive and negative ties) was *balanced* whenever the product across all ties was positive, and unbalanced whenever the product was negative, Cartwright and Harary (1956) developed the theorem that for all balanced networks, the network is either (1) entirely composed of positive ties or (2) subdivided into two distinct subsets, where all within-subset ties are positive and all between-subset ties are negative. Herein lies a key consequence of balance theory—*the tendency toward network balance creates network segregation.*

To the extent that perceptions of an object x (e.g., attitudes) reflect individual differences (such as personality or demographics), the balance principle should lead to segregation of the social network on the basis of these individual differences. Demographic network segregation is referred to by sociologists as *homophily* (see McPherson, Smith-Lovin, & Cook, 2001, for a review) and can be observed in Figure 6.1, where African American, Asian American, and Caucasian American respondents tend to be clustered in close proximity to one another, on average. In essence, these demographically homogeneous regions within the social network are formed through a local process of attraction to (Byrne, 1971), selection into, and attrition from the network cluster. These homogenizing forces will be limited only by physical and temporal barriers to voluntary tie formation and dissolution.

> Proposition 1: Within-group variability in individual differences (i.e., diversity) leads to the formation of cohesive social network subgroups.
>
> Proposition 2: Social network subgroups will be more homogeneous with respect to individual differences (i.e., less diverse) than will the overall organization.

Subgroup Climates

The balance hypothesis has another important consequence: As individuals in a network become friends, they will tend toward sharing perceptions of objects. When those objects are the policies, practices, and procedures of the organization that convey what is rewarded, supported, and expected, then these shared perceptions constitute an *organizational climate*. However, social segregation/homogenization processes, such as those described above, will often lead to emergence of distinct social regions within the network. These distinct social regions are then a divided architecture within which local, subgroup climates can emerge. A *subgroup climate* is reflected by a heightened level of psychological agreement among a cohesive network subgroup, regarding an organizational policy, practice, or procedure.

In order to contrast local (subgroup) climates with ambient organizational climates, it is useful to discuss the etiology of within-group agreement. Kenny's (1991) model of consensus suggests several factors that produce interpersonal similarity in perceptions, including (1) opportunity to observe the same target at the same time, (2) shared meaning systems held by two or more judges, and (3) direct communication between two or more judges. At the level of the entire organization unit, we suggest that group agreement reflects (1) opportunity to observe many of the same targets at the same times (including publicly announced and displayed practices, policies, and procedures) and (2) shared meaning systems created by personal factors (e.g., education, past work experience, personality) used to select individuals into the organization. These are the antecedents of ambient, organization-level climates. At the level of the informal social network subgroup, however, we suggest that group agreement reflects (1) greater opportunity to observe the same targets at the same times, (2) greater likelihood of possessing shared meaning systems (Rentsch, 1990), (3) *direct communication with social network peers*, and (4) *indirect communication with social network peers* through common acquaintances (Festinger, 1954; Leenders, 2002). This application of Kenny's consensus model to distinguish ambient, unit-level agreement from network-clustered, subunit-level agreement leads to the following propositions:

Proposition 3: Social network subgroups will display higher levels of agreement than will the overall organization (i.e., subgroup climate is stronger than ambient organizational climate).

Proposition 4: Subgroup climates will potentiate and constrain individual action more strongly than organizational climates.

In addition to forming new explanations for within-group variance, the subgroup climate concept also has implications for between-group variance. To explicate, overall (or ambient) organization-level climates are likely to vary between organizations as a result of differential practices, policies, and procedures across organizations. In contrast, subgroup climates (subunit level) express variation between clusters as a result of localized communication within cohesive subgroups. Thus, by adding the subunit level, we can now speak of (1) between-organization variance and (2) between-subgroup variance, within organizations. When one does not distinguish the network-subgroup level of analysis, then between-subgroup variance is lumped in with organization-level, within-group variance.

Proposition 5: Social network subgroups will display meaningful between-subgroup variation in climate perceptions.

Individual climate perceptions will be continuously reassessed in light of one's peers' perceptions. As cohesive network subgroups approach balance in the formation of shared perceptions of climate, many individuals' perceptions will undoubtedly change, upward or downward, toward convergence with the local subgroup. Because social network clusters can create pockets of heightened agreement within the larger organizational unit, we believe that an aggregation of climate perceptions across these local subgroups may become a biased representation of organization-level climate. That is, for individuals in cohesive network subgroups, climate perceptions reflect both (1) the initial perceptions of managerial policies, practices, and procedures, and (2) socially derived modifications of climate perceptions, grounded in social information processing (Salancik & Pfeffer, 1978; Zalesny & Ford, 1990). Therefore, to measure an accurate reflection of organization-level policies, practices, and procedures, it is helpful to focus on the perceptions of those who are less influenced by social information processing—the social network isolates. From this perspective, agreement (or shared perceptions) among social isolates is an excellent indication that an organization-level climate exists.

Proposition 6: Organizational climate, which involves ambient perceptions of organizational features, will be more adequately reflected by social network isolates than by members of cohesive social network subgroups.

Example of Subgroup Climates

To better understand what we mean by subgroup climates, refer to Figure 6.3. In these data, all members have provided ratings of a particular organizational feature, related to group leadership (90% response rate; Ramesh & Newman, 2005). In Figure 6.3, the size of each node corresponds to the level of that individual's perception, with a larger node suggesting more positive perceptions of the organizational feature. A cluster of same-sized nodes indicates local agreement. Across all respondents in the organization, the overall level of perceptual agreement is $r_{WG(J)} = .87$, $r_{WG(J)}^* = .62$ (James, Demaree, & Wolf, 1984; Lindell, Brandt, & Whitney, 1999), which is typically taken as adequate evidence for the presence of an organizational

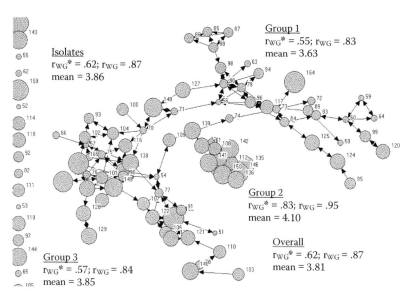

FIGURE 6.3 Organizational microclimates; larger node size = more positive perception of organizational features.

climate. In this sense, *organizational climate* reflects the *ambient* climate that is experienced by all members of the organization, independent of their specialized role relationships and network positions.

Groups 1 and 3 each display levels of perceptual agreement quite similar to the overall level of organizational agreement ($r_{WG(J)}$ = .83 and .84, $r_{WG(J)}^*$ = .55 and .57), although Group 1 has a lower mean-level perception compared to the overall mean level outside of Group 1 (mean = 3.63 vs. 3.87, d = −.30). What is most striking about Figure 6.3, however, is the presence of a strong subgroup climate in Group 2. For Group 2, $r_{WG(J)}$ = .95 and $r_{WG(J)}^*$ = .83. The variance of perceptions within Group 2 is .21, whereas the overall variance in perceptions outside of Group 2 is .66 (i.e., Group 2 variance is significantly smaller than the overall variance [$F_{(93, 12)}$ = 3.10, p < .05], approximately one-third its size). Also, aside from having more uniform perceptions (i.e., more agreement), Group 2 members have a much more positive set of perceptions, on average, than others in the overall organization (mean = 4.10 vs. 3.77, d = .42). Pictorially, this local climate is reflected in Figure 6.3 by moderately large nodes of uniform size for Group 2. Thus, consistent with our predictions, local subgroups identified by analyzing friendship networks differ measurably in their climate perceptions.

Finally, we have contended that agreement among isolates (i.e., individuals who are part of the organization, but are not tied into the social network) provides a more direct index of ambient organization-level climate. Because these individuals are unaffected by the local collective sensemaking (Weick, 1979) that inheres in cohesive network subgroups, their (shared) perceptions more accurately reflect organization-level policies, practices, and procedures. It is noteworthy, then, that the level of agreement for overall climate (as measured across all members of this organization) is identical to the agreement level for isolates ($r_{WG(j)}$ = .87 and r_{WG}* = .62). Mean-level climate perceptions are also similar between the isolates ($\bar{X}$ = 3.86) and the overall organization ($\bar{X}$ = 3.81). This suggests that, for this example, an overall aggregate measure of climate (and its agreement index) is a satisfactory substitute for the climate mean (and agreement index) that would be expected in the absence of social network influence.

Subgroup Climates and Organizational Climate Strength

Schneider et al. (2002) have recently introduced the concept of climate strength, which is "one of a class of variance constructs" (p. 220; see Chan, 1998) and is highly related to culture consensus (Martin, 1992). He and his colleagues have argued that mean climate perceptions must be considered in light of climate strength. Indeed, they obtained partial support for the moderating effect of service climate strength on mean service climate in predicting customer satisfaction (c.f., Brown & Hauenstein, 2005). The theoretical and methodological advancements implied by the concept of climate strength promise to improve the usefulness of the organizational climate construct.

The network-theoretic viewpoint elaborated in this chapter helps to add meaning and precision to the notion of climate strength. Specifically, when climate strength is low, it likely reflects the existence of multiple, subgroup climates. Not only is this perspective consistent with the climate strength literature, but it also follows from recent statistical developments indexing shared climate perceptions, which suggest that multiple subgroups may underlie low agreement results (LeBreton, James, & Lindell, 2005). The question for future research on climate strength, then, becomes one of identifying cohesive subgroups through the social network paradigm.

Network Clusters. The subgroups shown in Figure 6.1 and Figure 6.3 were fairly obvious and could be identified without the aid of mathematical analyses. However, this will not always be true. Terminology has been developed that more formally defines and identifies these cohesive network subgroups. In formal terms, cohesive network subgroups (which a layperson might call clusters) can take several forms: cliques, *n*-cliques, *n*-clans, and *k*-plexes (summarized by Wasserman & Faust, 1994). A *clique*, in mathematical terms, is a maximal complete subgraph of at least three nodes (Luce & Perry, 1949), or otherwise stated, it is a network region in which each member of the subgroup is connected to all other members. For example, there is an Asian American four-person clique at the top of Figure 6.1. An *n-clique* is a less restrictive definition of subgroup (Luce, 1950) that permits actors to be classified together so long as they are all interconnected by a social distance of *n* or less. For example, in a 2-clique, each member of the subgroup is at least a friend of a friend (social distance = 2) of all other members. A 1-clique is simply a clique. Because it is possible for an *n*-clique to involve individuals who are not members of the *n*-clique itself (e.g., a friend of a friend situation, where the intermediary friend is not in the *n*-clique), a more restrictive concept, *n*-clan, was developed (Mokken, 1979). A 2-clan is a 2-clique where each member of the subgroup is at least a friend of a friend (social distance = 2) of all other members, and all intermediary friends are also 2-clique members. A *k*-plex is another, less restrictive version of the clique concept (Seidman & Foster, 1978). In a 2-plex, each member of the subgroup is connected to at least *all but 2* ($k = 2$) of the other members.

NEURAL NETWORK PERSPECTIVE

In the current section, we switch gears somewhat from discussing networks of relationships among people, to discussing networks of associations among cognitive concepts within a single person. After this perspective is reviewed and applied to organizational climate, we provide some integration of the social network and the neural network approaches. Connectionism was originally developed in the cognitive sciences and has been widely discussed over the past decades (Hanges, Lord, & Dickson, 2000). While the early climate literature discussed the role of cognition in developing these perceptions (James, Hater, Gent, & Bruni, 1978), the emphasis on understanding the role of cognition in organizational climate has diminished since the shared/aggregate nature of the construct has been emphasized. We believe that this is unfortunate and that utility will be accrued by integrating the literature on shared organizational climate with the more recent developments in cognitive psychology.

In the section that follows, we first present the basic features of the connectionist model and then discuss how this model is consistent with the "climate as a gestalt" perspective from the organizational climate literature. We draw upon a recently proposed connectionist model of environmental perceptions (Lord, Hanges, & Godfrey, 2003) to develop a cognitive-network model of organizational climate. We will show how such a model yields some new insights into the measurement of organizational climate.

Basics of Connectionist Networks

Early work on cognitive interpretations of organizational climate used the old symbolic models of information processing. According to the symbolic models, the perceived attributes of the environment are clustered together in memory structures called schemas (Lord, Foti, & DeVader, 1984). Schemas are cognitive structures that "represent knowledge about a concept or type of stimulus, including its attributes and the relations among those attributes" (Fiske & Taylor, 1991, p. 98). Individuals are believed to have schemas about physical objects (e.g., chair, table, car), their social environment (e.g., leadership, gender roles, work roles), and perceptions of the broader business environment (e.g., customer needs, technological changes, supplier availability, labor market characteristics, sociopolitical environment, societal values) that they encounter (Daft, Sormunen, & Parks, 1988; Duncan, 1972; Hofstede, 1980, 2001; House, Hanges, Javidan, Dorfman, & Gupta, 2004; Lord & Maher, 1990; Rosch, 1973, 1978). Schemas are believed to facilitate the recall of old information as well as assist in the structuring, organizing, and interpreting of newly encountered information (Lord & Foti, 1986). In particular, schemas assist information processing by providing a standard to which people can compare the new object. The closer the match between the attributes contained in

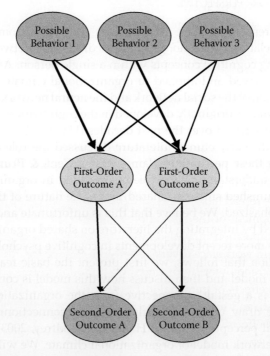

FIGURE 6.4 Connectionist neural network.

the schema and the attributes of the new object, the more likely people are to identify the new object as a member of the schema set (Lord & Maher, 1991).

The early cognitive categorization perspective primarily focused on the content of individuals' schemas. While schema content varied across individuals as a result of differences in experiences, values, and personality (Lord & Brown, 2004), it was maintained that schema content *could be* shared across individuals. These shared aspects of schemas are especially likely to be found when multiple individuals are sampled from intact groups. The old symbolic conceptualizations of cognition were applied to a variety of settings and phenomena. Indeed, this approach was applied to organizational climate as well (James et al., 1978).

Recently, however, researchers have been emphasizing the utility of a new model of information processing. This new model, called connectionist networks, has reconceptualized the way people think about information processing and schemas. Such theoretical models have been used to develop computational models of various phenomena. For example, connectionist networks have been developed for many types of cognitive and social processes, such as grapheme-to-phoneme conversion in speech coding (Clark, 2001), categorization of stimuli and extraction of category prototypes (Smith, 1996; Smith & DeCoster, 1998), causal attributions (Van Overwalle, 1998), and leadership perceptions (Lord, Brown, & Harvey, 2001; Lord, Brown, Harvey, & Hall, 2001), to provide just a few examples.

What exactly is a connectionist network? An example of a connectionist network is shown in Figure 6.4 to illustrate the properties of such networks. The building blocks of connectionist networks are the nodes represented by circles in Figure 6.4. The nodes are connected to one another, and these connections are represented by arrows in the figure. The strength of the connection between nodes can differ (represented by the differential thickness of the arrows in the figure). For example, the thick line in Figure 6.4 represents a strong connection/association between two nodes (e.g., the line connecting Possible Behavior 1 and First-Order Outcome A), whereas a thin line represents a weak connection/association between two nodes (e.g., the line connecting Possible Behavior 2 and First-Order Outcome A). As discussed above, the stronger the connection between two nodes, the more likely it is that one node will be activated when the other node is activated.

The sign of the relationship between nodes can also differ, so that a positive (or negative) connection between two nodes increases (or decreases) the likelihood that both nodes will be simultaneously activated. When information about some event is encountered, the activation level of individual nodes influences other nodes in the network, and this activation of individual nodes reverberates throughout the network. Eventually a stable activation pattern emerges, and it is this stable activation pattern that cognitive psychologists interpret as a schema. Such schemas are interpretative frameworks used to categorize the encountered event.

These schematic patterns of activity in the network become increasingly efficient (i.e., require less effort to evoke) as the number of encounters with the original source of information increases. Eventually, these patterns are so efficient that they are automatically activated (i.e., chronically accessible) even when encountering input stimuli that do not exactly match the input stimuli originally learned (Bechtel & Abrahamsen, 1991).

Connectionist networks have important consequences for the conceptualization of rewards and motivation. The probabilities that particular behaviors lead to first-order outcomes (Figure 6.4 arrows connecting behaviors to first-order outcomes) are what Vroom (1964) called expectancies. That is, these are probabilistic associations between the enactment of a possible behavior and the proximal outcome of that enactment (i.e., the expected chance that this behavior will result directly in said outcome). The primary outcomes eventually lead to secondary outcomes, such as obtaining promotions or providing for family. The probability that first-order outcomes lead to these various second-order outcomes (Figure 6.4 arrows connecting first-order outcomes to second-order outcomes) is called instrumentality. The conceptualization of expectancies and instrumentalities as strength and direction of the connections between nodes was first proposed by Lord et al. (2003). The advantage of using a connectionist approach for Vroom's (1964) Valence–Instrumentality–Expectancy (VIE) theory is that it enables the theory's predictions to hold without making the unrealistic assumption that individuals solve complex mutiplicative equations to determine their everyday behavior. Instead, the connectionist model of VIE suggests that motivational force will be generated in proportion to the theorized multiplicative functions, but that the determination of this motivational force is accomplished implicitly through the building of stable activation patterns among behaviors and outcomes.

Connectionism and Climate Perceptions

With this quick description of connectionist networks, we can now explain how such networks relate to organizational climate perceptions. Figure 6.5 illustrates a connectionist network model of organizational climate. The four circles at the top of this figure represent possible employee work behaviors. These behaviors could range from warmly welcoming customers, performing tasks in a fashion consistent with safety standards, or assisting co-workers, to things like taking frequent unscheduled breaks or sabotaging a co-worker's presentation. Each behavior has direct consequences, labeled "first-order outcomes." Examples of first-order outcomes include things like having friendly customer interaction, safely performing dangerous task, relaxing, increased stress, and *schadenfreude*. The primary outcomes eventually lead to secondary outcomes, such as receiving commissions, meaningful life, or providing for family.

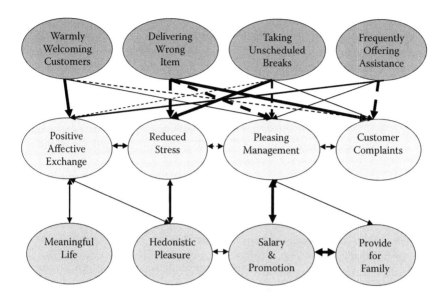

FIGURE 6.5 Connectionist schema of climate for service. Dotted line = negative association.

Lord et al. (2003) argued that people learn the associations between possible behaviors, first-order outcomes, and second-order outcomes based upon repeated exposure to environmental contingencies such as organizational practices, policies, and procedures. Thus, organizational practices, policies, and procedures influence the strength and direction of the connections between nodes of the network (i.e., expectancies and instrumentalities). Schneider and Reichers (1983) suggest a related conceptualization:

> Employee perceptions of the likelihood of certain behaviors "paying off," in the sense that the action will be reinforced by the organization's reward structure, may be a good indication of the climate for a particular behavior that the employee is considering. (p. 20)

Further, Reichers and Schneider (1990), in suggesting that climates convey what behavior is rewarded, supported, and expected, are defining organizational climate in a manner wholly consistent with the connectionist/neural network interpretation. The notion of a behavior being *rewarded* is captured by the associations or connections between possible behaviors and their positive outcomes. The notion that a behavior is *expected* is captured by connections between behaviors and the node, "pleasing management" (Figure 6.5). Finally, the concept that climates carry information about which behaviors are *supported* is represented by the initial range of possible behaviors considered in the schema. For instance, if a waiter works with an inadequate kitchen staff (i.e., no staff support), then "delivering the wrong item" (Figure 6.5) becomes a logical necessity and is no longer merely a *possible behavior* (Figure 6.4). Without support, the range of possible behaviors narrows. In sum, a learned pattern of associations such as the one shown in Figure 6.5 completely encapsulates the organizational climate concept.

Proposition 7: At the individual level, psychological climate perceptions can be comprehensively conceptualized as connectionist schemas.

While some of the learning of connectionist associations can occur at a conscious level, such as a person deliberately talking to co-workers or trusted others to make sense of the organizational contingencies, it does not have to be conscious. Indeed, some learning of the environmental contingencies occurs subconsciously as the individual encounters positive, negative, or neutral consequences for certain behavior in an organization.

Connectionist networks are different from the traditional symbolic models in that traditional models construe schemas as discrete and separate memory structures that can be modified, added to, and accessed independent of other schemas. Connectionist networks, on the other hand, conceive of schemas not as separate structures stored in memory, but rather as stable patterns of activity that emerge among the units in a network. It is this stable activation pattern that is the perceived organizational climate in connectionist networks.

Proposition 8: Individual-level climate schemas can be formed and modified with or without conscious information processing.

Implications of Connectionist Interpretation of Organizational Climate

At this point, the reader may be asking herself or himself what is gained by this connectionist interpretation of the organizational climate construct. We believe that this new model yields insights that can be tested. One implication of the connectionist model is that the structure—in addition to the content—of the activation pattern in a connectionist schema is an important characteristic of organizational climate. One characteristic of schema structure we believe to be particularly important is the *centrality* of a node in the climate schema. Centrality can be defined in a variety of ways, including (1) the simple number of connections to other nodes (*degree centrality*; Proctor & Loomis, 1951), (2) the reciprocal of the sum of shortest distances to all other nodes (*closeness centrality*; Sabidussi, 1966), and (3) the percentage of shortest paths between all other pairs of nodes that must travel through the focal node (*betweenness centrality*; Freeman,

1977). What centrality implies in the connectionist framework is that a central node will be frequently activated. Thus, the position of a concept within the structure of a connectionist climate schema will determine how salient that node is when one thinks of organizational climate. In Figure 6.5, for instance, "pleasing management" is a highly central node and is likely to be activated to some large degree whenever an individual considers the organization's climate. Having "pleasing management" as the central node would create a different climate than having another node, such as "positive affective exchange" as the central node. Thus, even though the content of the connectionist schema remains the same, the nature of the climate varies depending upon which node is central.

> Proposition 9: The more central a concept is within the connection-ist climate schema, the more salient it will be whenever climate is considered.
> Proposition 10: The more central a concept is within the climate schema, the more likely it will guide job attitudes and behavior.

Another characteristic of schema structure is its internal consistency, or what is called the *coherence* of a network. To oversimplify, coherence refers to the extent to which nodes of a network go together to form a meaningful whole (Miller & Read, 1991). A schema structure is said to be cohesive to the extent that the units in the network show a differential and hierarchical activation pattern. Indeed, coherence might be a useful, within-individual measure of climate strength.

> Proposition 11: The greater the coherence of an organizational climate, the stronger the regulation of employee behavior.

Finally, we note that it is possible to apply Heider's (1946) balance principle and Cartwright and Harary's (1956) balance-based theorem to connectionist climate schemas. In doing so, we suggest that the nodes in climate schemas will, over time, become segregated into two groups. Looking to Figure 6.5, it appears that the two supgroups that would emerge in a balanced climate schema would be (1) a subschema of negatively valenced behaviors and outcomes (i.e., delivering wrong item, taking unscheduled breaks, and customer complaints) and (2) a subschema of positively valenced behaviors and outcomes.

> Proposition 12: Connectionist climate schemas will tend to segregate into two subschemas: (1) a subschema reflecting positively valenced behaviors and outcomes and (2) a subschema reflecting negatively valenced behaviors and outcomes.

This schema segregation pattern is a unique property of each individual's climate map and reflects the points of view (e.g., employee, customer, manager) espoused by the individual respondent. A partitioning of the climate schema into positively and negatively valenced regions results directly from individual values at the time the schema is reported.

Measuring Connectionist Climate Schemas. Measuring the associations between nodes that make up climate schemas can be accomplished in a variety of ways. First, direct measurement can be used, in which individuals are explicitly asked to rate, for example, the extent to which warmly welcoming customers is related to customer complaints, on a scale from –5 (strongly negatively related) to 0 (unrelated) to +5 (strongly positively related). An example of direct schema measurement is given by Mathieu, Heffner, Goodwin, Salas, and Cannon-Bowers (2000). Self-reported connections can be optionally adjusted based upon a simplifying "pathfinder" algorithm (Schvaneveldt, 1990; see Day, Arthur, & Gettman, 2001). As an alternative to this explicit measurement method, connectionist climate schemas can also be ascertained implicitly, via response-time methods for judging the associations among concepts (Greenwald, Nosek, & Banaji, 2003; Ziegert & Hanges, 2005).

INTEGRATION: EXAMINING NETWORKS AT MULTIPLE LEVELS

In this chapter, we have presented two distinct sets of theoretical ideas, based upon a single representational device—the network. By considering individual climate perceptions as activated patterns of associations among behavioral and outcome concepts, and by considering organizational climate as determined by perceptual agreement at the level of the subgroup, we have attempted to expand the frontier of climate research. In the brief section that follows, we offer a few suggestions for how these two contributions can be integrated into a single, network model of organizational climate.

First, we propose that the component features of cognitive, connectionist climate schemas are subject to social influence. Following Proposition 9, we assert that conceptual nodes that are more central to an individual's climate schema (and therefore more frequently activated) are more likely to be communicated—and therefore interpersonally shared in social network subgroups. This more frequent activation and coactivation of particular nodes (e.g., pleasing management, hedonistic pleasure) among peers will lead those who are interpersonally connected (e.g., friends) to possess similar schemas.

Proposition 13: Cohesive social network subgroups will show high agreement in (1) their overall climate schemas, as well as in (2) the central schema concepts identified.

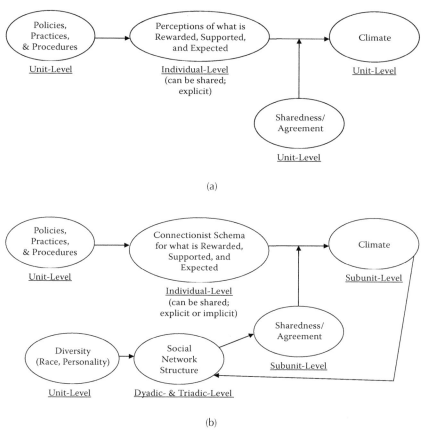

FIGURE 6.6 (a) Traditional model of organizational climate; (b) Network-connectionist model of organizational climate.

Methods for assessing this proposition are already under development in the teams literature, under the keyword *shared mental models* (Moham-med, Klimoski, & Rentsch, 2000). We suggest that these mental schemas come to be shared through interpersonal interaction that takes place in cohesive, informal social network clusters.

Network Model of Organizational Climate

Bringing together many of the propositions advanced in the present work, we introduce a diagram of our model in Figure 6.6 (see Table 6.1). As can be seen in Figure 6.6(a), the *traditional model of organizational cli-mate* is built upon individual-level perceptions of unit-level features (i.e., the psychological climate of Jones & Jones, 1974). In the *network model*

TABLE 6.1
Comparison of Organizational Climate Models

Dimension	Traditional Model of Organizational Climate	Network-Connectionist Model of Organizational Climate
Climate definition	Shared individual perceptions	Shared individual perceptions (explicit) and schema activation patterns (implicit)
Climate level of analysis	Unit	Subunit (cohesive social network subgroup)
Agreement level of analysis	Unit	Subunit (cohesive social network subgroup)
Source of agreement or sharedness	Common opportunity to observe organizational practices; common meaning system	Common opportunity to observe organizational practices; common meaning system; direct communication; indirect communication
Attraction-selection-attrition level of analysis	Unit (formal process)	Subunit (cohesive social network subgroup) (informal process)
Ambient (unit-level) climate measurement	Mean across all unit members	Mean across all network isolates
Climate strength	Deviation across all unit members	Existence of cohesive social network subgroups with differing perceptions
Climate outcomes	Group attitude and behavior (intercepts and slopes)	Subgroup attitude and behavior (intercepts and slopes); social network structure (dyads and triads)

(Figure 6.6(b)), individual-level climate perceptions need not be directly perceived, but rather need only constitute implicit associations among individual behaviors and their probabilistic, valenced outcomes. These connectionist climate schemas represent what is rewarded, supported, and expected for an individual. It is possible for entire schema patterns— or their constituent features—to be held in common among employees. While not entirely conscious, these schemas are likely to be shared more strongly at the subunit level (cohesive network subgroups) than at the level of the entire unit.

According to the traditional model, organizational climate is specified as a unit-level construct, dependent upon unit-level agreement among individual-level perceptions gathered from direct survey reports. In contrast, the network model of organizational climate specifies climate as a subunit-level construct (i.e., subgroup climate), dependent upon subunit-level agreement (i.e., consensus within cohesive network subgroups). Informal social network structure is posited as an antecedent of this agreement, where Heider's (1946) principle of balanced triads guides the sharing of climate perceptions among friends. The emergence of social network subgroups (i.e., subunit level), in which the local climates inhere, is itself the result of balance- (Cartwright & Harary, 1956) and attraction- (Byrne, 1971) based homophily processes. Such homophily processes, where "birds of a feather flock together," are endemic to organizational units with high dispersion/diversity (i.e., within-unit variation in individual differences). Relevant individual differences along which segregation occurs can be demographic, or based upon knowledge, skills, abilities, and personality. As such, the social networks enable a homogeneity process (Schneider, 1987) to operate at the subunit level, even in circumstances where attraction, selection, and attrition have failed to homogenize groups at the larger, unit level.

Sometimes, the psychological pull toward homogeneity is stifled by technological and pragmatic features of work. Physical work arrangements and formal organizational structures often constrain individuals to labor in close proximity to dissimilar others. When this occurs, absence of similar others in the local work setting can inhibit the formation of social ties, thereby reducing social capital (Coleman, 1990) and frustrating needs for belonging (Baumeister & Leary, 1995). In these (typical) instances, where employees are obliged to work among dispositionally dissimilar co-workers, how can personal needs for affiliation and belonging be met? We suggest that employees form interpersonal alliances in part through focusing on perceptual (rather than demographic) similarity. The availability of perceptual homogeneity (through shared perceptions of organizational features) can provide a basis upon which to form interpersonal ties while maintaining balance (Heider, 1946). In other words, mutual celebration or commiseration over company policies (i.e., shared climate) is a mechanism by which relationships are formed and maintained. From this viewpoint, there is a feedback loop from organizational climate to social network structure, as the availability of shared perceptions makes it easier to build friendship ties (i.e., co-workers bonding over their mutual agreement). This rationale supports our final proposition:

Proposition 14: Climate functions to build and maintain social structures.

CONCLUSION

In this work, we have taken the definition of organizational climate as shared individual perceptions of what is rewarded, supported, and expected (Reichers & Schneider, 1990) and elaborated upon the twin notions of *sharedness* and *reward/expectancy*. This was accomplished using the social network and neural network lenses, respectively. We suggested that climate emerges from two levels: the intraindividual level (from a set of concepts within a person's mind) and the interindividual level (from within a group of peers or friends who share similar perceptions and schemas). Both forms of networks were proposed to adhere to the balance principle, from which followed the theme of *maintaining microlevel homogeneity in the presence of macrolevel heterogeneity*. Both interpersonal networks and intraindividual connectionist schemas are proposed to develop cohesive clusters of similar nodes.

In the absence of the current perspective, both *organizational climate* and within-individual *psychological climate* concepts could be considered oversimplified. Climate researchers have traditionally operationalized climate with the overall group mean, regardless of communication patterns within the group. Further, individual climate perceptions are traditionally measured as the result of mental averaging and do not represent structures of connections among cognitive concepts, where some concepts are more central than others. With the *network-connectionist model*, we have now identified patterns within these climate concepts (i.e., previously undifferentiated groups are now seen as differentiated by social networks; overall climate perceptions are now seen as configured schemas) and constructed a series of propositions for how these climate patterns operate.

REFERENCES

Barnes, J. A. (1954). Class and committees in a Norwegian island parish. *Human Relations, 7,* 39–58.

Baumeister, R. F., & Leary, M. R. (1995). The need to belong: Desire for interpersonal attachments as a fundamental human motivation. *Psychological Bulletin, 117,* 497–527.

Bechtel, W., & Abrahamsen, A. (1991). *Connectionism and the mind.* Cambridge, MA: Blackwell.

Borgatti, S. P. (2005). *NetDraw network visualization software.* Harvard, MA: Analytic Technologies, Inc.

Borgatti, S. P., & Foster, P. C. (2003). The network paradigm in organizational research: A review and typology. *Journal of Management, 29,* 991–1013.

Brass, D. J., Galaskiewicz, J., Greve, H. R., & Tsai, W. (2004). Taking stock of networks and organizations: A multilevel perspective. *Academy of Management Journal, 47,* 795–817.

Brown, R. D., & Hauenstein, N. M. A. (2005). Interrater agreement reconsidered: An alternative to the r_{WG} indices. *Organizational Research Methods, 8,* 165–184.

Byrne, D. E. (1971). *The attraction paradigm.* New York: Academic Press.

Carr, J. Z., Schmidt, A. M., Ford, J. K., & DeShon, R. P. (2003). Climate perceptions matter: A meta-analytic path analysis relating molar climate, cognitive and affective states, and individual level work outcomes. *Journal of Applied Psychology, 88*, 605–619.

Cartwright, D., & Harary, F. (1956). Structural balance: A generalization of Heider's theory. *Psychological Review, 63*, 277–293.

Chan, D. (1998). Functional relations among constructs in the same content domain at different levels of analysis: A typology of composition models. *Journal of Applied Psychology, 83*, 234–246.

Clark, A. (2001). *Mindware: An introduction to the philosophy of cognitive science.* New York: Oxford University Press.

Coleman, J. S. (1990). *Foundations of social theory.* Cambridge: Belknap Press of Harvard University Press.

Daft, R. L., Sormunen, J., & Parks, D. (1988). Chief executive scanning, environmental characteristics, and company performance: An empirical study. *Strategic Management Journal, 9*, 123–139.

Davis, J. A. (1967). Clustering and structural balance in graphs. *Human Relations, 20*, 181–187.

Day, E. A., Arthur, W., & Gettman, D. (2001). Knowledge structures and the acquisition of a complex skill. *Journal of Applied Psychology, 86*, 1022–1033.

Doreian, P. (2002). Event sequences as generators of social network evolution. *Social Networks, 24*, 93–119.

Duncan, R. B. (1972). Characteristics of organizational environments and perceived environmental uncertainty. *Administrative Science Quarterly, 17*, 313–327.

Festinger, L. (1949). The analysis of sociograms using matrix algebra. *Human Relations, 2*, 153–158.

Festinger, L. (1954). A theory of social comparison process. *Human Relations, 7*, 117–140.

Fiske, S. T., & Taylor, S. E. (1991). *Social cognition.* New York: Guilford Press.

Freeman, L. C. (1977). A set of measures of centrality based on betweenness. *Sociometry, 40*, 35–41.

Glick, W. H. (1985). Conceptualizing and measuring organizational and psychological climate: Pitfalls in multilevel research. *Academy of Management Review, 10*, 601–617.

Glisson, C., & James, L. R. (2002). The cross-level effects of culture and climate in human service teams. *Journal of Organizational Behavior, 23*, 767–794.

Greenwald, A. G., Nosek, B. A., & Banaji, M. R. (2003). Understanding and using the implicit association test: An improved scoring algorithm. *Journal of Personality and Social Psychology, 85*, 197–216.

Hanges, P. J., Lord, R. G., & Dickson, M. W. (2000). An information-processing perspective on leadership and culture: A case for connectionist architecture. *Applied Psychology: An International Review, 49*, 133–161.

Harary, F., Norman, R. Z., & Cartwright, D. (1965). *Structural models: An introduction to the theory of directed graphs.* New York: John Wiley & Sons.

Heider, F. (1946). Attitudes and cognitive organization. *Journal of Psychology, 21*, 107–112.

Heider, F. (1958). *The psychology of interpersonal relations.* New York: Wiley.

Hofstede, G. H. (1980). *Culture consequences: International differences in work-related values.* Thousand Oaks, CA: Sage Publications.

Hofstede, G. H. (2001). *Culture consequences: Comparing values, behaviors, institutions and organizations across nations.* Thousand Oaks, CA: Sage Publications.

Homans, G. C. (1951). *The human group.* London: Routledge & Kegan Paul.

House, R. J., Hanges, P. J., Javidan, M., Dorfman, P., & Gupta, V. (2004). *GLOBE, cultures, leadership, and organizations: GLOBE study of 62 societies.* Newbury Park, CA: Sage Publications.

James, L. R., Demaree, R. G., & Wolf, G. (1984). Estimating within group interrater reliability with and without response bias. *Journal of Applied Psychology, 69,* 85–98.

James, L. R., Hater, J. J., Gent, M. J., & Bruni, J. R. (1978). Psychological climate: Implications from cognitive social learning theory and interactional psychology. *Personnel Psychology, 31,* 783–813.

James, L. R., & Jones, A. P. (1974). Organizational climate: A review of theory and research. *Psychological Bulletin, 81,* 1096–1112.

James, L. R., Joyce, W., & Slocum, J. (1988). Comment: Organizations do not cognize. *Academy of Management Review, 13,* 129–132.

Kenny, D. A. (1991). A general model of consensus and accuracy in interpersonal perception. *Psychological Review, 98,* 155–163.

Kilduff, M., & Tsai, W. (2003). *Social networks and organizations.* Thousand Oaks, CA: Sage Publications.

Krackhardt, D., & Kilduff, M. (1999). Whether close or far: Social distance effects on perceived balance in friendship networks. *Journal of Personality and Social Psychology, 76,* 770–782.

Lawler, E. E., Hall, D. T., & Oldham, G. R. (1974). Organizational climate: Relationship to organizational structure, process, and performance. *Organizational Behavior and Human Performance, 11,* 139–155.

LeBreton, J. M., James, L. R., & Lindell, M. K. (2005). Recent issues regarding rWG, r*WG, rWG(J), and r*WG(J). *Organizational Research Methods, 8,* 128–139.

Leenders, R. (2002). Modeling social influence through network autocorrelation: Constructing the weight matrix. *Social Networks, 24,* 21–47.

Lindell, M. K., Brandt, C. J., & Whitney, D. J. (1999). A revised index of interrater agreement for multi-item ratings of a single target. *Applied Psychological Measurement, 23,* 127–135.

Lord, R. G., & Brown, D. J. (2004). *Leadership processes and follower self-identity.* Hillsdale, NJ: Lawrence Erlbaum Associates.

Lord, R. G., Brown, D. J., & Harvey, J. L. (2001). System constraints on leadership perceptions, behavior, and influence: An example of connectionist level processes. In M. A. Hogg & R. S. Tindale (Eds.), *Blackwell handbook of social psychology: Group processes,* pp. 283–310. Oxford, UK: Blackwell Publishers.

Lord, R. G., Brown, D. J., Harvey, J. L., & Hall, R. J. (2001). Contextual constraints on prototype generation and their multilevel consequences for leadership perceptions. *Leadership Quarterly, 12,* 311–338.

Lord, R. G., & Foti, R. J. (1986). Schema theories, information processing, and organizational behavior, pp. 20–49. In H. P. Sims, Jr., & D. A. Gioia (Eds.), *The thinking organization.* San Francisco: Jossey-Bass.

Lord, R. G., Foti, R. J., & De Vader, C. (1984). A test of leadership categorization theory: Internal structure, information processing, and leadership perceptions. *Organizational Behavior and Human Performance, 34,* 343–378.

Lord, R. G., Hanges, P. J., & Godfrey, E. G. (2003). Integrating neural networks into decision-making and motivational theory: Rethinking VIE theory. *Canadian Psychology, 44,* 21–38.

Lord, R. G., & Maher, K. J. (1990). Alternative information-processing models and their implications for theory, research, and practice. *Academy of Management Review, 15,* 9–28.

Luce, R. D. (1950). Connectivity and generalized cliques in a sociometric group structure. *Psychometrika, 15,* 159–190.

Luce, R. D., & Perry, A. D. (1949). A method of matrix analysis of a group structure. *Psychometrika, 14,* 95–116.

Martin, J. (1992). *Cultures in organizations.* Oxford: Oxford University Press.

Mathieu, J. E., Heffner, T. S., Goodwin, G. F., Salas, E., & Cannon-Bowers, J. A. (2000). The influence of shared mental models on team process and performance. *Journal of Applied Psychology, 85,* 273–283.

Mayo, E. (1933). *The human problems of an industrial civilization.* New York: Macmillan.

McPherson, M., Smith-Lovin, L., & Cook, J. M. (2001). Birds of a feather: Homophily in social networks. *Annual Review of Sociology, 27,* 415–444.

Miller, L. C., & Read, S. J. (1991). On the coherence of mental models of persons and relationships: A knowledge structure approach. In G. J. O. Fletcher & F. D. Fincham (Eds.), *Cognition in close relationships* (pp. 69–99). Hillsdale, NJ: Erlbaum.

Mohammed, S., Klimoski, R., & Rentsch, J. R. (2000). The measurement of team mental models: We have no shared schema. *Organizational Research Methods, 3,* 123–165.

Mokken, R. (1979). Cliques, clubs and clans. *Quality and Quantity, 13,* 161–173.

Moreno, J. L. (1934). *Who shall survive? A new approach to the problems of human interrelations.* Washington, DC: Nervous and Mental Disease Publishing Company.

Moreno, J. L., & Jennings, H. H. (1938). Statistics of social configurations. *Sociometry, 1,* 342–374.

Ostroff, C., Kinicki, A. J., & Tamkins, M. (2003). Organizational culture and climate. In W. C. Borman, D. R. Ilgen, & R. J. Klimoski (Eds.), *Handbook of psychology: Industrial and organizational psychology* (Vol. 12, pp. 565–594). New York: John Wiley & Sons.

Proctor, C. H., & Loomis, C. P. (1951). Analysis of sociometric data. In M. Johada, M. Deutsch, & S. W. Cook (Eds.), *Research methods in social relations* (Part 2, pp. 561–586). New York: Holt, Rinehart, and Winston.

Ramesh, A., & Newman, D. A. (2005). Cognitive, social and affective influences on performance appraisal. In Y. Baruch (Chair), *New directions in performance management research.* Symposium conducted at the Annual Conference of the Academy of Management, Honolulu, Hawaii.

Reichers, A., & Schneider, B. (1990). Climate and culture: An evolution of constructs. In B. Schneider (Ed.), *Organizational climate and culture* (pp. 5–39). San Francisco: Jossey-Bass.

Rentsch, J. R. (1990). Climate and culture: Interaction and qualitative differences in organizational meanings. *Journal of Applied Psychology, 75,* 668–681.

Rosch, E. H. (1973). Natural categories. *Cognitive Psychology, 4,* 328–350.

Rosch, E. H. (1978). Principles of categorization. In E. Rosch & B. B. Lloyd (Eds.), *Cognition and categorization.* Hillsdale, NJ: Erlbaum.

Sabidussi, G. (1966). The centrality index of a graph. *Psychometrika, 31,* 581–603.

Salancik, G. R., & Pfeffer, J. (1978). A social information processing approach to job attitudes and task design. *Administrative Science Quarterly, 23,* 224–254.

Schneider, B. (1987). The people make the place. *Personnel Psychology, 40,* 437–453.

Schneider, B. (2000). The psychological life of organizations. In N. M. Ashkanasy, C. P. M. Wilderom, & M. F. Peterson (Eds.), *Handbook of organizational culture and climate* (pp. xvii–xxi). Thousand Oaks, CA: Sage Publications.

Schneider, B., & Reichers, A. E. (1983). On the etiology of climates. *Personnel Psychology, 36,* 19–40.

Schneider, B., Salvaggio, A. N., & Subirats, M. (2002). Climate strength: A new direction for climate research. *Journal of Applied Psychology, 87,* 220–229.

Schvaneveldt, R. W. (1990). *Path-finder associative networks: Studies in knowledge organization.* Norwood, NJ: Ablex.

Scott, J. (2000). *Social network analysis: A handbook.* Thousand Oaks, CA: Sage Publications.

Seidman, S., & Foster, B. (1978). A graph-theoretic generalization of the clique concept. *Journal of Mathematical Sociology, 6,* 139–154.

Simmel, G. (1908). *Sociology: Investigations on the forms of sociation.* Berlin: Duncker & Humblot.

Smith, E. R. (1996). What do connectionism and social psychology offer each other? *Journal of Personality and Social Psychology, 70,* 893–912.

Smith, E. R., & DeCoster, J. (1998). Person perception and stereotyping: Simulation using distributed representations in a recurrent connectionist network. In S. J. Read & L. C. Miller (Eds.), *Connectionist models of social reasoning and social behavior.* Mahwah, NJ: Lawrence Erlbaum.

Steel, R. P., Shane, G. S., & Kennedy, K. A. (1990). Effects of social-system factors on absenteeism, turnover intention, and job performance. *Journal of Business and Psychology, 4,* 423–430.

Van Overwalle, F. (1998). Causal explanation as constraint satisfaction: A critique and a feedforward connectionist alternative. *Journal of Personality and Social Psychology, 74,* 312–328.

Vroom, V. H. (1964). *Work and motivation.* New York: Wiley.

Warner, W. L., & Lunt, P. S. (1941). *The social life of a modern community.* New Haven, CT: Yale University Press.

Wasserman, S., & Faust, K. (1994). *Social network analysis: Methods and applications.* Cambridge, UK: Cambridge University Press.

Weick, K. E. (1979). *The social psychology of organizing* (2nd ed.). Reading, MA: Addison-Wesley.

Zalesny, M. D., & Ford, J. K. (1990). Extending the social information processing perspective: New links to attitudes, behaviors and perceptions. *Organizational Behavior and Human Decision Processes, 47,* 205–246.

Ziegert, J. C., & Hanges, P. J. (2005). Employment discrimination: The role of implicit attitudes, motivation, and a climate for racial bias. *Journal of Applied Psychology, 90,* 253–262.

Zohar, D. (1980). Safety climate in industrial organizations: Theoretical and applied implcations, *Journal of Applied Psychology, 65,* 96–102.

7

Cognitions in Organizations and Teams
What Is the Meaning of Cognitive Similarity?

JOAN R. RENTSCH
University of Tennessee

ERIKA E. SMALL
University of Tennessee

PAUL J. HANGES
University of Maryland

Bring two or more people together, give them a task, the proper resources, and contextual features, and something magical will happen. After some initial confusion and struggle they will make sense of how to work together. Team members develop beliefs, attitudes, and expectations about what is happening in the group (e.g., group efficacy), perceptions about how the team is treated and what is valued (e.g., justice, safety, innovation), and so on. They formulate understandings of such complex matters as how to accomplish and evaluate the task and how to interact with one another and with those outside of the team. The magic is that team members' understandings become similar. Eventually, these similar understandings may become strong enough that they appear to exert influence over team members and the team as a whole.

Organizational psychologists and sociologists are fascinated by this elusive phenomenon and have developed various conceptualizations and labels for "it," including *shared meaning, schema similarity, climate, culture, sensemaking,* and *collective climate.* Within organizations, "it" is assumed to exist at all levels of analysis, including the group or team, unit, and organization. Traditionally studied at the organizational and unit levels, similar understandings have received the most research attention in the forms of organizational climate and culture. More recently, in the past 15 or so years, the phenomenon has been studied within work teams in the forms of, for example, schema similarity, team climate, shared mental models, and group subculture. The purpose of this chapter is to review the empirical literature in which common meanings, understandings, and interpretations have been examined at the team level of analysis and to provide avenues for future research.

We begin by describing how we conceptualize "it" and why it is important to understand it in teams. At this point in the chapter, we offer *cognitive similarity* as the general term to describe "it" at any level of analysis. We refer to cognitive similarity at the team level as *team cognition.* Next, we describe how we approached the literature and present a focused review of the research on team cognition. Then, we discuss future research on cognitive similarity in general, but particularly with respect to team cognition. In addition, we describe forms of cognition, forms of similarity, and cognitive domains as underlying features of types of cognitive similarity. We propose that types of cognitive similarity in combination form configurations of cognitive similarity.

WHAT IS "IT"? SIMILAR MEANINGS IN ORGANIZATIONS AND TEAMS

Similar Meanings in Organizations

Perception, cognition, and behavior are intricately related. For example, a cat sees a woman, which it interprets as food. Naturally, this interpretation will affect the cat's interactions with the woman. The cat may approach the woman and meow in an attempt to get food from her. Another cat may interpret the woman as threatening and hide in her presence. Similarly, people in organizations may have differing interpretations of the same environmental stimuli. However, forces exist to cause their differing interpretations to converge, and in organizations, common meanings among members have been shown to be useful.

Common meanings among organizational members have been represented in the organizational socialization, climate, and culture literatures (James, Hater, Gent, & Bruni, 1978; Louis, 1980; Moreland & Levine, 1989; Rentsch, 1990; Schneider & Reichers, 1983). One outcome of organizational socialization is that newcomers learn how organizational events are interpreted within the organization (i.e., they learn how others interpret events and then adopt, assimilate, and internalize those interpretations). Interpretation is the process of making sense of organizational events by attributing meaning to them (Daft & Weick, 1984). Properly socialized organizational members are perceived to "fit in" and contribute functionally to the organization's performance in part because they interpret organizational events in the same way other members do. In doing so, they contribute to propagating the organization's climate and culture.

Evidence suggests that eventually organizational members' interpretations will achieve some degree of congruence or similarity. This similarity is a product of the social construction process that occurs when organizational members interact directly or indirectly with one another, particularly when they are solving problems (e.g., Berger & Luckmann, 1966; Schneider & Reichers, 1983). Interpretations that organizational members hold in common may be granted some degree of implicit or explicit power to influence behavior in the organization. This controlling force of a socially constructed reality tends to offer efficiencies to organizations because similar interpretations ease organizational functioning. For example, they enable organizational members to predict and understand the behavior of others, and they enable members to behave in ways that others in the organization will interpret as acceptable. Furthermore, similar interpretations aid in identifying and ousting deviants. Conversely, this controlling force may have deleterious effects on organizational functioning. For example, extreme homogeneity may be detrimental to the organization's adaptive capabilities (e.g., Schneider, 1987).

Schneider's (1987) attraction–selection–attrition (ASA) model explains how attraction to, selection by, and attrition from an organization perpetuate the process of converging meanings and interpretations within the organization. According to Schneider, similar people are attracted to and selected by an organization, and dissimilar people leave it, yielding an organization of highly similar people. These similar people tend to develop similar meanings for understanding organizational policies, practices, and procedures. These similar meanings are highly potent forces in organizations that may increase or decrease effectiveness.

Similar Meanings in Teams

Members of organizational work teams also engage in sensemaking processes to develop interpretations of ambiguous organizational and team-related events. Just as organizational newcomers are socialized into existing organizations, new team members are socialized into existing teams (Levine & Moreland, 1991). During the socialization process, they have the opportunity to learn how their teammates interpret team-related events and to assimilate those interpretations. In new teams, where all members are new concurrently, members negotiate interpretations of team-related events (Walsh, Henderson, & Deighton, 1988). Regardless of whether the team is new or preexisting, team members utilize their past experiences and interactions with one another to develop similar cognitive structures for understanding and attributing meaning to team-related events and factors, including one another, the task, and the team's context. Teams in which members interpret events similarly tend to benefit from smooth interactions and high performance.

As in organizations, similar understandings among team members may enhance or inhibit team performance, although most theoretical perspectives emphasize the positive effects. Assuming the cognitive content is functional and that the degree and form of the similarity is at an optimal level and of a beneficial type, it is reasonable to focus on the positive outcomes of similar meanings among team members. Under these assumptions, similar meanings among team members will facilitate group performance by creating efficient team process because team members will correctly interpret and predict each other's behavior (Cannon-Bowers, Salas, & Converse, 1993; Rentsch & Hall, 1994; Rentsch & Klimoski, 2001). It influences the kinds of environmental information that team members attend to and their interpretations of that information, which guides their behavior (Levy, 2005). Thus, similar meanings among team members enhance such team processes as communication (Weick, 1993), the experience and interpretation of conflict (Rentsch & Zelno, 2003), and the behaviors of team members (Greenberg, 1995; Naumann & Bennett, 2000; Xie & Johns, 2000; Zohar, 2000). Furthermore, similar meanings in teams have been theorized and found empirically to be positively related to team performance (e.g., Gibson, 2001; Kirkman, Tesluk, & Rosen, 2001; Levy, 2005; Naumann & Bennett, 2002; Rentsch & Klimoski, 2001; Smith-Jentsch, Mathieu, & Kraiger, 2005) and team member satisfaction (Mason & Griffin, 2003; Mohammed & Ringseis, 2001) either directly or mediated by team processes (e.g., Marks, Sabella, Burke, & Zaccaro, 2002; Marks, Zaccaro, & Mathieu, 2000).

Thus, we conceptualize "it" as cognitive similarity among individuals. We define cognitive similarity as forms of related meanings or understandings attributed to and utilized to make sense of and interpret internal and external events, including affect, behavior, and thoughts of self and others that exist among individuals (see Figure 7.1). Cognitive similarity is a general term that incorporates multiple types. Types of cognitive similarity are defined by the intersection of cognitive form, cognitive domain, and form of similarity. Different types of cognitive similarity in combination form configurations of cognitive similarity.

In this chapter, our interest is in cognitive similarity at the team level, which we refer to as team cognition. Below, we review the team-level empirical work that included some form of team cognition. Our aim was to determine how this phenomenon has been conceptualized and measured in the empirical literature and to offer a conceptual integration and highlight measurement challenges that we hope will provide promising avenues for future research on cognitive similarity, in general, and team cognition, in particular.

IDENTIFYING RESEARCH ON TEAM COGNITION

We searched the empirical articles published in major journals in the fields of industrial and organizational psychology and organizational behavior between 1990 and 2005 using search terms related to cognition and meaning in teams, including *schema, climate, culture, sensemaking,* and *mental model.* We limited the search to articles pertaining to work groups or teams (excluding sports and educational teams). We reviewed articles in which team cognition was assessed at or aggregated to the team level of analysis. The search yielded a small set of seemingly disjointed articles representing a variety of approaches to the study of meaning among team members. Interestingly, there was little overlap and few cross-references among the articles in the set. We deliberately disregarded several topics in team cognition, such as expertise and transactive memory. Expertise, although a cognitive variable, is typically associated with individual team members. Similarly, transactive memory within a team is characterized by differentiation of team members' cognitions (Hollingshead, 1998). Our focus was on some form of similarity among team members' meanings, interpretations, or understandings.

We reviewed the empirical works with respect to the following questions: How was team cognition conceptualized? How was team cognition measured? What was the form of the similarity? We used these issues to frame the literature review.

CONCEPTUALIZATIONS OF TEAM COGNITION IN THE EMPIRICAL RESEARCH

Three conceptualizations of team cognition were extracted from the empirical research: (1) perceptual, (2) structured, and (3) interpretive. Each represented some form of similar meaning, understanding, or

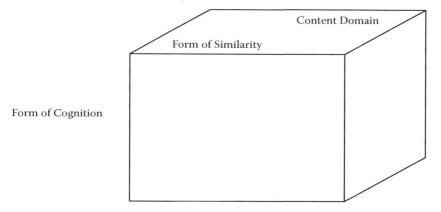

FIGURE 7.1 Features that form types of cognitive similarity.

interpretation among team members, and each is based on a set of assumptions regarding similar cognitions among team members.

Perceptual

One conceptualization of similar cognitions among team members is defined in terms of perceptions. The overlap or agreement among team members' perceptions is usually described as shared. In addition, research on aggregated individual-level constructs such as beliefs, expectations, and attitudes is based on the shared perceptions conceptualization.

Shared perceptions describe team-level climate. Glisson and James (2002) distinguished between psychological climate, which they defined as a set of individually held perceptions of the effect of the work environment on the individual's well-being, and organizational (or team) climate, which they defined as existing when there is a high level of agreement among individuals' perceptions. Thus, they clearly defined climate perceptions as cognition originating within individuals. They did not recognize the group as an entity capable of cognition. Furthermore, they specified the cognitive content to be the individual's interpretation of the environment's influence on his or her well-being. Within the team climate literature there is a high degree of consensus that team climate is defined as similar individual perceptions of team members (e.g., Bain, Mann, & Pirola-Merlo, 2001; Colquitt, Noe, & Jackson, 2002; Naumann & Bennett, 2000, 2002; Zohar, 2000; Zohar & Luria, 2005).

Many researchers studying teams from the perceptual perspective referred to Schneider's work (e.g., Schneider, 1975, 1990; Schneider & Reichers, 1983) when defining the relevance of shared perceptions or climate (e.g., Anderson & West, 1998; Hofmann, Morgeson, & Gerras, 2003; Naumann & Bennett, 2000, 2002). In particular, researchers relied on Schneider's (Schneider, 1990; Schneider & Reichers, 1983) definition of organizational climate as the "set of shared perceptions of the policies, practices, and procedures that an organization rewards, supports, and expects that is developed through group interaction" (Naumann & Bennett, 2000, p. 881). Thus, cognitive similarity is an explicit component of shared perceptions because shared perceptions represent meaning derived from observations of behavioral patterns existing in the environment.

Team researchers typically heed Schneider's (1975) call for identifying the relevant content of the perceptions under investigation. For example, climate for innovation, climate for creativity, climate for safety, and procedural justice team climate have been examined, and in these cases, climate was defined as shared perceptions (e.g., Anderson & West, 1998; Bain et al., 2001; Colquitt et al., 2002; Naumann & Bennett, 2000, 2002; Pirola-Merlo & Mann, 2004; Zohar, 2000; Zohar & Luria, 2005). For example, Zohar (2000) examined how group members interpreted patterns of supervisory behavior as indicating the priority supervisors placed on safety. Shared perceptions of the priority of safety goals were hypothesized to develop to the extent that a supervisor displayed similar patterns of behavior related to safety to all group members.

The above conceptualization of team cognition as perceptual is based on the assumption that meaning originates within individuals, and through their interactions with one another a socially constructed understanding emerges. The socially constructed meaning, although existing within each individual, is shared among individuals. It should be noted that some have referred to shared perceptions (climate) as a "distinct group-level cognition" (e.g., Colquitt et al., 2002) and as "cognitive representations" (e.g., Choi, Price, & Vinokur, 2003).

Shared beliefs also fit in the perceptual conceptualization (e.g., team members may share beliefs about team empowerment, failure, and team efficacy). One approach to the study of shared beliefs acknowledges beliefs as psychological variables existing within individuals that become shared among individuals. For example, team empowerment is a team-level variable that reflects team members' positive beliefs regarding their task and consists of a "set of shared cognitions" formed by team members developed through mutual influence and social construction (Kirkman et al., 2001, p. 652). Likewise, Cannon and Edmondson (2001) argued that team members share beliefs about how to respond to failure.

Another approach to shared beliefs explicates cognition as existing entirely within the group as a whole, thereby defining shared perceptions as residing within the team rather than within individuals, and differentiating team-level shared perceptions from aggregates of individual team member perceptions. For example, Gibson (2003) defines collective efficacy as a team's "collective belief in its capability to perform a task" (p. 2153). This collective belief is assumed to be cognition possessed and expressed by the group as a whole. The group as an entity approach permits the cognition to persist with the group regardless of membership changes. Nevertheless, Gibson (2001, 2003) assumed that this form of team cognition arises as a result of interaction and collective cognition processes. She stated, "Group efficacy forms as group members collectively acquire, store, manipulate, and exchange information about each other, their task, their context, process, and prior performance" (Gibson, 2001, p. 791).

Research on shared expectations presents another form of team cognition within the perceptual conceptualization (e.g., Earley & Mosakowski, 2000; Xie & Johns, 2000). For example, Xie and Johns (2000) focused on shared expectations about attendance level as the basis for shared understanding of absence behavior. In their study, they presented the notion of strength of shared perception, which they referred to as salience. Salience in their study was the extent of perceptual agreement about the appropriate level of absence for the group. (Other researchers working within the perceptual conceptualization have also discussed strength of shared perceptions [i.e., strength of team cognition]. For example, the extent to which a larger number of rules, expectations, and roles are shared serve as indications of the strength of shared perceptions [e.g., Earley & Mosa-kowski, 2000].)

Working within the perceptual conceptualization, Glisson and James (2002) defined organizational culture as the shared normative beliefs and shared expectations that prescribe team behavior. They argued that it is the assumptions and values underlying the expectations and beliefs that give meaning. Although they acknowledged that cognition exists in indi-viduals, they argue that the shared normative beliefs and expectations are properties of the social system.

Shared attitudes such as shared positive perceptions of the team con-text and group task satisfaction offer another conceptualization of team cognition as perceptual (Beersma & De-Dreu, 2002; Mason & Griffin, 2003). Mason and Griffin (2003) differentiated group task satisfaction, which refers to shared attitudes common to all members, from aggregated individual-level perceptual ratings, thereby steering away from conceptu-alizing team cognition as an aggregate of individual cognitions.

In summary, researchers working with perceptual conceptualizations of team cognition tend to (1) define sharedness as the degree of agree-ment in interpretations of environmental stimuli as reflected in percep-tions, beliefs, expectations, and attitudes; (2) identify the interpretive cognitive content (e.g., safety, innovation, justice); (3) prefer the use of the term *shared*, although less than perfect overlap in cognition appears to be acknowledged; (4) clearly identify either the individual or the team as the originating point of cognition; (5) develop theory regarding how percep-tions become shared, with a particular emphasis on social interaction and social construction; and (6) place no emphasis on cognitive structure (i.e., do not discuss how cognition in the forms of perceptions, beliefs, expecta-tions, and attitudes is organized).

Structured

Team cognition has also been conceptualized as organized knowledge structures or schemas. Approaches to team cognition using this concep-tualization center on the similarity of the structure of the cognition. Three basic approaches are defining structured cognition as mental models, as strategic consensus, and as team member schema similarity.

One perspective on structured cognition, the mental model approach, has roots in human factors psychology. In this approach, cognition is assumed to be structured in the form of a mental model. Mental mod-els are defined as "mechanisms whereby humans are able to generate descriptions of system purpose and form, explanations of system func-tioning and observed system states, and predictions of future systems states" (Rouse & Morris, 1986, p. 351). The organized knowledge in mental models is assumed to be about systems, responses to systems, and system environments. With respect to team cognition, individual team members are theorized to develop mental models representing knowledge about team characteristics, including its purpose, links among team members' actions and roles, and what it takes to complete collective action (Marks et al., 2002).

Team members are expected to develop shared or overlapping mental models, referred to as shared mental models, team mental models, and mental model similarity (defined as shared mental models) (e.g., Marks et al., 2000, 2002). Thus, sharedness is defined as the extent to which the individual mental models of team members are consistent with one another (Mathieu, Heffner, Goodwin, Cannon-Bowers, & Salas, 2005). Shared team mental models have been studied primarily within the context of military team training with the aim of using training to increase sharedness among team members' mental models (primarily with respect to the task or task performance).

Sharedness or sameness is the most studied form of mental models at the team level. According to Carley (1997), team (shared) mental models represent the knowledge that is shared or common among individuals, or social knowledge. She highlighted key characteristics of shared mental models, including the extent to which the team members are aware that they share mental models and the degree to which the mental representations are uniformly shared. Individuals are thought to posses multiple mental models and to utilize them differentially (Cannon-Bowers et al., 1993; Carley, 1997; Levesque, Wilson, & Wholey, 2001). Likewise, teams are also believed to develop multiple shared mental models associated with specific team domain contents (e.g., task work and teamwork).

Shared strategic cognition is another form of team cognition conceptualized as structured cognition. Ensley and Pearce (2001), working with top management teams (TMTs), referred to strategic consensus as understanding and agreeing on strategy. Thus, they defined shared strategic cognition as "the extent to which strategic mental models held in the hearts and minds of the TMT members overlap or agree" (p. 146). They argued that shared understanding results from the discussion of and debate over strategic decisions. These discussions and the associated cognitive conflict through which strategic ideas are examined and understood create shared strategic cognition.

Another perspective on structured cognition is based on the concept of schema and is grounded in the research on meanings in organizations and on climate and culture. Schemas are defined as knowledge structures that direct individuals' attention and guide their interpretations and expectations. They enable individuals to understand, interpret, and give meaning to stimuli (Rumelhart, 1980), thereby aiding in sensemaking processes. By affecting attention, encoding, and recall, schemas influence information processing and action. They may contain information related to a specific domain, be interrelated, and represent knowledge at all levels of abstraction (Rumelhart, 1980). Schemas are also implicit, active, and emergent. Essentially, schemas operate as knowledge units that are activated by stimuli existing in the environment. Once activated, the unit sets off a chain reaction that activates related units and inhibits unrelated units. Together, these units form the interpretive cognitive structure that provides meaning to the stimuli that initiated the sensemaking process (Rumelhart, Smolensky, McClelland, & Hinton, 1988). Schemas are powerful interpretive devices and their potential content domains are limitless (e.g., teamwork, team member, the task).

Rentsch and Klimoski (2001) conceptualized team cognition as structured cognition in the form of team member schema similarity (TMSS), which they defined as the degree to which team members have comparable cognitive structures or schemas for organizing team-related information. They emphasized that the cognitive structures may become similar, but they most likely would not achieve sameness or sharedness. The similarity of team members' schemas may take different forms, including schema agreement or congruence (i.e., a match between schemas), schema accuracy with respect to a predefined target (e.g., team members' schemas, task constraints, expert knowledge), or schema complementarity (Rentsch, Delise, & Hutchison, 2006; Rentsch & Woehr, 2004). Rentsch and Klimoski acknowledged the social aspect of the development of schema similarity, theorizing that TMSS develops through experience, interactions, and social construction processes.

In summary, researchers studying team cognition conceptualized as structured cognition tend to (1) focus on the organizational structure of knowledge; (2) not explicitly recognize the degree to which cognitive content is similar; (3) differ in their emphasis on antecedents of team cognition (e.g., mental model perspective emphasizes training, and schema similarity perspective emphasizes social construction); (4) emphasize shared cognitive structures (mental model perspective) or emphasize similarity of cognitive structures (schema similarity perspective); (5) recognize the individual as the source of structured cognition; and (6) expect structured cognition to include multiple content domains, which are usually specified.

Interpretive

Team cognition is also conceptualized as the interpretive convergence, which involves processes including sensemaking, interpretive systems, and collective learning. Sensemaking is the social process in which team members achieve an understanding of a complex situation. Similarly, a team as an interpretive system (Isabella & Waddock, 1994), yields team cognition referred to as cognitive consensus, common frames of reference, or common interpretations. Other perspectives within the interpretive category are collective learning and cognitive convergence processes.

The sensemaking perspective describes the retroactive, interactive process by which group members construct reality by attempting to impose order on, find rationality in, and otherwise make sense of their environment or past experiences (Greenberg, 1995; Weick, 1993). Team members are compelled to engage in sensemaking, particularly during times of change and confusion. This collaborative process yields emergent, shared meaning that is used to interpret the subjective environment (Weick, 1993).

Another form of interpretive convergence generally aims to explain meaning systems. For example, Gioia and Thomas (1996) studied a TMT's interpretative and meaning systems. In doing so, they considered the meaning system to be one of social construction, and they defined the interpretation system as "an intersubjectively negotiated framework of understanding" (p. 374). Of special interest to these researchers was how members of the TMT communicated interpretations of their experiences among themselves. The interpretation system was a shared process in which cognitive similarity was thought to exist and to be extracted.

A similar perspective describes interpretive convergence as the "process by which cognitive structures become more similar over time" through discussion and information sharing (Baba, Gluesing, Ratner, & Wagner, 2004, p. 547). Likewise, collective learning is the process of changing one's interpretation of events through developing a balance of diversity and consensus of viewpoints among group members (Fiol, 1994). Both processes are believed to result in cognitive consensus, which is defined as shared frames of reference or assumptions, or agreement about how issues are conceptualized (Baba et al., 2004; Fiol, 1994; Mohammed & Ringseis, 2001). This perspective defines team cognition in terms of cognitive categories used to interpret one's environment. Cognitive consensus (or dissensus) is also defined by interpretive content (i.e., labels, cognitive categories) and communication frames (breadth and rigidity; Fiol, 1994). This perspective acknowledges some of the complexity that may exist in team cognition. Within this perspective team members may simultaneously experience cognitive agreement and disagreement. For example, team members may share a broad frame but have different interpretations within the frame.

In summary, researchers studying team cognition conceptualized as interpretive convergence tend to (1) focus on the social construction, interaction, and negotiation processes for generating meaning (i.e., the process of convergence); (2) discuss complex formations of team cognition; (3) differ in their emphasis on the extent to which the team is the source of the cognition (i.e., team as interpretive system) or the individual is the source of cognition; (4) place little emphasis on cognitive structure; and (5) consider meaning at a broad and abstract level (i.e., not as a perception, belief, or cognitive structure).

MEASUREMENT OF TEAM COGNITION IN THE EMPIRICAL RESEARCH

The complex conceptualizations of team cognition as perceptions, structured cognition, and interpretive convergence create measurement challenges. Four measurement approaches found in the empirical research are (1) aggregated scale scores, (2) collective consensus, (3) structured assessments, and (4) qualitative methods. The measurement techniques are closely linked to the conceptualization category, but sometimes measurement methods cut across conceptualizations.

Aggregated Scale Scores

The research conceptualizing team cognition as shared perceptions tended to use some form of aggregation to represent team cognition. Usually, team members independently completed surveys regarding the relevant team cognition variable (e.g., perceptions, beliefs, expectations, and attitudes). The individual ratings were aggregated to form the team cognition variable (e.g., Bain et al., 2001; Beersma & De-Dreu; Choi et al., 2003; Ensley & Pearce, 2001). Typically, interrater agreement indices such as intraclass correlations or r_{wg} were calculated to justify aggregating individuals' ratings to the team level (e.g., Anderson & West, 1998; Cannon & Edmondson, 2001; Ensley & Pearce, 2001; Glisson & James, 2002; Hofmann et al., 2003; Kirkman et al., 2001; Levesque et al., 2001; Mason & Griffin, 2003; Naumann & Bennett, 2000, 2002; Xie & Johns, 2000). In addition to acceptable levels of agreement, analysis of variance was used to justify aggregation (e.g., Cannon & Edmondson, 2001; Ensley & Pearce, 2001).

Although much of the research using aggregated mean-level scores as the measure of team cognition was based on conceptualizing team cognition as shared perceptions, sharedness or the degree of similarity among members' cognitions was not utilized as the operationalization of team cognition. Instead, the level of the ratings on which team members agreed was the operationalization of choice because researchers were testing theoretical relationships between the level of the shared perceptions (e.g., how much justice or safety was valued in the team) and other variables (e.g., Naumann & Bennett, 2002; Zohar, 2000; Zohar & Luria, 2005). They were not necessarily interested in relationships between the degree of sharedness or similarity and other variables.

In other studies, questionnaire items were written to extract team members' ratings regarding the level of agreement among team members (e.g., Mason & Griffin, 2003; Xie & Johns, 2000). For example, team members might be asked, "What do you think the level of agreement would be in your team on [X issue]?" These individual-level ratings were then aggregated to the team level if measures of agreement achieved acceptable values (e.g., Mason & Griffin, 2003). Obviously, this approach yields a subjective assessment of perceptual agreement. Other researchers assessed the degree of similarity directly using a variance or interrater agreement index (e.g., r_{wg}, coefficient of variation; standard deviation) to capture the degree to which team members' ratings were in agreement (i.e., were similar) (e.g., Austin, 2003; Colquitt et al., 2002; Isabella & Waddock, 1994; Levesque et al., 2001; Mohammed & Ringseis, 2001).

Aggregated responses to questionnaire items highlight the content of the team cognition based on the perceptual content covered in the items. Regardless of the specific content domain, a critical component of the team cognition was the referent in the items. According to Glisson and James (2002), a salient distinction between shared perceptions (associated with climate) and normative beliefs and shared expectations (associated with culture) is the referent being rated. Shared perceptions about the work environment originate within individuals, whereas shared beliefs and expectations are properties of the group. Therefore, items should reference the individual (e.g., "I feel that ...") or the group (e.g., "Members of this team encourage one another"), respectively. Some researchers conformed to this distinction (e.g., Hofmann et al., 2003; Zohar, 2000) and others did not (e.g., Anderson & West, 1998).

Although aggregated scale scores were associated most closely with the perceptual conceptualization of team cognition, this measurement approach was also utilized to assess team cognition conceptualized as structured cognition (e.g., Ensley & Pearce, 2001; Levesque et al., 2001) and interpretive convergence (e.g., Isabella & Waddock, 1994; Mohammed & Ringseis, 2001).

Collective Consensus

Collective consensus is a measurement technique involving a group responding as a unit to each item on a questionnaire. Gibson (2001) reported that collective consensus ratings of shared efficacy beliefs are highly correlated with aggregated individual scores on the same set of questions. However, she used the collective consensus method in order to enhance the consistency between the conceptual and operational variables in her study. Collective consensus, she believed, enabled an assessment of team cognition that captured the interaction processes within the team. In general, collective consensus was used to assess team cognition conceptualized as shared perceptions (Gibson, 2001, 2003; Kirkman et al., 2001). This method did not afford information regarding the degree to which team members' understandings were in agreement.

Structural Assessments

When researchers conceptualized team cognition as structured cognition, they tended to assess it using structural assessments that captured the structure of the cognition and the degree to which team members' structured cognitions were similar. Structural assessments were not used when team cognition was conceptualized as shared perceptions or interpretive convergence. Typically, researchers used analysis of paired comparison ratings (ratings provided by individual team members) or concept mapping techniques (maps provided by individual team members or the entire team).

For example, Marks and colleagues (2002) measured shared team interaction mental models using team members' relatedness ratings of 10 critical task concepts (e.g., identify enemy, adjust speed, adjust altitude, select target). These relatedness ratings were subjected to Pathfinder, and the resulting C statistic was used as the index of team cognition. Relatedness ratings have also been analyzed using network analysis, which provided an index of convergence that was used to represent team cognition (e.g., Marks et al., 2002; Mathieu, Heffner, Goodwin, Salas, & Cannon-Bowers, 2000). Likewise, Rentsch and Klimoski (2001) assessed team member teamwork schema agreement using paired comparison similarity ratings produced by individual team members and analyzed them using multidimensional scaling analysis. The resulting R^2 statistic was used as the measure of team cognition (team member teamwork schema agreement; Rentsch, 1990; Rentsch & Klimoski, 2001).

Concept mapping techniques have been used to assess shared mental models of team interaction. For example, team members selected concepts from a set provided by the researcher (e.g., shoot pillbox) and placed them in a prespecified hierarchical structure forming a concept map (e.g., Marks et al., 2000, 2002). Aggregated sharedness scores reflected the degree of content and structural overlap existing at the team level (e.g., the percentage of concepts placed identically on the map; Marks et al., 2002). Marks et al. (2000) collected subjective data to assess the accuracy of mental models using doctoral students' ratings of the overlap of the concept maps with task objectives.

In addition, some researchers coded the content of text to extract the structure of team cognition. For example, Carley (1997) used a textual analysis technique to extract the task-related mental models of software engineering teams. By analyzing the content of each individual's answer to open-ended questions regarding the task of developing software, Carley was able to construct cognitive maps of each team member's task mental model and to analyze the degree of overlap among these models. Similarly, Levy (2005) used content analysis to examine letters to shareholders as a means to extract and analyze how a top management team as a whole interprets the environment (i.e., the foci of their attention).

Qualitative Assessments

Team cognition conceptualized as interpretive convergence was assessed using such qualitative data as case studies, observations, interviews, essays, e-mails, and teleconferences. These data were transformed into descriptions of interpretive convergence content and of the processes yielding the convergence.

For example, in a unique case study, Weick (1993) reanalyzed the Mann Gulch disaster as it was presented in an award-winning book. His idiosyncratic analysis focused on what caused the team's interpretive system to unravel and how the team could have increased its resilience. He concluded from his analysis that a combination of pressure and incomprehensible events (e.g., an engulfing fire) can cause team members to abandon their roles and can inhibit their ability to interpret the environment.

Several researchers applied coding schemes to qualitative data. For example, Fiol (1994) and a research assistant coded 1,128 entries of a communication log of more than 2,000 pages. They coded the log content using prespecified dimensions and evaluated the coded data using content analysis and structural analysis. The interpretive convergence conceptualization of team cognition was evaluated by analyzing the means and confidence intervals associated with scores for each coded dimension. Similarly, Gruenfeld and Hollingshead (1993) applied a coding scheme to analyze the integrative complexity of individually produced and group-produced essays on group activities. Researchers evaluated the essays for differentiation (the recognition of multiple perspectives) and integration (the recognition of connections or integration among different perspectives). Although analyzing qualitative data, they established a set of scores for each dimension of integrative complexity and used these scores to compare the individually written essays to the group-written essays. They were able to quantitatively demonstrate that team cognition is a fundamentally collective phenomenon, unique from the collection of individual cognitions.

Another qualitative assessment approach involved integrating qualitative data provided by a combination of sources. For example, Gioia and Thomas (1996) collected data using interviews and questionnaires. They conducted in-depth ethnographic interviews over a 6-month period and applied complex coding schemes (e.g., categorization and theme analysis, and domain analysis) in an effort to triangulate on convergent sensemaking processes and meaning. They used these coding schemes to identify terms, concepts, and themes that were common to the members of the team and used to interpret their environment. These data were then used to develop a questionnaire for their quantitative study of interpretive convergence.

Baba et al. (2004) also integrated qualitative data from multiple sources to assess convergence processes. They constructed a narrative case history based on multiple data gathering techniques that included observing meetings, listening in on teleconferences, conducting individual interviews, and reviewing documents and e-mails. Using these data they recounted the story of a globally distributed team over time. Team cognition was operationalized as the increase in shared understanding, which they inferred based on their analysis of the text and conversational data. They intuitively drew conclusions about the similarity of individuals' interpretations.

Summary of the Measurement of Team Cognition

The measurement of team cognition has proven to be challenging for researchers. Various measurement techniques have been employed for each of the three conceptualizations of team cognition (perceptual, structured, and interpretive). Although there are exceptions, there appears to be some consistency between the conceptualization of team cognition and the measurement of it such that (1) aggregated scale scores and collective consensus were used primarily by researchers conceptualizing team cognition as perceptual, (2) structural assessments were used by researchers conceptualizing team cognition as structured, and (3) researchers conceptualizing team cognition as interpretive relied primarily on qualitative data. A summary of the empirical research is presented in Table 7.1.

FORMS OF SIMILARITY EXAMINED IN THE EMPIRICAL RESEARCH

Implicit in the conceptualizations and measurement of team cognition is the nature of the similarity of meanings among team members, which has been referred to in the literature as sharedness, agreement, salience or strength, similarity, collectiveness, consensus, commonality, and convergence.

Cognitive sharedness, agreement, similarity, salience, and strength are based on comparing each team member's cognition (perceptions, cognitive structures, or interpretations) with other members' cognitions. Researchers who conceptualized team cognition as shared perceptions preferred the term *shared* or *agreement* to denote the overlap or similarity of cognition among team members. The use of agreement indices signals that researchers implicitly acknowledge nonidentical perceptions among team members. However, as mentioned above, the agreed-upon level of the perceptual ratings, rather than the degree of similarity (or sharedness) in the ratings, was used as the measure of team cognition when testing hypotheses. Some researchers, however, operationalized similarity using variance indices, thereby measuring the degree of sharedness, which was referred to as the salience or strength of the shared perceptions (e.g., Colquitt et al., 2002; Xie & Johns, 2000). Within the structured cognition perspective, researchers who studied team member schemas preferred the term *similar* to identify cognitions among team members that were somehow alike, whereas those who studied team mental models preferred the term *shared*. However, both used measurement methods that provided assessments of the degree of likeness (i.e., similarity).

Team cognition in the form of collective consensus is not a comparison of meaning among team members. Rather, team members presented with

TABLE 7.1
Summary of Empirical Research

Conceptualization of Team Cognition	Approach Using This Conceptualization	Measurement of Team Cognition	Form of Similarity
Perceptual	Team climate Team culture Shared beliefs Shared expectations Shared attitudes	Aggregated scores Collective consensus	Agreement Strength Salience Consensus

Structured	Shared mental
	  models
	Shared strategic
	  consensus
	Team member
	  schema similarity
		Aggregated scores
		Structured
		  assessment
			Similarity
			Accuracy

Interpretive	Sensemaking process Interpretive systems Cognitive convergence	Aggregated scores Qualitative data	Overlapping Consensus

a stimulus must negotiate and achieve consensus on their interpretation of the stimulus. Specifically, team members must achieve consensus on the team's responses to a set of questionnaire items. The item responses are interpreted as indicators of meaning. However, it is possible, and quite likely, that although each member may be willing to agree with a response that is acceptable to other team members, the extent to which each team member agrees with the response differs. For example, one member may be willing to go along with the team consensus, but is 30% in agreement with the team's response, whereas another team member may be 90% in agreement with the response. The consensus measures tend not to detect this type of similarity.

Those who conceptualized team cognition as interpretive tended to assume that a significant level of convergence in the form of agreement or likeness existed among team members. Thus, analysis of the degree of similarity among team members is not common in this research. The exception occurred in some work on cognitive consensus (dissensus) where similarity was assessed as a variance index based on individual responses to questionnaire items (e.g., Mohammed & Ringseis, 2001).

DIRECTIONS FOR FUTURE RESEARCH

As teams become increasingly prevalent in organizations, serving as the foundation of organizational structure and as strategic decision-making forces, organizational and team research is experiencing a resurgence of interest in "it." Clearly, team cognition has been examined from many and varied perspectives using a mix of measurement techniques, and we encourage future research on the topic. The varied approaches have obtained promising results. For example, team cognition has been found to be related to many types of outcomes, including helping behavior (Naumann & Bennett, 2000), positive attitudes (Glisson & James, 2002), and trust (Klimoski & Mohammed, 1994) at the individual level, and to microaccidents (Zohar, 2000), team satisfaction (Mason & Griffin, 2003; Mohammed & Ringseis, 2001), team creativity (Pirola-Merlo & Mann, 2004), absenteeism (Colquitt et al., 2002; Xie & Johns, 2000), and team effectiveness (Gibson, 2001; Kirkman et al., 2001; Marks et al., 2000; Naumann & Bennett, 2002; Rentsch & Klimoski, 2001) at the team level. In addition, several variables show strong potential as antecedents of team cognition, including leader behavior, training, and work group characteristics such as team size and cohesion (Greenberg, 1995; Naumann & Bennett, 2000; Rentsch & Klimoski, 2001; Zohar, 2000).

Understanding team cognition is essential to managing behavior using mechanisms such as rewards, training, leadership, and so on. Some research effort must be devoted to assisting teams in acquiring self-managing skills that include the ability to manage the development of similar cognitions among team members. In particular, team cognition must be managed such that team members' interpretations promote functional team processes and effective team outcomes. Although research on team cognition, in general, is progressing, additional research is needed. Below, we offer an integrative framework of cognitive similarity and methodological challenges that we hope will be helpful in guiding future research.

Cognitive Similarity

The three broad conceptualizations of team cognition illustrate the conceptual complexity of the variable under investigation. We offer cognitive similarity as an overarching concept that integrates previous work. We define cognitive similarity as meanings or understandings that are alike among individuals and utilized to make sense of, attribute meaning to, and interpret internal and external events, including affect, behavior, and thoughts of self and others. We deliberately select the term *similar* rather than the term *shared*. *Shared* implies identical. We wish to make the distinction that individuals will likely not develop identical interpretations as is implied by *shared*, but rather, they will develop *similar* interpretations. From this perspective, cognition is assumed to exist exclusively within the individual. An individual's cognitions will be influenced by personal experiences, including direct and indirect interactions with others. Cognitive similarity is a general term that incorporates multiple types that are defined by the intersection of three features: (1) the form of similarity, (2) the form of the cognition, and (3) the cognitive content domain. Types of cognitive similarity in combination produce configurations of cognitive similarity.

Forms of Similarity

In the majority of studies reported above, similarity, agreement, sharedness, and consensus of meaning were regarded as a match existing among team members' meanings. We wish to emphasize that imperfect or non-identical overlap will likely exist. However, similarity may take a variety of forms, including congruence, accuracy, complementary, and others. In order to enhance theoretical development, we suggest investigators clearly articulate the form of similarity they are studying.

One form of similarity that cognition among individuals may take is congruence. Cognitive congruence defines the degree of match in cognition among individuals where there is no target or "correct" value. Cognitive congruence, then, is a generic term that leaves open the cognitive form (e.g., perceptual, structured, interpretive) and the cognitive content domain (e.g., work environment, task work, teamwork).

Another form of cognitive similarity is cognitive accuracy. Rentsch and Hall (1994) highlighted team member schema accuracy as a form of schema similarity, and Marks et al. (2000) had judges rate the accuracy of mental models. In general, accuracy as a form of cognitive similarity is empirically unexplored. We define cognitive accuracy as reflecting the degree of match in cases where a "true score" or target value exists. Other team members' characteristics (or cognitions), task and contextual features, and so on, may serve as targets. Training effectiveness, for example, could be evaluated by examining the degree to which trainees' schemas match the instructor's schema (i.e., the target value) at the conclusion of training (Smith-Jentsch et al., 2005). Likewise, a team member may be the target of cognitive accuracy. For example, team members may form accurate schemas of their teammates' schemas (target) (Rentsch & Zelno, 2003).

Similarity may also take a complementary form. That is, team members' cognitions may be complementary in structure or content, fitting together like puzzle pieces. For example, team members with differing areas of expertise (e.g., marketing, production, research and development) may have complementary understandings of task components from the perspective of their expertise. This form of cognitive similarity may enhance team performance. Cognitive convergence and divergence, integration and differentiation are example forms of cognitive complementarity.

Additional forms of similarity may be derived from the social relations model (Rentsch & Woehr, 2004). The social relations model (SRM) differentiates person perceptions as influences due to the perceiver, influences due to the target, and influences due to the idiosyncratic interaction of the perceiver and the target (Kenny, 1994). The SRM elicits such research questions as "Does Chris know how he is seen by his teammates?" (referred to as meta-accuracy) and "Do Chris and Pat view each other similarly?" (referred to as reciprocity). Applying the SRM to cognitive similarity suggests additional possible forms of similarity. For example, cognitive similarity within a team might be described using team meta-accuracy (i.e., the degree to which all team members are accurate in understanding how their teammates view them). Rentsch and Woehr articulated several possible forms of similarity among team cognitions inspired by the social relations model.

Dimensions associated with each form of similarity include level, variability, stability, and, when examining multiple types of cognitive similarity, profile shape. Typically, similarity assessments will involve a comparison of members to one another. The average of these comparisons is an indicator of the level of cognitive similarity among the individuals. The variability of the comparisons reveals additional information about the similarity. As seen earlier, level and variability are used regularly in the empirical research. Similarity may also be examined in terms of its stability or reliability. When multiple types of cognitive similarity are assessed, profile shape may also be evaluated. In addition, all forms of similarity may be related to various cognitive forms (e.g., perceptual, structured, interpretive) and to various cognitive content domains (e.g., work environment, task, equipment, rewards). Regarding form of similarity, the challenge for researchers is to clearly articulate and measure the dimension(s) of the form(s) of similarity under investigation.

Forms of Cognition

Just as several forms of similarity exist, multiple forms of cognition also exist. The research literature reviewed above revealed conceptualizations and measurements of cognition that addressed different aspects of meaning.

Perceptual cognition addresses meaning reflected in descriptions or expectations constructed on the basis of patterns identified from accumulated observations developed to alleviate uncertainty and to facilitate prediction. This type of meaning does not provide deep understanding of causal, relational, or explanatory links. For example, new team members will begin making sense of the team by observing events and constructing descriptive meanings such as "The team expects members to make mistakes" or "Team members critique one another's ideas." Therefore, perceptual cognition is more closely associated with cognitive content than with cognitive structure. Perceptions provide content nodes, which are essential for developing structured cognition. The forms of cognition in the perceptual perspective include beliefs, attitudes, values, perceptions, prototypes, and expectations.

Structured cognition provides information in addition to perceptual cognition. Structured cognition, such as schemas, is the organization of knowledge and incorporates causal, relational, and explanatory connections among nodes of content. Structured cognition has defining underlying characteristics, including integration, differentiation, centrality, density, content and directionality of linkages, and so on. It reflects expertise level with respect to a given domain. For example, a very dense structure would consist of many connections among all or most content nodes, reflecting a high degree of integration among concepts in the content domain. Such features have not been the subject of much investigation in the team cognition research, but present avenues for future work on cognitive similarity. How team members interpret such events will depend on how they cognitively organize relevant information. Cognitive structure is the basis of interpretive meaning. Forms of cognition in the interpretive conceptualization include schema and mental model.

Interpretive cognition involves value-laden explanations or frames for ascribing meaning to events. Interpretive meaning is based on an individual's past experiences, physiological and biological makeup, the culture in which he or she is embedded, and his or her interactions with others (e.g., Lord & Maher, 1991). This socially constructed reality will be reflected in similar interpretative structures, or schemas, among team members. These interpretations will affect the actions performed by members. Perceptual cognition provides the cognitive content that becomes structured, and the linkages among the cognitive structures produce interpretive cognition. Forms of cognition in the interpretive conceptualization include frames, underlying dimensions, and interpretive categories.

Other forms of cognition that are relevant to cognitive similarity may exist. For example, formations of knowledge from the expertise and cognitive science literature (e.g., declarative, procedural) present additional forms of cognition. Regarding form of cognition, the challenge for researchers is to clearly articulate and measure the characteristics and form(s) of cognition under investigation.

Cognitive Content Domains

Individuals may develop cognitive content with respect to any domain. Content domains relevant to teams include self, team members, people external to the team, national culture, typical events, time and space, team leadership, the task, and so on. Researchers should elaborate on and specify the domain of relevant cognitive content under investigation.

Dimensions underlying content domains include degree of abstraction, level of articulation (depth), breadth, functionality, and stability. For example, Cannon-Bowers et al. (1993) pointed out that team members may develop multiple mental models (including equipment, task, team interaction, and team models) and suggested that there may be variance in the stability of the content of different models (e.g., equipment models are more stable than team interaction models). Also, the degree to which the cognitive content is functional should be addressed (e.g., Mathieu et al., 2005; Rentsch & Hall, 1994). Regarding cognitive content domains, the challenge for researchers is to clearly articulate and assess the underlying dimension(s) and content domain(s) of the cognition studied.

Cognitive Similarity Types

The notion of cognitive similarity will contribute to theoretical development to the extent that the features of cognitive similarity (i.e., similarity form, cognitive form, and cognitive content domain) are specified (see Table 7.2). Doing so creates *types of cognitive similarity*. Types of cognitive similarity are limitless due primarily to the domain dimension. However, any given type of cognitive similarity will likely be associated with specific outcomes and antecedents. Thus, clearly defining the type of cognitive similarity should increase understanding of specific nomological networks. This type of specificity will have basic and applied implications. Several sample types are presented in Table 7.3. For example, if team members have accurate (form of similarity) beliefs (form of cognition) about one another's competence (content domain), then they should be better able to assign tasks appropriately to team members. Likewise, if team members hold congruent (form of similarity) schemas (form of cognition) about teamwork (content domain), then they should be better able to more easily and efficiently work together, avoiding conflict and misinterpretation of team-related behavior.

TABLE 7.2
Features of Cognitive Similarity That May Be Combined to Form Types of Cognitive Similarity

Form of Similarity	Form of Cognition	Sample Content Domain	Possible Units of Analysis
Cognitive congruence	Schema	Teamwork	Dyads
Cognitive accuracy	Mental model	Task	Groups
Cognitive complementary	Beliefs	Equipment	Teams
Form based on the SRM	Climate perceptions Expectations Dimensions Frames	Team members Innovation Justice Creativity	Organizational units Organizations Communities Nations

TABLE 7.3
Sample Types of Cognitive Similarity

Conceptual Category of Team Cognition	Content Domain	Form of Cognition	Form of Similarity
Structured	Team members' cognition	Schema	Accuracy
Structured	Task	Schema	Complementary
Structured	Teamwork	Mental model	Congruence
Perceptual	Competence	Beliefs	Accuracy
Perceptual	Leadership	Expectations	Complementary
Perceptual	Innovation	Climate perceptions	Congruence
Interpretive	Customers	Dimensions	Accuracy
Interpretive	Product development	Frames	Complementary
Interpretive	Strategic vision	Frames	Congruence

Cognitive Similarity Configurations

Although specifying similarity forms, cognitive forms, and cognitive content domains in combination to define cognitive similarity types will likely reveal relationships in nomological networks, the greatest theoretical advances are expected to be produced by *cognitive similarity configurations*. Combinations of cognitive similarity types form cognitive similarity configurations.

For example, a cognitive similarity configuration consisting of (1) accurate schemas of team members, (2) complementary interpretations of the task, and (3) congruent perceptions of the reward system (as motivating) may be highly related to team effectiveness. The complementary interpretations of the task may enable the team to identify all task constraints, the accurate schemas of team members enable the team to extract and utilize each member's expertise that is required to meet the task constraints, and the congruent perceptions of the reward system provide members with the motivation to seek and meet the task constraints.

Future research should explore the usefulness of cognitive similarity configurations. Several features of such configurations to consider include identifying (1) the optimal levels of similarity forms, (2) the appropriate balance of cognitive forms, (3) the best configuration of integration and differentiation with respect to particular content domains, and (4) the overall best set of cognitive forms given any particular outcome or antecedent of interest (i.e., identifying "shapes" of cognitive similarity configurations).

Measurement Challenges

Measurement presents a continual challenge for psychology, and team cognition researchers have been inventive and daring in their measurement techniques. Four measurement challenges facing researchers are to (1) maintain consistency between conceptual and operational variables, (2) compare and evaluate measurement techniques, (3) incorporate advanced statistical methods, and (4) attempt to triangulate on team cognition.

Researchers appear to be striving to meet the first challenge and, for the most part, have maintained consistency between conceptual and operational variables. For example, those conceptualizing structured cognition tended to use structured assessments. However, in a few cases, although the conceptual variable was structured cognition, the measurement was the mean of the aggregated scores. Researchers must be cautioned that aggregated survey scores of items containing descriptive content rated on agree–disagree scales usually do not provide information regarding cognitive structure. However, they may provide information regarding cognitive content. We challenge researchers to be aware of what their measures are actually assessing with respect to team cognition.

The second challenge follows from the first. Measurement techniques require evaluation. Perhaps this challenge is being partially addressed among researchers conceptualizing team cognition as structured cognition. The complexity associated with measuring structured cognition has prompted two reviews of measurement techniques (Langan-Fox, Code, & Langfield, 2000; Mohammed, Klimoski, & Rentsch, 2000). Langan-Fox et al. (2000) reviewed knowledge elicitation and representation techniques in terms of their advantages and disadvantages, whereas Mohammed et al. (2000) focused on methods that provide a measure of the degree of similarity between cognitive structures (i.e., multidimensional scaling, Pathfinder, and text- and interaction-based cause maps). These reviews provide some comparative evidence for the measurement techniques. However, additional empirical comparative examination of the alternative methods and the situational contingencies (e.g., task type, team type) that affect the appropriateness or effectiveness of each measurement method is needed. Comparison and evaluation of measurement techniques used to assess interpretive convergence is also needed.

The third challenge is to incorporate advanced research methods in the study of team cognition. For example, researchers have used hierarchical linear modeling and other cross-level analytic techniques to investigate the effects of team cognition on individual- and team-level outcomes. Some climate researchers have already begun this line of investigation (e.g., Glisson & James, 2002; Hofmann et al., 2003; Naumann & Bennett, 2000, 2002), allowing for an examination of the effects of climate (shared perceptions) on individual outcomes (e.g., attitudes, turnover, citizenship, and helping behavior) and team outcomes (e.g., team performance).

The fourth challenge is for researchers to attempt to triangulate on team cognition using multiple methods. The variable, as should be evident from the above review, is complex. In order to fully understand the multifaceted aspects of team cognition, researchers must attempt to triangulate on it. In doing so, one must keep in mind the first challenge and be sure to use operationalizations that are congruent with well-developed conceptualizations.

CONCLUSION

In conclusion, the study of team cognition is an intriguing and challenging venture, which researchers have approached using a variety of conceptual and measurement approaches. We propose the cognitive similarity configuration approach for future research on cognitive similarity in teams (i.e., team cognition) and in organizations. We propose that the various configurations of cognitive similarity will interact to explain many team (and organizational) processes and outcomes.

REFERENCES

Anderson, N. R., & West, M. A. (1998). Measuring climate for work group innovation: Development and validation of the team climate inventory. *Journal of Organizational Behavior, 19,* 235–258.

Austin, J. R. (2003). Transactive memory in organizational groups: The effects of content, consensus, specialization, and accuracy on group performance. *Journal of Applied Psychology, 88,* 866–878.

Baba, M. L., Gluesing, J., Ratner, H., & Wagner, K. H. (2004). The contexts of knowing: Natural history of a globally distributed team. *Journal of Organizational Behavior, 25,* 547–587.

Bain, P. G., Mann, L., & Pirola-Merlo, A. (2001). The innovation imperative: The relationships between team climate, innovation, and performance in R&D teams. *Small Group Research, 32,* 55–73.

Beersma, B., & De-Dreu, C. K. W. (2002). Integrative and distributive negotiation in small groups: Effects of task structure, decision rule, and social motive. *Organizational Behavior and Human Decision Processes, 87,* 227–252.

Berger, P. L., & Luckmann, T. (1966). *The social construction of reality.* New York: Doubleday.

Cannon, M. D., & Edmondson, A. C. (2001). Confronting failure: Antecedents and consequences of shared beliefs about failure in organizational work groups. *Journal of Organizational Behavior, 22,* 161–177.

Cannon-Bowers, J. A., Salas, E., & Converse, S. A. (1993). Shared mental models in expert team decision making. In N. J. Castellan, Jr. (Ed.), *Individual and group decision making: Current issues* (pp. 221–246). Hillsdale, NJ: Erlbaum.

Carley, K. M. (1997). Extracting team mental models through textual analysis. *Journal of Organizational Behavior, 18,* 533–558.

Choi, J. N., Price, R. H., & Vinokur, A. D. (2003). Self-efficacy changes in groups: Effects of diversity, leadership, and group climate. *Journal of Organizational Behavior, 24*, 357–372.

Colquitt, J. A., Noe, R. A., & Jackson, C. L. (2002). Justice in teams: Antecedents and consequences of procedural justice climate. *Personnel Psychology, 55*, 83–109.

Daft, R., & Weick, K. E., (1984). Toward a model of organizations as interpretation systems. *Academy of Management Review, 9*, 284–295.

Earley, P. C., & Mosakowski, E. (2000). Creating hybrid team cultures: An empirical test of transnational team functioning. *Academy of Management Journal, 43*, 26–49.

Ensley, M. D., & Pearce, C. L. (2001). Shared cognition in top management teams: Implications for new venture performance. *Journal of Organizational Behavior, 22*, 145–160.

Fiol, C. M. (1994). Consensus, diversity, and learning in organizations. *Organization Science, 5*, 403–420.

Gibson, C. B. (2001). Me and us: Differential relationships among goal-setting training, efficacy, and effectiveness at the individual and team level. *Journal of Organizational Behavior, 22*, 789–808.

Gibson, C. B. (2003). The efficacy advantage: Factors related to the formation of group efficacy, *Journal of Applied Social Psychology, 33*, 2153–2186.

Gioia, D. A., & Thomas, J. B. (1996). Institutional identity, image, and issue interpretation: Sensemaking during strategic change in academia. *Administrative Science Quarterly, 41*, 370–403.

Glisson, C., & James, L. R. (2002). The cross-level effects of culture and climate in human service teams. *Journal of Organizational Behavior, 23*, 767–794.

Greenberg, D. N. (1995). Blue versus gray: A metaphor constraining sensemaking around a restructuring. *Group and Organization Management, 20*, 183–209.

Gruenfeld, D. H., & Hollingshead, A. B. (1993). Sociocognition in work groups: The evolution of group integrative complexity and its relation to task performance. *Small Group Research, 24*, 383–405.

Hofmann, D. H., Morgeson, F. P., & Gerras, S. J. (2003). Climate as a moderator of the relationship between LMX and content specific citizenship: Safety climate as an exemplar. *Journal of Applied Psychology, 88*, 170–178.

Hollingshead, A. B. (1998). Retrieval processes in transactive memory systems. *Journal of Personality and Social Psychology, 74*, 659–671.

Isabella, L. A., & Waddock, S. A. (1994). Top management team certainty: Environmental assessments, teamwork, and performance implications. *Journal of Management, 20*, 835–858.

James, L. R., Hater, J. J., Gent, M. J., & Bruni, J. R. (1978). Psychological climate: Implications from cognitive social learning theory and interactional psychology. *Personnel Psychology, 31*, 783–813.

Kenny, D. A. (1994). Using the social relations model to understand relationships. In R. Erber & R. Gilmour (Eds.), *Theoretical frameworks for personal relationships* (pp. 111–127). Hillsdale, NJ: Lawrence Erlbaum.

Kirkman, B. L., Tesluk, P. E., & Rosen, B. (2001). Assessing the incremental validity of team consensus ratings over aggregation of individual-level data in predicting team effectiveness. *Personnel Psychology, 54*, 645–667.

Klimoski, R., & Mohammed, S. (1994). Team mental model: Construct or metaphor? *Journal of Management, 20*, 403–437.

Langan-Fox, J., Code, S., & Langfield, K. (2000). Team mental models: Techniques, methods, and analytic approaches. *Human Factors, 42,* 242–271.

Levesque, L. L., Wilson, J. M., & Wholey, D. R. (2001). Cognitive divergence and shared mental models in software development project teams. *Journal of Organizational Behavior, 22,* 135–144.

Levine, J. M., & Moreland, R. L. (1991). Culture and socialization in work groups. In L. B. Resnick, J. M. Levine, & S. D. Teasley (Eds.), *Perspectives on socially shared cognition* (pp. 257–279). Washington, DC: American Psychological Association.

Levy, O. (2005). The influence of top management team attention patterns on global strategic posture of firms. *Journal of Organizational Behavior, 26,* 797–819.

Lord, R. G., & Maher, K. J. (1991). Cognitive theory in industrial and organizational psychology. In M. D. Dunnette & L. M. Hough (Eds.), *Handbook of industrial and organizational psychology* (Vol. 2, pp. 1–62). Palo Alto, CA: Consulting Psychologists Press.

Louis, M. R. (1980). Surprise and sense making: What newcomers experience in unfamiliar organizational settings. *Administrative Science Quarterly, 25,* 226–251.

Marks, M. A., Sabella, M. J., Burke, C. S., & Zaccaro, S. J. (2002). The impact of cross-training on team effectiveness. *Journal of Applied Psychology, 87,* 3–13.

Marks, M. A., Zaccaro, S. J., & Mathieu, J. E. (2000). Performance implications of leader briefings and team-interaction training for team adaptation to novel environments. *Journal of Applied Psychology, 85,* 971–986.

Mason, C. M., & Griffin, M. A. (2003). Identifying group task satisfaction at work. *Small Group Research, 34,* 413–442.

Mathieu, J. E., Heffner, T. S., Goodwin, G. F., Cannon-Bowers, J. A., & Salas, E. (2005). Scaling the quality of teammates' mental models: Equifinality and normative comparisons. *Journal of Organizational Behavior, 26,* 37–56.

Mathieu, J. E., Heffner, T. S., Goodwin, G. F., Salas, E., & Cannon-Bowers, J. A. (2000). The influence of shared mental models on team process and performance. *Journal of Applied Psychology, 85,* 273–283.

Mohammed, S., Klimoski, R., & Rentsch, J. R. (2000). The measurement of team mental models: We have no shared schema. *Organizational Research Methods, 3,* 123–165.

Mohammed, S., & Ringseis, E. (2001). Cognitive diversity and consensus in group decision making: The role of inputs, processes, and outcomes. *Organizational Behavior and Human Decision Processes, 85,* 310–335.

Moreland, R. L., & Levine, J. M. (1989). Newcomers and oldtimers in small groups. In P. B. Paulus (Ed.), *Psychology of group influence* (2nd ed., pp. 143–186). Hillsdale, NJ: Lawrence Erlbaum.

Naumann, S. E., & Bennett, N. (2000). A case for procedural justice climate: Development and test of a multilevel model. *Academy of Management Journal, 43,* 881–889.

Naumann, S. E., & Bennett, N. (2002). The effects of procedural justice climate on work group performance. *Small Group Research, 33,* 361–377.

Pirola-Merlo, A., & Mann, L. (2004). The relationship between individual creativity and team creativity: Aggregating across people and across time. *Journal of Organizational Behavior, 25,* 235–257.

Rentsch, J. R. (1990). Climate and culture: Interaction and qualitative differences in organizational meanings. *Journal of Applied Psychology, 75,* 668–681.

Rentsch, J. R., Delise, L., & Hutchison, S. (in press). Cognitive similarity configurations in teams: In search of the Team MindMeld™. In E. Salas, G. F. Goodwin, & C. S. Burke (Eds.), *Team effectiveness in complex organizations and systems: Cross-disciplinary perspectives and approaches.* San Francisco, CA: Jossey-Bass.

Rentsch, J. R., & Hall, R. J. (1994). Members of great teams think alike: A model of team effectiveness and schema similarity among team members. In M. M. Beyerlein, D. A. Johnson, & S. T. Beyerlein (Eds.), *Advances in interdisciplinary studies of work teams: Theories of self-managing work teams* (Vol. 1, pp. 223–261). Greenwich, CT: JAI Press.

Rentsch, J. R., & Klimoski, R. J. (2001). Why do "great minds" think alike? Antecedents of team member schema agreement. *Journal of Organizational Behavior, 22,* 107–120.

Rentsch, J. R., & Woehr, D. J. (2004). Quantifying congruence in cognition: Social relations modeling and team member schema similarity. In E. Salas & S. M. Fiore (Eds.), *Team cognition: Understanding the factors that drive process and performance* (pp. 11–31). Washington, DC: American Psychological Association.

Rentsch, J. R., & Zelno, J. A. (2003). The role of cognition in managing conflict to maximize team effectiveness. In M. A. West, D. Tjosvold, & K. G. Smith (Eds.), *International handbook of organizational teamwork and cooperative working* (pp. 131–150). New York: John Wiley & Sons.

Rouse, W. B., & Morris, N. M. (1986). On looking into the black box: Prospects and limits in the search for mental models. *Psychological Bulletin, 100,* 349–363.

Rumelhart, D. E. (1980). On evaluating story grammars. *Cognitive Science, 4,* 313–316.

Rumelhart, D. E., Smolensky, P., McClelland, J. L., & Hinton, G. E. (1988). Schemata and sequential thought processes in PDP models. In A. M. Collins & E. E. Smith (Eds.), *Readings in cognitive science: A perspective from psychology and artificial intelligence* (pp. 224–249). San Mateo, CA: Morgan Kaufmann.

Schneider, B. (1975). Organizational climates: An essay. *Personnel Psychology, 28,* 447–479.

Schneider, B. (1987). The people make the place. *Personnel Psychology, 40,* 437–453.

Schneider, B. (1990). The climate for service: An application of the climate construct. In B. Schneider (Ed.), *Organizational climate and culture* (pp. 383–412). San Francisco: Jossey-Bass.

Schneider, B., & Reichers, A. E. (1983). On the etiology of climates. *Personnel Psychology, 36,* 19–39.

Smith-Jentsch, K. A., Mathieu, J. E., & Kraiger, K. (2005). Investigating linear and interactive effects of shared mental models on safety and efficiency in a field setting. *Journal of Applied Psychology, 90,* 523–535.

Walsh, J. P., Henderson, C. M., & Deighton, J. (1988). Negotiated belief structures and decision performance: An empirical investigation. *Organizational Behavior and Human Decision Processes, 42,* 194–216.

Weick, K. E. (1993). The collapse of sensemaking in organizations: The Mann Gulch disaster. *Administrative Science Quarterly, 38,* 628–652.

Xie, J. L., & Johns, G. (2000). Interactive effects of absence culture salience and group cohesiveness: A multi-level and cross-level analysis of work absenteeism in the Chinese context. *Journal of Occupational and Organizational Psychology, 73,* 31–52.

Zohar, D. (2000). A group-level model of safety climate: Testing the effect of group climate on microaccidents in manufacturing jobs. *Journal of Applied Psychology, 85,* 587–596.

Zohar, D., & Luria, G. (2005). A multi-level model of safety climate: Cross-level relationships between organization and group-level climates. *Journal of Applied Psychology, 90,* 661–628.

8

Linking Various Perspectives on Service

DAVID E. BOWEN
Thunderbird School of Global Management

It has been over 25 years since Ben Schneider and colleagues (1980) published the *Administrative Science Quarterly* (*ASQ*) article "Employee and Customer Perceptions of Service in Banks," which stated:

> Research on the daily customers of retail service organizations is essentially missing in the literature (Schneider, 1973), and little published information exists about the ways in which organizational functioning may be reflected in consumer behavior. The present study details a strategy for evaluating the effectiveness of retail service organizations in relation to the customers of the organization.... Specifically, the present research concerns branch customer perceptions of service at branch banks and the relationship of the customer perceptions to employee views of the practices and procedures that characterize branch service. (pp. 252–253)

Since 1980, Schneider and his colleagues have pursued a program of research that links the views of employees and customers to reveal that employee experiences of the service climate of the organization at which they work predicts various customer outcomes such as customer satisfaction. This linkage research, also conducted by others (e.g., Heskett, Sasser, & Schlesinger, 1997; Pugh, Dietz, Wiley, & Brooks, 2002), has been part of a broader effort to specify how *services make organizations a different type of place from goods-producing organizations*. This effort has had a multidisciplinary perspective, with contributions from marketing, operations management (OM), and organizational behavior/human resources management (OB/HRM) in particular.

As a festschriftian overview, this chapter links, in a broad sense of the word, various perspectives on service organizations—across multiple stakeholders and several decades. By *multiple stakeholders*, reference is to both the actual parties to service encounters (employees and customers) and leadership's role in shaping those encounters, and in terms of the academic disciplines that have undertaken defining the nature of those encounters and specifying the dimensions of their effectiveness. By *decades*, reference is to the evolution of services thought from the 1970s to the present, during which the focus has evolved from differentiating between services and goods, differentiating within services, addressing how goods-producing firms shift to being services based, to proposing new paradigms that, in a sense, integrate goods and services within a reframed perspective of the meaning of service in which *all economic exchanges are service* (Vargo & Lusch, 2004). We will touch on this emerging new service paradigm at chapter's end.

Of the disciplinary stakeholders (marketing, OM, and OB/HRM), the primary focus will be OB/HRM, although services as a subject have attracted far fewer contributors from that discipline than is true for marketing, certainly, and OM, arguably. Despite the passing of 25 years, the study of service in the OB/HRM discipline has drawn only a handful of contributors, with Schneider certainly being the most frequent. Indeed, a recent special issue of the *Academy of Management Executive* was introduced with an article titled "Suppose We Took Service Seriously" (Bowen & Hallowell, 2002), and more recently, the same journal had a contribution from Schneider (2004) in the "Research Briefs" section titled "Welcome to the World of Services Management."

Thus, this chapter will be more descriptive than analytical and critical, in consideration of the many likely to be unfamiliar with the academic field of services management, and will move across both stakeholders and time. The goals are to provide a feel for services, in theory and practice, and also to highlight some of Ben Schneider's contributions. The focus on service will be primarily business to consumer/client (B2C), with contact between the customer and the employee as service provider.

SERVICES *ARE* DIFFERENT: "THAT'S INTERESTING"

All "interesting" theories deny some part of the taken for granted worlds of their audiences, at both a theoretical and practical level. They take the form of "what seems to be X is in reality non-X" or "what is accepted as X is actually non-X." Furthermore, to be interesting, it must refute some ongoing practical activity; otherwise, the response will be "So what?" or "Who cares?" (Davis, 1971).

Reading now that services and the organizations that deliver them are significantly different from goods and the organizations that produce them sounds more obvious (affirms assumptions) than interesting (challenges some assumptions). However, in the 1970s, the scholarly and applied literature had tended to ignore these distinctions, implicitly or even explicitly accepting theories of marketing and organizational behavior that emerged from studies of goods organizations as essentially comprising general principles equally applicable to both goods and services.

This began to change in the 1970s with contributions from both marketing and OB. In marketing, there was the article many view as the breakthrough piece on "services marketing," titled "Breaking Free From Product Marketing." Shostack (1977), an executive with Banker's Trust, emphasized that there were meaningful differences between marketing tangible goods and intangible services—what is accepted as effective practice for marketing X (all output) may in reality have a non-X component (services). Also in marketing, Kotler (1973) wrote of "atmospherics as marketing tool." In OB, Schneider was writing not on service atmospherics per se, but had published "The Perception of Organizational Climate: The Customer's View" (1973) and "The Service Organization: The Climate is Crucial" (1980), as well as the 1980 *ASQ* article cited in the opening.

So what? As Davis (1971) would challenge, what are the meaningful implications of these differences? One was that both disciplines were underscoring the importance of creating an *intangible experience* in services, different from goods. Two, both disciplines were focusing on how *customers*, often in close proximity to employees, evaluated the service they received and interacted with providers and overall organizational context in service consumption and assessment. These were two significant implications for both theory and practice.

The focus on the customer was obviously a long-standing tenet of the marketing discipline but was fairly new to the management literature. This absence of the customer had been earlier noted in the best-seller *In Search of Excellence*, which noted that management theory does not help explain the role of the customer in the prototypical excellent company (Peters & Waterman, 1982). Even earlier, Brenda Danet (1981) had noted in Nystrom and Starbuck's *Handbook of Organizational Design* that organization theorists have viewed organizations from the top looking down (management's perspective) and the inside looking around (employees' perspective), but rarely from the outside looking in (which would include the clients'/customers' perspective).

In sum, these earlier contributions, starting in the 1970s, were interesting in denying the taken for granted worlds that theories of marketing and organization developed from the study of goods, and manufacturing organizations were fully generalizable to services and the organizations that provide them. Two overarching differences between goods and services noted were the relatively greater intangibility of the experience and customer contact during the provision of that experience. These differences were likely a part of Davis's (1983) conclusion that using industrial models to manage service-based organizations makes no more sense than using farm models to run factories. Appropriately, then, the disciplines of marketing, OM, and OB/HRM began to answer the "so what" question of the unique nature of services more fully.

CHARACTERISTICS OF SERVICES AND THEIR ORGANIZATIONAL IMPLICATIONS: EARLY PERSPECTIVES FROM MARKETING, OM, AND OB/HRM

In the late 1970s and through the 1980s, the academic disciplines' views of service organizations focused considerably on further specifying the unique characteristics of services that differentiated them from goods. In turn, each discipline developed how these service characteristics required examining, and sometimes revising, how the discipline dealt with theoretical constructs and mangement practices in its respective areas.

Marketing

This examination was particularly pronounced in marketing and took the form of what has been labeled the IHIP view of services (see Lovelock & Gummesson, 2004, for a more complete description and critique). Starting with services broadly defined as acts, deeds, performances, or efforts, IHIP referred to the following specific characteristics of services: *intangibility, heterogeneity* or nonstandardization, *inseparability* of production and consumption or the simultaneity of those two activities, and *perishability* or inability to inventory services.

In turn, scholars in marketing then developed how these characteristics of services required different marketing strategies and approaches than was true for goods (e.g., Zeithaml, Parasuraman, & Berry, 1985). A central example of this explication is how intangibility invited a user-based approach to the assessment of service quality, as opposed to a technical approach. The former measures quality from the perspective of the user/ customer; the latter bases quality assessment on conformance to objective and readily measurable standards set for the attributes of output (for a more complete discussion, see Schneider & White, 2004). Additionally, a measurement tool, driven by the user-based approach, was introduced, SERVQUAL (Parasuraman, Zeithaml, & Berry, 1985, 1988), which conceptualized service quality along five dimensions (reliability, assurance, tangibles, empathy, and responsiveness) and defined and measured service quality as the gap between what customers expected to receive and their perceptions of what they actually did receive. The five dimensions were essentially a further elaboration of Gronroos's (1990) distinction between technical quality (what was delivered) and functional quality (how it was delivered). In both conceptualizations, an emphasis is placed on the creation of a service experience in the eyes of the customer.

Obviously, many other implications have been developed for services marketing (for a more complete specification, see, e.g., Zeithaml,

Bitner, & Gremler, 2006; Lovelock & Wirtz, 2003). In this festschrift spirit, it is worth noting that Schneider (2004) highlighted the following contributions from marketing: service recovery (what firms do to set things right when customers experience a service failure); the impact and design of physical spaces, which have been labeled "servicescapes" (Bitner, 1992); and understanding the long-term relationship between consumer and firm in what has become known as customer relationship management (CRM). Also, we should mention the work on the financial returns on quality, and the customer equity approach (Rust, Zeithaml, & Lemon, 2000).

Operations Management (OM)

A primary early "so what" focus in the operations management literature has been, "Where does the customer fit in a service operation?" (Chase, 1978; Chase & Tansik, 1983). The debate, both theoretical and applied, has been on the advantages and disadvantages of customer contact, not only their physical proximity as a consumer, but also their physical presence as they help to coproduce the services they receive. With customer contact, there is the apparent trade-off between marketing effectiveness and operations efficiency. Customer contact enhances opportunities to leverage marketing opportunities, but, on the other hand, customer contact can induce additional input uncertainty and variance into the operations of the core technology.

Interestingly, the potential resolution, or relaxation, of this trade-off that can result in customer contact's advantages with fewer disadvantages is to manage how customers perform their coproduction roles. That is, if the firm can create "high-performance customers," then their presence contributes to organizational effectiveness. Managing customers in this way can be guided by the same individual performance frameworks used with employees, as specified in the OB/HRM literature to which we turn next.

Before leaving the topic of OM, however, it should be noted that, as was true with marketing, there are many other implications of service characteristics for OM theory and research (see, e.g., Chase, Aquilano, & Jacobs, 1998; Johnston & Clark, 2005). Also, Schneider (2004) offered the following highlighted OM contributions: the importance of demand and capacity trade-offs versus revenue generation; the consequences (e.g., customer satisfaction, revenues) of waiting/queuing; and the relationship between various service operations characteristics, such as maintenance schedules, spatial configurations, and customer outcomes and revenues.

This brief overview of early work in marketing and OM was to present, with breadth more than depth, some of the uniqueness of services—to help provide context for the somewhat deeper review of the organizational behavior and human resources management perspective that now follows and is the primary focus for the rest of the chapter.

ORGANIZATIONAL BEHAVIOR/HUMAN RESOURCES MANAGEMENT (OB/HRM): CLIMATE FOR SERVICE, LINKAGE RESEARCH, AND UNIQUE HUMAN RESOURCES

The related fields of OB and HRM also addressed the issue of the organizational implications of the unique characteristics of service. As one example, Bowen and Schneider (1988) explained how three unique service attributes (intangibility, simultaneous production and consumption, customer participation) posed distinct organizing contingencies that, in turn, should influence organizing principles for management practice. For example, intangibility is associated with an organizing contingency of limited objective reference points for assessing value, which in turn indicates an organizing principle to enhance the climate for service, the contextual cues arising from organizational practices and service delivery processes, which is visible to both employees and customers.

As to these three service attributes, or those of the IHIP model, there are emerging challenges to the validity of such specifications. Again, these will be mentioned at chapter's end. However, Schneider's (2004) assertion that these services versus goods distinctions are issues of degree, not kind, is true. Prototypic services do possess relatively more intangibility than prototypic goods, and the provision of a service does tend to have more customer physical proximity and coproduction than the manufacture of the prototypic good.

Climate for Service

An important conceptual origin for OB/HRM perspectives on service was Schneider's (1975) article "Organizational Climate: An Essay," which made a strong case for the study of climate *for* some specific organizational referent, for example, safety or innovation. The point was for climate research to move from global, generic treatments of climate to a climate with a specific focus, even a climate associated with a strategic emphasis or initiative.

Climate for service has been presented in a number of Schneider's studies. Here is a recent definition:

> The shared employee perceptions of the policies, practices, and procedures that get rewarded, supported, and expected with regard to customer service and customer service quality. Basically, a climate for service represents the degree to which the internal functioning of an organization is experienced as one focused on service quality. (Schneider & White, 2004, p. 100)

A typical approach to the assessment of employees' perceptions of climate for service is to start by conducting focus groups with employees, asking them to respond to general, open-ended questions about their organization in order to identify the kinds of experiences they have had that indicated to them whether service was important in that setting. These responses are then content analyzed to yield dimensions of the climate for service. Then survey items are built into an employee survey (e.g., Schneider & Bowen, 1985; Schneider, Parkington, & Buxton 1980). Climate for service and its dimensions are conceptualized and measured at the unit level, for example, the branch of a bank. An example of service climate dimensions is the following: branch management (e.g., setting service goals), customer attraction/retention (e.g., active attempts to retain customers), systems support (e.g., employees felt that other personnel and activities such as marketing supported their efforts to provide service), and logistics support (e.g., equipment and supplies were sufficient and reliable enough to support service delivery efforts). Again, this is one example of service climate, but one that identifies dimensions likely to be relevant in many service settings. Nevertheless, whereas the SERVQUAL measure in marketing has tended to dominate as the measure of service climate, there is not one measure of service climate (Schneider & White, 2004).

Linkage Research: Climate for Service "Shows" to Both Employees and Customers

The early service climate studies (Schneider & Bowen, 1985; Schneider et al., 1980) also collected data from customers to assess whether employees' perceptions of service climate and service quality would be linked or correlated with customers' perceptions of the service they received, both on various aspects of the service and on service quality overall. In both studies, results included a strong, significant correlation between employee and customer assessments of overall service quality, as well as various significant correlations between employee perceptions of service climate dimensions and customers' perceptions of aspects of service delivery.

Conclusions included that the climate for service shows, so to speak, both to employees and customers. Furthermore, this effect, and the strength of resulting shared assessments and perceptions, reflected the physical and psychological closeness that exists between employees and customers in many service encounters.

Linkage research has made numerous contributions to a multiple-perspective understanding of service organizations: First, it has avoided the tendency in management thought and practice to separate internal climate issues from customer experiences. More broadly, it has demonstrated that the design of the internal organization, and the way that employees experience it, has important consequences for customer experiences. Second, it has externally validated, via shared customer reports, employees' perceptions about their organization's activities, and effectiveness. Employee experiences of the service climate in which they work significantly predict customer satisfaction; it demonstrated that employee reports, such as employee attitude surveys, are reflected in customer satisfaction. This elevates the role of employees as reporters as possible valid "sensors" of how well the organization is aligned to address the demands of not only customers, but multiple constituencies and goals (Schneider, Paul, & White, 1998). Third, it indicates which facets of the employee experience most strongly relate to customer satisfaction, thereby indicating where management/leadership should invest in affecting the employee experience most likely to enhance customer satisfaction. For example, do employee perceptions of their organization's training, compensation, or some other practice correlate most strongly with customer satisfaction (Schneider & Bowen, 1993)? Finally, it modeled a chain of linkages that runs from leadership/management through internal (employee) and external (customer) perceptions and attitudes, even on to profits themselves, that is, the service profit chain, (Heskett, Sasser, & Schlesinger, 1997).

Linking Antecedents and Consequences of Climate for Service

Figure 8.1 presents a general model of internal and external linkages with organizational outcomes. It begins with leadership creating the organizational climates necessary for subsequent linkages. As Schneider and White (2004) note, the very early work on climate (Lewin, Lippitt, & White, 1939) emphasized the role of leadership in creating the climate of the situation for those in it. In turn, leadership in service has as its central responsibility to create the "climates for" associated with positive experiences for the often tightly linked employees and customers.

Leaders need to create both a climate for service and an employee-oriented climate, or *internal* service climate, the latter being the foundation on which climate for service can be built (Schneider & Bowen, 1985, 1995; Schneider & White, 2004). The employee-oriented/internal service climate has been conceptualized as "climate for work facilitation" (Schneider, White, & Paul, 1998; see also Burke, Borucki, & Hurley, 1992) or "climate for

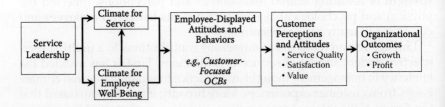

FIGURE 8.1 Linkages, internal and external, with organizational outcomes (a general perspective).

employee well-being" (Schneider & Bowen, 1993). Both focus on creating an internal work environment that enables employees to meet both customer expectations and their own workplace needs. Additionally, an organizational climate that emphasizes fairness in the treatment of employees has been suggested as a necessary foundation for service quality (Bowen et al., 1999). Leaders can then build a climate for service, as described earlier, upon this internal/employee-oriented foundation to link to external customer service quality and desired organizational outcomes.

To further strengthen the final linkage to organizational outcomes such as profits, "leadership" should refine climate for service, generically, to climate for a particular type of service, *strategically* matched to an intended customer market segment (Bowen, Schneider, & Kim, 2000; Schneider & Bowen, 1995). For example, type of service could be differing levels of emphasis, focus really, on three different types of service in terms of customer expectations for speed (quick and immediately available), tender loving care (TLC; attentive and empathetic at a deep level), or customization (uniquely offered; customer has wide degree of freedom in tailoring the service offering). In turn, depending on the focus, the human resource management philosophy and mix of selection, training, rewards, and so on, would need to be designed to build a climate for a particular type of service, say focused on speed rather than TLC.

An example of matching strategy climate for a particular type of service, and the design of HRM philosophy and practice, can be found in the contingency approach to employee empowerment in services (Bowen & Lawler, 1992, 1995). Bowen and Lawler suggested that if a service firm had a strategy aligned with a market segment around speed and low price, then low employee discretion (a production line approach to service delivery) would be the right match. Alternatively, if the strategy and market segment focused on TLC, or customization for that matter, then high employee discretion (an employee empowerment approach) would be the appropriate match.

Finally, it is also leadership's responsibility to create these as strong, not weak, climates (Schneider, Salvaggio, & Subirats, 2002) in which all employees are in shared agreement that management is committed to the for's that are the focus of the climate: for internal and external service to employees and customers. This requires a set of human resource management practices that possess the HRM strength to build potentially divergent employees' perspectives into a "strong situation" with a shared sense of what goals to pursue and the behaviors expected to do so (Bowen & Ostroff, 2004).

Refining the Linkages: Some Mediators and Moderators

The early linkage theory and research built a number of mediated associations across internal employee experiences to customer experiences to outcomes of interest to the organization such as growth and profitability. In the 1990s, a line of research emerged on organizational citizenship behaviors (OCBs) as a "spillover" mechanism that mediates between the employee and customer experience (Bowen, Gilliland, & Folger, 1999; Masterson, 2001; Schneider, Erhart, Mayer, Saltz, & Niles-Jolly, 2005). OCBs are essentially unrewarded behaviors to "go above and beyond the call of duty" in performing one's job (Organ, 1988). Generic OCBs have been clustered as displays of altruism, courtesy, sportsmanship, conscientiousness, and civic virtue (Organ, 1988). In a service-based, customer contact perspective, customer-focused OCBs have been defined as extra-role behaviors directed toward customers (Bettencourt & Brown, 1997). These OCBs have a service quality flavor that would be positively associated with customer experiences of the service they receive.

As to the antecedent mediator variables that would then link to customer-focused OCBs, the emerging literature suggests employee perceptions of either the firm's climate for service (Schneider et al., 2005) or fair treatment (e.g., Bowen et al., 1999; Masterson, 2001; Maxham & Netemeyer, 2003), as part of a climate for employee well-being. A climate for service would send employees signals about service quality to customers as an organizational imperative, which in turn would facilitate customer-focused OCBs. The justice perspective builds on earlier work by Moorman (1991), for example, that reported the relationship between employee justice perceptions and their displays of OCBs. More recent work has examined employee engagement as a mediator in linkage models (Macy & Schneider, 2006).

Moderators of the Linkages.   This line of work has concentrated on specifying the boundary conditions, such as type of service, that influence the strength of the relationship between employee and customer reports (for a more complete discussion, see Pugh et al., 2002; Schneider & White, 2004). Schneider (2004) briefly summarized this work by noting that although employee–customer linkages appear robust across different service settings, most of the linkage research has been done with services with high customer contact, high intangibility, and high interdependence among service deliverers.

Are, then, the findings of positive employee service climate perceptions and customer satisfaction generalizable to all services? There do appear to be boundary conditions: For example, the linkage between service climate and customer satisfaction was found to be low when customer contact is low (Dietz, Pugh, & Wiley, 2004). The same diminished linkage is true for low intangible services.

A Shift in Focus in "That's Interesting" from Between to Within.   This discussion of linkage moderators, and the earlier point about climates for a particular type of service, have in common a focus on differences *within* the service sector, as opposed to the earlier focus on the difference *between* services and goods. Recall that what was "interesting" in the earliest descriptions of services was their "non-X" attributes vis-à-vis goods. Efforts to demonstrate this, then, were much in evidence in the late 1970s to mid-1980s. Attention to differences *within* services focus began earlier in marketing than in OB/HRM. Zeithaml et al. (1985) had underscored that there were important differences *among* service firms, not just in contrast to goods-producing firms. This *within* focus emerged a bit later in OB/HRM, but in both fields it was a shift, or expansion, in what was now interesting about services versus in the mid-1970s.

Unique Human Resources: Employees and Customers

The oftentimes close linkage between employees and customers, both physically and psychologically, challenged scholars to address how this degree of customer contact, as an ongoing task characteristic, could be managed, in both theoretical and practical terms. Theories and models in the OB/HRM literature were built largely on the premise of a thick boundary between the organization's core technology and environmental disturbances (e.g., Thompson's [1967] buffered core). There are theoretical treatments in which employee–customer contact is addressed, such as the passing inclusion of customer contact as a feedback strategy in the job characteristics model (Hackman, Oldham, Janson, & Purdy, 1975) and more macro and general discussions, such as in Thompson's own mediating technology, but there had been really no focused theoretical treatment of customer contact, and certainly not customer coproduction, as an ongoing part of the employee work experience relevant to the effective and efficient workings of the core technology.

In the 1980s, then, this led to a number of contributions, such as how to select employees with a service orientation (e.g., Hogan, Hogan, & Busch, 1984) who could meet customer needs. This example can be viewed as an extension of the ongoing focus in industrial and organizational (I–O) psychology of building valid screening technologies for different individual competencies. However, the following two contributions to managing this linkage exemplify the unique nature of both employees and customers as human resources in services.

Employee Emotional Labor. The employee–customer linkage in service organizations adds emotional labor to other forms of employee labor, such as physical, technical, and cognitive. Daniel Bell (1973) foreshadowed the emergence of emotional labor in his book *The Coming of Post-Industrial Society.* Bell offered a metaphorical description of the evolution of work over time in which first there was a "game against nature," in which competencies such as brawn and energy were necessary for fishing and farming. This was followed by a "game against fabricated nature" around the time of the industrial revolution, which required new forms of organization and new competencies, evidenced largely in principles associated with scientific management.

With the late 1970s, though, the nature of work in an information and service-driven (U.S.) economy became a game between persons. This required interpersonal competencies and organizational arrangements that arguably extend organizational boundaries to include the customer.

Including the customer in the employee work experience can place an emotional toll on workers, obviously, but also for a reason not always obvious—employees must sometimes display false emotions in order to satisfy multiple stakeholders, such as management's demands and customers' expectations. The emotional labor involved in this was well expressed in an early book on the subject titled *The Managed Heart: The Commercialization of Human Feeling* (Hochschild, 1982), which reported on flight attendants having to smile at passengers who may be acting rudely and stay outwardly upbeat, no matter if they were having personal problems themselves.

In sum, emotional labor was an interesting addition to the literature that received considerable impetus from the emergent study of the non-X nature of service organizations. In turn, for those curious about this subject, much of the really interesting work on this in services has been done by Anat Rafaeli, who has looked at emotional displays, the struggle for control of the service encounter between employees and customers, and so on (e.g., Rafaeli, 1989; Sutton & Rafaeli, 1988); also see Pugh's (2001) work on emotional contagion in the service encounter.

Managing Customers as Human Resources.   Recall from our earlier discussion of OM contributions that if firms can create high-performance customers, then the firm can successfully resolve the trade-off from customer contact between marketing effectiveness and operational efficiency. This led to theoretically framing customers as "partial employees" or additional human resources of the service organization, whose performance needs to be managed (Bowen, 1986; Mills & Morris, 1986).

The framework presented to manage customer performance is essentially derived from established models of how to manage individual employee performance (e.g., Vroom, 1964). In other words, for customers to perform their coproduction roles well requires that they possess role clarity (understanding what tasks they are expected to perform), motivation (a perception that performing as expected leads to valued outcomes), and ability (a capacity to perform as expected). In turn, service firms must leverage these three variables via communication of role expectations, clear consequences for performing as expected, and selecting and training the "right type" of customer to fit the performance requirements of the service delivery system (Tax, Colgate, & Bowen, 2006).

In recent years, this more micro treatment of customer performance has been supplemented by more macro and strategic discussions of how to co-opt or utilize customer competencies to enhance organizational effectiveness (Bettencourt, Ostrom, Brown, & Roundtree, 2002; Lengnick-Hall, 1996; Prahalad & Ramaswamy, 2000). These contributions help lay a foundation for more encompassing perspectives on how service logic around intangible experiences and customer closeness and coproduction can frame organization–customer exchange, generally.

FUTURE PERSPECTIVES ON SERVICE ORGANIZATIONS: WHAT IS INTERESTING LOOKING AHEAD?

As was true throughout this chapter, the objective of this closing perspective is to provide a feel for the answer, not an exhaustive reply. Two perspectives will be offered. One is a series of possible directions for future inquiry that are important and continuous extensions of past perspectives of service organizations. Second is a more discontinuous perspective in the form of emerging work on what have been labeled new services paradigms.

Directions for Future Inquiry

The possibilities here are endless and even suggested by the limited service focus of this chapter on primarily B2C, face-to-face service settings. Thus, obvious candidates for future inquiry include subjects such as service over the Internet, business to business (B2B) services, all the issues associated with formerly predominantly goods-based organizations transitioning to services based, cross-cultural differences, service networks that require links across more than two parties, and so forth.

More *contingency* perspectives are needed in the service management literature. For example, as Schneider and White (2004) note, although the services literature emphasizes the importance of service employee personality in influencing service-oriented behavior, and thus customer satisfaction, the empirical evidence for these sorts of associations is mixed (e.g., Frei & McDaniel, 1998; Rogelberg, Barnes-Farrell, & Creamer, 1999). One explanation is that personality matters most, if at all, in high customer contact services. More broadly, despite the strategic HRM perspective on the linkage between climates for different types of service and different market segments of customer expectations, there is a need for more empirical work on how service firms best match their employees and HRM practices to different segments.

At a more organizational theory level, much of the service literature emphasizes a need for cross-functional integration in order to satisfy the customer and to be effective overall. However, the overall perspective found in the organizational theory literature is that an integrated organization is more effective only under certain conditions, for example, a contingency perspective, as found in Lawrence and Lorsch (1967). This contingency perspective on the effects of integration has not been dealt with in a systematic manner in the services literature (Schneider & White, 2004).

Finally, linkage research still needs more studies on moderators and boundary conditions. Schneider and White (2004) suggest, for example, examining the pattern of correlations between SERVQUAL customer scores and employee scores on various internal climates for service dimensions.

More research is needed on the strength of the linkage to profits. Empirically validating this linkage is essential to addressing the "so what" question as to how interesting the antecedent linkages really are, and thus how interested executives really should be in these linkages overall.

Additional attention should be given to customers as coproducers of their own services. Services of all sorts are requiring additional levels of customer coproduction and even self-service (see the considerable work in marketing on self-service technologies, e.g., Bitner, Ostrom, & Meuter, 2002). Schneider and White (2004) also suggest examining how this phenomenon affects employee job retention prospects, employee responsibility to supervise coproducing customers, and employees' workplace attitudes and performance.

Reframing the Perspective on Service: Toward a New Paradigm?

We can move to concluding this overview of perspectives on services in the manner in which the chapter began, with another observation from Schneider, 20 years after the *ASQ* quotation, commenting on the state of the study of services:

> We need a new paradigm. I wish I knew what it should be, but I know we need one.... Services marketing has been successful because it differentiated itself in the marketplace with a conceptual paradigm shift—services are different from goods. All else has followed from this conceptual leap—and with increasing refinement. We have had a happy 20 year run ... but we need some new energy and new directions. (Schneider, 2000, p. 180)

In other words, how to make the study of services interesting again. The marketing discipline has recently addressed this challenge and advanced two possible paradigms: a "rental/access" versus ownership perspective on the nature of services (Lovelock & Gummesson, 2004) and the "service-dominant logic," which reframes the nature of all market exchange—goods or services (Vargo & Lusch, 2004). The ownership paradigm on services is based on the idea that marketing transactions that do not involve a transfer of ownership are distinctively different from those that do. Services, then, "involve a form of 'rental' or 'access' in which customers obtain benefits by gaining the right to use a physical object, to hire the labor and expertise of personnel, or to obtain access to facilities and networks" (Lovelock & Gummesson, 2004, p. 34). The authors argue for this perspective as an alternative to the long-standing IHIP paradigm in services marketing. In turn, other disciplines, for example, OM and OB/HRM, can now grapple with the "so what" implications of this rental or access perspective for theory and practice.

The service-dominant logic (Vargo & Lusch, 2004) is a perspective that applies to all marketing offerings, including those that involve tangible output (goods) in the process of service provision. Service provision, then, is fundamental to all economic exchange, and services are defined as "the application of specialized competencies (knowledge and skills) through deeds, processes and performances for the benefit of another entity or the entity itself" (p. 2). In this service-dominant logic paradigm, goods are viewed as a distribution mechanism for service provision. Additionally, value is not embedded in the offering, no matter whether it is a good or service. Value is only created at the point of customer consumption. Thus, the service-dominant logic also assumes that all exchange involves customer coproduction; that is, it is necessary for value creation, and also is inherently customer oriented and relational.

This service-dominant logic paradigm in marketing poses interesting theoretical and practical issues for OM and OB/HRM. As Vargo and Lusch (2004) observe, this new marketing logic, grounded as it is on value creation for the customer via a bundle of intangible organizational resources, places marketing "at the center of the integration of business functions and disciplines" (p. 5) and "is also compatible with emerging theories of the firm" that view the firm as an organization of capabilities and competencies (p. 6).

In sum, these new paradigms suggest new links among exchange parties in the creation of value and can encourage the forging of new links among the various disciplinary perspectives on this value creation process. Finally, although they are new paradigms, they are grounded in old concepts of intangibles and psychological closeness between customer and service providers that were initially advanced by the service pioneers of the 1970s—such as Ben Schneider.

REFERENCES

Bell, D. (1973). *The coming of post-industrial society: A venture in social forecasting.* New York: Basic Books.

Bettencourt, L., & Brown, S. W. (1997). Contact employees: Relationships among workplace fairness, job satisfaction, and pro-social behaviors. *Journal of Retailing, 73,* 39–61.

Bettencourt, L. A., Ostrom, A. L., Brown, S. W., & Roundtree, R. I. (2002). Client coproduction in knowledge-intensive services. *California Management Review, 44,* 100–128.

Bitner, M. J. (1992). Servicescapes: The impact of physical surroundings on customers and employees. *Journal of Marketing, 56,* 57–71.

Bitner, M. J., Ostrom, A. L., & Meuter, M. (2002). Implementing successful self-service technologies. *Academy of Management Executive, 16,* 96–109.

Bowen, D. E. (1986). Managing customers as human resources in service organizations. *Human Resource Management Journal, 25,* 371–384.

Bowen, D. E., Gilliland, S., & Folger, R. (1999). HRM and service fairness: How being fair with employees spills over to customers. *Organizational Dynamics, 27,* 7–23.

Bowen, D. E., & Hallowell, R. (2002). Suppose we took service seriously? An introduction to the special issue. *Academy of Management Executive, 16,* 69–72.

Bowen, D. E., & Lawler, E. E., III. (1992). The empowerment of service workers: What, why, how, and when. *Sloan Management Review, 33,* 31–39.

Bowen, D. E., & Lawler, E. E., III. (1995). Empowering service employees. *Sloan Management Review, 36,* 73–84.

Bowen, D. E., & Ostroff, C. (2004). Understanding HRM-firm performance linkages: The role of the "strength" of the HRM system. *Academy of Management Review, 29,* 203–221.

Bowen, D. E., & Schneider, B. (1988). Services marketing and management: Implications for organizational behavior. In B. Staw & L. L. Cummings (Eds.), *Research in organizational behavior* (Vol. 10, pp. 43–80). Greenwich, CT: JAI Press.

Bowen, D. E., Schneider, B., & Kim, S. (2000). Shaping service cultures through strategic human resource management. In T. A. Swartz & D. Iacobucci (Eds.), *Handbook of services marketing and management* (pp. 439–454). Thousand Oaks, CA: Sage Publications.

Burke, M., Borucki, C., & Hurley, A. (1992). Reconceptualizing psychological climate in a retail service environment: A multiple stakeholder perspective. *Journal of Applied Psychology, 77,* 717–729.

Chase, R. B. (1978). Where does the customer fit in a service operation? *Harvard Business Review, 56,* 137–142.

Chase, R. B., Aquilano, N. J., & Jacobs, F. R. (1998). *Production and operations management: Manufacturing and services.* San Francisco: Irwin/McGraw-Hill.

Chase, R. B., & Tansik, D. A. (1983). The customer contact model for organization design. *Management Science, 49,* 1037–1050.

Danet, B. (1981). Client-organization relationships. In P. C. Nystrom & W. H. Starbuck (Eds.), *Handbook of organizational design* (p. 382). New York: Oxford University Press.

Davis, M. S. (1971). That's interesting. Towards a phenomenology of sociology and a sociology of phenomenology. *Philosophy of Social Science, 1,* 309–344.

Davis, S. M. (1983, Spring). Management models for the future. *New Management,* 12–15.

Dietz, J., Pugh, S. D., & Wiley, J. (2004). Service climate effects on customer attitudes: An examination of boundary conditions. *Academy of Management Journal, 47,* 81–92.

Frei, R. L., & McDaniel, M. A. (1998). Validity of customer service measures in personnel selection: A review of criterion and construct evidence. *Human Performance, 11,* 1–27.

Gronroos, C. (1990). *Service management and marketing: Managing the moments of truth in service competition.* Lexington, MA: Lexington Books.

Hackman, J. R., Oldham, G., Janson, R., & Purdy, K. A. (1975). A new strategy for job enrichment. *California Management Review, 17,* 57–71.

Heskett, J. L., Sasser, W. E., Jr., & Schlesinger, L. A. (1997). *The service profit chain: How leading companies link profit and growth to loyalty, satisfaction, and value.* New York: Free Press.

Hochschild, A. (1982). *The managed heart: The commercialization of human feeling.* Berkeley, CA: University of California Press.

Hogan, R. T., Hogan, J., & Busch, A. (1984). How to measure service orientation. *Journal of Applied Psychology, 69,* 167–173.

Johnston, R., & Clark, R. G. (2005). *Service operations management: Improving service delivery.* London: Financial Times/Prentice Hall.

Kotler, P. (1973). Atmospherics as a marketing tool. *Journal of Retailing, 49,* 48–63.

Lawrence, P. K., & Lorsch, J. W. (1967). *Organization and environment: Managing differentiation and integration.* Cambridge, MA: Harvard.

Lengnick-Hall, C. (1996). Customer contributions to quality: A different view of the customer-oriented firm. *Academy of Management Review, 21,* 791–824.

Lewin, K., Lippitt, R., & White, R. K. (1939). Patterns of aggressive behavior in experimentally created "social climates." *Journal of Applied Psychology, 10,* 271–299.

Lovelock, C., & Gummesson, E. (2004). Whither services marketing? In search of a new paradigm and fresh perspectives. *Journal of Service Research, 7,* 20–41.

Lovelock, C. H. & Wirtz, J. (2003). Services marketing: People, technology, and strategy, 5th edition. New Jersey: Pearson/Prentice Hall.

Macy, W. H. & Schneider, B. (2006). Employee experiences and customer satisfaction. In A. I. Kraut (Ed.) *Getting Action from Organizational Surveys* (pp. 53–75). San Francisco, CA: Jossey-Bass.

Masterson, S. (2001). A trickle-down model of organizational justice: Relating employees' and customers' perceptions of and reactions to fairness. *Journal of Applied Psychology, 86,* 594–604.

Maxham, J. G., & Netemeyer, R. G. (2003). Firms reap what they sow: The effects of shared values and perceived organizational justice on customers' evaluations of complaint handling. *Journal of Marketing, 67,* 46–62.

Mills, P. K., & Morris, J. H. (1986). Clients as "partial employees" of service organizations: Role development in client participation. *Academy of Management Review, 11,* 726–735.

Moorman, R. (1991). The relationship between organizational justice and organizational citizenship behaviors: Do fairness perceptions influence employee citizenship? *Journal of Applied Psychology, 86,* 594–604.

Organ, D. W. (1988). *Organizational citizenship behavior: The good soldier syndrome.* Lexington, MA: Lexington Books.

Parasuraman, A., Zeithaml, V., & Berry, L. (1985). A conceptual model of service quality and some implications for future research. *Journal of Marketing, 49,* 41–50.

Parasuraman, A., Zeithaml, V., & Berry, L. (1988). SERVQUAL: A multi-item scale for measuring consumer perceptions of service quality. *Journal of Retailing, 64,* 41–50.

Peters, T., & Waterman, R. H. (1982). *In search of excellence.* New York: Harper & Row.

Prahalad, C. K., & Ramaswamy, V. (2000). Co-opting customer competence. *Harvard Business Review, 78,* 79–87.

Pugh, S. D. (2001). Service with a smile: Emotional contagion in the service encounter. *Academy of Management Journal, 44,* 1018–1027.

Pugh, S. D., Dietz, J., Wiley, J. W., & Brooks, S. M. (2002). Driving service effectiveness through employee-customer linkages. *Academy of Management Executive, 16*, 73–84.

Rafaeli, A. (1989). When cashiers meet customers: An analysis of the role of supermarket cashiers. *Academy of Management Journal, 32*, 245–273.

Rogelberg, S. G., Barnes-Farrell, J. L., & Creamer, V. (1999). Customer service behavior: The interaction of service predisposition and job characteristics. *Journal of Business and Psychology, 13*, 421–435.

Rust, R., Zeithaml, V., & Lemon, K. N. (2000). *Driving customer equity: How customer lifetime value is reshaping corporate strategy.* New York: The Free Press.

Schneider, B. (1973). The perception of organizational climate: The customer's view. *Journal of Applied Psychology, 57*, 248–256.

Schneider, B. (1975). Organizational climates: An essay. *Personnel Psychology, 28*, 447–470.

Schneider, B. (2000). In R. P. Fisk, S. J. Grove, & J. John (Eds.), *Services marketing self-portraits: Introspections, reflections, and glimpses from the experts* (pp. 173–188), Chicago: American Marketing Association.

Schneider, B. (2004). Welcome to the world of services management. *Academy of Management Executive, 18*, 144–150.

Schneider, B., & Bowen, D. E. (1985). Employee and customer perceptions of service in banks: Replication and extension. *Journal of Applied Psychology, 70*, 423–433.

Schneider, B., & Bowen, D. E. (1995). *Winning the service game.* Boston: Harvard Business School Press.

Schneider, B., Erhart, M., Mayer, D., & Saltz, J. L. (2005). Understanding organizational-customer linkages. *Academy of Management Journal.*

Schneider, B., Parkington, J. J., & Buxton, V. M. (1980). Employee and customer perceptions of service in banks. *Administrative Sciences Quarterly, 25*, 252–267.

Schneider, B., Salvaggio, A. N., & Subirats, M. (2002). Climate strength: A new direction for climate research. *Journal of Applied Psychology, 87*, 220–229.

Schneider, B., & White, S. S. (2004). *Service quality: Research perspectives.* Thousand Oaks, CA: Sage.

Schneider, B., White, S. S., & Paul, M. C. (1998). Linking service climate and customer perceptions of service quality in banks: Test of a causal model. *Journal of Applied Psychology, 83*, 150–163.

Shostack, G. L. (1977). Breaking free from product marketing. *Journal of Marketing, 41*, 73–80.

Sutton, R. I., & Rafaeli, A. (1988). Untangling the relationship between displayed emotions and organizational sales: The case of convenience stores. *Academy of Management Journal, 31*, 461–487.

Thompson, J. D. (1967). *Organizations in action.* New York: Wiley.

Vargo, S. L., & Lusch, R. F. (2004). Evolving to a new dominant logic for marketing. *Journal of Marketing, 68*, 1–17.

Vroom, V. (1964). *Work and motivation.* New York: Wiley.

Zeithaml, V. A., Bitner, M. J., & Gremler, D. D. (2006). *Services marketing: Integrating customer focus across the firm.* New York: McGraw-Hill/Irwin.

Zeithaml, V. A., Parasuraman, A., & Berry, L. (1985). Problems and strategies in services marketing. *Journal of Marketing, 49*, 33–46.

9

The "Good" Corporation*

JILL C. BRADLEY
California State University, Fresno

ARTHUR P. BRIEF
University of Utah

KRISTIN SMITH-CROWE
University of Utah

> Silver and gold are not the only coin; virtue too passes current all over the world.
>
> —*Euripides (480–406 B.C.E.)*

We cannot remember the last time we read a newspaper or watched a television news program that was absent stories of scandals or crimes involving public figures, celebrities, elected officials, or corporate entities. Stories about people and organizations doing the "right" thing, however, seem to be less commonly told. In terms of organizational research, scholars too have tended toward a negative slant (see Cameron, Dutton, & Quinn, 2003; but see Lazarus, 2003). Here, we are concerned with the moral nature of organizations and thus are sensitive to the apparent emphasis in the organizational literature on *unethical* behaviors and their causes and cures (e.g., Brief, Buttram, Elliot, Reizenstein, & McCline, 1995; Brief, Dukerich, & Doran, 1991; Kelman & Hamilton, 1989; Tenbrunsel & Messick,

---

* The second and third authors contributed equally and are therefore listed alphabetically. The authors would like to offer their sincere thanks to Ben Crowe and Joshua Margolis for their help and guidance on earlier drafts of this chapter.

1999; Tenbrunsel, Smith-Crowe, & Umphress, 2003; Trevino & Weaver, 2003; Trevino & Youngblood, 1990). To understand the moral nature of organizations requires one to examine both sides of the coin—the good and the bad. Our aim in this chapter, therefore, is to explore the concept of the "good corporation"[1] and, drawing heavily on the works of Benjamin Schneider (e.g., 1975, 1987, 1990), to speculate about the ways in which corporations come to be good and stay good. In this way, we attempt to bring balance to that domain of the organizational literature addressing issues of morality.

While organizational scholars have been relatively negligent in considering goodness, they have not ignored it completely. For example, one can readily find reference to the notion of "corporate social responsibility" (e.g., Margolis & Walsh, 2003) and the more nascent concept of "positive deviance" (e.g., Quinn, 1996; Spreitzer & Shonenshein, 2003b; Sternen, 2002). However, we will argue that the "good corporation" is not necessarily equivalent to a positively deviant or a socially responsible one. Indeed, much of this chapter will be devoted to defining "goodness" and, more specifically, the "good corporation." Our examination of the meaning of goodness requires us to move beyond the organizational literature; thus, even though they are largely foreign territories to us, we sample heavily from philosophy and religion. Because scholars within these traditions tend to discuss morality and goodness with respect to *individuals*, we must first tackle the notion that moral attributes of individual persons can be applied to *organizations*. Those readers well versed in religion or the philosophy of ethics will find our approach to corporate goodness to be an amalgamated one; that is, we do not adopt any one sect or school of thought.

After addressing what being a good corporation entails, we briefly turn to how such a corporation might be distinguished empirically from one that is not good. The serious student of measurement will not find our discussion especially comforting as we will provide more challenges than answers. We then proceed to examine the means by which a corporation might come to be good and maintain its goodness. Our examination will be guided by the attraction–selection–attrition (ASA) framework (Schneider, 1987) and the literature on organizational climate, especially contributions by Benjamin Schneider and his colleagues (e.g., Schneider & Reichers, 1983). The chapter will close with a few personal observations.

CAN A CORPORATION BE GOOD?

Philosophy, religion, and conventional wisdom tell us that human beings are moral agents (e.g., Augustine, 426/1950; Blackburn, 2001), capable of both good and evil. Charting out our concept of the good corporation necessitated our thinking about the moral agency of an organization in humanlike terms.[2] Consequently, we became concerned with the legitimacy of ascribing moral agency to organizations. Numerous scholars, we discovered, have contemplated such an analogy (e.g., Curtler, 1986; Danley, 1984; Donaldson & Werhane, 1996; Goodpaster & Matthews, 1982; Horwitz, 1992; Nash, 1993; Ozar, 1979; Paine, 2003). Some (e.g., French, 1984) strongly support the analogy, but others (e.g., Fox, 1996) deem the likening of organizations to people as anthropomorphic and, as such, unjustifiable. Philosophers and legal scholars (e.g., Hobbes, Marshall, 1819; Wolgast, 1992) often use the term *artificial persons* when describing corporations, bestowing them a status comparable to people in some ways but not in others. Hopefully not too naively, we adopt the position that many of the attributes of individual goodness are applicable to corporations (see Park & Peterson, 2003).

Clear support for this position is found in the U.S. legal system. Since 1819, the Supreme Court has regarded corporations as persons (*Trustees of Dartmouth College v. Woodward*). Legally, corporations are holders of natural rights such as life, liberty, and property under the 14th Amendment of the Constitution (*Santa Clara County v. Southern Pacific Railroad*), and like people, corporations have the right to free speech (*First National Bank of Boston v. Bellotti*). In addition to possessing rights, corporations also can be held responsible for acts of wrongdoing (see U.S. Sentencing Commission, 2003). Royal Caribbean Cruise Ltd., for example, was charged with and pled guilty to the crime of routinely dumping oil and toxic chemicals and lying about doing so to U.S. Coast Guard officials. Moreover, like individual citizens, corporations can be punished; Royal Caribbean was fined $18 million for its transgressions. However, quite unlike individuals, corporations cannot be imprisoned, nor can they feel guilt or remorse for their crimes.

Reflecting on the complexity of the artificial person, Wolgast (1992) reasoned that while corporations are like people in some ways, carrying out actions like buying, selling, or negotiating, they are unlike people in moral capacities (see also, for instance, Donaldson, 1982; Ladd, 1970):

> I conclude that it is implausible to treat a corporation as a member of the human community, a member with a personality (but not a face), intentions (but no feelings), relationships (but no family or friends), responsibility (but no conscience), and susceptibility to punishment (but no capacity for pain). (Wolgast, 1992, p. 86)

While we see Wolgast's strong position as having merit, we contend that it is insufficient to relegate corporations to the status of completely amoral entities. Indeed, we suggest that corporations might even be thought of as having a conscience (Goodpaster & Matthews, 1982), at least as reflected by its corporate policies, norms, and culture (Velasquez, 1998). Also attempting to justify the notion of an organizational conscience, Buchholz (1989) reasoned that corporate actions are the result of a collective and cannot always be linked back to specific individuals: "Policies are truly acts of the corporation, and the corporation as such can be held responsible for their effects" (p. 112). Similar arguments are found, for example, in the literature on organizational climate (e.g., Reichers & Schneider, 1990) and on transactional memory systems (e.g., Austin, 2003; Wegner, 1986), the latter of which suggests that knowledge possessed by individuals can become intricately linked within a group-level memory system that has "emergent properties" not attributable to any one person.

Importantly, our position that corporations are moral entities should not be mistaken as a claim that corporations are equivalent to human beings or that individuals should be relieved of moral obligations. Again, corporations here are understood to be artificial persons, and because corporations both operate through and influence human actors, individuals *and* corporations hold moral responsibility (Valasquez, 1998). Our view, then, is a tempered one suggesting that counterparts to many, but not all, characteristics typically assigned to persons can be thought of as existing at the corporate level (Park & Peterson, 2003). Accordingly, we began our search for the meaning of corporate goodness by considering the good person. Such a consideration called for an exploration of territories foreign to us, those populated by philosophers and theologians. In embarking on this journey, we feared that we would not discover a clear, crisp, indisputable definition of goodness. As you will see below, our fears were well founded; no such definition was found. Goodness, as we anticipated, is an elusive concept whose meaning is difficult to pin down. Although we cannot provide clear directions, in the sections that follow we will provide clues that guide the search for the meaning of corporate goodness. We are certain the "hidden treasure" is there to be found; as of yet, however, we are unsure where to find it.

CLUE 1: A GOOD CORPORATION IS MORE THAN "NOT BAD"

The first clue in our journey is that a good corporation is much more than "okay," "so-so," or "not bad." While being decent and avoiding morally repugnant behavior obviously is desirable, this is not goodness (also see Solomon, 1994). Paine (2003) identified two levels of commitment companies can exhibit in attempting to do the right thing. The basic level entails, for example, fulfilling contracts, obeying the law, and avoiding harm to the community. In contrast, the full level of commitment includes things such as helping others, improving the community, and upholding the spirit of the law.[3] Goodness occurs at this second level of commitment and embraces, for instance, being generous, courageous, and promoting human dignity. What we will call "decent corporations" operate at Paine's basic level of commitment; "bad corporations" are those that do not meet this basic level, engaging in illegal acts and demonstrating a lack of consideration for people, animals, and the environment. Importantly, goodness, decency, and badness are conceptualized here as categorically distinct rather than as lying at varying points along a single continuum.

That is, behaviors defined as good, for instance, are not necessarily the polar opposite of those defined as bad. Theft, for instance, is a bad action that has no correspondent in the goodness category because abstaining from theft is not enough to be labeled good.

Unfortunately, determining a corporation's place within our typology is complicated by the fact that a corporation can be good in one domain (e.g., human rights) but decent or bad in other domains (e.g., environmental concerns). Additionally, corporations might be good at one time, but merely decent at another. Virtually any corporation is likely to exhibit a mixture of goodness, decency, and badness. Take the case of Altria Group, Inc. This corporation contributes substantially to causes aimed at alleviating social ills like AIDS, hunger, and domestic violence (good); it complies with applicable environmental laws and regulations (decent); and it is the parent company of tobacco giant Philip Morris, whose noxious products kill nearly half a million Americans each year and result in the loss of approximately $157 billion annually in health-related costs (bad; Centers for Disease Control [CDC], 2002).

It seems, then, that no corporation, just like no person, is all good, all decent, or all bad. Thus, attempting to evaluate the overall goodness of a corporation requires the consideration of multiple domains, such as product safety, community relations, and employee relations—each of which can be viewed in terms of being good, decent, or bad. The mathematics of weighing and combining these various domains into an overall rating is far beyond the scope of this chapter, but recognizing the potential importance and difficulty of doing so is not. A significant problem in creating an overall scoring system stems from the fact that corporations operate under a variety of pressures and are beholden to numerous stakeholders (see Donaldson & Preston, 1995; Evan & Freeman, 1988), many of whom may differentially categorize the same corporation. For example, the environmental group Sierra Club might view Ford Motor Company as bad for manufacturing gas-guzzling SUVs, whereas the British Museum, a recipient of Ford's largesse, might label Ford a good corporation.

In sum, Clue 1 tells us that decency is a prerequisite to goodness but does not equal it, and that all corporations likely exhibit a combination of goodness, decency, and badness. Formulae for aggregating such combinations are yet to be advanced and verified. The following clue takes us closer to an understanding of what corporate goodness is.

CLUE 2: DON'T LOOK TO OUTCOMES … IT'S INTENTIONS THAT COUNT

The second clue as to the meaning of corporate goodness cautions against definitions that weigh outcomes too heavily (e.g., profits and employee satisfaction) and factors like intentions, actions, and virtues too lightly (e.g., as does Friedman, 1970). In the language of philosophers, we will argue—as have others (e.g., Kant, 1785/1964; Rawls, 1971)—against a strictly consequentialist definition of goodness, or one that looks only to the consequences of actions in assessing goodness. For instance, utilitarianism (e.g., Mill, 1962), a specific consequentialist theory, holds that actions are good to the extent that they maximize pleasure or happiness and minimize pain or unhappiness for everyone affected by them. On the surface, the goal of maximizing pleasure sounds pretty good; however, for the reasons provided below, an outcome-focused approach to corporate goodness is problematic.[4]

A primary shortcoming of utilitarianism, according to some scholars (e.g., Donaldson & Werhane, 1996; Hartman, 1996), is its inability to ensure individual rights (e.g., life, liberty, and freedom from slavery; United Nations, 1948) and justice (e.g., fair procedures for all people; see, for instance, Rawls, 1971; United Nations, 1948). To illustrate this point, Donaldson and Werhane (1996) described a scenario in which the world's overall maximum pleasure is achieved by enslaving a small percentage of the population. In this example, strict utilitarianism would support slavery; yet most people, we hope, would agree that slavery is not good because it tramples on the rights of the enslaved individuals. Another example commonly used to illustrate this particular deficiency of utilitarianism is that of an involuntary organ donor killed to save the lives of five other people. From the strict utilitarian perspective, the murder is justified because the happiness of five people is more valuable than that of one. Again, however, utilitarianism disregards the rights of the individual, in this case the donor. Those in opposition to utilitarian-like thinking (including us) assert that the greatest good for the greatest number does not warrant denying some individuals their basic rights (for a listing of basic human rights, see Rawls, 1971; United Nations, 1948).

Another difficulty with the consequentialist perspective is that outcomes are not always under one's control (Kant, 1785/2002). Industrial-organizational psychologists, for instance, have argued convincingly that job performance should not be measured in terms of outcomes (e.g., number of widgets made or sold), but by those job-relevant behaviors under one's control (e.g., communicating with supervisors, supporting team efforts; Burke, Sarpy, Tesluk, & Smith-Crowe, 2002; Campbell, McCloy, Oppler, & Sager, 1993). This perspective on job performance is rooted in the idea that even the best of intentions and greatest of efforts might not result in desired outcomes—a notion that we think applies to corporate goodness as well.[5] Suppose, for example, that a corporation intends to assist survivors of a natural disaster by donating food to them. Now suppose that the food is not properly stored and handled by some intermediary distributors, resulting in a number of people suffering from food poisoning. Examining the situation through a consequentialist lens, one might conclude that the company had done wrong because of the negative outcomes of its charity. Alternatively, one could argue that the corporation's actions were good because they were driven by the good intention of assisting people in need. Put simply, we recognize that bad outcomes can occur despite good intentions.

On the other hand, good outcomes can occur despite bad intentions. For instance, we would not consider a company good if it intends to take advantage of lenient or nonexistent labor laws by opening a factory in a third world country, submitting employees there to harsh work environments and unfair wages. Arguably, because sweatshop workers frequently have no alternatives for work, the opening of such a factory can improve the lives of individuals who work there by providing wages where none existed. Nevertheless, the company has not intended to help the people; rather, its intention was to prey upon a vulnerable and needy population to minimize labor costs. Because the company's intentions are bad, it should not be credited as being good.

In many instances, people and corporations do not necessarily have good or bad intentions, but rather have no intention other than to fulfill self-serving purposes. These morally neutral intentions, nonetheless, may be associated with outcomes that could be deemed good or bad. Even under such circumstances, we claim that a good outcome should not be used to infer goodness. Good intentions are critical to the moral goodness of both people and corporations. Goodness is that which derives not from good outcomes, but from the *explicit intention* to do good. To illustrate this point, consider the following question: Should one judge a woman to be good if she tosses her shabby, ill-fitting clothes into the garbage and a homeless person finds and wears them? As a more organizationally relevant example, envision a pharmaceutical company that profits by developing a miracle disease-curing drug. Curing the sick certainly is a positive outcome, but this alone does not make the company good in our view; profits, not necessarily the intent to help others, may have driven development of the drug. What would one infer if the company stopped production of the drug if the venture was no longer profitable—if most of the people with the disease could not afford the drug? Similarly, what would one infer about a pharmaceutical company that possessed the capabilities to develop such a drug but does not do so because a relatively small number of people are afflicted by the disease (see Clinton, 2004) or because of costly research and development (Abating, or exploding, 2004)—both of which would undermine profits (Abating, or exploding, 2004)? Personally, we would label such companies decent; they are profiting through legal means, but they are not going above and beyond the basic level of functioning to serve societal needs. At the extreme, Aristotle might describe such corporations as parasites—the word he used to refer to business conducted solely for selfish gains (as cited in Solomon, 1994, p. 50). Likewise, Blackburn (2001) argued that people who obey God's commandments for the self-serving reasons of avoiding "horrendous punishments" and gaining "delicious rewards" are not practicing religion for the good and right reason:

It is not good enough if I think: "Well, let me see, the gains are such-and-such, but now I have to factor in the chance of God hitting me hard if I do it. On the other hand, God is forgiving and there is a good chance I can fob him off by confession...." These are not the thoughts of a good character. (p. 16)

In conclusion, we reiterate that good intentions rather than good outcomes are critical to defining the concept of corporate goodness. We have alluded to the notion that good actions are those actions driven by good intentions. Below we explain that good actions too are crucial to defining corporate goodness.

CLUE 3: GOOD CORPORATIONS WALK THE TALK

The third clue to defining corporate goodness is short and sweet—or short, at the least. Good intentions are not enough; for a corporation to be good, good actions also are necessary. More explicitly, intentions not supported by actions are vacuous. The idea that both intentions and actions are necessary to define goodness is consistent with Kant (1785/2002), who wrote of actions that follow from respect for moral law (i.e., good intentions). The notion that actions should follow intentions is supported not only by philosophy, but also by folk morals like "practice what you preach" or "walk the talk." Such sayings reflect societal cynicism of people and corporations who voice laudable intentions and make big promises, but then do not follow through. Holding good intentions often is easier than acting on them. For one thing, enacting intentions typically requires a bigger commitment in terms of time and resources—and in some cases courage, too—than merely believing in or stating them.

Outside the realm of goodness, many of us, as individuals, have difficulty carrying through with intentions such as exercising, quitting smoking, or even organizing the hall closet. Until we move from intentions to actions, however, can we consider ourselves to be healthy or organized? Likewise, should an organization within the restaurant industry be deemed good if it states opposition to the exploitation of farm workers but purchases produce from farmers that rely on underpaid immigrants and sharecroppers to harvest their crops (see Cockburn, 2003; Schlosser, 2003)? If actions do not follow from good intentions, one can infer that other intentions have taken priority over the initial good intentions. For example, corporate intentions to conserve time, money, or other resources might overcome its good intentions to refrain from contributing to the plight of migrant workers, thus preventing action that supports those intentions.

In sum, then, we have argued in Clue 3 that intentions without actions are void; as such, a good corporation is one that follows good intentions with supportive actions. In the next section, we begin to illuminate the content of good intentions and actions.

CLUE 4: GOODNESS IS NOT CONTENT-FREE

Goodness, to this point, has been described in terms of intentions and actions. Missing, however, is an articulation as to the specific *content* of goodness; that is, how can one determine whether a particular intention or action is a good one? Our claim that a good corporation is one with good intentions and actions is relatively meaningless unless we know what is meant by *good* (see Soule, 2002). In searching for such meaning, we again turned to philosophy and religion, and we noticed a number of recurring themes. For example, words like *honesty, compassion, justice, wisdom, moderation, courage, fidelity*, and *charity* appeared repeatedly in discussions of the goodness and virtue of individuals (e.g., Aristotle, 384–322 B.C.E./1984; Franklin, 1790/1962; Kant, 1785/1964; Kofi Annan in Ramo, 2000; Petersen & Seligman, 2004; Stackhouse, McCann, Roels, & Williams, 1995). Commenting on this convergence, a number of scholars (e.g., Donaldson & Dunfee, 1999; Langlois & Schlegelmich, 1990; Pincoffs, 1986; Stackhouse et al., 1995) have concluded that the world's religions and philosophies largely agree on the content of goodness. Kant (1785/1964), in fact, believed that certain moral principles are universally self-evident, or inherently known by all people—a point echoed by Moore (1903).

Compassion, wisdom, courage, honesty, and the other contents of goodness can be thought of as either intentions or actions; that is, one can *intend* to be courageous and one can actually *act* courageously, for example, by blowing the whistle on unethical behavior at work. From here on, we shall refer to the content (or focus) of good intentions and actions as good or moral "virtues."[6] In the remainder of this clue, we will elaborate briefly on the virtue of charity to exemplify what we mean by the content of goodness.

Charity

Charity, or the giving of money, time, or other resources to those in need, is a widely recognized virtue. Aristotle (ca. 384–322 B.C.E./1984), for instance, espoused generosity as a virtue, and W. D. Ross (1930) listed beneficence—a concept similar to charity—as a duty by which one should abide. Outside of philosophy, the world's religions seem to agree that to give is better than to receive. For example, charity is one of the five pillars of Islam; the Koran instructs followers to be charitable: "Give in alms of the wealth you have lawfully earned and of that which we have brought out of the earth for you" (2:267). Mosaic law instructs followers to distribute God's resources such to provide all people with the necessities to live even if they cannot provide anything in return: "When you reap the harvest of your land, you shall not reap to the very edges of your field.... You shall not strip your vineyard bare, or gather the fallen grapes of your vineyard; you shall leave them for the poor" (Leviticus 19:9–10, Holy Bible).

Moreover, Jesus taught through his telling of the story of Lazarus that charity is the obligation of his followers (Luke 16:20–31, Holy Bible). Giving anonymously, for example, is an especially honorable form of giving, as it is not done to boost one's reputation and can also prevent embarrassment on the part of the recipient.

Despite relative consensus that charity is good at the individual level, charity at the corporate level has been criticized by those who argue that the primary obligation of the corporation is to make money for its shareholders—a criticism voiced most notably, perhaps, by Milton Friedman (1970, 1988), recipient of the 1976 Nobel Memorial Prize for economics. Many, however, fervently oppose Friedman's view (e.g., Cavanagh, 1984; Evan & Freeman, 1988; Schlosser, 2003). Legal precedent too contradicts the belief that a corporation's sole duty is to its shareholders. For example, President Roosevelt's tax act of 1936 helped legitimize corporate giving by allowing corporations to deduct charitable contributions of up to 5% of pretax profit from their federal income taxes. Almost 20 years later, when A. P. Smith Manufacturing Company was sued by a shareholder for donating money to Princeton University, the New Jersey Supreme Court ruled in favor of A. P. Smith, asserting that corporate donations do not have to provide a direct benefit to the company. Today, corporate giving not only is accepted, but is almost expected by some consumers (for instance, see Margolis & Walsh, 2003).

For these reasons, we assert that charity can be thought of as virtue that guides the intentions and actions of both individuals and corporations. Charity ranges from giving begrudgingly to giving freely and abundantly to giving such that others may be self-reliant and no longer in need of charity (Salamon, 2003)—the latter type of giving being more consistent with the teachings of religions such as Christianity, Islam, and Judaism. As such, a good corporation does not give begrudgingly; rather, its words and deeds are directed at helping others become independent in ways that avoid recipients feeling shame or disparagement (Kahaner, 2003): "Charity vaunteth not itself, is not puffed up" (I Corinthians 13:4, Holy Bible). Additionally, a good corporation does not engage in charity only to advance the corporation's economic agenda or to gain approval from consumers: "To be charitable in public is good, but to give alms to the poor in private is better" (2:267, Koran).

Other Virtues and the Vagueness of Virtues

As noted previously, a number of moral principles are common to various religions and philosophical perspectives (e.g., compassion, fidelity, and justice). Above, we have illustrated charity as an exemplar of that which philosophers and theologians recognize to be the content of goodness. We will not elaborate on the other virtues, in part due to the interest of space, but also because we view any finite list of moral virtues as neither comprehensive nor useful for practical application. Previous attempts of such listings (e.g., Aristotle, 384–322 B.C.E./1984; Franklin, 1790/1962) have proven incomprehensive; despite considerable overlap, no two lists contain the exact same content (but see Soule, 2002).

Even if a comprehensive list of virtues could be compiled, we are doubtful of its utility. Arguably, a list of virtues does not tell one how to act upon these virtues or which virtue is most relevant in a particular situation (e.g., Berlin, 1991; Tetlock, 1986). These shortcomings seriously call into question the usefulness of such a list. Consistent with this point, Hosmer (1987) criticized corporate ethical codes because they do not prioritize the moral virtues that are most important, and it is this prioritization that reflects the true values of a corporation. In other words, a company can list honesty and compassion as virtues in its ethical code, but if the two virtues conflict in a particular situation, the virtues alone do not dictate a resolution or course of action.

Such conflicts among virtues are not uncommon. For example, University of Iowa Hospital employees recently were fired for knowingly lying and breaking the law by giving away expensive medications of deceased patients to patients who could not afford them (O'Neal, 2004). The employees were acting in accordance with the virtue of charity, but in doing so, they were acting in a dishonest and criminal manner. To further illustrate this point, we tell the story common in philosophy primers of a mother who lies to a deranged gunman concerning the whereabouts of her children (see Bok, 1989). Is the mother obligated, according to good virtue, to tell the gunman the truth? Honesty appears to be a universally valued moral virtue (Hart, 1961, as cited in Paine, 2003; Stackhouse et al., 1995), yet most of us would insist that the mother is obligated to protect her children by being dishonest. Honesty, it seems, is something that is "generally desirable" (see Pincoffs, 1986), but not always more desirable than other moral virtues, such as compassion and justice, a point recognized even by the typically obstinate Augustine and Kant (but see Bok, 1989). Augustine, for example, acknowledged that some lies were more excusable (though not allowable) than others. Thus, we suspect that Augustine would "excuse" the lying mother more readily than he would a corporation that lies about toxic chemicals it is dumping in a nearby river to avoid fines.

As with the virtue of honesty, we question whether the virtue of charity should be applied blindly such as if a corporation donates to the Ku Klux Klan. Personally, we would not consider charity to be good in this case because of the Klan's egregious posture toward people who are Black, Catholic, or Jewish. Here, charity conflicts, for example, with compassion and justice. Discussing the current struggle to secure both personal security and liberty in the war on terror, Amnesty International U.S. Executive Director William Schulz (2004) lamented: "If you try to pursue two or more virtues at the same time, you may need to compromise one of them or the other" (p. 20). Thus, choosing between virtuous intentions and translating the chosen intention into action can pose a significant challenge.

Thus, despite general agreement about the contents of goodness, any listing of virtues quickly becomes cumbersome, if not meaningless, in some circumstances. As such, without an overarching set of guidelines to organize and prioritize virtues, one is often left wondering exactly how to apply virtues or even if they should be applied in the first place. In the next clue, we will explain further the issue of conflicting virtues and attempt a resolution. Before moving on, however, it is important to reiterate the value of moral virtues to defining corporate goodness. Simply, without these virtues, intentions and actions are morally content-free. Virtues tell us, at least in a broad sense, what intentions and actions are to be considered good. However, like intentions and actions, virtues are necessary, but not sufficient, to defining corporate goodness.

CLUE 5: GOODNESS ENTAILS PRINCIPLED REASONING

With this clue, we pick up where the last clue left off; specifically, we intend to address how a good corporation translates moral virtues into specific intentions and actions. We build upon our recognition of the potential for moral conflict and, in doing so, suggest principles that enable a good corporation to reason through potential conflicts among good intentions and also to "walk the talk" by translating good intentions into good actions.

Discussed below are those decision principles that appeared most dominant in our readings and most applicable to weighing intentions and translating intentions into actions. Although the decision principles are presented as distinct, in actuality they can be viewed as a family of related principles. This point is important, because we would expect that regardless of the specific decision principle adopted, the conclusions reached or actions chosen could arguably be construed as good. Moreover, and most important, these decision principles are salient to our current purpose for they contribute to framing the definition of the good corporation; that is, part of being a good corporation entails relying upon the sorts of principles outlined below.

Decision Principle 1: The Golden Rule

We suspect that the first principle to be described—the "golden rule"—will be familiar to most readers. According to Morris (1997), the golden rule is present in some variation in all of the world's cultures and religions (see also Blackburn, 2001). In Judaism and Christianity, for example, the golden rule is stated as "Do unto others as you would have them do unto you." The Buddhist variant reads: "See for others the happiness you desire for yourself. Hurt not others with that which pains you." Islamic followers are taught: "No one of you is a believer until he loves for his brother what he loves for himself" (Morris, 1997, pp. 146–147).

The golden rule, of course, advises against unethical or hurtful behavior, but importantly, it also encourages us to be good to others in the same way we would want them to be good to us. Volunteering to cover the work of a sick colleague, for example, is a good action that most of us would want someone to do for us if we were in need of such assistance. Organizationally, the rule would imply, for example, that managers treat employees with the same respect and dignity with which they would want to be treated. A commendable example of the golden rule in action is the policies and procedures at SAS Institute, which is the world's largest privately held software company and consistently appears on *Fortune* magazine's list of best employers. Fishman (1999) reported that SAS has implemented a 7-hour workday and a limitless supply of sick days—concepts foreign to most of today's American workers. The company touts other benefits, including state-of-the-art fitness equipment and classes, as well as a company health clinic. Commenting on the rationale behind the company's exemplary treatment of employees, CEO and cofounder Jim Goodnight cites golden rule-like reasoning: "What we tried to do was to treat people who joined the company as we ourselves wanted to be treated" (in Pfeffer, 1998, p. 5).

Although the golden rule does not always provide a simple solution to the often difficult problems of weighing and enacting intentions, it is a straightforward message recognized by people throughout the world. As such, it may appeal intuitively to corporate decision makers, leading them to more thoroughly evaluate their intentions and actions. For instance, the golden rule does not solve a supervisor's dilemma in deciding whether to give a raise to a mediocre performer who supports four children on his own (virtue of compassion), or to an excellent performer who supports only herself (virtue of justice). Rather, it offers a familiar means of reasoning by which to evaluate the situation from the perspective of the parties involved and to consider what might constitute a good course of action.

Decision Principle 2: Kant's Universalization Test

Similar to but more comprehensive than the golden rule is Kant's (1785/1964) "universalization test." "Act only on that maxim through which you can at the same time will that it should become a universal law" (p. 88).[7] An action cannot be morally good if it, stated as a maxim, cannot be a universal law (i.e., an imperative for every person in every situation); it cannot be a universal law if it would be logically incoherent or contradictory (Bowie, 1999).[8] In part, Kant's universalization test suggests that we should act (or not act) in a way that we would want everyone to act (or not act). On the surface, this principle sounds much like the golden rule, yet according to Ciulla (2003), it is a "more detailed rendering" (p. 94). For example, use of the golden rule entails thinking only in terms of the self and the other persons directly involved in a situation. In contrast, the universalization test requires one to think beyond these parties, imagining *all people* carrying out the act in question.

To illustrate his principle, Kant used the example of an insincere promise. Suppose, for example, that a supervisor promises an employee that she will be promoted to a job for which the supervisor knows there will not be an opening. Such a promise, according to Kant, is immoral because the supervisor could not will logically that everyone make promises without intent to fulfill them. For Kant, the ethicality of insincere promises hinges on the question of whether as a universal law the maxim would be contradictory, as indeed it is; if everyone broke promises, promises would be meaningless and people would stop making them. Thus, as a universal law, insincere promises make no sense and, according to Kant, are therefore immoral. Other types of lying not uncommon in the business world also are shown to be immoral by Kant's universalization test. Take, for example, what is euphemistically known as "cooking the books" or "aggressive/optimistic accounting." Suppose that a chief financial officer thinks to herself, "I will fraudulently report my company's profits when not doing so could result in negative consequences for my company and myself." As a universal law, however, cooking the books is incoherent; corporations operate on the expectation of fair exchange, and fair exchange is based in part upon accurate financial reports. If all corporations were to fraudulently report their finances, then there would be no expectation of fair exchange, and a fundamental assumption of commerce would be undermined. Because cooking the books would be self-contradictory as a universal law, Kant would argue that it is an immoral activity.

In the examples above, use of the universalization test identified bad behavior, but more germanely, its use, like the golden rule, also can lead to goodness. For instance, Kant (1785/2002) described a case in which a wealthy man, upon witnessing a poor and struggling man, thinks: "What do I care? … I won't deprive him of anything … but I don't feel like contributing anything to his well-being or to helping him in his distress" (p. 224). To Kant, such thinking and lack of helping fails the universalization test. If the man were to will that everyone thought and acted as he did, this universal law would be incoherent and self-contradictory; all people, at some time or another, need the help of another person, whether in the form of monetary assistance, emotional support, medical care, and so forth. As such, moral goodness derives not from merely going about one's business and avoiding harm to others; rather, it comes from actively helping people when they need it. Reflecting this idea, Bob Dunn, past vice president of Levi Strauss and current chairperson of the nonprofit organization Business for Social Responsibility, has argued that if companies only meet minimal ethical standards, "our society is the worse for it. It would be like citizens saying 'the only responsibility I have as a citizen is not to violate the law. I'm not required to vote, so I'm not going to do that. I'm not required by law to make the schools better in my community, so

I won't bother.' We have to think about what kind of a society we want to have" (as cited in Makower, 1994, p. 227). Returning to religion, an analogous theme is depicted in the Judeo-Christian story of brothers Cain and Abel. After Cain murdered Abel, God asked Cain where his brother was, to which Cain responded, "I know not, am I my brother's keeper?" (Genesis 4:9, Holy Bible). The response to Cain's question undoubtedly is yes. This theme is depicted elsewhere in the Bible: "Whoever has the world's goods, and beholds his brother in need and closes his heart against him, how does the love of God abide in him?" (John 3:17).

The universalization test also can be applied in the environmental domain. Picture, for instance, that a corporation operates under the maxim "we will use the earth's finite resources with no attempt to preserve or replenish them." Although a corporation might gain financially under this mode of operation, it cannot rationally will that every corporation act according to the same maxim. Such a universal law would be incoherent because corporations depend on these very resources to exist, and with no efforts to preserve or replenish them, they will be eradicated. Corporations, if operating according to the universalization test, would act to protect and preserve the environment.[9]

An example of corporate goodness regarding the environment is Aveda, a cosmetics and hair care company that was the first American corporation to sign the Coalition for Environmentally Responsible Economies (CERES) principles. These principles guide corporate behavior toward environmental sustainability and include goals of protecting the biosphere and environmental restoration. Key to our current discussion of goodness, the CERES principles not only condemn actions harmful to the environment, but also advocate actions that benefit the environment. Aveda proclaims: "Our mission at Aveda is to care for the world we live in, from the products we make to the ways in which we give back to society. At Aveda, we strive to set an example of environmental leadership and responsibility, not just in the world of beauty, but around the world" (Rechelbacher, n.d.). Reasoning suggestive of the universalization test is reflected in the latter portion of the mission; the company strives to be a role model in the environmental domain, acting in a ways that it hopes would become a universal law followed by all corporations. Again, corporate goodness is that which goes beyond merely upholding the law. Use of the universalization test as a decision principle in weighing intentions and actions can help corporations move beyond decency toward goodness by considering the implications of one's actions if all people were to engage in the same behavior.

Decision Principle 3: The Respect Principle

Kant's (1785/2002) "respect principle" asserts that one should "act in such a way that you always treat humanity, whether in your own person or in the person of any other, never simply as a means, but always at the same time as an end." Reflecting a similar perspective, Jewish theologian Martin Buber (1923/1987) distinguishes between I–It relations, in which people are valued only if they fulfill some need or purpose, and I-Thou relations, in which people are regarded as intrinsically valuable regardless of any outcomes or services they can provide. Consistent with Kant and Buber, the respect principle applied to corporations would focus on respecting and valuing people—employees, customers, and humanity in general—not merely as a means to profits, but also simply for being people. Thus, a good corporation's intentions and actions support human dignity by treating individuals as valued ends in and of themselves.

A corporate example of the respect principle in action is the well-known Tylenol recall invoked by Johnson & Johnson after the drug was linked to the deaths of seven people in Chicago (see Foster, 1999). The company responded immediately by contacting the Food and Drug Administration as well as the media to caution consumers about the potential danger. But why did Johnson & Johnson choose this course of action? Reportedly, upon hearing about the Tylenol-related deaths, Johnson & Johnson executives turned to the company credo for answers. The credo, which was written in the mid-1940s by Robert Wood Johnson, who cofounded and then led the company for nearly 50 years, contains elements similar to the respect principle. The first line of the credo reads: "We believe our first responsibility is to the doctors, nurses, and patients, to mothers and fathers and all others who use our products and services." This statement reflects Johnson's consideration of consumers as more than a source of revenue, as more than a means to an ends—a consideration that seems to have played a role in the decision to recall Tylenol. The credo also states: "Everyone must be considered as an individual. We must respect their dignity and recognize their merit.... We must be mindful of ways to help all employees fulfill family responsibilities." Clearly, this statement reflects Johnson & Johnson's commitment to treating people as ends, not merely as means.

Another corporate example of respecting people as valuable ends rather than merely as means to profits comes from Cummins, Inc. At its San Luis Potosi, Mexico, location, the Cummins Engine Foundation funds an educational training program to teach blind people carpentry skills and to help them gain employment (Asmus, 2003). In Brazil, where poor children were stealing scrap metal from the company's plant, Cummins responded by building a local school and community health center for the children and their parents. In its hometown of Columbus, Indiana, Cummins Engine Foundation has revitalized the community by footing the bill for architectural fees for more than 50 new public buildings (Makower, 1994). Use of respect principle-like reasoning is reflected in Cummins' vision of "making people's lives better by unleashing the Power of Cummins" (Cummins, Inc., n.d.).

Thus, as Johnson & Johnson and Cummins exemplify, good corporations consider how to treat people as valued ends rather than just as a means to profits. As such, in deciding, for instance, whether to make use of limited funds by making charitable donations to a worthy cause, the good corporation would focus on the importance of treating people as ends in themselves, rather than gaining public attention and approval. Like the golden rule and the universalization test, principled reasoning aligned with the respect principle is indicative of a corporation's goodness.

Decision Principle 4: The Original Position

We have lamented the fact that moral values will at times conflict with one another (e.g., Ross, 1930). In addition to the decision principles reviewed earlier, a solution to this dilemma that a good corporation might employ is supplied by philosopher John Rawls' (1971, 1993) notion of the "original position." The original position is a hypothetical situation in which reasonable and rational individuals can generate principles of justice from behind a "veil of ignorance," meaning that they are ignorant with regard to their place in society (e.g., race, gender, intelligence, personality, religion, physical capacities, and so forth).[10] The veil of ignorance helps ensure that reasonable and rational people will not unfairly favor particular groups or individuals when deciding on a scheme for distributing basic goods in a just manner.

An oft-used analogy (e.g., Hartman, 1996) to Rawls' proposal is one in which two people sharing a piece of cake do so fairly by one person slicing the cake and the other person choosing his or her half. The cake slicer knows that she should try her best to divide the cake as fairly as possible because the cake chooser can select the larger piece. What this example makes clear is that the primary issue facing the hypothetical parties in the original position is the fair distribution of a finite quantity of goods. Hartman (1996) has related the Rawlsian societal strategy to organizations by arguing that "a morally sound organization is one that would be designed by a group of people who value being free and politically equal and desire to be responsible citizens, who know they are going to represent stakeholders of the organization but do not know which kind" (p. 109).

Rawls (1971) argued that in the original position, behind the veil of ignorance, reasonable and rational individuals would agree to two principles of justice with the aim of assuring a fair distribution of basic goods. The first is that of greatest equal liberty: "Each person is to have an equal right to the most extensive scheme of equal basic liberties compatible with a similar scheme of liberties for others" (p. 53). In other words, barring the infringement of another's rights, individuals should be allowed to enjoy such freedoms as those of person, speech, and thought. The second is that of the fair distribution of goods and opportunities: "Social and economic inequalities are to be arranged so that they are both (a) reasonably expected to be to everyone's advantage, and (b) attached to positions and offices open to all" (p. 53). These principles derived by Rawls reveal a key advantage of applying the original position to corporate decisions—the provision of the fair distribution of goods and opportunities and the provision of individuals' rights. Given our previous argument against a consequentialist approach to understanding corporate goodness, we are particularly interested in Rawls's principle of greatest equal liberty.

Rawls obviously is not alone in advocating the importance of individual rights. The United Nations' Universal Declaration of Human Rights (1948) upholds, for all people, such basic rights as life, liberty, property, and free speech. The declaration outlines principles of justice that are particularly pertinent for corporations. It states, for instance, that businesses should support and protect human rights and that businesses should grant employees the right to association and collective bargaining. Additionally, the declaration affirms that all people have the right to work, the right to "just and favourable conditions of work," and "the right to rest and leisure, including ... periodic holidays with pay." Notably, religious leaders and organizations such as the National Conference of Catholic Bishops and Pope John XXIII have issued statements paralleling those of the United Nations regarding inalienable human rights, arguing that people should be free to pursue their own fulfillment.

While the Catholic Bishops' proclamation and the United Nations' declaration, as well as similar other statements regarding basic human rights, are meant to apply to all people, societies do exist in which these ideals are not widely realized due to variance in cultural practices and norms. This fact poses a dilemma for companies that operate globally: Should they apply their own country's standards for ethical business conduct or those of their host countries (see Donaldson & Dunfee, 1999, for a discussion of this issue)? The particular danger represented in this dilemma is that companies will adopt a relativistic stance, which is problematic for reasons articulated by Donaldson and Dunfee:

> The relativist view is grounded in the assumption that a person or culture *believing* an act is morally correct, helps *make* it morally correct—or at least to make it correct for *that* person or *that* culture. In its pure form, relativism would allow any individual or community to define ethically correct behavior in any way they wished. No matter how inhumane, no matter how bizarre, their ethics would be on a par with everyone else's. (1999, p. 20)

Conceivably, badly intentioned companies can use relativism to justify taking advantage of vulnerable worker populations in poor countries, offering them only a fraction of the pay workers in their own, more wealthy countries would receive, as well as subjecting them to working conditions that would be illegal in their own countries.

Bowie (1996) addressed the issue of differing societal practices concluding that "the mere fact that a culture considers a practice moral does not mean that it is moral" (p. 93). Blackburn (2001) too criticized "moral relativism," arguing that we should not take differences in societal practices to mean that all practices are morally equivalent. He also noted that not all people within a society necessarily support its practices: "After all, it is typically only the oppressors who are spokespersons for *their* culture.... It is not the slaves who value slavery" (p. 27). Thus, if individuals considered the issue from the perspective of the original position, slavery and other systems that deny certain people basic liberties would not exist because reasonable and rational people would not agree to a conception of justice that would allow their enslavement or their basic liberties to be otherwise limited.

But if not relativism, then what is the answer to globally operating companies' question of whose standards to apply? Donaldson (1989) indirectly supplied an answer by discussing the minimal duties of multinational corporations in dealing with the issue of fundamental rights. He argued that "it would be unfair, not to mention unreasonable, to hold corporations to the same standards for enhancing and protecting social welfare to which we hold civil governments" (p. 172). While we agree that corporations likely cannot and perhaps should not be required to promote social welfare, this is, in fact, a prime example of what we mean by corporate goodness: going above and beyond the minimal duties of not violating laws and protecting individual rights.

Decent corporations are those that do not violate the rights of or act unjustly toward employees, the public, or shareholders, but good corporations are those that, beyond merely upholding their own obligations to stakeholders, actually attempt, consistent with the application of the original position as a decision procedure, to promote human rights. For instance, a good corporation operating in Africa, where as many as 28 nations practice female genital mutilation, might develop an educational program to protect women from this painful and dangerous custom (Amnesty International, 1997). Likewise, a good corporation located in Nigeria, where women and children are commonly forced into prostitution ("Sick and Tired About Lying", 2004), might provide job training and assistance in finding safe and legitimate employment for these individuals.

While these examples might seem far-fetched, we are not alone in making such suggestions (see Cockburn, 2003). In all of these examples, the corporations are deemed good because they were not directly responsible for the subjected women and children, but acted nevertheless. The original position decision principle encourages corporations to move beyond the immediate concern of survival and profits by requiring decision makers to imagine that their position in society is not fixed or secure. As a result, members of traditionally privileged groups (e.g., White males) might make more aggressive attempts to correct past and prevent future injustices. Weighing intentions and actions based on principled reasoning reflective of the original position is suggestive of a corporation's goodness.

Synopsis of Principled Reasoning

The objective of Clue 5 was to present a number of reasoning principles that corporate decision makers might utilize in selecting and enacting intentions. Because good intentions frequently conflict and strategies for enacting intentions are not always clear, a good corporation will engage in principled reasoning to resolve such dilemmas. Here, we have identified the golden rule, Kant's universalization test and respect principle, and Rawls's original position as decision principles that might be employed for such purposes. Importantly, these principles were selected for discussion not because we believe them to be the exclusive means by which to engage in principled reasoning, but because they (1) are prominent within philosophy and religion, (2) are readily applicable to corporations, and (3) do not require a strict focus on outcomes (as prohibited by Clue 2). Accordingly, corporations may engage in principled reasoning that fit these criteria but were not noted here. Moreover, decision makers do not need to explicitly recognize the intricate details of each principle or be able to quote them verbatim so long as they engage in reasoning characteristic of the types of principles discussed here. Rather, we believe it possible that decision makers without any formal training in ethics and who are completely unaware of the specific decision rules stated herein can nevertheless engage in some sort of principled reasoning. Moreover, due to the limitations of focusing purely on lists of virtues, or the content of goodness, we assert that good corporations will in fact engage in principled reasoning.

SYNOPSIS OF CLUES

Through a series of five clues we have attempted to map the territory of corporate goodness. In doing so, we have ascertained what goodness is not; specifically, it is not merely the absence of badness, nor is it defined by good outcomes. Instead, good intentions and good actions were identified as critical components of corporate goodness. In further delineating the intentions and actions of the good corporation, we have noted several moral virtues (charity in particular) as well as decision principles (e.g., the golden rule) by which to weigh conflicting intentions and virtues and to translate good intentions into good actions. In the following section, we compare and contrast our crude construal of corporate goodness with similar constructs in the organizational literature in order to further delineate its meaning.

DIFFERENTIATING CORPORATE GOODNESS FROM SIMILAR CONSTRUCTS

In introducing this chapter, we noted the discrepancy between scholarly attention devoted to negative and positive organizational phenomena. At the same time, we recognized several recent attempts to remedy this situation—in particular, the well-established corporate social responsibility literature and the burgeoning positive organizational scholarship movement (e.g., Cameron et al., 2003). Below, we address key differences between corporate goodness and two other positive constructs represented in those literatures.

Corporate Social Responsibility and Corporate Social Performance

The terms *corporate social responsibility* (CSR) and *corporate social performance* (CSP) have become catchphrases in both the academic literature and popular press (e.g., Cochran & Wood, 1984; Griffin & Mahon, 1997; Makower, 1994; Ruf, Muralidhar, & Paul, 1998; Stevenson, 1996; Wood, 1991). CSR largely refers to processes and principles, and CSP refers to actions. Despite common usage of the CSP and CSR terminology, there is little agreement as to their exact meaning. CSR, for example, sometimes is taken to mean fulfilling basic social obligations and refraining from unethical behavior, while at other times it is held to a more rigorous standard of positively impacting society. Obviously, the former is not what we mean by corporate goodness.

By and large, CSR research and initiatives are focused on the relationship between social and financial performance (e.g., Menon & Kahn, 2003; Orlitzky, Schmidt, & Rynes, 2003). We, however, dismiss this work as exemplifying what we are not interested in pursuing. Like Margolis and Walsh (2003) and Paine (2003), we believe that questions of whether "ethics pays" are misguided and can send the wrong message:

> On the surface "ethics pays" seems to endorse values. At a deeper level, it is doing just the opposite.… Managers who base their appeal solely on the financial benefits of ethical commitment are only reinforcing the patterns of reasoning and justification that make it difficult for people to take moral considerations seriously. (Paine, 2003, p. 135)

While we certainly do not consider financial gains that may occur as a side effect of goodness to be a bad thing, we emphasize that corporate goodness cannot be justified by profits. Unlike CSR, corporate goodness is an end in and of itself; moreover, we hope that researchers pay heed to the advice of Margolis and Walsh (2003), who suggest investigations of the conditions under which organizations can and do have a positive impact on society, rather than the conditions under which organizations profit from CSR efforts. However, because Margolis and Walsh are concerned with outcomes (albeit at the societal rather than the corporate level), even this line of research is qualitatively different from what we would envision research on corporate goodness to look like; in particular, corporate goodness research should entail an emphasis on intentions, actions, and decision principles rather than outcomes—societal or otherwise. Thus, both definitionally and in terms of how CSR and CSP have been treated in the literature, they are distinct from our vision of corporate goodness. Arguably, conceptions of CSR and CSP often reflect a more traditional view of the role of corporations in society than does the notion of goodness, which is intended to embrace a higher moral standard and encourage a different research path.

Positive Deviance

In comparison with CSR and CSP, positive deviance is a new term that has yet to be adopted widely outside the positive organizational scholarship movement (e.g., Quinn, 1996; Quinn & Quinn, 2002). Spreitzer and Sonenshein (2003b) define it as "intentional behaviors that depart from the norms of a referent group in honorable ways" (p. 209). Quinn (1996) defines deviance in more statistical terms, but the message remains the same: Positive characteristics or behaviors are a form of deviance. Of course, a corporation that deviates positively from its peers is not necessarily good because the entire lot could be scoundrels; thus, we would not equate corporate goodness with positive deviance. A related difficulty with the deviance concept is that it does not allow for goodness to be the norm among corporations. That is, if being good means being deviant from other organizations, then there necessarily must be organizations that are not good. Consequently, the ideal of all corporations being good ones becomes incoherent when goodness is defined in relativistic terms.

For these reasons, we see clear distinctions between the construct of corporate goodness and existing positive constructs like corporate social responsibility and positive deviance. Whereas corporate goodness focuses on intentions, actions, and decision principles, other constructs place great emphasis on outcomes and, in the case of positive deviance, only allow for a fraction of companies to be considered good, and only then in a relative sense. Now that we have addressed what corporate goodness looks like (in the previous section) and what it does not look like (in the current section), we turn to issues of measurement.

MEASURING CORPORATE GOODNESS

Naturally, because we derived our notion of goodness from the literature to which ethicists typically attend, our construct is closely aligned with the ideas found there. Ethicists, however, likely would view corporate goodness as more exclusively normative than we do (see Donaldson, 2003); our bent as organizational scholars, in contrast, is to approach the construct as an object of descriptive, empirical study. Therefore, in this section, we turn—briefly and tentatively—from conceptual to measurement issues, considering how corporate goodness might be assessed. Although we provide some answers, we also present issues and pose questions with which we have become intrigued and would love to see researchers pursue.

Discerning Goodness From Reputation

The first issue we raise stems from our concern with the import of separating indices of a corporation's *reputation* from those of its *goodness*. That is, one might assume a pharmaceutical company to be good merely because its products alleviate pain. Please recall, however, our argument that a pharmaceutical company might be interested in helping the sick only to the extent that doing so is profitable. More generally, one might conclude falsely that a corporation with a reputation for being good is, in fact, good. We fear, as lamented by Shakespeare, "Reputation is an idle and most false imposition; oft got without merit, and lost without deserving" (*Othello*, Act 2, Scene 3). Substantiating our fears is research suggesting that the two primary determinants of a corporation's reputation are its economic performance and its variability in profits (Fombrun & Shanley, 1990)—neither of which has much, if anything, to do with goodness. Although we do not discount the merit of current indices of corporate reputation, we do view them with healthy skepticism. Unlike such indices, our intent in measuring goodness is neither to assess outcomes nor to sing the praises of good corporations; rather, the goal is to describe and understand corporations' intentions, actions, and decision strategies.

Multilevel Measurement: Intentions, Actions, and Principled Reasoning

As illustrated by our "corporation as person" analogy, corporate goodness is a construct existing at multiple levels; although it is ultimately a corporate-level phenomenon, corporate goodness has its roots in the intentions, actions, and principled reasoning of individuals. Given its multilevel nature, opportunities for measuring corporate goodness exist at both the individual and organizational levels. At the individual level, measuring corporate goodness could be achieved by surveying organizational members, asking them to report relevant intentions, actions, and decision principles used. Alternatively, one could employ policy capturing methodologies (see Brief & Aldag, 1994) by presenting work scenarios to people and asking them to select one of a number of actions that reflect various good intentions, like honesty, wisdom, and courage. Researchers could instruct the individuals to "talk out" their thoughts while deciding which action to take—information that could be content analyzed to determine if the individuals were engaging in any of the reasoning principles discussed here (e.g., Smith-Crowe, 2004). For yet greater realism, one could ask people to recall actual instances in which they had to make moral decisions and the reasoning used to arrive at their decisions. Whatever method used in collecting individual-level data, the data will have to be aggregated to the corporate level as specified by a theoretically relevant composition model (Chan, 1998). Likely, aggregation can be reasonably justified on the basis of agreement among organizational members (e.g., Burke & Dunlap, 2002; Burke, Finkelstein, & Dusig, 1999; Dunlap, Burke, Smith-Crowe, 2003); an organization characterized by people enacting good intentions on the basis of principled reasoning is a good organization.

At the corporate level of analysis, researchers might turn to more objective indicators of corporate goodness, such as corporate mission statements or the percentage of profits allocated to charity. We recognize the potential disconnect between a corporation's publicly voiced intentions, such as in a mission statement, and its true intentions. Thus, actions that follow from good intentions will become critical in inferring the sincerity of stated intentions. Regarding corporate-level measurement of principled reasoning, we look to the Bradford studies (e.g., Cray, Mallory, Butler, Hickson, & Wilson, 1991), in which, for instance, researchers investigated organizational decision processes by interviewing senior executives and other informants after organizational decisions had been made. The advantage of the Bradford studies methodology over more traditional surveys is that corporate decision makers likely will not recognize or state decision principles in such explicit terms as we have here; to study principled reasoning then, researchers can observe decisions as they are made or examine the reasons stated post hoc for a particular decision, and then determine whether the reasoning fits the criteria for good decision principles as discussed in Clue 5. Ideally, reflecting the multilevel nature of corporate goodness, measurement strategies at both levels (the individual and the corporate) will be utilized and shown to converge, thus providing some confidence the construct is being gauged accurately.

Consistency Across Domains and Time

The final, broad issues we raise are the consistency of goodness across the domains in which corporations exist (e.g., the environment, public health, human rights, and employee welfare) and the stability of goodness across time. What these two issues have in common is that they both represent obstacles to pinpointing a company's true level of goodness. Inconsistency across domains and time represents both complicated conceptual and measurement problems for which we cannot offer clear solutions.

Previously, we recognized that corporations enact virtues (e.g., honesty, courage, and wisdom) and vices (e.g., deceit, cowardice, or ignorance) within a variety of domains. Thus, it is entirely possible (and probably very typical) for an organization to be good in one domain while bad or decent in another. To once again use Altria Group, Inc., as an example, this corporation might be deemed good in the domain of human rights based on its attempts to alleviate domestic violence, but might be considered decent—or bad even—in the domain of public health for advertising tobacco products to young and influential audiences by teaming with Hollywood to show movies in which celebrities like Renee Zellweger and Mel Gibson glamorize smoking (Mekemson & Glantz, 2002). Given such inconsistency in goodness across domains, how should one arrive at an overall judgment concerning a corporation's goodness? Can goodness in one domain balance or cancel out badness in another domain? What does one make, for example, of the corporation that withholds information from shareholders about the fact that it makes substantial donations to a charitable organization despite losses in shareholder profits? Arguably, badness and goodness should not necessarily carry equal heft in deeming a corporation good or bad, as some bad acts simply cannot be expunged. Supporting this view is the fact that KLD Research & Analytics, Inc., one of the largest reporters of CSR, excludes industries such as tobacco and gaming from their CSR indices. Thus, any good done by R. J. Reynolds, for example, cannot compensate for the fact that use of its products is the leading cause of preventable death in the United States (CDC, 2002).

Similar to this problem of inconsistency across domains is the problem of inconsistency across time. That is, we recognize that corporate goodness likely fluctuates over time, with an organization demonstrating a greater level of goodness at Time 1 than Time 2. A key question related to the issue of time is whether the stability of goodness matters. For example, how does one compare a corporation that is consistently good with a corporation that is not consistently good over the same time frame, assuming that their mean levels of goodness across time are the same? Brief, Buttram, and Dukerich (2001) suggested that corporations depend upon consistency and predictability and cannot rely on the vicissitudes of an inconstant human nature. Can the same be said of corporate goodness? If the stability of corporate goodness is an important factor, how should we reconsider the measurement strategies previously noted? Are corporations with consistently decent intentions, for example, better than those that fluctuate between good and bad intentions? Additionally, what if corporate decision makers do not consistently demonstrate principled reasoning in deciding between good intentions and actions? As with the problem of inconsistency across domains, regarding instability, we are only able to raise the issue with the hope that researchers will be able to address our questions in the future.

Measurement Synopsis

Our point in this section was not necessarily to provide a measurement toolkit for researchers to use in gauging corporate goodness. Rather, we attempted to raise a number of issues that need attention should one attempt to empirically study corporate goodness; for some we have provided answers, while other issues are merely raised without the offer of clear solutions. These issues included discerning goodness from reputation; measuring intentions, actions, and principled reasoning; and the consistency of goodness across domains and time. Now that we have addressed what corporate goodness is and is not, as well as relevant measurement issues, we now turn to a discussion of how organizations can achieve and maintain goodness.

BECOMING AND STAYING GOOD: A SCHNEIDERIAN APPROACH

The remainder of this chapter will be devoted to utilizing Schneiderian ideas—specifically his attraction–selection–attrition (ASA) framework (Schneider, 1987) and organizational climate research (e.g., Schneider, 1975, 1990)—to understand how organizations might become good and stay that way. Additionally, we will consider how corporations might change overtime—either intentionally or unintentionally—to become good, decent, or bad. We especially focus our discussion on the extremes of badness and goodness. As in our discussion of measurement issues, our goal here is to raise questions, particularly regarding the applicability of ASA and climate theory to the corporate goodness concept, rather than provide answers. Before launching into those questions stimulated by Schneider's research, however, we will review briefly the underlying premises and assumptions of both his ASA and organizational climate research.

ASA theory is a quintessential "meso" (e.g., House, Rousseau, & Thomas-Hunt, 1995) perspective in that it describes the interplay between individual- and organization-level factors. According to Schneider and his colleagues (1987; Schneider, Goldstein, & Smith, 1995), people are differentially attracted to, selected by, and retained within organizations based on the similarity or fit between the personality, attitudes, and values of each party. A number of studies have, in fact, supported Schneider's predictions (e.g., Eagleson, Waldersee, & Simmons, 2000; Judge & Bretz, 1992; Judge & Cable, 1997), and researchers have attributed to the ASA process empirical observations that organizational members are relatively homogeneous with regards to personality and certain demographic variables (e.g., Jordan, Herriot, & Chalmers, 1991; Schaubroeck, Ganster, & Jones, 1998; Schneider, Smith, Taylor, & Fleenor, 1998).

Organizational climate, defined as "incumbents' perceptions of the events, practices, and procedures and the kinds of behaviors that get rewarded, supported, and expected in a setting" (Schneider, 1990, p. 384), is a natural companion to ASA theory because it can be viewed as both a cause and a result of differential attraction, selection, and attrition processes. That is, an organization's climate is, in part, what leads to the attraction, selection, and retention of particular types of persons—or to use Schneider's terminology, the "homogeneity" of people within organizations. Homogeneity, in turn, helps explain why an organization's climate is what it is; a homogeneous group of people hold "similar perceptions and attach similar meanings to organizational events because the members themselves are in some ways similar to each other" (Schneider & Reichers, 1983, p. 27).

According to Schneider and Reichers's (1983) interactionist view of the etiology of organizational climate, individuals seek meaning in the world around them, and this meaning arises from interactions among individuals. Specifically, workers gather information about the practices, policies, and procedures enacted by their organizations (Schneider, Brief, & Guzzo, 1996; Schneider & Gunnarson, 1996; Schneider, Gunnarson, & Niles-Jolly, 2001)—information that is filtered through social interactions, where meaning is ascribed. Because climate perceptions within organizations are derived from common stimuli and understood through interactions of relatively similar organizational members (due to ASA), these perceptions come to be shared. Thus, Schneiderian principles tell us that people within organizations will be relatively homogeneous with respect to personality, attitudes, and values (Schneider et al., 1995), and that employees will come to share similar perceptions about the organizations' practices, policies, and procedures, and the behavior that is expected and rewarded.

Application of ASA and Climate Research to the Good Corporation

Previously, we asserted that corporate goodness is distinct—though not completely so—from the goodness of the people within it. Here, we expand on the relationship between individual and corporate goodness and argue, in accordance with the ASA framework, that good corporations will tend to attract, select, and retain good individuals. Some preliminary support for this view—at least in the attraction process—is offered by Scott (2000), who found that applicants were influenced by organizations' moral values as depicted in brochures and other materials such that the fit between an applicant's and an organization's moral values predicted attraction to that organization. In a more informal survey, 76% of respondents indicated that their choice of employer would be influenced by the employer's integrity (Lewis, 2003, *Boston Globe*). In short, we expect that good corporations will be comprised of good individuals—a rather humdrum prediction in light of ASA's tenets.

The goodness of individuals alone, however, does not guarantee corporate goodness. We know, both anecdotally and empirically, that good people sometimes do bad things (e.g., Brief, Buttram, & Dukerich, 2000). We also know that good acts spring up spontaneously (e.g., Rochat & Modigliani, 1995). While the former statement is clearly an unfortunate fact of life in general, the latter, though positive on the surface, is nonetheless an unfortunate fact for organizations. When it comes to corporate goodness, more than the spontaneity of goodness is required; what is needed to ensure corporate goodness with any degree of consistency is an environment that makes goodness relevant and therefore brings out the good in people (e.g., Trevino, 1986). Unless policies, practices, and procedures are in place that encourage goodness and support decency, good people may be relatively ineffectual in terms of the influence they exert on a corporation's morality:

> Obviously, if the organization has the right people in place in the various subsystems, then the probabilities for success are improved; that is why good staffing is so important ... the point here is that there is a tendency in organizations to put all the blame for ineffectiveness on the people in the organization and fail to realize that those people may simply not have created the structures, processes, and procedures under which they could have been more successful. (Schneider & Schmitt, 1986, p. 409)

What, then, is necessary for corporate goodness is an organizational climate for goodness, or the shared perception that goodness is valued and rewarded within the organization. A climate for goodness, according to Schneider (e.g., 1987; Schneider et al., 1995), in part will originate with and be cultivated by the founder (see Dickson, Smith, Grojean, & Ehrhart, 2001; Victor & Cullen, 1988).

What Is the Role of the Founder in the Good Corporation?

On numerous occasions, Schneider has asserted that founders play a particularly important formative role in an organization's development (e.g., 1987; Schneider et al., 1995). One explanation for the import of the founder is that his or her personality, values, and attitudes come to be reflected in the corporation's policies, practices, and procedures (Schneider et al., 1995), which are, in turn, captured by its climate. Another means by which a founder can impart influence, according to Schneider et al. (1995; see also Schein, 1993), is by attracting and selecting "lieutenants" or top management teams (e.g., Daboub, Rasheed, Priem, & Gray, 1995; Jackson et al., 1991) with values and assumptions similar to those of the founder. Top management teams, then, will have considerable impact on an organization's intentions, actions, and decision strategies, and thus its goodness. Once the founder and the freshly obtained top management team are in place, then—according to ASA theory—new applicants who are similar to these upper-echelon members will be differentially attracted to and selected by the organization. At the same time, the organizational climate is expected to perpetuate as new employees come to learn and share perceptions of the policies, practices, and procedures established by the core organizational members.

Despite speculation about the ways in which founders influence the values and climate for ethics in organizations (e.g., Dickson et al., 2001;

Victor & Cullen, 1988), no empirical investigations, to our knowledge, have been conducted on the matter (for a review of founders' impact on organizational climate in general, see Hofstede, Neuijen, & Ohayv, 1990). To explore the issue, researchers might assess the relationship between the goodness of founders and the goodness of their organizations by, for instance, conducting organizational ethnographies that trace the development of an organization and the policies, practices, and procedures as they were established and nurtured over time. For example, Tom's of Maine cofounders Tom and Kate Chappell have been lauded with numerous awards, including the New England Environmental Leadership Award and the Governor's Award for Business Excellence. The Chappells are known for infusing their business activities with personal values and spiritual faith, as can be seen in both the company's mission statement and their positive actions toward the environment and animal protection (Tom's of Maine, n.d.). In his book *The Soul of a Business*, Tom Chappell (1993) described his attempt to quash the traditional business planning strategy in which business leaders ask questions about end results like, "Where do we want to be in five years, and how do we get there?" Instead, he asked questions about the company values like "Who are we?" and "What do we believe?" (p. 26). "Our values," wrote Chappell, "informed every decision we made at Tom's of Maine" (p. 24). Interestingly, Chappell also discussed the influence of Kant's respect principle on his personal thinking and how it reinforced his company's belief that customers should be treated as ends rather than as a means to profit.

Organizational scholars, using narratives such as Chappell's or by conducting interviews or observational analyses, could begin to test empirically the impact of the founder on the development of a climate for goodness. We believe that the founder's goodness will play an instrumental role in forming and maintaining a climate for goodness (e.g., Dickson et al., 2001). While this prediction follows rather directly from Schneiderian principles, we attempt in the following section to be a bit more provocative, raising challenges concerning the applicability of ASA and climate theory to the corporate goodness construct. First, we will work our way through each of the processes within the attraction-selection-attrition framework, questioning assumptions of the model at each step. Next, we will present two critical obstacles to creating a climate for goodness. We then will consider processes by which a corporation might change from good to bad or bad to good, followed by a brief discussion of ASA processes at the industry and occupational level of analysis.

Will Good Applicants Be Fooled by Bad Corporations?

Consistent with the ASA frame, we begin with the assumption that good applicants will be attracted to good corporations and that decent and bad applicants will be attracted to decent and bad organizations, respectively. Despite the fact that studies have been supportive of the notion that individuals are differently attracted to organizations based on their personality, values, and attitudes, one might question the generalizability of such studies to both the corporate goodness construct and to real-world organizations outside of the laboratory. Indeed, many of the studies conducted on organizational attraction have been laboratory based and have examined hypothetical paper organizations (e.g., Turban & Keon, 1993). Arguably, applicants will have more trouble discerning the personality, values, and attitudes of a real organization than hypothetical organizations in which these characteristics are made to be less complex and clearly spelled out by the researchers. Take, for example, the now defamed Enron corporation. Before this corporate scandal was made public, would applicants have been able to see beyond the company's stated values of excellence, respect, and integrity (Enron, 2000)?

If applicants are not able to distinguish between a corporation's reputation and its true characteristics, then they might be attracted to something other than what they believe it to be. Especially in the case of goodness, a socially desirable characteristic, corporations might try to present an image of goodness, even if it is false. If so, a big question is whether applicants will recognize the difference. And if they do, will only good people be attracted to a good corporation, or might bad people also be attracted to a good corporation? To evoke a common metaphor (e.g., Trevino & Youngblood, 1990), is it possible that bad apples will be attracted to an otherwise good barrel?

Will Bad Applicants Seek Out Good Corporations?

"Bad apples" plausibly might be attracted to a good corporation in hopes of taking advantage of the goodness of others. Indicative of this perspective are "prisoner's dilemma" studies (e.g., Wildschut, Insko, & Gaertner, 2002) in which two people must decide separately whether they want to cooperate with or defect against the other person, such as in the case of two partners in crime sitting in isolated cell blocks each being told by police that if one of them confesses to the crime, that person will go free, but the other one will go to prison. If both partners defect and confess, then they both go to prison, but if both partners cooperate with each other, there is a chance that neither will go to prison. If people in the prisoner's dilemma are fairly certain that their partners will cooperate, it is in their best self-interest to defect. Generalizing this rationale to corporations, people who intend to "defect" against other people at work might seek out good, or "cooperating," corporations. Bad apples in such a context could find themselves in a position to "free ride" or otherwise take advantage of others.

Essentially, the attraction process in the ASA framework is dependent on the fact that applicants can judge, with some accuracy, characteristics of organizations. Given the possibility that applicants can discern a corporation's goodness, we have conjectured as to whether bad applicants will prey on good corporations for selfish gains. That the motivations of people with bad intentions might lead them to act in ways not predicted by ASA theory prompts us to question whether similar exceptions to this theory might occur during the selection and attrition phases.

Can Organizations Discriminate Between Good and Bad Applicants?

According to ASA theory, organizational members will select applicants who are similar to, or fit, the organizational personality, values, and attitudes. However, just as we questioned the tenability of applicants' judgments about an organization's goodness, we question the ability of interviewers to discern the goodness of applicants. Interviews, in particular, might most aptly be considered maximum ability tests in which applicants put their best—but not typical—face forward (see Sackett, Zedeck, & Fogli, 1988, for a discussion of maximum vs. typical performance). If all applicants are motivated to present themselves as good, or at least as better than they really are, how can a good corporation sift through them and select only those people who are actually good? Integrity tests, which are utilized by some organizations to screen out people prone to lying, stealing, and other counterproductive behaviors (see Sackett & Wanek, 1996), might not be as effective in identifying goodness as they are in identifying a lack of badness.

Will Corporations Ever Intentionally Select Morally Bad Applicants?

If we assume that interviewers can, in fact, determine an applicant's goodness, decency, or badness, an additional question arises about whether the selection of good, decent, and bad apples will be symmetric across all types of organizations. In other words, will all organizations—good, decent, and bad—select applicants that fit with their goodness, decency, or badness? We do not question whether good organizations will select, if able, good applicants, as this would best preserve the climate for goodness and the maintenance of good intentions, actions, and decision principles within the organization. The precepts of ASA also suggest that bad organizations will select bad applicants more readily than good ones. Organizations in which lying, stealing, and cheating are part of everyday business arguably might not want to hire "goody two shoes" applicants who might refuse to comply with such activities—or worse, might blow the whistle. A shady used car dealership, for instance, probably would prefer not to employ people who empathize with buyers, conveying all information accurately and trying to give the buyer the best deal possible. Also plausible, however, is that bad organizations might attempt to attract and select do-gooders if they can keep them unaware of dubious activities taking place. Enron, for instance, might have preferred to hire good employees over bad ones because they would be more likely to act in morally good ways toward the organization itself. Conceivably, bad organizations that hire bad applicants run the risk of these employees taking unethical actions against the organization, rather than working in concert with other bad organizational members toward unethical ends on behalf of the organization.

Will Attrition Be Symmetric Across Good and Bad Barrels?

Plausibly, individuals who have passed through the attraction and selection phases to become organizational members might display asymmetrical attrition patterns based on whether the employees are good or bad apples and whether they are in good or bad barrels. For example, might a good person have a more difficult time surviving in a corporation where lying, stealing, and malicious gossip run rampant than would a bad person in a corporation characterized by honesty, charity, and compassion? More than the former, a good misfit in a bad corporation likely would feel uncomfortable with the actions of others in the work environment. Additionally, morally good people might be considered bad performers if in refusing to engage in bad behavior they fall behind other employees who are willing to engage in unscrupulous acts and "play the game." In contrast, a good organization, upon discovery of a bad employee, likely would be motivated to rid itself of the bad apple before the rest of the barrel spoils.

ASA predicts that turnover will be higher for those individuals who do not fit—as such, we would expect good people to leave bad organizations and bad people to leave good organizations. However, ASA does not specify the type of attrition for organizational misfits, that is, whether such people leave the organization voluntarily or involuntarily. The type of attrition that misfits display is conceivably asymmetric across good and bad corporations. As discussed previously, bad apples might enjoy being in a good or decent barrel, as it is an advantageous environment for taking advantage of others. If this is the case, such people are unlikely to turn over voluntarily, but are likely to stay in the organization until their rottenness is smelt and they are forced to leave. In contrast to this scenario, good apples who find themselves in a bad barrel are more likely to leave voluntarily because they do not want to be a part of the badness (Cialdini, Petrova, & Goldstein, 2004). Also plausible is that good apples will not survive in the bad barrel and will be fired for lack of compliance with bad policies, practices, and procedures.

As with attraction and selection, corporate goodness appears to pose some difficulties for the attrition portion of ASA theory. Given the issues the corporate goodness construct imposes on ASA theory, we wondered whether it might introduce difficult issues regarding organizational climate theory as well. The result of our inquiry, discussed in the next section, is the suggestion of two barriers to the creation of organizational climate.

Can a Climate for Goodness Exist?

The Negativity Bias. We began this chapter by saying that journalists and organizational scholars are fixated with all things negative. According to Baumeister, Bratslavsky, Finkenauer, and Vohs (2001), the allure of the negative is not unique to these two groups but is shared by people in general. In their comprehensive review on the topic, Baumeister et al. presented evidence that most everyone can discriminate between positive and negative, with people reacting more strongly to negative events and information than their positive counterparts in almost all cases. Specifically, people have been shown to process negative information more thoroughly than positive information (e.g., Klinger, Barta, & Maxeiner, 1980), and barring a few exceptions (Baumeister et al., 2001), people remember negative information better than positive information (e.g., Dreben, Fiske, & Hastie, 1979; Krietler & Krietler, 1968). Research also suggests that while we have neurological structures dedicated to processing certain negative stimuli, we lack similar structures for dealing with analogous positive stimuli (Luu, Collins, & Tucker, 2000; Miltner, Braun, & Coles, 1997).

The sum of the evidence led Baumeister et al. (2001) to the general conclusion that "bad is stronger than good" (p. 323). If this conclusion is accurate, what is the implication for organizational climate for goodness? Perhaps human nature itself represents a barrier to the formation of a climate for corporate goodness; perhaps climates that lend themselves to negative frames will be more easily created and sustained than those that lend themselves more exclusively to positive information frames. For instance, an organizational climate for safety (Smith-Crowe, Burke, & Landis, 2003; Zohar, 1980) might consist, in large part, of negatively framed perceptions such as "If I don't wear my gas mask, I'll be exposed to radiation, and I could develop cancer." According to the research cited above, organizational members will process such negative information more thoroughly and remember it better than positive information such as "My organization values goodness." We do not suggest, however, that a negativity bias represents an insurmountable obstacle for the formation of a climate for corporate goodness. Rather, we suggest that there might be a discernable and constant power differential between such negative and positive information, similar to that proposed by Gottman (1994), who said that close relationships are likely to fail unless the ratio of positive events to negative ones is at least 5 to 1. Generalizing this information, perhaps it takes five times as many organizational policies, practices, and procedures that reflect corporate goodness to have an equal climate impact as would each negatively framed organizational policy, practice, and procedure.

The Reward Dilemma.   Along with the negativity bias, the reward dilemma constitutes another barrier to creating a climate for corporate goodness. As mentioned previously, Schneider (1990) defined organizational climate in part as the perceptions of what behaviors are rewarded; individuals seek out information about what constitutes proper behavior in their organizations and rely on organizational reward structures as a primary source for this information. Of course, it follows that individuals act so as to be rewarded—a self-interested transaction. Herein lies the sticky issue: A climate for corporate goodness would have people doing good in order to be rewarded materially or with some other careerist gain, but as we have argued already, people are not really doing good if they primarily are motivated out of self-interest (e.g., Kant, 1785/1964). Thus, the question becomes whether a climate for corporate goodness can exist in the absence of a supportive organizational reward structure. We see this as an important empirical question stimulated by philosophical concerns.

To this point, implicit in our discussion of how organizations can come to be good and stay that way is the assumption that beginning with the founder and continuing through the mechanisms of ASA and organizational climate, an organization arrives at goodness, decency, or badness, end of story. This is not, however, the end of the story, for organizations can change from good to bad, from bad to good, and so forth. Given the veracity of the previous statement, how then do corporations change?

How Do Corporations Change?

ASA and climate tell us much about how organizations come to be relatively homogeneous with respect to personality, values, and attitudes, and they inform us about how policies, practices, and procedures are reified by the shared perceptions of organizational members. This research reveals less, however, about how organizational change occurs—how good organizations come to be decent or bad over time, or how bad organizations move on to become decent or good. In this section, we explore several issues related to organizational change, asking questions of how and why change might occur.

Previously, we conjectured, based on ASA and climate research, that good founders will construct good organizations. Can we generalize beyond this statement to conclude that organizations founded by good people will be good and remain good across time? In our best estimation, the answer to this question is "not necessarily"; given some thought, one can probably recall scandals that have occurred in corporations founded by good individuals (or at least people with a reputation for being good). For example, Arthur E. Andersen, founder of the now disparaged Arthur Andersen public accounting firm, has been described as a man of integrity who insisted that doing the right thing was more important than profits: "Think straight, talk straight" was a favorite saying of Andersen's (Toffler

& Reingold, 2003, p. 12). At some point over the course of the company's 80-plus year existence, however, this message was lost and the firm's involvement in the Enron scandal eventually led to the "fall of the house of Andersen" (Toffler & Reingold, 2003).

The disconnect between founder and corporate goodness at Arthur Andersen seems in conflict with the prior illustration of Tom's of Maine, the ASA framework, and climate research, all of which suggest that a founder's goodness will influence the organization's goodness through differential attraction, selection, and attrition of employees and through employees' shared perceptions of policies, practices, and procedures—thus perpetuating itself. How, then, can we explain cases such as Arthur Andersen where the founder's and the corporation's goodness do not correspond? One likely explanation is that founders eventually retire, die, or otherwise leave their organizations, being replaced by new leaders who may or may not act in ways that reinforce the founders' influence. Additional explanations include the size or age of the corporation (also see Miller, Kets de Vries, & Toulouse, 1982). Specifically, the founder's role might be more critical in the nascent stages of an organization's development than in later stages when it has grown and the policies, practices, and procedures are crafted and carried out by an increasing number of different employees. In other words, might the relationship between founder goodness and corporate goodness decline as a firm grows and ages? Statements by Anita Roddick (2001), founder of the Body Shop—a corporation frequently praised for being environment friendly—support the notion that growth and time can diminish the impact of the founder: "Rapid growth has been really difficult.… One of the things that eroded our culture very fast was the bringing in of such a huge amount of new people from blue-chip corporations" (in Makower, 1994).

Perhaps the seeming inconsistency between corporate change and Schneiderian notions can be resolved upon a more careful examination of assumptions underlying those ideas. Specifically, we will address how employees different from those in place surface as an organization grows and develops. ASA processes are not claimed to produce perfectly homogeneous organizations. Indeed, a few bad apples might slip their way into an otherwise good barrel. Arguably, if enough bad individuals get into and remain within the organization—perhaps in a tight labor market when organizations have less choice over whom to hire and retain—the organizational climate may begin to change. What was once a strong climate (see Schneider, Salvaggio, & Subirats, 2002, for a discussion of climate strength) for goodness could weaken and eventually change valence to become merely decent or even bad (see Dickson et al., 2001). How many bad apples, then, can be tolerated before the whole barrel begins to rot?

How Might Rotten Apples Spoil the Barrel?

Perhaps it is not the number of bad apples so much as their location within the barrel. Lack of goodness at the top of the barrel might impact those apples at the bottom of the barrel more so than the converse. We already have suggested that the founder and top management team play an important role in ASA processes and in formulating the policies, practices, and procedures that are the basis for organizational climate. Thus, can one assume that corporate goodness will be more a function of top apples than those lower in the barrel? For example, a former senior executive at Royal Dutch/Shell reported being "sick and tired of lying" to cover up the "aggressive/optimistic" accounting of the firm's reserves at the behest of "top apple" Sir Philip Watts, former chairman of the company ("Sick and Tired About Lying", 2004). The executive's dilemma clearly reflects the power of people at the top in terms of influencing moral decisions and actions of an organization.

But what does one make of the corporation that is good at the top but contains a number of bad apples at the bottom? Imagine, for instance, that a corporation has good intentions to contribute to the community by donating money and employee time to building homes for Habitat for Humanity. If lower-level employees participate only begrudgingly, can the corporation still be deemed good? Our tentative answer is yes because of the relative influence wielded by those at the top in comparison to the bottom. However, we note that top apples are not completely in control of the barrel; unless bad apples at the bottom are tossed out, their presence may eventually lead to the rotting of the entire barrel.

In addition to the number and location of apples within the barrel, might the clustering of the apples be important, such that a few bad apples dispersed in the barrel have a different impact than if those apples were bunched together in one location? Conceivably, a clustering of bad apples could act like a cancerous tumor that metastasizes to other parts of the organization (Cialdini et al., 2004). Also plausible is that bad apples that are dispersed, rather than clustered in one location, have a direct impact on a greater number of other apples, and thus the spreading of rot is more pervasive than if the bad apples are limited to one location in the barrel. These considerations of how bad apples can spread rot through a previously good barrel, suggest our next question: Can the barrel be saved?

Can a Rotten Barrel Be Saved?

Thus far, in discussing organizational change, we have addressed how good corporations might slide unintentionally off the moral high ground. To end this section on a more positive note (in line with the theme of the chapter), we consider how a corporation might change from bad or decent to good. Consider, for example, a corporation that historically has not been good but wants to become so. Unlike change from goodness to badness, we argue that transforming from badness to goodness will require a more concerted effort and will not happen unintentionally. Because goodness is, in fact, contingent upon good intentions, a person or corporation cannot become good accidentally. We speculate that efforts to change a decent corporation into a good one will be less arduous than those to transform from badness to goodness. Skeptics might wonder whether it is even possible for a really bad corporation to become good. Reflecting this skepticism, Mehta (2003) noted:

> Business historians are hard-pressed to name corporations that have transformed themselves into shining examples of virtue in areas in which they were once prime practitioners of vice. Sure Exxon cleaned up its act after the Exxon Valdez debacle, but no one equates [them] with environmental friendliness. Many other damaged companies, such as Arthur Andersen, go out of business before they have a chance to reinvent themselves. (p. 117)

Following from Schneiderian ideas, skepticism is not unwarranted; would not the bad organization, for instance, be less attractive and amenable to good applicants and therefore less able to populate its barrel with good apples (see Cialdini et al., 2004)? And might not bad organizations have deeply ingrained cultures in which people cling to shared perceptions of bad policies, practices, and procedures? If the answer is yes, and we presume it is, then how can a bad organization become good? Our presumption is based on the notion that bad corporations, more so than good ones, will find it difficult to attract and retain people whose goodness could bring about change.

One strategy is to clean house. One of the first moves by MCI, the company until recently known as WorldCom, in its attempt to shed the WorldCom image of having committed financial fraud resulting in the largest bankruptcy in U.S. history (Mehta, 2003), was to "ax" the old WorldCom board of directors and fire employees directly involved in cooking the books and those who stood by and watched but did nothing to prevent the fraud. Also present in this example is another strategy—losing the old company name in an attempt to dissociate from its former self. The second strategy, however, perhaps better meets the goals of changing the corporate reputation rather than its actual goodness or character. Corporations, however, do not exist in a vacuum; a greater understanding of corporate goodness requires a consideration of the context.

What About Occupation and Industry Effects on Corporate Goodness?

Until this point, we have discussed Schneiderian ideas at the organizational level. Now, we consider their application to both occupational and industry levels—considerations that Schneider himself has discussed (e.g., Schneider, 1987; Schneider et al., 1998). In fact, according to Schneider (1987), the ASA model was constructed, in part, by building on research in the vocational domain that suggested that people are attracted to occupations based on their fit with the people within the occupation (e.g., Holland, 1973). Additionally, in an empirical test of ASA, Schneider et al. (1998) assessed and found homogeneity of personality both within organizations and within industries. Can these findings be generalized to goodness? That is, will the goodness, decency, or badness of individuals influence attraction to particular occupations and industries? If so, can certain occupations and industries be characterized as more or less good, decent, or bad? To call on crude stereotypes, are social workers, for example, more generally good than used car dealers? Are good people more likely to work in health service or education industries, for instance, than in the banking or tobacco industries?

We do know, based on empirical evidence, that criminal activity is more prevalent in some industries than others and that organizations within certain industries succumb to corruption at rates comparable to other organizations within that industry (e.g., Baucus & Near, 1991). If ASA for goodness occurs at either or both the occupational and industry levels, will these effects be stronger than ASA processes at the corporate level? For example, if someone has decided to work as a lobbyist for the tobacco industry, the goodness of this individual might not impact whether she works for Philip Morris (of the Altria Group, Inc.) as opposed to R. J. Reynolds. Likewise, for a man who receives a law degree with hopes of protecting civil liberties of minority groups, his goodness might have little influence on whether he ends up working for the American Civil Liberties Union or the National Association for the Advancement of Colored People. Clearly, factors other than one's goodness, such as personality, life history, and so forth, could influence choice of occupation, industry, and organization. In the case of goodness, however, it is possible that occupational or industry norms for goodness, decency, or badness could overwhelm any differences among corporations within a particular industry.

Synopsis: Corporate Goodness and Schneiderian Ideas

In this section, we have explored corporate goodness through the lens of Schneiderian ideas of ASA and organizational climate by discussing how organizations might come to be good and remain good. We have suggested straightforward propositions directly stemming from Schneiderian ideas (e.g., good organizations will attract good applicants), and we have posed a number of questions and challenges raised by these same ideas (e.g., Will bad applicants be attracted to good organizations?). In the end, our goal was to stimulate study of the good corporation. The questions we posed may not be the right ones, but if they have stimulated the reader's own questions, then we have succeeded.

FINAL WORDS

In this chapter we have explored the concept of corporate goodness. We have offered clues that we believe point to the heart of the corporate goodness construct. Our first clue was that being good is categorically distinct from being not bad or merely decent. The second, third, and fourth clues focused on the necessity of good intentions, actions, and the content of goodness, respectively. In the fifth and final clue, we outlined several decision principles through which good corporations might weigh various intentions and translate intentions into actions. Following the definitional clues of goodness, we briefly addressed measurement issues and the ways in which corporate goodness differs from other positive organizational constructs. The latter portion of the chapter was devoted to utilizing Benjamin Schneider's ASA theory and organizational climate research to speculate as to the ways in which corporate goodness can develop and flourish; along the way we challenged the full applicability of ASA and climate theory to the special case of corporate goodness.

Although our attempt has been to define and discuss the good corporation from a scientific and objective standpoint, we cannot pretend our chapter is value-free.[11] Labeling something as good or bad is inherently a value-laden task, and indeed, our values are infused throughout. The mere fact that we undertook to write this chapter is a reflection of our values. That our values are embedded within the context of our work is not unique to this particular endeavor; the scientific enterprise in its entirety is value-laden (often unrecognizedly so). Kaplan (1998) argued that the notion of value-free science is nothing more than a myth—that the questions we ask and the ways in which we ask them are steered by our values. In accordance with Kaplan, we believe business, like science, is not value-free. Below we will tread farther into the domain of personal beliefs and values, offering our ideal role of the good corporation within society. In doing so, we move clearly out of a descriptive realm and into a normative one (see Donaldson, 2003).

First, and perhaps most critically, we see corporations as moral entities striving for more than profits and financial success. In the words of past Quaker Oats president Kenneth Mason, "Making a profit is no more the purpose of a corporation than getting enough to eat is the purpose of life" (as cited in Makower, 1994). We do not mean, however, that every corporation is responsible for improving all aspects of society; clearly, corporations cannot be expected to contribute to every cause or to cure every social ill. Kanter (2002) urged corporations to direct their social efforts at those things in which the company excels, or the core of the company. Intel and Microsoft specialize in computer technology; thus, their Teach to the Future Program is aptly matched for training teachers in technology (Kanter, 2002). Likewise, the Grateful Dead has funded school music programs, and the herbal tea company Celestial Seasonings has directed charitable efforts at pesticide and crop management issues

(Scott & Rothman, 1992). Because each corporation has unique capabilities and resources to offer, Kanter suggested the formation of coalitions such that corporations can coordinate their individual specialized efforts to address a variety of causes. In this way, each corporation can seek to satisfy the needs of those people it is best suited to serve, and all corporations—working together—can strive to help meet the needs of all.

Corporations are uniquely positioned to positively impact the world. They certainly have more resources at their disposal to do good than do most individuals and even some governments. A report by Anderson and Cavanaugh (n.d.) revealed that 51 of the 100 largest economies in the world are corporations and that the world's largest 200 corporations account for an impressive 27.5% of the world gross domestic product. Clearly, corporations have become increasingly powerful world forces (see Fox, 1996), and with this power comes the ability to have a positive impact on the lives of individuals and society at large (Donaldson, 1982; Margolis & Walsh, 2003). The final question is, Will corporations choose goodness?

ENDNOTES

1. Although we recognize that many organizations, such as the Red Cross and Planned Parenthood, are created and exist primarily to promote social welfare, our focus here is on corporations: for-profit organizations that have the ability to be positive agents of change in society but do not necessarily do so.

2. Alternatively, one could start with the state or society rather than the person (e.g., Rawls, 1971). However, in line with Schneider's (1987, p. 437) dictum that "the people make the place," we have built our argument around the analogy of the corporation as a person.

3. Paine's (2003) distinction is consistent with that of Kant's (1785/1964) between acting in accordance with duty (upholding the letter of the law) and acting from duty (upholding the spirit of the law).

4. Our intention is not to refute utilitarianism in particular, or consequentialist approaches to ethics in general. Rather, we wish to argue that these types of approaches are ill-suited for understanding the concept of corporate goodness.

5. Although we prefer and use the term *intention* to Kant's *will*, we perceive similar meanings between the two.

6. We note that our usage of the term *virtue* does not perfectly coincide with its usage by philosophers such as Aristotle (ca. 384–322 B.C.E./1984), who view virtues more in terms of the characteristics of individuals rather than any particular actions they might perform or potential outcomes achieved.

7. The "universalization test" is the name often used to refer to the first formulation of Kant's categorical imperative, the moral imperative across all situations. The respect principle is the second formulation of the categorical imperative.

8. We note that Kant's approach to morality was a strict and decidedly rational one; morality to him was not about actions done out of feelings such as love or compassion. Kant did not consider love and compassion to be bad, but as feelings they were not enough to ensure moral goodness because feelings may be fleeting and can even lead to wantonness. If people rely solely on their feelings as a basis for action, they might not always "feel like" doing good things, and thus can be led astray from the morally good path. Because of this concern over the sometimes capricious nature of feelings, Kant's moral philosophy is duty based rather than emotion based. Kant's focus on fulfilling duties has lead to questions of whether his philosophy allows for the notion of goodness. The word *duty* implies an obligation that if fulfilled merely prevents one from being bad. Hill and Zweig (2002) stated this thought as follows: "If all morally worthy acts are done from duty, however, there must be no special moral worth in heroic and saintly acts that are, as we say, 'above and beyond the call of duty'" (p. 35). Hill and Zweig admitted that this feature of Kant's theory has been criticized by some scholars, but they also pointed out that Kant's own class of "imperfect duties" reveals that some acts are good beyond those that are required.

9. This judgment is supported not only by Kantian philosophy, but also by religion. The Hebrew scriptures, for example, teach followers that God is the creator and owner of all the earth and that we, as humans of the earth, are stewards entrusted with care for the earth: "The Earth belongs to God! Everything in all the world is his!" (Psalms 24:1). As such, the Israelites were instructed to allow the land to restore itself by leaving it unsown every seventh, or Sabbath, year (Stackhouse et al., 1995). That God is the owner of the earth can be taken to mean that corporations do not truly own land or resources. The idea is admittedly controversial and at odds with common beliefs and practices in the modern business world. People and corporations certainly can and do own land in a legal sense. Much less radical, however, is the idea that corporations and people who are fortunate enough to "own" land and resources have important obligations and capabilities to do good with their blessings.

10. Rawls's original position assumes that individuals, in generating rules of justice, will be reasonable (i.e., capable of complying with principles of justice) and rational (i.e., capable of pursuing their interests).

11. Not only are our values reflected in this chapter, but when asked to write a paper in celebration of Ben Schneider's career, we immediately thought of his basic goodness as a person, leading to the current topic.

REFERENCES

Abating or exploding? (2004, April 17–23). *Economist*, 21–23.

Amnesty International. (1997). Female genital mutilation: A human rights information pack (AI index, ACT 77/05/97). London: Author.

Anderson S. & Cavanaugh, J. As referenced in DellaMattera, N. and Gaudet, J., "Coming to a Town Near YOU: Corporate Globalization & Its Impact on Massachusetts Workers," retrieved December 1, 2004, from http://www.uml.edu/Dept/RESD/globalization%20reportqa.pdf

Aristotle. (1984). *Nicomachean ethics* (H. G. Apostle, Trans.). Grinnell, IA: Peripatetic Press. (Original work written ca. 384–322 B.C.E.)

Asmus, P. (2003). 100 best corporate citizens. *Business Ethics*. Retrieved on December 1, 2004, from http://www.business-ethics.com/100best.htm

Augustine. (1950). *The city of God* (D. B. Zema & G.G. Walsh, Trans.). In *Fathers of the church* (Vol. 8). New York: Catholic University of America Press. (Original work published 426)

Austin, J. R. (2003). Transactive memory in organizational groups: The effects of content, consensus, specialization, and accuracy on group performance. *Journal of Applied Psychology, 88*, 866–878.

Baucus, M. S., & Near, J. P. (1991). Can illegal corporate behavior be predicted? An event history analysis. *Academy of Management Journal, 34*, 9–36.

Baumeister, R. F., Bratslavsky, E., Finkenauer, C. & Vohs, K. D. (2001). Bad is stronger than good. *Review of General Psychology, 5*, 323–370.

Berlin, I. (1991). *The crooked timber of humanity*. New York: Knopf.

Blackburn, S. (2001). *Being good: An introduction to ethics*. New York: Oxford University Press.

Block, P. (1993). *Stewardship: Choosing service over self-interest*. San Francisco: Berrett-Koehler.

Bok, S. (1989). *Lying: Moral choice and public and private life*. New York: Vintage Books.

Bowie, N. E. (1999). Business ethics: A Kantian perspective. Malden, MA: Blackwell Publishers.

Bowie, N. E. (1996). Cultural and moral relativism. In T. Donaldson & P. Werhane (Eds.), *Ethical issues in business: A philosophical approach* (5th ed., pp. 91–95). Englewood Cliffs, NJ: Prentice Hall.

Brief, A. P., & Aldag, R. J. (1994). The study of work values: A call for a more balanced perspective. In I. Borg & P. Ph. Mohler (Eds.), *Trends and perspectives in empirical and social research* (pp. 99–110). Berlin: Walter de Gruyter.

Brief, A. P., Buttram, R. T., & Dukerich, J. M. (2000). Collective corruption in the corporate world: Toward a process model. In M. E. Turner (Ed.), *Groups at work: Advances in theory and research* (pp. 471–499). Hillsdale, NJ: Lawrence Erlbaum Associates.

Brief, A. P., Buttram, R. T., Elliot, J. D., Reizenstein, R. M., & McCline, R. L. (1995). Releasing the beast: A study of compliance with orders to use race as a selection criterion. *Journal of Social Issues, 51*, 177–193.

Brief, A. P., Dukerich, J. M., & Doran, L. I. (1991). Resolving ethical dilemmas in management: Experimental investigations of values, accountability and choice. *Journal of Applied Social Psychology, 21*, 380–396.

Buber, M. (1987). *I and thou* (R. G. Smith, Trans.; T. E. Hill, Jr., & A. Zweig, Eds.). New York: Collier Books. (Original work published 1923)

Buchholz, R. A. (1989). *Fundamental concepts and problems in business ethics*. Englewood Cliffs, NJ: Prentice Hall.

Burke, M. J., & Dunlap, W. P. (2002). Estimating interrater agreement with the average deviation (AD) index: A user's guide. *Organizational Research Methods, 5*, 159–172.

Burke, M. J., Finkelstein, L. M., & Dusig, M. S. (1999). On average deviation indices for estimating interrater agreement. *Organizational Research Methods, 2*, 49–68.

Burke, M. J., Sarpy, S. A., Tesluk, P. E., & Smith-Crowe, K. (2002). General safety performance: A test of a grounded theoretical model. *Personnel Psychology*, 55, 429–457.

Cameron, K. S., Dutton, J. E., & Quinn, R. E. (2003). *Positive organizational scholarship: Foundations of a new discipline.* San Francisco: Berret-Koehler.

Campbell, J. P., McCloy, R. A., Oppler, S. H., & Sager, C. E. (1993). A theory of performance, (pp. 35–70). In N. Schmitt & W. C. Borman (Eds.), *Personnel selection in organizations.* San Francisco: Jossey-Bass.

Cavanagh, G. F. (1984). *American business values* (2nd ed.). Englewood Cliffs, NJ: Prentice Hall.

Centers for Disease Control. (2002). *Annual smoking-attributable mortality, years of potential life lost, and economic costs—United States, 1995–1999.* 51: 300–303.

Chan, D. (1998). Functional relations among constructs in the same content domain at different levels of analysis: A typology of composition models. *Journal of Applied Psychology, 83*, 234–246.

Chappell, T. (1993). *The soul of a business.* New York: Bantam Books.

Cialdini, R. B., Petrova, P. K., & Goldstein, N. J. (2004). The hidden costs of organizational dishonesty. *MIT Sloan Management Review*, 67–73.

Ciulla, J. B. (2003). *The ethics of leadership.* Toronto: Thomson Wadsworth.

Clinton, H. R. (2004, April 18). Now can we talk about health care? p. 26. *New York Times Magazine.*

Cochran, P. L., & Wood, R. A. (1984). Corporate social responsibility and financial performance. *Academy of Management Journal, 27*, 42–56.

Cockburn, A. (2003, September). 21st-century slaves. *National Geographic, 204*, 2–25.

Cray, D., Mallory, G. R., Butler, R. J., Hickson, D., & Wilson, D. C. (1991). Explanations of strategic decision making processes. *Journal of Management Studies, 28*, 227–251.

Cummins, Inc. (n.d.). *Our vision.* Retrieved October 21, 2004, from http://www.cummins.com/cmi/content.jsp?siteId=1&langId=1033&menuId=1&overviewId=2&menuIndex=1

Curtler, H. (1986). *Shame, responsibility and the corporation.* New York: Haven.

Daboub, A. J., Rasheed, A. M. A., Priem, R. L., & Gray, D. A. (1995). Top management team characteristics and corporate illegal activity. *Academy of Management Review, 20*, 138–170.

Danley, J. R. (1984). Corporate moral agency: The case for anthropological bigotry. In W. M. Hoffman & J. M. Moore (Eds.), *Business ethics: reading and cases in corporate morality* (pp. 173–179). New York: McGraw-Hill.

Dickson, M. W., Smith, D. B., Grojean, M. W., & Ehrhart, M. (2001). An organizational climate regarding ethics: The outcome of leader values and the practices that reflect them. *Leadership Quarterly, 12*, 197–217.

Donaldson, T. (1982). *Corporations and morality.* Englewood Cliffs, NJ: Prentice Hall.

Donaldson, T. (1989). Moral minimums for multinationals. *Ethics and International Affairs, 3*, 163–182.

Donaldson, T. (2003). Editor's comment: Taking ethics seriously—A mission now more possible. *Academy of Management Review, 28*, 363.

Donaldson, T., & Dunfee, T. W. (1999). *The ties that bind: A social contracts approach to business ethics.* Boston: Harvard Business School Press.

Donaldson, T., & Preston, L. E. (1995). The stakeholder theory of the corporation: Concepts, evidence, and implications. *Academy of Management Review, 20*, 65–91.

Donaldson, T., & Werhane, P. H. (1996). *Ethical issues in business: A philosophical approach* (5th ed.). Upper Saddle River, NJ: Prentice Hall.

Dreben, E. K., Fiske, S. T., & Hastie, R. (1979). The independence of evaluative and item information: Impression and recall order effects in behavior based impression formation. *Journal of Personality and Social Psychology, 37*, 1758–1768.

Dunlap, W. P., Burke, M. J., & Smith-Crowe, K. (2003). Accurate tests of statistical significance for r_{WG} and average deviation interrater agreement indexes. *Journal of Applied Psychology, 88*, 356–362.

Dworkin, R. (1977). *Taking rights seriously*. Cambridge, MA: Harvard University Press.

Eagleson, G., Waldersee, R., & Simmons, R. (2000). Leadership behaviour similarity as a basis of selection into a management team. *British Journal of Social Psychology, 39*, 301–308.

Enron. (2000). Annual report. Retrieved October 22, 2004, from www.enron.com/corp/investors/annuals/2000

Evan, W. M., & Freeman, R. E. (1988). A stakeholder theory of the modern corporation: Kantian capitalism. In T. L. Beauchamp & N. E. Bowie (Eds.), *Ethical theory and business* (3rd ed., pp. 97–106). Englewood Cliffs, NJ: Prentice Hall.

Euripides. (480–406 B.C.) Œdipus. Frag. 546.

First National Bank of Boston v. Bellotti, 435 U.S. 765 (1978). U.S. Supreme Court.

Fishman, C. (1999). Sanity Inc. *Fast Company*, 84.

Fombrun, C., & Shanley, M. (1990). What's in a name? Reputation building and corporate strategy. *Academy of Management Journal, 33*, 233–258.

Foster, L. G. (1999). *Robert Wood Johnson: The gentleman rebel*. State College, PA: Lillian Press.

Fox, D. R. (1996). The law says corporations are persons, but psychology knows better. *Behavioral Sciences and the Law, 14*, 339–359.

Franklin, B. (1962). *The autobiography of Benjamin Franklin*. New York: Touchstone. (Original work published 1790)

French, P. A. (1984). *Collective and corporate responsibility*. New York: Columbia University Press.

Friedman, M. (1970, September 13). The social responsibility of business is to increase its profits. p. sm 17–sm 20. *New York Times Magazine*.

Friedman, M. (1988). The social responsibility of business. In J. C. Callahan (Ed.), *Ethical issues in professional life* (pp. 349–350). London: Oxford University Press.

Goodpaster, K. E., & Matthews, J. B., Jr. (1982). Can a corporation have a conscience? *Harvard Business Review, 60*, 132–142.

Gottman, J. (1994). *Why marriages succeed or fail*. New York: Simon & Schuster.

Griffin, J. J., & Mahon, J. F. (1997). The corporate social performance and corporate financial performance debate: Twenty-five years of incomparable research. *Business and Society, 36*, 5–31.

Hartman, E. M. (1996). *Organizational ethics and the good life*. New York: Oxford University Press.

Hobbes, T. (1651). *Leviathan, or the matter, forme, and power of a commonwealth, Ecclesiasticall and civil*. London: Andrew Crooke.

Hofstede, G., Neuijen, B., & Ohayv, D. D. (1990). Measuring organizational cultures: A qualitative and quantitative study across twenty cases. *Administrative Science Quarterly, 35*, 286–316.

Holland, J. L. (1973). *Making vocational choices: A theory of careers*. Englewood Cliffs, NJ: Prentice Hall.

Horwitz, M. (1992). *The transformation of American law, 1870–1960: The crisis of legal orthodoxy*. New York: Oxford University Press.

Hosmer, L. T. (1987). *The ethics of management*. Homewood, IL: Irwin Press.

House, R., Rousseau, D. M., & Thomas-Hunt, M. (1995). The meso paradigm: A framework for the integration of micro and macro organizational behavior. In L. L. Cummings & B. M. Staw (Eds.), *Research in organizational behavior* (Vol. 17, pp. 71–114). Greenwich, CT: JAI Press.

Jackson, S. E., Brett, J. F., Sessa, V. I., Cooper, D. M., Julin, J. A., & Peyronnin, K. (1991). Some differences make a difference: Individual dissimilarity and group heterogeneity as correlates of recruitment, promotions, and turnover. *Journal of Applied Psychology*, Vol. 76, pp. 675–689.

Jordan, M., Herriot, P., & Chalmers, C. (1991). Testing Schneider's ASA theory. *Applied Psychology: An International Review, 40*, 47–53.

Judge, T. A., & Bretz, D. (1992). Effects of work values on job choice decisions. *Journal of Applied Psychology, 77*, 261–271.

Judge, T. A., & Cable, D. M. (1997). Applicant personality, organizational culture, and organization attraction. *Personnel Psychology, 50*, 359–394.

Kahaner, L. (2003). *Values, prosperity, and the Talmud: Business lessons from the ancient Rabbis*. Hoboken, NJ: John Wiley & Sons.

Kant, I. (1964). *Groundwork of the metaphysics of morals* (H. J. Paton, Trans.). New York: Harper & Row. (Original work published 1785)

Kant, I. (2002). *Groundwork of the metaphysics of morals* (A. Zweig, Trans.; T. E. Hill, Jr., & A. Zweig, Eds.). New York: Oxford University Press. (Original work published 1785)

Kanter, R. M. (2002). Rising to rising expectations. p. 70–74. *WorldLink: Magazine of the World Economic Forum*.

Kaplan, A. (1998). *The conduct of inquiry: Methodology for behavioral science*. New Brunswick, NJ: Transaction.

Kelman, H. C. & Hamilton, V. L. (1989). Crimes of obedience: Toward a social psychology of authority and responsibility. New Haven: Yale University Press.

Klinger, E., Barta, S. G., & Maxeiner, M. E. (1980). Motivational correlates of thought content frequency and commitment. *Journal of Personality and Social Psychology, 39*, 1222–1237.

Krietler, H., & Krietler, S. (1968). Unhappy memories of the "happy past": Studies in cognitive dissonance. *British Journal of Psychology, 59*, 157–166.

Ladd, J. (1970). Morality and the ideal of rationality in formal organizations. *The Monist, 54*, 488–516.

Langlois, C., & Schlegelmich, B. B. (1990). Do corporate codes of ethics reflect national character? Evidence from Europe and the United States. *Journal of International Studies, 21*, 519–539.

Lazarus, R. S. (2003). Does the positive psychology movement have legs? *Psychological Inquiry, 14*, 93–109.

Lewis, D. E. (2003, November 23). Corporate trust a matter of opinion, p. G2. *Boston Globe.*

Lewis, S. (2003). Reputation and corporate responsibility. *Journal of Communication Management, 7,* 356–364.

Luu, P., Collins, P., & Tucker, D. M. (2000). Mood, personality, and self-monitoring: Negative affect and emotionality in relation to frontal lobe mechanisms of error monitoring. *Journal of Experimental Psychology: General, 129,* 43–60.

Makower, J. (1994). *Beyond the bottom line: Putting social responsibility to work for your business and the world.* New York: Simon & Schuster.

Margolis, J. D., & Walsh, J. P. (2003). Misery loves companies: Rethinking social iniatives by business. *Administrative Science Quarterly, 48,* 268–305.

Marshall, J. J. (1819). *Dartmouth vs. Woodward.*

Mehta, S. N. (2003, October 27). MCI: Is being good good enough? *Fortune,* 117–124.

Mekemson, C., & Glantz, S. A. (2002). How the tobacco industry built its relationship with Hollywood. *Tobacco Control, 11,* 81–91.

Menon, S., & Kahn, B. E. (2003). Corporate sponsorships of philanthropic activities: When do they impact perception of sponsor brand? *Journal of Consumer Psychology, 13,* 316–327.

Mill, J. S. (1962). Utilitarianism. In M. Warnock (Ed.), *Utilitarianism and other writings* (pp. 251–321). New York: Penguin Books.

Miller, D., Kets de Vreis, M. F. R., & Toulouse, J. M. (1982). Top executive locus of control and its relationship to strategy-making, structure, and environment. *Academy of Management Journal, 25,* 237–253.

Miltner, W. H., Braun, C. H., & Coles, M. G. H. (1997). Event-related brain potentials following incorrect feedback in a time-estimation task: Evidence for a "generic" neural system for error detection. *Journal of Cognitive Neuroscience, 9,* 788–798.

Moore, G. E. (1903). *Principia ethica.* Cambridge, UK: Cambridge University Press.

Morris, T. (1997). *If Aristotle ran General Motors: The new soul of business.* New York: Henry Holt.

Nash, L. L. (1993). *Good intentions aside: A manager's guide to resolving ethical problems.* Boston: Harvard Business School Press.

O'Neal, J. (2004, February 21). University hospital nurses fired for giving away medication, p. B1. *Cedar Rapids Gazette.*

Orlitzky, M., Schmidt, F. L., & Rynes, S. L. (2003). Corporate social and financial performance: A meta-analysis. *Organizational Studies, 24,* 403–441.

Ozar, D. (1979). The moral responsibility of corporations. In T. Donaldon & P. Werhane (Eds.), *Ethical issues in business* (pp. 294–300). Englewood Cliffs, NJ: Prentice Hall.

Paine, L. S. (2003). *Value shift: Why companies must merge social and financial imperatives to achieve superior performance.* New York: McGraw-Hill.

Park, N., & Peterson, C.M. (2003). Virtues and organizations. In K. S. Cameron, J. E. Dutton, & R. E. Quinn (Eds.), *Positive organizational scholarship: Foundations of a new discipline* (pp. 33–47). San Franciso: Berret-Koehler.

Peterson, C., & Seligman, M. E. P. (2004). *Character strengths and virtues: A handbook and classification.* New York: Oxford University Press.

Pfeffer, J. (1998). *SAS Institute (A): A different approach to incentives and people management practices in the software industry.* Board of Trustees of the Leland Stanford Junior University.

Pincoffs, E. (1986). *Quandaries and virtues: Against reductionism in ethics.* Lawrence, KS: University Press of Kansas.

Quinn, R. E. (1996). *Deep change: Discovering the leader within.* San Francisco: Jossey-Bass.

Quinn, R. E., & Quinn, G. T., (2002). *Letters to Garrett: Stories of change, power, and possibility.* San Francisco: Jossey-Bass.

Ramo, J. C. (2000, September 14). The five virtues of Kofi Annan. *Time Magazine,* 35–42.

Rawls, J. (1971). *A theory of justice.* Cambridge, MA: Harvard University Press.

Rawls, J. (1993). *Political liberalism.* New York: Columbia University Press.

Rechelbacher, H. M. (n.d.). *Aveda mission statement.* Retrieved October 21, 2004, from http://aveda.aveda.com/about/beliefs_vision/default.asp

Rochat, F. & Modigliani, A. (1995). The ordinary quality of resistance: From Milgram's Laboratory the Village of Le Chambon. *Journal of Social Issues, 51,* 195–210.

Roddick, A. (2001). Business as unusual: The triumph of Anita Roddick. New York: Thorsons.

Ross, W. D. (1930). *The right and the good.* Indianapolis: Hackett.

Ruf, B. M., Muralidhar, K., & Paul, K. (1998). The development of a systematic, aggregate measure of corporate social performance. *Journal of Management, 24,* 119–133.

Sackett, P. R., & Wanek, J. E. (1996). New developments in the use of measures of honesty, integrity, conscientiousness, dependability, trustworthiness, and reliability for personnel selection. *Personnel Psychology, 49,* 787–829.

Sackett, P. R., Zedeck, S., & Fogli, L. (1988). Relations between measures of typical and maximum job performance. *Journal of Applied Psychology, 73,* 482–486.

Salamon, J. (2003). *Rambam's ladder: A mediation on generosity and why it is necessary to give.* New York: Workman Publishing Company.

Santa Clara County v. Southern Pacific Railroad.

Schaubroeck, J., Ganster, D. C., & Jones, J. R. (1998). Organization and occupation influences in the attraction–selection–attrition process. *Journal of Applied Psychology, 83,* 869–891.

Schein, E. H. (1993). *Organizational culture and leadership* (2nd ed.). San Francisco: Jossey-Bass.

Schlosser, E. (2003). *Reefer madness: Sex, drugs, and cheap labor in the American black market.* Boston: Houghton Mifflin.

Schneider, B. (1975). Organizational climates: An essay. *Personnel Psychology, 18,* 447–479.

Schneider, B. (1987). The people make the place. *Personnel Psychology, 40,* 437–453.

Schneider, B. (1990). The climate for service: An application of the climate construct. In B. Schneider (Ed.), *Organizational climate and culture* (pp. 383–412). San Francisco: Jossey-Bass.

Schneider, B., Brief, A. P., & Guzzo, R. A. (1996). Creating a climate and culture for sustainable organizational change. *Organizational Dynamics, 24,* 7–19.

Schneider, B., Goldstein, H. W., & Smith, D. B. (1995). The ASA framework: An update. *Personnel Psychology, 48,* 747–773.

Schneider, B., & Gunnarson, S. (1996). Organizational climate and culture: The psychology of the workplace. In J. James, B. Steffy, & D. Bray (Eds.), *Applying psychology in business* (pp. 542–551). Lexington, MA: Lexington Books.

Schneider, B., Gunnarson, S. K., & Niles-Jolly, K. (2001). Creating the climate and culture of success. *Organizational Dynamics, 23,* 17–29.

Schneider, B., & Reichers, A. E. (1983). On the etiology of climates. *Personnel Psychology, 36,* 19–39.

Schneider, B., Salvaggio, A. N., & Subirats, M. (2002). Climate strength: A new direction for climate research. *Journal of Applied Psychology, 87,* 220–229.

Schneider, B., & Schmitt, N. (1986). *Staffing organizations* (2nd ed.). Glenview, IL: Scott, Foresman & Company.

Schneider, B., Smith, D. B., Taylor, S., & Fleenor, J. (1998). Personality and organizations: A test of the homogeneity of personality hypothesis. *Journal of Applied Psychology, 83,* 462–470.

Schulz, W. F. (2004, April 18). Security is a human right, too: Have rights advocates failed to face up to terrorism? *New York Times Magazine,* 20.

Scott, E. D. (2000). Moral values fit: Do applicants really care? *Teaching Business Ethics, 4,* 405–435.

Scott, M., & Rothman, H. (1992). *Companies with a conscience: Intimate portraits of twelve firms that make a difference.* Secaucus, NJ: Carol Publishing Group.

Sick and tired about lying. (2004, April 24). *Economist,* 63–64.

Smith-Crowe, K. 2004. *An interactionist perspective on ethical decision-making: Integrative complexity and the case of worker safety.* Unpublished doctoral dissertation, Tulane University, New Orleans.

Smith-Crowe, K., Burke, M. J., & Landis, R. S. (2003). Organizational climate as a moderator of safety knowledge—safety performance relationships. *Journal of Organizational Behavior, 24,* 861–876.

Solomon, R. C. (1994). Business and the humanities: An Aristotelian approach to business ethics. In T. Donaldson and R. E. Freeman (Eds.) *Business as humanity.* (pp. 45–75). New York: Oxford University Press.

Soule, E. (2002). Managerial moral strategies: In search of a few good principles. *Academy of Management Review, 27,* 114–124.

Spreitzer, G., & Sonenshein (2003a). Toward the construct definition of positive deviance. *American Behavioral Scientist, 47.*

Spreitzer, G. M., & Sonenshein, S. (2003b). Positive deviance and extraordinary organizing. In K. S. Cameron, J. E. Dutton, & R. E. Quinn (Eds.), *Positive organizational scholarship: Foundations of a new discipline* (pp. 207–224). San Francisco: Berret-Koehler.

Stackhouse, M. L., McCann, D. P., Roels, S. J., & Williams, P. N. (1995). *On moral business: Classical and contemporary resources for ethics in economic life.* Grand Rapids, MI: WM. B. Eerdmans Publishing.

Sternen, J. (2002). Positive deviance: A new paradigm for addressing today's problems today. *Journal of Corporate Citizenship,* Vol. 5, pp. 57–62.

Stevenson, R. W. (1996, May 9). Minding more than the bottom line: Two companies and two different views of corporate responsibility, p. D1. *New York Times.*

Taylor, S. E. (1991). Asymmetrical effects of positive and negative events: The mobilization-minimization hypothesis. *Psychological Bulletin, 110,* 67–85.

Tenbrunsel, A. E., & Messick, D. M. (1999). Sanctioning systems, decision frames, and cooperation. *Administrative Science Quarterly, 44*, 684–707.

Tenbrunsel, A. E., Smith-Crowe, K., & Umphress, E. E. (2003). Building houses on rocks: The role of ethical infrastructure in the ethical effectiveness of organizations. *Social Justice Research, 16*, 285–307.

Tetlock, P. E. (1986). A value pluralism model of ideological reasoning. *Journal of Personality and Social Psychology, 50*, 819–827.

Toffler, B. L., & Reingold, J. (2003). *Final accounting: Ambition, greed and the fall of Arthur Andersen.* New York: Broadway Books.

Tom's of Maine. (n.d.). *Tom Chappell: Co-founder and president.* Retrieved October 21, 2004, from http://www.tomsofmaine.com/about/bio_tom.asp

Trevino, L. K. (1986). Ethical decision making in organizations: A person–situation interactionist model. *Academy of Management Review, 11*, 601–617.

Trevino, L. K., & Weaver, G. R. (2003). *Managing ethics in business organizations: Social scientific perspectives.* Stanford, CA: Stanford University Press.

Trevino, L. K., & Youngblood, S. A. (1990). Bad apples in bad barrels: A causal analysis of ethical decision-making behavior. *Journal of Applied Psychology, 75*, 378–385.

Turban, D. B., & Keon, T. L. (1993). Organizational attractiveness: An interactionist perspective. *Journal of Applied Psychology, 78*, 184–193.

United Nations. (1948). *Universal declaration of human rights.* Retrieved from www.ohchr.org. September 4, 2004.

U.S. Sentencing Commission. (2003). *Federal sentencing guideline manual: Sentencing of organizations* (chap. 8). Retrieved from www.ussc.gov/orgguide.htm

Velasquez, M. G. (1998). *Business ethics: Concepts and cases* (4th ed.). Upper Saddle River, NJ: Prentice Hall.

Victor, B., & Cullen, J. B. (1988). The organizational bases of ethical work climates. *Administrative Science Quarterly, 33*, 101–125.

Wegner, D. M. (1986). Transactive memory: A contemporary analysis of the group mind. In B. Mullen & G. R. Goethals (Eds.), *Theories of group behavior* (pp. 185–208). New York: Springer-Verlag.

Wildschut, T., Insko, C. A., & Gaertner, L. (2002). Intragroup social influence and intergroup competition. *Journal of Personality and Social Psychology, 82*, 975–992.

Wolgast, E. (1992). *Ethics of an artificial person: Lost responsibility in professions and organizations.* Stanford, CA: Stanford University Press.

Wood, D. J. (1991). Social issues in management: Research and theory in corporate social performance. *Journal of Management, 17*, 383–406.

Zohar, D. (1980). Safety climate in industrial organizations: Theoretical and applied implications. *Journal of Applied Psychology, 65*, 96–102.

10

Variability Within Organizations
Implications for Strategic Human Resources Management

LISA H. NISHII
Cornell University

PATRICK M. WRIGHT
Cornell University

Strategic human resources management (SHRM) refers to the pattern of planned human resource deployments and activities intended to enable an organization to achieve its goals (Wright & McMahan, 1992). It involves all of the activities that are implemented by an organization to affect the behavior of individuals in an effort to implement the strategic needs of a business. Over the last decade or so, the field of strategic human resources management has witnessed a progression through a number of stages, including (1) initial excitement and energy around the convincing argument that HR practices should be considered as a system that, when implemented appropriately, can enhance organizational performance; (2) empirical tests of this argument; and (3) critiques of the growing field accompanied by propositions for how thinking on the topic can be expanded and improved. Of the critiques that have been levied at the field, the most common contend that the "black box" through which HRM practices are thought to impact organizational performance remains insufficiently specified. Less common, but no less valuable, are critiques surrounding the conceptualization and measurement of fit or alignment, and the need to identify the boundary conditions that influence the effectiveness of high-performance HRM systems. Even more critiques and proposed theoretical extensions to the field are likely, as it is through such endeavors that we will improve upon and advance our science (cf. Reichers & Schneider, 1990).

In this chapter, we introduce and discuss another potential critique of the SHRM field, and, in so doing, hope to illuminate a number of important research questions for the future. In particular, we are concerned with the lack of attention that has been paid to variability within SHRM research. By variability we mean variability at all relevant levels of analysis, but particularly variability within organizations (i.e., individual and group levels). It is our contention that by failing to examine the potential role of variability in SHRM research, we miss a very interesting and important part of the picture.

THE CONCEPT OF VARIABILITY WITHIN SHRM RESEARCH

First, consider the typical study within the empirical research on the HR practices to performance relationship. A single respondent, usually a senior HR professional, completes a survey regarding the HR practices that exist within his or her organization. Sometimes the practices are with regard to large categories of employees (e.g., hourly or managerial/technical/professional employees; Huselid, 1995) and sometimes with regard to a specific group (e.g., bank teller; Delery & Doty, 1996; or assembly line workers; MacDuffie, 1995). Then, the responses from the HR professional are statistically related to some measure of firm performance. Note that such methods implicitly assume that all employees receive the same practices. Such methods also implicitly assume that the single organizational respondent can accurately represent the opinions and experiences of all organizational members with regard to HR practices, or that variability in employees' experiences of HR practices need not be captured when examining the HR-performance relationship.

In essence, we have hitherto failed to explicitly recognize the many ways in which individuals and groups may experience and respond differentially to HR systems within organizations (see Bowen & Ostroff, 2004, for an exception). Examining such variability is important for a number of reasons. These sources of variability may operate as moderators on the HR practices–performance link. That is, holding all else constant, variability in any one or more of these factors across organizations may be cause for meaningful variability in the HR practices–performance relationship. Without explicit consideration of these factors, this variability might erroneously be considered "noise," or lead to incomplete or inaccurate conclusions regarding the HR practices–performance relationship. Research that fails to more fully consider the range of issues within organizations that impact the HR practices–performance relationship is likely to have limited usefulness for understanding the complexity of this relationship. It may even obscure important components of this relationship. In order to progress to the next stage of SHRM knowledge, in which

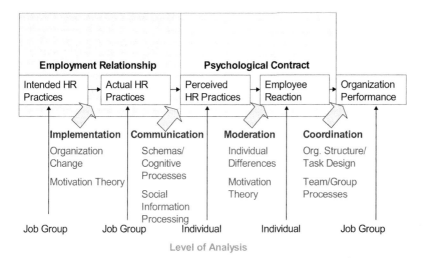

FIGURE 10.1

inconsistent research findings are explained through expanded theories and an examination of the boundary conditions that are relevant to the relationships of interest, we believe it is critical for scholars to give fuller consideration to the sources of variability at multiple levels of analysis. In this chapter, we begin exploring these sources of variability.

But before we turn to this task, a few caveats are in order. First, we do not claim to propose an exhaustive analysis of variability, although we do hope to identify areas worthy of future research attention. Second, we base our discussion on the assumption that HR practices are ultimately associated with desirable organizational outcomes through their influence on a number of mediating variables. Overall, the process through which HR practices lead to enhanced performance is not well understood; thus, it is not clear whether HR practices exert their effects through similar means across organizations. As we argue in this chapter, they most likely do not, as suggested by the variability in and around each of the mediating links in the HR practices–performance relationship.

The mediators that we see as particularly critical are represented in Figure 10.1. First, we recognize the very real possibility that actual HR practices may differ from intended HR practices as a function of the way that HR practices are implemented. Second, we contend that the effect of actual HR practices does not reside in those practices, but rather in the perceptions that employees have of those practices. We expect that employee perceptions of HR practices vary as a function of differences in schemas and associated values, personality, and other individual difference variables (as described later). It is these employee perceptions that are in turn associated with attitudinal and behavioral reactions on the part of employees, which, in the aggregate, are associated with organizational performance. The extent to which employee attitudes and behaviors are associated with performance at higher levels of analysis is a function of group process variables, such as team structure, task interdependence, leadership, and group cohesion.

The model just described represents an expansion on the more typical model that has been implied in the SHRM literature, in which HR practices are presumed to be associated with performance through their influence on employee skills, attitudes, and motivation (Huselid, 1995; Parker et al., 2003; Wright, McMahan, & McWilliams, 1994; Wright, McCormick, Sherman, & McMahan, 1999). Two key features of our model are the explicit attention we give to the potential difference between intended and actual HR practices and to employee perceptions of those HR practices. The latter is an area that has not received much theoretical or empirical attention. For example, researchers within the field of SHRM have long stressed the importance of commitment in the relationship between HR practices and organizational effectiveness; according to many researchers, appropriately designed HR practices are an important predictor of commitment and satisfaction (e.g., Arthur, 1992; Osterman, 1994; Tsui, Pearce, Porter, & Hite, 1995; Tsui, Pearce, Porter, & Tripoli, 1997; Whitener, 2001). This vein of research assumes that the effect of HR practices on employee attitudes and behaviors is inherent in the HR practices themselves—commitment-enhancing HR systems will enhance employee commitment, while control HR systems will not.

Yet psychologists would agree that it makes little sense to assume that employees will respond similarly in their attitudes and behaviors to HR practices. Employees react to environments as a function of the meaning and significance that those environments have for them (Gray, Bougon, & Donnellon, 1985; Jackson & Dutton, 1988; James, James, & Ashe, 1990; Thomas, Clark, & Gioia, 1993). The essence of our argument is based on theories of social cognition, according to which cognition is an important precursor of subsequent attitudes and actions. People attach different meanings to social stimuli based on differences in the cognitive frameworks that they use to make sense of social information (Fiske & Taylor, 1991). Therefore, based on the way that people perceptually filter external information, their attitudinal and behavioral responses to that information may differ.

Virtually our entire discussion regarding variability in the effects of HR practices is related to the groundbreaking work of Benjamin Schneider. It is he who advanced the now famous mantra "the people make the place." In relation to SHRM research, this reminds us that failing to pay explicit attention to the role of people and their varying personal characteristics in influencing the qualities of organizations and their performance is a critical oversight because we cannot fully understand organizations without first understanding the people who comprise them. The attraction–selection–attrition (ASA) model also highlights the likelihood that individuals who react negatively to their organization's HR practices may leave, thereby (1) enhancing the desired effects of HR on organizational performance over the long run and (2) reminding us that HR practices may not be reacted to similarly by all individuals (i.e., highlighting individual-level variability). Furthermore, in his pioneering work on organizational climate, Schneider emphasized the importance of sharedness in employees' perceptions of an organization's HR and other practices. In so doing, he brought attention to the fact that such perceptions are not always shared, nor are they necessarily aligned with the espoused messages of organizational practices as intended by management.

VARIABILITY AT THE INDIVIDUAL LEVEL OF ANALYSIS

Most of the SHRM literature to date has focused almost exclusively on the relationship between managerial reports of HR practices and organizational effectiveness. The content of HR systems, or the specific practices that are said by key managers to be adopted by organizations, have not been distinguished from (1) the process through which HR systems are enacted within organizations or (2) the perceptions of those practices by the very human resources the practices are hypothetically implemented to affect. This ignores the possibility that the actual effect of HR practices may differ from the expected effect of HR practices as a function of employees' perceptions of the HR practices to which they are subjected (as depicted in Figure 10.1). While researchers agree that employee experiences of HR practices are important in understanding the connection between HR practices and organizational effectiveness, little research exists on the link between employee perceptions of HR practices and unit or organizational effectiveness.

Most cognitive, social, and organizational psychology theories clearly support the idea that individuals bring different information processing networks (i.e., schemas; Fiske & Taylor, 1991), motivations (e.g., Locke & Latham, 1990), past experiences (e.g., Rousseau, 2001), demographic backgrounds (Cox, 1993), values (e.g., Judge & Bretz, 1992; Meglino & Ravlin, 1998), personalities (e.g., Hough & Schneider, 1996), and attitudes (e.g., Brief, 1998) to bear on their interpretations of, and reactions to, organizational experiences. Common SHRM methodologies have not allowed researchers to examine the effect of these sources of variability, but given the need to illuminate the black box, this variability is important to consider. We discuss some of these sources of variance in this section.

Employee Perceptions of HR Practices

As previously mentioned, the hypothesis that employees' perceptions of HR practices are likely antecedents of employee reactions (attitudes and behaviors) has received little theoretical and empirical attention in the SHRM literature. Yet whether employees respond to HR practices in ways desired by their employers—that is, with increased satisfaction, commitment, and motivation; improved skills; and greater likelihood of exerting positive discretionary effort—depends on their perceptions and evaluations of HR practices. HR practices serve a signaling function by sending messages that employees use to define the psychological meaning of their work situation (Rousseau, 1995). Thus, the very same set of HR practices can be perceived positively by some employees but not others, depending on the level of perceived fit between those practices and individual values, personality, goals, and schematic expectations (Guzzo & Noonan, 1994). According to social exchange theory, employees gauge their contribution to the organization based on what they perceive the organization to be providing them (i.e., the norm of reciprocity; cf. Ostroff & Bowen, 2000; Schmitt & Allscheid, 1995; Whitener, 2001).

The idea that it is people's subjective perceptions of the environment, rather than any objective environment, that drives behavior, and that individuals differ in those subjective perceptions of the environment, is the cornerstone of psychological climate research (James et al., 1990; Rentsch, 1990). Indeed, scholars in this area view psychological climate perceptions as the mediating link between organizational characteristics and individual outcomes such as employee attitudes, motivation, and performance (Parker et al., 2003). Consistent with Kurt Lewin's (1936) pioneering notion of "life space," psychological climate perceptions are thought to provide individuals with cognitive representations of their organizational environment that act as a lens through which they attach meaning to organizational events and determine the attitudes and behaviors that will result in desired outcomes. To the extent that psychological climate perceptions engender feelings of satisfaction and commitment, employees are expected to be motivated to expend discretionary effort on behalf of the organization. In support of this idea, a recent meta-analysis of psychological climate research concluded that affective, cognitive, and instrumental dimensions of climate influence job performance, withdrawal, and psychological well-being through their impact on satisfaction and organizational commitment (Carr, Schmidt, Ford, & DeShon, 2003).

The mediating role of psychological climate perceptions in the relationship between HR systems and performance has also been highlighted by Bowen and Ostroff (2004; Ostroff & Bowen, 2000). They argue that psychological climate perceptions must be shared by employees if they are to lead to enhanced performance at higher levels of analysis. Building on communication and attribution theories, they propose that when the HRM system is perceived by employees as being high in distinctiveness, consistency, and consensus, it will be perceived as a strong HRM system. In strong HRM systems, variability in individual-level climate perceptions is reduced and shared climate perceptions emerge, and it is when shared climate perceptions emerge at the group and organizational levels of analysis that desired performance outcomes accrue, for when employees share their perceptions, they are better able to coordinate their behaviors toward the collective achievement of the organization's strategic objectives. As convincing as their model is, however, it has yet to be tested empirically.

Another potentially important mediator in the relationship between actual HR practices and employee reactions is the attributions that employees make regarding the "why" of HR practices. Nishii (2006) argued that employees are not passive recipients of HR practices, and that the attributions that they make for HR practices can have a significant influence on their satisfaction, commitment, and organizational citizenship behaviors (OCBs), and ultimately on organizational performance. She hypothesized that individual employees would make varying attributions for HR practices based on differences in how they selectively attend to information regarding HR practices and how they process that information (Mischel & Shoda, 1995).

Nishii (2006) relies on social exchange theory to explain how HR attributions are associated with employee reactions. Specifically, when employees perceive that the underlying intentions of an organization's HR practices translate into positive and beneficial circumstances for them, she argues that they will feel an obligation to reciprocate in positive and beneficial ways, as evidenced by higher levels of commitment, satisfaction, and OCBs. Furthermore, HR attributions are thought to serve as guidelines for employee behavior. Employees observe the HR practices to which they and others in the organization are subjected in order to deduce conclusions about the organization's priorities and expectations for employee behavior. These conclusions in turn serve as frames of reference against which the appropriateness of behavior can be judged (Schneider, 1975; Schneider, Gunnarson, & Niles-Jolly, 1994). Thus, it is upon these attributions that employees base their judgments regarding where they should focus their energies and competencies.

Nishii's (2006) results support the notion that the same HR practices can be perceived quite differently by employees and that HR attributions are associated with department-level satisfaction, commitment, and OCBs, and ultimately with customer satisfaction (Nishii, Lepak, & Schneider, in press). Two main implications stem from this research. First, the managerial accounts of HR practices often used in SHRM studies may not adequately represent reality because those reports might represent intended, rather than actual, HR practices and because they ignore the variability in employee perceptions and attributions regarding those practices. Second, some of the inconsistent research findings to date in SHRM may be accounted for by the failure to capture the complexity of the relationship between HR practices and employees' perceptions of and experiences with them. The results showed that even a relatively constant set of HR practices can be associated with different employee attitudes and behaviors, and ultimately unit performance because employees make varying attributions about those HR practices. Thus, the observed relationship between single respondent reports of HR practices and firm performance may be subject to an unmeasured variance problem that mis-specifies the true nature of the relationship.

Predictors of Employees' Perceptions of HR Practices

Given that people's perceptions of HR practices can differ and that those differential perceptions are associated with valued outcomes, the next important question becomes: What factors account for these perceptual differences among employees? Variations in the perceptions and valuations that constitute psychological climate perceptions and HR attributions likely result from individual differences, differences in features of the organizational environment to which they are subjected (i.e., the situation), as well as an interaction between the person and the situation (Brown & Leigh, 1996; Schneider, 1987). We review relevant aspects of the environment in the section on the group level of analysis and focus here on some of these individual difference variables.

Perceptions and evaluations of HR systems will depend on employees' values, personalities, goals and needs, social roles and identities, and past experiences, competencies, and expectancies. In essence, the meaning of an HR system depends on whether it is seen as relevant for the fulfillment of an individual's personal goals (Bowen & Ostroff, 2004; Vroom, 1966). For example, younger workers without children might be more favorably disposed toward jobs that offer minimal benefits but above-market pay levels, whereas older employees might prefer more comprehensive benefits (Milkovich & Newman, 1999). Or, employees with young children who have highly accessible self-schemas about being a parent or otherwise have a "balanced careerist" orientation may be particularly critical of work–family balance and employee flexibility practices, as well as relevant benefits such as superior medical coverage for children. By contrast, for a person with a "fast-tracker" career orientation, HR practices that allow for developmental opportunities (e.g., training) and reward excellence should be considered particularly important. In sum, individuals perceive HR practices through different lenses and make varying conclusions about the extent to which the practices satisfy their needs.

Although little empirical work has examined the moderating role of employee characteristics on their perceptions of, and reactions to, HR systems (c.f. Wright & Boswell, 2002), support does exist for the moderating role of employee characteristics on reactions to single HR practices. For example, individuals high in need for achievement are more attracted to organizations that reward performance as opposed to seniority (Turban & Keon, 1993) and have individual-oriented reward systems as opposed to organization-oriented reward systems (Bretz, Ash, & Dreher, 1989). They also respond more favorably to high job scope than individuals low on need for achievement (Steers & Spencer, 1977). In addition, pay for performance is more strongly associated with motivation for individuals that have a high need for control (Eisenberger, Rhoades, & Cameron, 1999). The personality dimensions of extroversion and agreeableness have been found to interact with job autonomy in predicting contextual performance (Gellatly & Irving, 2001), neuroticism is positively associated with a preference for jobs with high pay (Lawler, 1971), and individuals high in conscientiousness are more attracted to organizations with cultures characterized by need for achievement (Judge & Cable, 1997).

The underlying explanation for these findings is that the favorability of an HR practice depends on its perceived instrumentality in helping individuals to accomplish personal goals or satisfy personal needs (Locke, 1976; Vroom, 1966) and express one's array of personality traits (Tett & Burnett, 2003). As such, the HR strategy that might be most appropriate for improving the performance of one segment of employees may differ from the motivational strategies that are required for other segments of employees. In other words, great variability may exist in the way that employees respond to HR practices. Indeed, research on person–organization (P–O) fit has clearly shown that when people's values and personalities match the characteristics of their organizations, they experience higher satisfaction and commitment (Erdogan, Kraimer, & Liden, 2004; Meglino, Ravlin, & Adkins, 1989), organizational identification and perceived organizational support (Cable & DeRue, 2002), and less stress (Ivancevich & Matteson, 1984). In addition, they engage in more citizenship behaviors (Cable & DeRue, 2002), report higher intentions to stay with the organization (Posner, Kouzes, & Schmidt, 1985), and are less likely to turn over (O'Reilly, Chatman, & Caldwell, 1991). According to the principles of Schneider's ASA framework (Schneider, 1987; Schneider, Goldstein, & Smith, 1995) and research findings on P–O fit, we might expect that variability in employees' perceptions of, and reactions to, HR practices diminishes over time, as individuals who are dissatisfied with their organization's HR practices are likely to turn over.

Another major factor influencing employee perceptions of a firm's HR practices is their past experiences with HR practices in different organizations. According to Rousseau (2001), differences in people's preemployment experiences influence their expectations about the employment. Such preemployment schemas direct people's information-seeking activities once in the organization. In addition, recruitment and socialization experiences are thought to be particularly influential in the formation of one's beliefs regarding the employment relationship. Recruiting experiences can differ widely based on the recruiting representative with whom an individual has contact, demographic characteristics of the applicant, the specific recruiting messages that an individual receives, and market conditions (Rynes & Barber, 1990). These experiences help to set one's expectations regarding what it will be like as an employee of the organization, which in turn influences the way that individuals make sense of subsequent organizational events, especially when, for example, people look for schema-confirming information. Thus, the assumption is that the same organizational context can give rise to differential perceptions regarding HR practices, depending on the cognitive processes, that is, preemployment schemas, of individuals.

People's perceptions are also likely to be influenced by their organizational roles; an individual's place in the organizational hierarchy, reporting relationships, patterns of informal social interaction, personal experiences with leaders, and experienced schedules of reinforcement contingencies affect the way people evaluate organizational information. Through sensemaking, social interaction, and shared experiences, employees influence one another's perceptions and attributions of HR practices (James, Joyce, & Slocum, 1988; Kozlowski & Hattrup, 1992; Weick, 1995).

In addition, the position that people occupy within their organization's informal networks influences their perceptions of HR practices because it impacts their access to valued resources and career opportunities (Dabos & Rousseau, 2004). Individuals who are centrally positioned in informal networks have greater control over the allocation and use of valued resources, and hence enjoy better opportunities for obtaining their desired goals. As a result, they develop more favorable perceptions of the employment relationship (Dabos & Rousseau, 2004) and HR practices. This underscores the importance of social interaction patterns in shaping employees' perceptions of HR practices. Similarly, when individuals successfully negotiate "idiosyncratic deals" (Rousseau, 2005) with their managers or other individuals in control of valued resources, they may develop different interpretations of HR practices than co-workers who have different deals.

Support for the notion that managers play a critical role in shaping individuals' perceptions of HR practices can be found in the work of Daniel (1985), who found that management style is related to subordinates' psychological climate perceptions. Likewise, Tierney (1999) found that the quality of one's relationship with his or her manager (i.e., leader–member exchange [LMX]) positively influences climate perceptions. In related research, Kristof (1996) found that when employees perceive that their values are not similar to those of the organization (i.e., low person–organization fit)—as evidenced, for example, by HR practices—those employees with high LMX relationships with their managers are better able to create desirable organizational experiences that help compensate for low person–organization fit. Together, these results suggest that employee perceptions of the broader organization, including HR practices, are partially a function of experiences with, and attitudes toward, the focal supervisor.

VARIABILITY AT THE GROUP LEVEL OF ANALYSIS

Almost as scarce as research recognizing variability in HR perceptions at the individual level of analysis is empirical attention focused on understanding group-level variability and its impact on the HR practices–performance relationship. Wright and Nishii (2005) noted specifically that while firms may have policies that declare what and how HR practices are to be implemented, variability often exists at the work group level because supervisors may differ in how they implement them. Consequently, real differences may exist in the actual practices that employees are subjected to even within the same job.

Group leaders influence employees' perceptions of, and reactions to, HR practices primarily through their role as implementers of organizational policies and practices (Offermann & Malamut, 2002; Tierney, 1999; Zohar, 2002; Zohar, 2000; Zohar & Luria, 2004). Group leaders, or line managers, have the task of executing organizational policies by translating them into situation-specific action directives during their interactions with subordinates (Zohar, 2000). Because organizational procedures cannot possibly cover every contingency that might arise, managers have a certain level of discretion in the way they implement policies, thereby resulting in different perceptions of those policies and practices at the subunit level (Zohar, 2000). For example, Gully, Phillips, and Tarique (2003) found that the more collectivistic a manager's values and the larger the merit increases, she or he is likely to give to low-performing subordinates. Within a single organization, this can lead to inconsistencies in the treatment and reward of subordinates, thereby affecting employee perceptions and the effectiveness of a merit pay system. Leaders also influence employees' perceptions of HR practices through their leadership styles (Daniel, 1985), personalities, and behaviors (Schneider & Reichers, 1983; Schneider, Ehrhart, Mayer, Saltz, & Niles-Jolly, 2005), and by communicating their own perceptions of HR practices to employees.

In addition to leaders, other group members also influence employee perceptions of HR practices. Group members develop shared meanings and attitudes because of social interactions and common experiences among members of the group (James et al., 1988; Kozlowski & Hattrup, 1992). Social interaction among group members leads to collective sense-making, or to the shared development of attitudes and perceptions of the environment (Weick, 1995). Common experiences and working conditions, such as exposure to relatively homogeneous situational factors and events, shared leadership, working conditions, policies and practices, and general task goals (among other factors), lead group members to share their perceptions of the work environment (Kozlowski & Klein, 2000). Even job satisfaction and other work-related attitudes, which have traditionally been thought to contain a large dispositional component, have been linked to environmental influences such that members of a group come to develop shared job attitudes (Gutek & Winter, 1992; Judge & Hulin, 1993; Ostroff, 1992, 1993; Watson & Slack, 1993).

Furthermore, because of the workings of the attraction–selection–attrition model (Schneider, 1987), it is reasonable to expect that people in work units become increasingly homogeneous in attitudes over time as dissimilar individuals leave the group. George (1990), for example, found that groups develop homogeneous affective tones as a function of the attraction–selection–attrition cycle. The extent to which group members come to share climate perceptions will likely be influenced by group factors such as cohesion and task interdependence—cohesion because it is associated with communication (Evans & Jarvis, 1980) and task interdependence because it leads to shared experiences and sensemaking. Mayer (2006), for example, found that task interdependence predicted justice climates in a sample of departments within a supermarket chain. Thus, to the extent that employees share more experiences with members of their units than with employees outside of their units, unit-level differences in collective perceptions of, and reactions to, HR practices should emerge. In turn, shared cognition is important for group performance because it provides the foundation for communication, coordination, and cooperation (Kozlowski, Gully, McHugh, Salas, & Cannon-Bowers, 1996).

In addition to being influenced by membership in formal organizational units, perceptions of HR practices may also vary according to informal group memberships. Specifically, perceptions of HR practices may depend on membership in social identity groups. According to social identity theory (Tajfel, 1982; Tajfel & Turner, 1979) and embedded intergroup relations theory (Alderfer, 1986; Alderfer & Smith, 1982), the ways in which people perceive social realities are largely determined by their group memberships, particularly when experiences with organizational practices and access to valued organizational resources are associated with group membership (Ilgen & Youtz, 1986). When members of a particular group perceive that organizational practices are not fairly implemented, they are excluded from social and information networks, or they are not provided with the opportunities necessary to succeed within the organization, then these perceptions are likely to be reflected in their interpretations of HR practices. There is indeed some research that suggests that women and racial minorities report less positive climate perceptions than men and Caucasians, suggesting that demographic groupings may moderate the HR practices to performance relationship (Hicks-Clarke & Iles, 2000; Kossek & Zonia, 1993). However, it is important to recognize that such perceptions of discriminatory or unfair treatment about HR practices may vary according to membership groups other than race and gender. Nishii and Raver (2003), for example, found that climate perceptions cluster according to the group memberships that are salient within a particular organizational context. In their sample, position status and racial minority status were significantly associated with perceptions of diversity climate, but gender was not, presumably because only the former was associated with organizational power and thus influenced the way that employees experienced and attached psychological meaning to their organizational environments.

In addition to moderating the relationships between actual HR practices and employees' experiences of those HR practices, group-level characteristics should also moderate later links in the SHRM process model depicted in Figure 10.1. Specifically, a number of cognitive, affective, and behavioral group process variables influence the extent to which individual attitudes and behaviors become reflected in aggregate levels of group and organizational performance (see Kozlowski & Bell, 2003, for a review). Relevant cognitive factors, for example, might include a group's transactive memory and learning levels. The transactive memory that characterizes a group is presumed to relate positively to the cognitive efficiency of the group by reducing redundancy of effort through the specialization of knowledge and expertise (Hollingshead, 1998). As for team learning, a key component of team performance, group differences emerge due to differences in team psychological safety (Edmonson, 1999) and the quality of the coaching that is available to the team (Cannon & Edmondson, 2000).

Affective group constructs such as cohesion and collective efficacy also influence the extent to which group members come together to perform at superior levels. Task cohesion, which refers to a group's shared attraction and commitment to the group goal, is positively associated with group performance (Mullen & Copper, 1994), particularly when combined with interpersonal cohesion, or interpersonal liking among group members (Zaccaro & McCoy, 1988). Collective efficacy is also positively associated with group performance, as concluded in a meta-analysis by Gully, Joshi, and Incalcaterra (2001). Thus, subunits within a single organization that are subjected to the same set of HR practices may still differ in their performance—and therefore the observed HR practices–performance relationship for those groups—as a result of differences in these affective group factors. An interesting question, then, is: What can organizations do to influence these group-level factors in ways that optimize the HR practices–performance relationship?

Finally, group coordination and cooperation are behavioral process mechanisms that positively impact group performance (Kozlowski & Bell, 2003). For example, coordination behaviors such as delegating team tasks, asking team members for input, and helping one another are positively related to performance (Stout, Salas, & Carson, 1994). Cooperative behaviors are also positively related to task and psychosocial outcomes (Pinto & Pinto, 1990), as well as financial outcomes (Smith et al., 1994).

That group-level constructs influence group performance is not news, but an explicit examination of their moderating effects on the HR practices–performance relationship within organizations would be. Indeed, as researchers focus more attention on cross-level and emergent processes as a means of more fully explicating the process of SHRM, attention needs to be paid to such group-level moderators.

VARIABILITY AT THE JOB LEVEL OF ANALYSIS

Until relatively recently, SHRM research has treated HR systems as almost monolithically uniform across the organization. However, Huselid's

(1995) distinction between the HR practices aimed at hourly employees and those aimed at managerial professional employees, and MacDuffie's (1995) and Delery and Doty's (1996) focus on core employee groups began the recognition that multiple HR strategies might exist within the same organization. Most recently, Lepak and Snell's (1999) human capital model made explicit the importance of recognizing the variation in HR systems that exists across jobs.

Lepak and Snell (1999) debunk the assumption that one type of employment relationship with its corresponding HR practices is appropriate for all employees. Rather, they argue that employment relationships should be dictated by the value and uniqueness of human capital. They suggest that human capital varies along two dimensions: value-creating potential, or the ratio of strategic benefits relative to costs incurred in human capital investments; and uniqueness, or the extent to which the human capital in question is idiosyncratic to a firm. According to their model, organization-focused employment relationships that are characterized by long-term mutual investment and a commitment-maximizing HR system are only appropriate for human capital that is high in both uniqueness and value-creating potential. Human capital that is high in value but low in uniqueness, however, should be acquired from the external market rather than developed internally. This is mainly because the low idiosyncratic nature of the human capital means that it can be easily employed by competitors, and thus firms would not gain returns on investments in training and development should the employees leave to work for competitors. They further identify the alliance mode for highly unique human capital with low value-creating potential and the contracting employment mode for human capital that is low in both uniqueness and value-creating potential. In later work, they suggest that these different HR systems imply different psychological contracts with the employees (Lepak, Takeuchi, & Snell, 2000). Note that the previous discussion recognized variability in individual psychological contracts, whereas Lepak and Snell suggest that there should also be job-level variance in these contracts.

Tsui et al. (1995) similarly propose that employment relationships should vary based on the types of job in question. Their model suggests that jobs requiring technological and skill complexity should be correlated with the use of organization-focused employment relationships, which are characterized by broad, open-ended obligations between the employer and employee. This contrasts with economic exchange relationships, which are more common for jobs with an abundant labor supply and lower-skilled jobs and which involve tight monitoring, explicit rules, and rigidly defined employment contracts that lack benefits and training.

It is also possible that there may be variability in some of the links pictured in Figure 10.1 according to occupational lines. Rousseau (2001), for example, argues that people's psychological contract perceptions may differ according to occupational ideologies such that people come to expect from their organizations treatment that is consistent with occupational norms and philosophies. Based on differential norms across occupations, this can translate into differences across occupational groups in the expectations of HR practices and henceforth evaluations of a firm's HR practices. There is also some support for the idea that members of high-status occupations (e.g., professional) not only have higher expectations of their organization than members of low-status occupations (e.g., blue collar), but also are less likely to respond to extrinsic rewards with organizational commitment (Cohen, 1992). Instead, because they attribute the rewards that they receive to their qualifications, their commitment tends to be directed toward their occupation rather than the organization per se. This suggests that there may be occupational differences in the perceived HR practices–employee reactions link; that is, members of different occupations might respond differently to the same set of HR practices.

THEORETICAL IMPLICATIONS

Currently, cross-level or multilevel theories of SHRM are almost nonexistent. With the exception of Ostroff and Bowen (2000) and Bowen and Ostroff (2004), virtually no SHRM researchers have attempted to theorize across levels of analysis, yet exactly such theorizing may provide the foundation for renewed energy around research in this area.

Vast literatures on social information processing (Salancik & Pfeffer, 1978) have focused on understanding how social processes impact the perceptions and reactions of individual employees to organizational phenomena such as job characteristics. These same social processes surely play a role in what aspects of the HR practices employees attend to, how they are interpreted, and the reactions that they feel are appropriate. Future research needs to explore these issues.

Similarly, at the group level of analysis, little attention has been paid to variability across groups. Work group leaders likely implement HR policies quite differently, yet we know little as to what might explain the differences in implementation as well as the variability in outcomes that result from such differences. At the job level, Lepak and Snell's (1999) HR architecture has provided at least a rationale for moving away from looking for one HR strategy across an organization. In addition, Lepak and his colleagues have begun empirically exploring how firms manage multiple HR systems across multiple jobs.

In addition, future research would certainly benefit from exploring within-organization variability in employee perceptions and attributions of HR practices in studies of external fit (i.e., the notion that alignment between HR practices and other external factors such as strategy or technology yields enhanced performance). The inconsistent findings to date regarding external fit may be partially explained by the commonly used large-scale firm-level studies in which single respondents are asked to report on a firm's HRM system and strategies. Employees' reactions to and interpretations of a firm's HR practices and strategy might lead the same inputs (HRM systems and strategy), ceteris paribus, to varying levels of firm effectiveness.

In recognition of such an idea, some researchers have argued that because external fit is highly idiosyncratic and the way strategy is linked to HR practices, and in turn to firm performance, involves causal ambiguity (Becker & Huselid, 1998), it is time to move beyond traditional contingency frameworks and extend the domain of external fit to include other organizational phenomena (Snell, Youndt, & Wright, 1996). The above discussion suggests that employees' perceptions of HR practices may represent one set of employee experience variables with the potential to deepen our understanding of the relationships among HR systems, strategy, and firm performance.

Similarly, employees' perceptions of HR practices may also prove useful when thinking about internal fit. For example, it is possible that a firm's employees might have perceptions about internal fit that differ from those reported by the HR representatives of their company or from researchers' calculations of internal fit. If one of the main objectives of achieving internal fit is to send consistent messages to employees regarding the firm's goals and expectations for employee behavior, it makes sense to explore notions of fit from the employees' perspective. In particular, how coherent or internally aligned are the HRM-related messages that employees receive from the HR practices to which they are subjected, and is there agreement across employees (cf. Bowen & Ostroff, 2004)? It is entirely reasonable to expect that in some cases, even if a firm's HR practices (as described in a very generic form in SHRM research surveys) appear to be internally consistent on paper, they may not be experienced as such by employees.

In practical terms, examining employee perceptions of internal consistency can be a useful tool for organizations seeking to enhance their internal fit; it can provide organizations with specific leverage points on which to focus their attention. For example, which HR practices are failing to send the message that service quality is the organization's primary strategic objective? Which HR practices do employees disagree with regard to the underlying strategic goal? Identifying the specific HR practices that are the culprit and then focusing efforts to revise either the HR practices themselves or the communication surrounding those HR practices may prove to be helpful.

In addition, future research that includes qualitative methods aimed at uncovering why and how employees develop the perceptions and attributions that they do would also be useful. For example, what pieces of organizational information are the most influential in forming employees' perceptions? How are perceptions and attributions shaped by the volume, presentation, and timing of discrepant information regarding HR practices? What are the conditions under which employees are motivated to seek information about the goals of management that drive HR practices? How is information gathered from various sources weighted differently in the formation of HR perceptions and attributions based on the credibility of the information source or the clarity of the information? How, explicitly, do employees' preemployment experiences influence the perceptions and attributions that they subsequently develop? Once formed, how susceptible to change are employees' perceptions and attributions? What are the organizational and individual competencies that contribute to the formation of HR attributions with desirable consequences for organizations? Is it the HR practices themselves, or other signals that accompany them that shape employees' HR attributions?

Furthermore, research that examines the relationship between individual personality and values on the one hand, and perceptions of the system of HR practices on the other, would be valuable. Previous research has shown how personality is related to reactions to a particular HR practice. However, still unexamined is how people respond to the pattern of HR practices. Given the emphasis placed on internal consistency of HR practices, it makes sense to assume that people's perceptions of a particular HR practice (especially as presented to them in a lab study, as has been the case in many such studies) may differ from their perceptions of that practice when evaluated in conjunction with other potentially synergistic HR practices.

Finally, although we restricted our discussion of variability to sources of within-organization variance, we recognize that there are many important sources of variability in the HR practices–performance relationship outside of organizations. In particular, we urge future research to more explicitly examine variability according to industry sector, regulatory environment, and national culture.

PRACTICAL IMPLICATIONS

Recognizing the potential variability in perceptions of and reactions to HR systems in organizations suggests a number of implications for practice. First, while Lepak and Snell's (1999) HR architecture rightly notes that firms manage different employee groups differently, they do not discuss how each group reacts to what might be perceived as inequitable treatment. Such an approach to managing multiple employee groups may increase the inequality of outcomes, and the practical impact of such a situation is not clear.

Second, the recognition that work groups within the same job may experience different practices focuses on the critical role that work group leaders play in representing the organization. Because employee reactions can be shaped by both the perceived practices they experience and their attributions for the motivations behind those practices, work group leaders may strongly determine the effectiveness of an HR system developed by a firm.

Finally, the model presented in Figure 10.1 highlights the importance of redundancy and consistency of communication in order to effectively implement HR practices that align with strategy and drive performance. As Ostroff and Bowen (2004) noted, HR practices serve as communication devices, and as MacDuffie (1995) noted, part of the value of the HR system is realized through the redundancy of practices. However, the communications that are derived from HR practices must be internally consistent with other forms of organizational communication (e.g., supervisory, written, leader verbal messages, etc.) in order to achieve maximum effect.

SUMMARY AND CONCLUSIONS

While considerable research attention has focused on the empirical link between HR practices and firm performance, little empirical or theoretical attention has been devoted to recognizing the cross-level nature of this phenomenon. Future SHRM theorizing and research must be willing to acknowledge the variability that exists within a firm regarding how HR practices are implemented, perceived, and interpreted by the employees who are the targets of these practices, and whose behavioral reactions serve as the only way through which the practices can impact performance.

REFERENCES

Alderfer, C. P. (1986). An intergroup perspective on group dynamics. In J. W. Lorsch (Ed.), *Handbook of organizational behavior* (pp. 190–222). Englewood Cliffs, NJ: Prentice Hall.

Alderfer, C. P., & Smith, K. K. (1982). Studying intergroup relations embedded in organizations. *Administrative Science Quarterly, 27*, 35–65.

Arthur, J. B. (1992). The link between business strategy and industrial relations in American steel minimills. *Industrial and Labor Relations Review, 45*, 488–506.

Becker, B. E., & Huselid, M. A. (1998). High performance work systems and firm performance: A synthesis of research and managerial implications. *Research in Personnel and Human Resource Management, 16*, 53–102.

Bowen, D. E., & Ostroff, C. (2004). Understanding HRM-firm performance linkages: The role of the "strength" of the HRM system. *Academy of Management Review, 29*, 203–221.

Bretz, R. D., Ash, R. A., & Dreher, G. F. (1989). Do people make the place? An examination of the attraction–selection–attrition hypothesis. *Personnel Psychology, 42*, 561–581.

Brief, A. P. (1988). *Attitudes in and around organizations.* Thousand Oaks, CA: Sage Publications.

Brown, S. P., & Leigh, T. W. (1996). A new look at psychological climate and its relationship to job involvement, effort, and performance. *Journal of Applied Psychology, 81*, 358–368.

Cable, D. M., & DeRue, S. D. (2002). The convergent and discriminant validity of subjective fit perceptions. *Journal of Applied Psychology, 87,* 875–884.

Cannon, M., & Edmondson, A. (2000). *Confronting failure: Antecedents and consequences of shared learning-oriented beliefs in organizational work groups.* Paper presented at the Annual Meeting of the Academy of Management Conference, Toronto.

Carr, J. Z., Schmidt, A. M., Ford, J. K., & DeShon, R. P. (2003). Climate perceptions matter: A meta-analytic path analysis relating molar climate, cognitive and affective states, and individual level work outcomes. *Journal of Applied Psychology, 88,* 605–619.

Cohen, A. (1992). Antecedents of organizational commitment across occupational groups: A meta-analysis. *Journal of Organizational Behavior, 13,* 539–558.

Cox, T. (1993). *Cultural diversity in organizations: Theory, research and practice.* San Francisco: Berrett-Koehler.

Dabos, G. E., & Rousseau, D. M. (2004). Social interaction patterns shaping employee psychological contracts. *Academy of Management Best Papers Proceedings,* OB, N1-N6.

Daniel, T. L. (1985). Managerial behaviors: Their relationship to perceived organizational climate in a high-technology company. *Group and Organization Studies, 10,* 413–428.

Delery, J. E. & Doty, D. H. (1996). Modes of theorizing in strategic human resource management: Tests of universalistic, contingency and configurational performance predictions. *Academy of Management Journal, 39,* 802–835.

Edmonson, A. C. (1999). Psychological safety and learning behavior in work teams. *Administrative Science Quarterly, 44,* 350–383.

Eisenberger, R., Rhoades, L., & Cameron, J. (1999). Does pay for performance increase or decrease perceived self-determination and intrinsic motivation? *Journal of Personality and Social Psychology, 77,* 1026–1040.

Erdogan, B., Kraimer, M. L., & Liden, R. C. (2004). Work value congruence and intrinsic career success: The compensatory roles of leader-member exchange and perceived organizational support. *Personnel Psychology, 57,* 305–332.

Evans, N. J., & Jarvis, P. A. (1980). Group cohesion: A review and reevaluation. *Small Group Behavior, 11,* 359–370.

Fiske, S. T., & Taylor, S. E. (1991). *Social cognition* (2nd ed.). New York: McGraw-Hill.

Gellatly, I. R., & Irving, G. (2001). Personality, autonomy, and contextual performance of managers. *Human Performance, 14,* 229–243.

George, J. M. (1990). Personality, affect, and behavior in groups. *Journal of Applied Psychology, 75,* 107–116.

Gray, B. M., Bougon, G., & Donnellon, A. (1985). Organizations as constructions and deconstructions of meaning. *Journal of Management, 11(2),* 83–98.

Gully, S. M., Joshi, A., & Incalcaterra, K. A. (2001, April). *A meta-analytic investigation of the relationships among team-efficacy, self-efficacy, and performance.* Presented at the 16th Annual Conference of the Society for Industrial and Organizational Psychology, San Diego.

Gully, S. M., Phillips, J. M., & Tarique, I. (2003). Collectivism and goal orientation as mediators of the effect of national identity on merit pay decisions. *International Journal of Human Resource Management, 14,* 1368–1390.

Gutek, B. A., & Winter, S. (1992). Consistency of job satisfaction across situations: Fact or artifact? *Journal of Vocational Behavior, 41,* 61–78.

Guzzo, R., & Noonan, K. (1994). Human resource practices as communications and the psychological contract. *Human Resource Management, 33*, 447–462.

Hicks-Clarke, D., & Iles, P. (2000). Climate for diversity and its effects on career and organizational attitudes and perceptions. *Personnel Review, 29*, 324–343.

Hollingshead, A. B. (1998). Communication, learning, and retrieval in transactive memory systems. *Journal of Experimental Social Psychology, 34*, 423–442.

Hough, L. M., & Schneider, R. J. (1996). Personality traits, taxonomies and applications in organizations. In M. Kevin (Ed.), *Individual differences and behavior in organizations* (pp. 31–88). San Francisco: Jossey-Bass.

Huselid, M. A. (1995). The impact of human resource management practices on turnover, productivity and corporate financial performance. *Academy of Management Journal, 38*, 635–672.

Ilgen, D. R., & Youtz, M. (1986). Factors affecting the evaluation and development of minorities in organizations. In K. M. Rowland & G. R. Ferris (Eds.), *Research in personnel and human resource management* (Vol. 4, pp. 81–124). Greenwich, CT: JAI Press.

Ivancevich, J. M., & Matteson, M. T. (1984). A type A–B person–work environment interaction model for examining occupational stress and consequences. *Human Relations, 37(7)*, 491-513.

Jackson, S. E., & Dutton, J. E. (1988). Discerning threats and opportunities. *Administrative Science Quarterly, 3*, 370–387.

James, L. R., James, L. A., & Ashe, D. K. (1990). The meaning of organizations: The role of cognition and values. In B. Schneider (Ed.), *Organizational climate and culture* (pp. 40–84). San Francisco: Jossey-Bass.

James, L. R., Joyce, W. F., & Slocum, J. W. (1988). Organizations do not cognize. *Academy of Management Review, 13*, 129–132.

Judge, T. A., & Bretz, R. D. (1992). Effects of work values on job choice decisions. *Journal of Applied Psychology, 77*, 261–271.

Judge, T. A., & Cable, D. M. (1997). Applicant personality, organizational culture and organization attraction. *Personnel Psychology, 50*, 359–394.

Judge, T. A., & Hulin, C. L. (1993). Job satisfaction as a reflection of disposition: A multiple source causal analysis. *Organizational Behavior and Human Decision Processes, 56*, 388–421.

Kossek, E. E., & Zonia, S. C. (1993). Assessing diversity climate: A field study of reactions to employer efforts to promote diversity. *Journal of Organizational Behavior, 14*, 61–81.

Kozlowski, S. W. J., & Bell, B. S. (2003). Work groups and teams in organizations. In W. C. Borman, D. R. Ilgen, & R. J. Klimoski (Eds.), *Handbook of psychology: Industrial and organizational psychology* (Vol. 12, pp. 333–375). New York: Wiley.

Kozlowski, S. W. J., Gully, S. M., McHugh, P. P., Salas, E., & Cannon-Bowers, J. A. (1996). A dynamic theory of leadership and team effectiveness: Developmental and task contingent leader roles. In G. R. Ferris (Ed.), *Research in personnel and human resource management* (Vol. 14, pp. 253–305). Greenwich, CT: JAI Press.

Kozlowski, S. W. J., & Hattrup, K. (1992). A disagreement about within-group agreement: Disentagling issues of consistency versus consensus. *Journal of Applied Psychology, 77*, 161–167.

Kozlowski, S. W. J., & Klein, K. J. (2000). A multilevel approach to theory and research in organizations: Contextual, temporal, and emergent processes. In K. J. Klein & S. W. J. Kozlowski (Eds.), *Multilevel theory, research, and methods in organizations: Foundations, extensions, and new directions* (pp. 3–90). San Francisco: Jossey-Bass.

Kristof, A. L. (1996). Person–organization fit: An integrative review of its conceptualizations, measurement, and implications. *Personnel Psychology, 49,* 1–49.

Lawler, E. (1971). *Pay and organizational effectiveness.* New York: McGraw-Hill.

Lepak, D. P., & Snell, S. A. (1999). The human resource architecture: Toward a theory of human capital allocation and development. *Academy of Management Review, 24,* 31–48.

Lepak, D. P., Takeuchi, K., & Snell, S. A. (2003). Employment flexibility and firm performance: Examining the interaction effects of employment mode, environmental dynamism, and technological intensity. *Journal of Management,* 29: 681–703.

Lewin, K. (1936). *Principles of topological psychology.* New York: McGraw-Hill.

Locke, E. (1976). Nature and causes of job satisfaction. In M. D. Dunnette (Ed.), *Handbook of industrial and organizational psychology* (pp. 1297–1349). Chicago: Rand McNally.

Locke, E., & Latham, G. (1990). *A theory of goal setting and task performance.* Englewood Cliffs, NJ: Prentice Hall.

MacDuffie, J. (1995). Human resource bundles and manufacturing performance: Organizational logic and flexible production systems in the world auto industry. *Industrial and Labor Relations Review, 48,* 197–221.

Mayer, D. M. (2006, May). A group-level examination of the relationship between LMX and justice. In H. H. M. Tse & N. M. Ashkanasy (Chairs), *Leaders and followers: How social exchange and influence impact outcomes.* Symposium conducted at the 21st Annual Conference of the Society of Industrial and Organizational Psychology, Dallas, TX.

Meglino, B. M., & Ravlin, E. C. (1998). Individual values in organizations: Concepts, controversies, and research. *Journal of Management, 24,* 351–389.

Meglino, B., Ravlin, E., & Adkins, C. (1989). A work values approach to corporate culture: A field test of the value congruence process and its relationship to individual outcomes. *Journal of Applied Psychology, 74,* 424–432.

Milkovich, G. T., & Newman, J. M. (1999). *Compensation* (6th ed.). Homewood, IL: Irwin.

Mischel, W., & Shoda, Y. (1995). A cognitive-affective system theory of personality: Reconceptualizing situations, dispositions, dynamics, and invariance in personality structure. *Psychological Review, 102,* 246–268.

Mullen, B., & Copper, C. (1994). The relation between group cohesiveness and performance: An integration. *Psychological Bulletin, 115,* 210–227.

Nishii, L. H. (2006). *The role of employee attributions of HR practices in SHRM.* Poster presented as the recipient of the 2005 S. Rains Wallace Dissertation Research Award at the 21st Annual Conference of the Society for Industrial and Organizational Psychology, Dallas, TX.

Nishii, L. H., Lepak, D. P., & Schneider, B. (in press). Employee attributions of the "why" of HR practices: Their effects on employee attitudes and behaviors, and customer satisfaction. *Personnel Psychology.*

Nishii, L. N., & Raver, J. L. (2003). *Collective climates for diversity: Evidence from a field study.* Paper presented at the 18th Annual Conference of the Society for Industrial and Organizational Psychology, Orlando, FL.

Offermann, L. R., & Malamut, A. B. (2002). When leaders harass: The impact of target perceptions of organizational leadership and climate on harassment reporting and outcomes. *Journal of Applied Psychology, 87*(5), 885–893.

O'Reilly, C. A., Chatman, J., & Caldwell, D. F. (1991). People and organizational culture: A profile comparison approach to assessing person–organization fit. *Academy of Management Journal, 34,* 487–516.

Osterman, P. (1994). How common is workplace transformation and who adopts it? *Industrial and Labor Relations Review, 47,* 174–188.

Ostroff, C. (1992). The relationship between satisfaction, attitudes, and performance: An organizational level analysis. *Journal of Applied Psychology, 77,* 963–974.

Ostroff, C. (1993). Comparing correlations based on individual-level and aggregated data. *Journal of Applied Psychology, 78,* 569–582.

Ostroff, C., & Bowen, D. E. (2000). Moving HR to a higher level: HR practices and organizational effectiveness. In K. J. Klein & S. W. J. Kozlowski (Eds.), *Multilevel theory, research, and methods in organizations: Foundations, extensions, and new directions* (pp. 211–266). San Francisco: Jossey-Bass.

Parker, C. P., Baltes, B., Young, S., Altmann, R., LaCost, H., Huff, J., & Roberts, J. E. (2003). Relationships between psychological climate perceptions and work outcomes: A meta-analytic review. *Journal of Organizational Behavior, 24,* 389–416.

Pinto, M. B., & Pinto, J. K. (1990). Project team communication and cross-functional cooperation in new program development. *Journal of Product Innovation Management, 7,* 200–212.

Posner, B. Z., Kouzes, J. M., & Schmidt, W. H. (1985). Shared values make a difference: An empirical test of corporate culture. *Human Resource Management, 24,* 293–309.

Reichers, A. E., & Schneider, B. (1990). Climate and culture: An evolution of constructs. In B. Schneider (Ed.), *Organizational climate and culture* (pp. 5–39). San Francisco: Jossey-Bass.

Rentsch, J. R. (1990). Climate and culture: Interaction and qualitative differences in organizational meanings. *Journal of Applied Psychology, 75*(6), 668–681.

Rousseau, D. M. (1995). *Psychological contracts in organizations: Understanding written and unwritten agreements.* Newbury Park, CA: Sage.

Rousseau, D. M. (2001). Schema, promise and mutuality: The building blocks of the psychological contract. *Journal of Occupational and Organizational Psychology, 74,* 511–541.

Rousseau, D. M. (2005). *I-deals: Idiosyncratic deals employees bargain for themselves.* New York: M.E. Sharpe.

Rynes, S. L., & Barber, A. E. (1990). Applicant attraction strategies: An organizational perspective. *Academy of Management Review, 15,* 286–310.

Salancik, G. R., & Pfeffer, J. (1978). A social information processing approach to job attitudes and task design. *Administrative Science Quarterly, 23,* 224–253.

Schein, E. H. (1992). *Organizational culture and leadership* (2nd ed.). San Francisco: Jossey-Bass.

Schmitt, M. J., & Allscheid, S. P. (1995). Employee attitudes and customer satisfaction: Making theoretical and empirical connections. *Personnel Psychology, 48,* 521–536.

Schneider, B. (1975). Organizational climate: An essay. *Personnel Psychology, 28,* 447–479.

Schneider, B. (1987). The people make the place. *Personnel Psychology, 40,* 437–454.

Schneider, B., Ehrhart, M. G., Mayer, D. M., Saltz, J. L., & Niles-Jolly, K. (2005). Understanding organization-customer links in service settings. *Academy of Management Journal, 48,* 1017–1032.

Schneider, B., Goldstein, H. W., & Smith, D. B. (1995). The ASA framework: An update. *Personnel Psychology, 48,* 747–773.

Schneider, B., Gunnarson, S. K., & Niles-Jolly, K. (1994). Creating the climate and culture of success. *Organizational Dynamics, 23,* 17–29.

Schneider, B., & Reichers, A. E. (1983). On the etiology of climates. *Personnel Psychology, 36*(1), 19–39.

Smith, K. G., Smith, K. A., Olian, J. D., Smis, H. P., Jr., O'Bannon, D. P., & Scully, J. A. (1994). Top management team demography and process: The role of social integration and communication. *Administrative Science Quarterly, 39,* 412–438.

Snell, S. A., Youndt, M. A., & Wright, P. M. (1996). Establishing a framework for research in strategic human resource management: Merging resource theory and organizational learning. In G. R. Ferris (Ed.), *Research in personnel and human resources management* (Vol. 14, pp. 61–90). Greenwich, CT: JAI Press.

Steers, R. M., & Spencer, D. G. (1977). The role of achievement motivation in job design. *Journal of Applied Psychology, 62,* 472–479.

Stout, R. J., Salas, E., & Carson, R. (1994). Individual task proficiency and team process behavior: What's important for team functioning. *Military Psychology, 6,* 177–192.

Tajfel, H. (1982). *Human groups and social categories: Studies in social psychology.* Cambridge, UK: Cambridge University Press.

Tajfel, H., & Turner, J. (1979). An integrative theory of intergroup conflict. In W. G. Austin & S. Worchel (Eds.), *The social psychology of intergroup relations* (pp. 33–47). Monterey, CA: Brooks/Cole.

Tett, R. P., & Burnett, D. D. (2003). A personality trait-based interactionist model of job performance. *Journal of Applied Psychology, 88,* 500–517.

Thomas, J. B., Clark, S. M., & Gioia, D. A. (1993). Strategic sensemaking and organizational performance: Linkages among scanning, interpretation, action, and outcomes. *Academy of Management Journal, 36,* 239–270.

Tierney, P. (1999). Work relations as a precursor to a psychological climate for change: The role of work group supervisors and peers. *Journal of Organizational Change Management, 12,* 120–134.

Tsui, A. S., Pearce, J. L., Porter, L. W., & Hite, J. (1995). Choice of employee-organization relationship: Influence of external and internal organizational factors. In G. R. Ferris (Ed.), *Research in personnel and human resources management* (Vol. 13, pp. 17–151). Greenwich, CT: JAI Press.

Tsui, A. S., Pearce, J. L., Porter, L. W., & Tripoli, A. M. (1997). Alternative approaches to the employee-organization relationship: Does investment in employees pay off? *Academy of Management Journal, 40,* 1089–1121.

Turban, D. B., & Keon, T. L. (1993). Organizational attractiveness: An interactionist perspective. *Journal of Applied Psychology, 78,* 184–193.

Vroom, V. H. (1966). Organizational choice: A study of pre- and post-decision processes. *Organizational Behavior and Human Performance, 1,* 212–225.

Watson, D., & Slack, A. K. (1993). General factors of affective temperament and their relation to job satisfaction over time. *Organizational Behavior and Human Decision Processes, 54,* 181–202.

Weick, K. E. (1995). *Sensemaking in organizations.* Thousand Oaks, CA: Sage.

Whitener, E. M. (2001). Do "high commitment" human resource practices affect employee commitment? A cross-level analysis using hierarchical linear modeling. *Journal of Management, 27,* 515–535.

Wright, P., & Boswell, W. (2002). Desegregating HRM: A review and synthesis of micro and macro human resource management research. *Journal of Management, 28,* 247–276.

Wright, P. M., McCormick, B., Sherman, S., & McMahan, G. (1999). The role of human resource practices in petro-chemical refinery performance. *International Journal of Human Resource Management. 10,* 551–557.

Wright, P. M., & McMahan, G. C. (1992). Theoretical perspectives for strategic human resource management. *Journal of Management, 18,* 295–320.

Wright, P. M., McMahan, G. C., & McWilliams, A. (1994). Human resources as a source of sustained competitive advantage: A resource-based perspective. *International Journal of Human Resource Management, 5,* 301–326.

Wright, P. M., & Nishii, L. H. (in press). Strategic HRM and organizational behavior: Integrating multiple levels of analysis. In D. Guest (Ed.), *Innovations in HR.* Oxford: Blackwell Publishing.

Zaccaro, S. J., & McCoy, M. C. (1988). The effects of task and interpersonal cohesiveness on performance of a disjunctive group task. *Journal of Applied Social Psychology, 18,* 837–851.

Zohar, D. (2000). A group-level model of safety climate: Testing the effect of group climate on microaccidents in manufacturing jobs. *Journal of Applied Psychology, 85,* 587–596.

Zohar, D. (2002). The effects of leadership dimensions, safety climate, and assigned priorities on minor injuries in work groups. *Journal of Organizational Behavior, 23,* 75–92.

Zohar, D., & Luria, G. (2004). Climate as a social-cognitive construction of supervisory safety practices: Scripts as proxy of behavior patterns. *Journal of Applied Psychology, 89,* 322–333.

11

Colleges of Business That Moved to New Buildings
The Places Changed, but the People Did Not—What Happened?

JOHN P. WANOUS
Ohio State University

ARNON E. REICHERS
Ohio State University

Beginning in the mid-1990s, a flurry of new construction began at colleges of business administration throughout the United States. About one-third of the top 50 MBA programs ranked by *U.S. News and World Report* moved into new buildings or into extensively renovated facilities. In addition, 29 MBA programs outside that top 50 also moved into new buildings. This means that two assessments of moving can be made: (1) changes in rankings for the movers that were in the top 50, and (2) whether the movers outside the top 50 entered the top 50 after moving.

The mover schools represent a situation where the place changed, but the people did not. The attraction–selection–attrition (ASA) theory predicts that moving to new buildings will have little or no effect on MBA program rankings. The primary reason for this is that there was no meaningful change in the faculty or staff at these schools.

ASA theory is not known outside of academia. Conventional wisdom (held by deans, alumni, and wealthy donors) makes the opposite prediction from ASA theory. According to conventional wisdom, spending a lot of money on new buildings is justifiable because the buildings enhance the reputation of the college vis-à-vis its competitors. The belief is that there will be a one-time "bump up" in a college's ranking because of the move. This is because only a minority of business colleges actually move in any given period. Thus, moving, per se, is assumed to give an advantage to those who moved to nicer physical facilities versus those who have not yet moved.

There are several assumptions underlying conventional wisdom, and together they appear to make a convincing argument for moving to new buildings. First, new buildings are a tangible sign of financial success, as well as a prestige symbol. This symbol of success may be attractive to students, alumni, recruiters, local corporations, and executives interested in further education. Schools offering the executive MBA or various programs for senior managers typically charge much higher tuition. New buildings may be especially important in establishing credibility with this particular group. As is sometimes said in similar situations, "Beware of the physician (lawyer, dentist, etc.) having a small, drab, inexpensive office."

Second, colleges of business are ranked by several media outlets, for example: *U.S. News & World Report* (annually since 1990), *Business Week* (every other year since 1988), and the *Wall Street Journal* (annually since 2001). These rankings create a very public competitive environment for the best known colleges of business. Thus, it is reasonable to assume that most business school deans feel pressure to "keep up with the competition." Deans may also worry that failing to keep up might lead to a decrease in MBA rankings, which is something that no dean wants. Schools outside the top 50 may view new buildings as a way to move into the top 50.

The title of an article in the *Chronicle of Higher Education* captures the essence of the second assumption: "The New 'Arms Race' in Business-School Buildings" (Mangan, 2002). Several examples of colleges moving to new buildings at both ranked and unranked colleges were cited in this article. In some cases the costs of new buildings exceed $120 million, as was the case at our school, Ohio State University. Several deans were quoted by Mangan (2002) about their expectations for the effect of new buildings. They all espoused conventional wisdom in one way or another. However, Mangan had a skeptical conclusion: "Whether these new buildings will live up to their billing remains to be seen" (Mangan, 2002). ASA theory was not cited as the reason for Mangan's skepticism. However, we use ASA theory to contradict conventional wisdom.

WHAT DO THEORY AND RESEARCH HAVE TO SAY ABOUT CONVENTIONAL WISDOM?

The ASA Model: Conventional Wisdom Is Wrong

We consider the ASA model developed by Schneider (1987) quite relevant for assessing the results of moving to new buildings. This is because it represents a viewpoint directly opposite from conventional wisdom.

The title of Schneider's much cited work (1987) expresses his main point: "The people make the place." He argued that organizations are strongly affected by three interrelated processes: (1) attraction of new personnel, (2) selection of them by the organization, and (3) attrition of those who do not fit with the organization.

One consequence of these three processes is that organizations develop their own internal climates and culture, as represented by employees who are more similar to one another than they are different in terms of both skills and personality. For example, Southwest Airlines practices very careful recruitment and selection so that new hires fit their "work hard and have fun" culture that is distinctive in the airline industry. Some observers believe that their strong culture is one reason why Southwest has been the most financially successful U.S. airline in the past 30 years (O'Reilly & Pfeffer, 2000). Southwest has earned profits every year since 1972, with a history of no layoffs and no fatal crashes. It is the only U.S. airline to be profitable in the four years following the 9/11 terrorist attack. Competitors try to match their business strategy, which is no secret. However, no competitor has yet matched the winning internal culture at Southwest, which is why it remains unique.

In the years since its initial publication, the ASA model has been difficult to assess empirically, as described some years later by Schneider, Goldstein, and Smith (1995). According to them, the type of data needed to assess the ASA model should be at the organization level and with repeated measures over time. Further, researchers are advised to avoid assessing the unique contributions of the three ASA processes (attraction–selection–attrition), and instead focus on *organizational-level outcomes*. Finally, Schneider et al. recommend gathering data from multiple organizations rather than a single organization. This is because ASA concerns interorganizational differences, as illustrated by Southwest Airlines versus all other airlines. Our research project meets all of these criteria, as discussed later.

We believe that Schneider's ASA framework can be interpreted to predict that merely moving to new buildings will fail to produce long-lasting organizational change. This is because the people inside the buildings are more important to organizational performance than the buildings themselves. As applied to moving to new buildings, the place changes, but the people do not. If "the people make the place" has validity, then the high expectations about moving to a new place will be shattered. Long-term change requires changes in people, not bricks and mortar.

With regard to the place changing but not the people, we need to distinguish between two groups of people inside graduate business school buildings. There is relatively little turnover among the faculty and staff on a year-to-year basis. However, there is considerable turnover among the students. In the typical two-year full-time MBA program a new class enters each year as one leaves. This is a 50% yearly turnover among students. ASA theory can also be extended to predict that certain kinds of students might be attracted to and selected by some schools and not others as a result of differences in internal learning climates for different schools. For example, colleges of business can differ on several dimensions: teaching pedagogy, size of classes, emphasis on teamwork, diversity within the student body, and so on. Thus, because of ASA effects on students, the typical 50% turnover among full-time MBA students may be less dramatic than this high turnover rate might seem to indicate.

OB Theory and Research That Support Conventional Wisdom

Over 30 years ago, Steele (1973) was one of the earliest advocates for incorporating physical surroundings into the study of organizational behavior (OB) and organizational development (OD). Unfortunately for our research, he did not report any empirical studies of moving to entirely new buildings. Rather, he reported on how physical structure affects interpersonal interactions, communication, status hierarchies, interdepartmental conflict versus cooperation, and so on.

Some years after Steele's pioneering work, a thorough review about the psychology of the physical workplace was conducted by Sundstrom and Sundstrom (1986). They, too, found no research on moving to new buildings (out of 290 citations in their book). In fact, they lamented the almost complete absence of field experimental research on physical factors of any type.

Since these two reviews were published, two more OB-oriented reviews of physical factors have been conducted by Baron (1994) and Oldham, Cummings, and Zhou (1995). However, both of these reviews focused exclusively on *within*-organization physical factors. Because ASA theory concerns *between*-organizational differences, the results of these two reviews have limited relevance.

Finally, from an OD orientation, Macy and Izumi (1993) reviewed 131 field studies of various types of OD interventions. They found just nine concerning changes in physical factors, but none about moving to new buildings. Thus, it appears that the conclusion reached decades ago by Sundstrom and Sundstrom (1986, p. 403) still applies today: "Research and theory are least well developed at the level of the organization." With little guidance from empirical research on the effect of moving to new buildings, we next turned to what OB theory might suggest.

Positive Affect Created by Moving to New Buildings.   Isen and Baron (1991) reviewed the accumulated research on positive affect. This is a concept initially developed in social psychology that they extended to organizational behavior. Briefly, positive affect is related to a wide variety of social behavior (e.g., generosity, helping behavior, less hostility, less competition, and so on), as well as to cognitive processes (decision making, memory, judgment, creativity, and so on). With regard to OB topics, positive affect has been related to the level of interpersonal conflict, pro-social organizational behaviors, decision making, performance appraisals, interview judgments, job satisfaction, and so on.

Unfortunately, the experimental studies of positive affect conducted to date have concerned those actions that are likely to produce only short-term positive affect. For example, one study examined how subjects reacted to a supportive versus condescending supervisor during a role play simulation (Baron, 1984). Another study examined how subjects reacted to a person who is only seen on videotape (Borman, 1977).

What has not yet been studied is how to create long-lasting positive affect in naturalistic settings, as contrasted with the somewhat contrived experiments that have been conducted thus far. Isen and Baron (1991) proposed two ways that long-lasting positive affect might be created. First, changes in the physical environment might produce long-lasting positive affect because the physical environment changes are stable and concrete (both literally and figuratively). Second, changes in organizational climates or culture might be another source of enduring positive affect. However, changing climates or culture is admittedly more difficult than changing physical facilities. Our research directly addresses their first suggestion, but may have implications for their second one.

Our research is reported in two studies. In Study 1 we assess the before-to-after *U.S. News and World Report* rankings of the top 50 MBA programs. We separated the top 50 into those that moved versus those that did not. For those that moved, we then compared average rankings for the 3 years before a move with the average for the 3 years after. For those who did not move, we compared their rankings over the first 3 years versus the last 3 years of the period we examined for this study. Finally, we examined schools outside the top 50 *U.S. News* colleges that moved to new buildings in order to see if they were able to move up into this group. Because those outside the top 50 do not have specific rankings, we could only assess whether they moved from outside to inside the top 50.

In Study 2 we focus on our MBA program at Ohio State, which moved to (dramatically better) new buildings. We were able to obtain additional data beyond *U.S. News* rankings: (1) the number of recruiter visits 3 years before versus 3 years after the move, and (2) student ratings of MBA classroom instructors for 3 consecutive years: before, during, and after the move.

STUDY 1

The Web site for the Association to Advance Collegiate Schools of Business (AACSB), www.aacsb.edu/communities/interestgrps/bldg.asp, listed 47 business schools that moved to new buildings (or had major renovations of existing ones) from 1996 through 2003. Of the 47, 18 have been consistently ranked among the top 50 during the past 10 years by *U.S. News*. The other 29 schools that moved have historically been outside the top 50. We identified three groups for examination: (1) 18 top-ranked schools that moved, (2) 28 other top-ranked schools that did not, and (3) 29 unranked schools that moved to new buildings.

We used the *U.S. News* rankings instead of those from *Business Week* for two important reasons. First, the *U.S. News* rankings have been done annually since 1990, whereas *Business Week*'s rankings are done just every other year. Second, *U.S. News* has ranked the top 50 since 1994, whereas *Business Week* used to rank just the top 25 until recently, moving up to specific rankings for 30 graduate schools of business. Thus, *U.S. News* provides more data points and a larger sample for analysis than *Business Week*. The *Wall Street Journal* rankings, which started in 2001, are too new to be useful for longitudinal research.

Method

U.S. News & World Report first ranked business schools in 1987. The next ranking was not until 1990, but it has been done annually since then. During the early 1990s there were changes in the method used to produce the rankings. Fortunately for our research, their method has remained fairly stable in the past 10 years or so. As a result, we will focus on the 10-year period from 1994 through 2003 for several reasons. First, the number of schools ranked was increased to 50 in 1994 and has remained at 50 since then. (In 1992 and 1993 the top 25 were ranked and a second tier of 25 was listed alphabetically. In the years before 1992, only 25 schools were ranked.) Second, the number of factors used to produce the rankings went from four to three starting in 1995 (graduation rate was dropped). Third, survey respondents have been both deans and recruiters since 1994. Prior to 1994 it was deans and CEOs. With respect to these factors, there has been little change in the method used to produce the rankings. There is one exception to this, as described next.

The wording of the survey question about a school's perceived reputation is the only factor that changed during the 10-year period we examined. From 1994 to 1998 survey respondents were asked to nominate those schools "in the top 25." Since 1999, a 5-point Likert-type rating scale has been used.

We used the published school rankings in three ways. First, we examined the 18 top 50 schools that had moved to new or renovated buildings. We intended to do a before-to-after comparison, so we needed to know precisely when the buildings actually opened. The AACSB Web site provided us with the initial list of 18 schools, but was sometimes imprecise in terms of opening dates. For example, a groundbreaking date was reported, but the opening date was not. A research assistant contacted all of the 18 schools, but some would not return phone calls or e-mails from the assistant. The first author then e-mailed his friends at the nonresponding schools to obtain the missing information.

Once we confirmed the opening dates for the 18 schools, we tabulated the school's average rank for 3 years prior to the move with the 3 years after the move, and also recorded each school's rank during the move itself (typically the first year). Because there are frequent ties in the rankings, we took the average rank when schools were tied. For example, if three schools were tied at number 25, this meant that rankings 25, 26, and 27 were involved because the next ranked school was identified as number 28. We used the average rank of number 26, which we believe is more accurate than designating all three schools by the lowest possible rank (number 25).

For the 32 top 50 schools that did not move, we faced a different problem because there was no clear before-and-after period. Because most data for the 18 that moved to new buildings involved the 10-year period from 1994 through 2003, we decided to compare the first 3 years of this period (1994, 1995, and 1996) with the last 3 years (2001, 2002, and 2003).

Making a comparison over this 10-year period meant that the sample size was reduced from 32 to 28, because a school needed to be in the top 50 over the entire 10-year period in order to make a comparison. Finally, for those 29 schools that were unranked when they moved, we looked to see if any moved up into the top 50 afterwards.

Results

The 18 schools that moved are (in alphabetical order): Case-Western Reserve, Chicago, Columbia, Cornell, Emory, Georgia, Harvard, Indiana, North Carolina, Ohio State, Pennsylvania, Purdue, Rice, Southern California, Texas A&M, Tulane, Washington University, and Wisconsin. The 28 schools that did not move are (in alphabetical order): Arizona, Arizona State, Berkeley, BYU, Carnegie-Mellon, Duke, Georgetown, Georgia Tech, Illinois, Iowa, Maryland, Michigan, Michigan State, Minnesota, MIT, Northwestern, NYU, Penn State, Pittsburgh, Rochester, SMU, Stanford, Texas, UCLA, Vanderbilt, Virginia, Washington, and Yale.

After comparing the 3-year before and the 3-year after average rankings, there is no supporting evidence for the so-called ratings bump predicted by conventional wisdom. The average before-to-after change in rank is actually a .24 decline. This is a very small number and essentially means that there is no difference in MBA ranking associated with moving to new buildings.

The second analysis concerned those mover schools below the top 50 to see whether any of them moved up into that group. Of the 29 schools listed on the AACSB's Web site, none have yet broken into the top 50 after moving to new buildings. This is further evidence that moving to new buildings does not produce the expected change in national rankings, according to conventional wisdom.

The third analysis concerned those schools in the top 50 that did not move during the period we studied. Their average rankings show remarkable stability on an overall basis. The net average change in ranking between the first 3 years versus the last 3 years of the 1994–2003 period is just –.63. This is no change at all. However, if one looks more closely at the results, there does appear to be evidence of regression to the mean. That is, those schools near the top of the rankings tended to experience a slight loss in average rank, whereas those at the bottom tended to show a slight gain in average rank.

Discussion

The *U.S. News* rankings data disconfirm the positive results believed to result from moving to new buildings. This raises the question as to whether the rankings themselves are the wrong measures to reach such a conclusion or whether conventional wisdom about moving needs to be reexamined. An important question that needs to be addressed is the logical connection of how new buildings might produce changes in their *U.S. News* ranking. We address this next.

The first factor used by *U.S. News* is selectivity of students (25% of the overall ranking). Selectivity of students is composed of three weighted components: (1) acceptance rate (5% weight), (2) average undergraduate grade point average (30% weight), and (3) average GMAT scores (65% weight). We think it is reasonable to expect an improvement in the quality of applicants if the school moves to new buildings. Furthermore, this would seem to be especially true for those who visit several campuses before deciding where to apply. However, we do note that Web sites can provide pictures for those who do not visit in person. Schools with new facilities often tout them in their recruitment literature, for example, having T1 Internet connections in classrooms, state-of-the-art audio/visual technology in classrooms, break-out rooms for team meetings, video conferencing capability, and so on.

The second factor is job placement success at a school (35% of the overall ranking). This factor is composed of three weighted components: (1) the average of salary and bonus (40% weight), (2) the percentage with employment at graduation (20% weight), and (3) the percentage with employment 3 months after graduation (40% weight). It seems less clear to us, however, as to how new buildings might affect this particular component. This is because recruiters are primarily looking for specific job competence and for the fit of job candidates to their organization (Wanous, 1980, 1992). In the long run, if better students are attracted to new buildings, this could be reflected in the job placement indicators. However, in the short run, it seems to us that new buildings are less likely to affect job placement than student recruitment.

The third factor (40% of the overall ranking) is the perceived reputation of a school. Perceived reputation itself is composed of two weighted factors: (1) ratings by deans (62.5%) and (2) ratings by recruiters (37.5%). In other words, the ratings by deans constitute 25% of the overall ranking (i.e., 40% × 62.5% = 25%), and those by recruiters constitute 15% of the overall ranking (i.e., 40% × 37.5% = 15%). Thus, perceived reputation is the most important component of the overall ranking.

It seems reasonable to assume that new buildings might influence recruiters as they travel to various locations. Recruiters are in a position to know the facilities at a number of business schools. Deans may travel to other schools less than recruiters, but they do meet and tend to stay in touch with each other. Among the top schools, it is probably safe to say that deans know what is going on at most of their competitors' schools.

Based on the above, we believe it is reasonable to assume there might be a rankings increase associated with new buildings because of direct connections between the first and third factors, and an indirect connection with the second factor. That said, there are other factors that might be influenced by new buildings that are excluded from the *U.S. News* method. To the extent that these are important indicators, the *U.S. News* ranking method itself is deficient, as discussed next.

The new arms race article by Mangan (2002) mentions several factors that might be positively affected by moving to new buildings. These factors are not part of the *U.S. News* method: (1) financial donations by alumni, (2) financial donations by local corporations, (3) increased attractiveness to executives because they are used to nice surroundings in their own organizations and want the same at these business schools, (4) increases in the number of corporate recruiters, and (5) better classroom teaching or research mission accomplishment.

Despite all these additional measures, the rankings done by print media, of which *U.S. News* is just one, are probably the most widely accepted yardstick. One reason is that they are widely available to anyone who is interested. In contrast, the factors cited by Mangan (2002) are internal measures that are not available to those outside a particular school, and that includes us.

STUDY 2: WHAT HAPPENED AT OUR SCHOOL?

In Study 2 we will examine two additional measures that might be affected by moving to new buildings in order to try to understand the absence of empirical support based on the *U.S. News* rankings. We think these additional data may be instructive because our new buildings were dramatically better than the old ones. If new buildings have a measurable impact, it ought to be found at our school, Ohio State.

Our move was from very old, poorly maintained buildings to brand new, very high quality buildings. This move was a dramatic change in physical facilities. Some observers said it was from the worst buildings in the entire United States to the best buildings. It was not a change in fundamental educational philosophy (e.g., from lectures to case discussions), nor was there a change in class sizes.

Method

Research Setting.   We moved from a very rundown two-building complex to a brand new five-building campus within a campus. The new campus has its own courtyard and other amenities that made our business school look more like a stand-alone college than a component of the largest university in the world. Table 11.1 summarizes the factors that were both different and similar between the old versus the new buildings.

As can be seen in Table 11.1, most of the differences were a change from old to new, especially new technology for course delivery. There

TABLE 11.1
Physical Changes in Moving to New Buildings

Type of Change	Old Buildings	New Buildings
Buildings: Differences	1. 2 buildings	1. 5 buildings
	2. Mixed purposes: faculty offices and classrooms not separated	2. Each building has its own clear purpose
	3. Partial air-conditioning	3. Consistent air-conditioning
	4. "Hard" seating	4. Cushioned seating
	5. "Crash carts" for classroom technology	5. Permanently installed technology
	6. No classroom Internet connections	6. Internet available in larger rooms
	7. Few computer labs and small capacity	7. Many computer labs and large capacity
	8. No student lounges	8. MBA and honors lounges
	9. Status symbols not consistent with status	9. Status symbols consistent with status
Buildings: Similarities	1. Wide hallways	
	2. High ceilings	
	3. Room sizes (50, 85, and 250)	
	4. Room configuration (flat vs. tiered)	
	5. Mix of room sizes and configurations	
Location: Differences	1. Expensive parking in ramp next door	1. Cheap parking on surface lots within 1 to 3 blocks
	2. Nearby fast food and abundant choices	2. No fast food nearby
	3. No internal food available	3. MBAs can buy food in their own lounge
Location: Similarities	1. Abundant parking	

was no intended change in the basic pedagogy of course delivery, nor was there a new educational philosophy. One exception to this is that MBA and undergraduate classes are now held in different buildings. Faculty offices, the library/computer center, and executive education are housed in separate buildings. In the old two-building complex, faculty offices, the library, undergraduate classes, and graduate classes were mixed together, whereas each now has its own building.

A second change that may be more than merely cosmetic is that faculty offices and the classroom buildings more clearly reflect the internal status hierarchy. In the old buildings there were status differences, but they were less obvious and less consistent than in the new ones. Specifically, there are now four sizes of faculty offices: (1) regular faculty, (2) endowed professorships and department chairs, (3) associate deans, and (4) the dean.

Furnishings inside the different classroom buildings (seating, lighting fixtures, woodwork and trim, etc.) also reflect status differences. Although the MBA, executive education, and undergraduate classroom buildings are similar to one another in size and outside appearance, the lowest quality classroom furnishings are in the undergraduate classroom building, followed by the MBA classroom building, with the executive education building having the highest level of furnishings. Keep in mind that while the undergraduate classroom building furnishings are of slightly lower quality within our college, they are vastly superior to other classroom buildings at our university.

Measures: Recruiter Visits and Student Ratings of Classroom Teaching.   The number of recruiter visits to this college was obtained from the office in charge of student placement. Because this office serves both MBA and undergraduate students, they did not separate recruiters into those seeking MBAs versus undergraduates. Thus, the measure we will report here is the total number of different companies who sent recruiters to this business school in the years before, during, and after the move.

The Student Evaluation of Instruction (SEI) is the measure of classroom teaching performance used at our university. The SEI was developed in 1994 for the singular purpose of evaluating teaching performance for personnel decisions such as promotion, tenure, and merit pay. It replaced a much longer rating form (developed in 1977) that was designed to provide both evaluative and developmental feedback.

Student ratings of classroom teaching are affected by many factors, although class size and whether the class is a requirement versus an elective are the two most influential factors at our university, based on considerable internal research. In order to make a fair comparison (Cooper & Richardson, 1986) between teaching ratings from before to after the move, student ratings were based on within-instructor and within-course comparisons. This meant that an individual instructor had to teach the same class more than once during the 3-year period for which we examined student ratings of classroom instruction.

Because of the decision to restrict data to within-instructor and within-course, a number of courses taught during these 3 years were omitted. However, failing to control for both instructor and course differences would have biased the ratings in an unacceptable way.

The SEI is a one-page form. Classroom instruction is measured with nine specific facets that concern teaching and one overall rating. The nine facet items are worded in somewhat general terms (e.g., "The instructor communicated the subject matter clearly") because they were designed to apply to the entire portfolio of classes offered at our university. The nine facet items are measured with a 5-point agree/disagree scale. The overall rating of the instructor is a single-item 5-point scale having two anchors: 5 = excellent and 1 = poor. In addition to these 10 items, other questions on the SEI include class standing (freshman, sophomore, graduate student, etc.), self-reported cumulative grade point average, and the reason for enrolling in the class (required vs. elective).

The overall single-item rating of classroom teaching performance from the SEI is the measure used here. In practice, it is the primary (and typically the only) measure used for evaluating classroom teaching. Because it is a global, summary evaluation of the course instructor, it is more appropriate than any of the nine facet items for two reasons. First, the relevance of the specific teaching facet items varies from class to class, depending on the class level (graduate vs. undergraduate), class size, and instructor teaching methods (lecture vs. the Socratic method). Differences in the relevance of specific teaching facet items among classes mean that using the global, summary item allows for reasonably fair comparisons (Cooper & Richardson, 1986) across different types and sizes of classes.

Summing the nine facets to form a scale would not resolve the fair comparison issue for the very same reasons. That is, the relative emphasis of any particular item varies according to the type of class. Further, there is no guarantee that a sum of these nine facets is comparable to an overall rating, which is an important point that has been made with respect to summing up job facet satisfaction ratings versus an overall measure of job satisfaction (Scarpello & Campbell, 1983).

Although the SEI measure is a single-item measure, it has been found to be reliable. In a study using the SEI, Wanous and Hudy (2001) concluded that a reasonable estimate of its reliability is .80, despite the fact that it is a single-item measure. This estimate is higher than the .70 reliability estimate for single-item measures of overall job satisfaction previously reported by Wanous, Reichers, and Hudy (1997).

The reason for the higher reliability estimate for the SEI versus job satisfaction is that the SEI data are aggregated at the class level, a procedure recommended for this situation (Cranton & Smith, 1990). This aggregation reduces some sources of variance and thus increases the reliability of the class mean rating (Hanges, Schneider, & Niles, 1990).

Results

The *U.S. News* rankings and the number of recruiter visits represent an interrupted time series design for two organizational-level criteria. Specifically, the 3-year *U.S. News* average ranking before the move was 25 versus an average of 25.3 for 3 years after the move was completed. (During the 2-year move-in, the MBA program average ranking was 26.5.) The number of recruiter visits was constant over a 3-year period: (1) 261 visits in the year before the move, (2) 260 visits in the first year of the move, and (3) 267 visits in the second year of the move.

Thus, both organization-level factors (rankings and recruiter visits) show no effect of moving to the new buildings. We next discuss student ratings of classroom teaching, which is a group-level measure. As such, it is possible that it might be more sensitive in detecting the effects of moving to new buildings.

The median SEI rating in MBA classes went from 4.3 the year before our move up to 4.5 the first year classes were held in the new buildings ($p < .01$, $N = 46$). However, during the second year in the new buildings, the median SEI rating went back to the same 4.3 level observed in the year prior to the move ($p < .01$, $N = 30$). Remember that all data points are within-instructor and within-course when two different years are compared. The Wilcoxon Signed Rank Test (Siegel, 1956) was used to determine the statistical significance of the median SEI ratings between these different time periods.

A potential confounding factor in any time series analysis is the possibility of a general, campuswide trend in SEI ratings. However, this did not occur. The overall average for the university is recalculated each quarter, and it remained constant ($M = 4.3$) throughout all 3 years we examined (i.e., nine consecutive academic year quarters).

Discussion

We singled out our own move for two reasons. First, the change in facilities was dramatic—almost breathtaking, and that is no overstatement. Because of this, we assumed that if new buildings affect business school rankings we would see it here. Second, additional "local" data were available to us, that is, number of recruiter visits and student ratings of classroom teaching. Both of these local measures are within-school measures that are not factored into the *U.S. News* rankings.

We think that the pattern of results for the SEI teaching evaluations is best explained as *temporary positive affect* created by the contrast between the old and new buildings. It seems reasonable that positive affect would be more easily created by experiencing a contrast between the old versus the new buildings than by experiencing new buildings without the knowledge of the old ones. During the first year of use, only the second-year MBAs had experienced the old buildings. By the second year of use, none of the MBA students had experienced the old buildings. In some ways, the year before the move and the second year of use are similar, that is, there was no contrast between the old versus new buildings. The only year that a contrast effect could occur was during the first year of use, and it would only occur for those in the second year of the MBA program.

Besides students feeling good about new buildings, it is possible that faculty members might have behaved in ways that increased their SEI ratings. If this happened, it would most likely occur in the first year inside the new buildings because faculty would experience the same contrast effect as the second-year MBA students.

It is, of course, possible that ratings of classroom instruction are not the best way to make an inference about the creation of positive affect because they are indirect measures. We believe, however, that the student ratings of teaching are preferable to measuring positive affect directly, such as by a survey, for two reasons. First, simply asking students and faculty if they notice the difference between new versus old buildings—and if they like what they see—could easily lead to a "so what" response by a skeptical reader. For example, one might argue that such a survey would produce results comparable to asking people if they notice the difference between good versus inclement weather and whether they prefer the former to the latter. We believe that an opinion survey would only "prove" the obvious, that is, that most people enjoy nice new surroundings to old dirty ones. The second reason for not measuring positive affect directly is that merely asking this question is considered so reactive that most of the experiments on positive affect have inferred its presence as we did (Isen & Baron, 1991).

In some ways the temporary nature of the positive affect is going to be disappointing for those who have suggested that long-lasting positive affect might be created by physical facilities/surroundings (Isen & Baron, 1991). On the other hand, these results are consistent with Schneider's ASA framework (1987). The present situation is a very close approximation to "changing the place, but not the people." Because of this, we believe that it does allow inferences to be made regarding the ASA framework. Furthermore, the ASA framework is organizational level in nature, also consistent with the rankings data presented here.

DISCUSSION OF BOTH STUDIES

It is interesting that the (within-instructor and within-course) student ratings of instruction did appear to show sensitivity in measuring the effect of moving to new buildings. This is because some previous research on the stability of student ratings of classroom teaching has found that these ratings are quite stable, suggesting that they are insensitive measures.

Specifically, Hanges, Schneider, and Niles (1990) looked at the stability of college professor teaching ratings (seven facets and a composite) over 6.5 years. They found that the most stable ratings were the within-course/within-instructor ratings (mean correlation = .63), compared to same-course/different-instructor (mean correlation = .36) or same-faculty/different-course (mean correlation = .54) ratings. With this inherent stability of within-course and within-instructor data in mind, the significant differences found here might actually be stronger than they appear.

The *U.S. News* rankings did not show the anticipated results for those who moved, that is, there was no rankings "bump," nor did any unranked schools break into the top 50. In addition, there was no increase in the number of recruiters coming to our school. As noted earlier, these organization-level measures can be influenced by a host of factors, perhaps more so than student ratings of classroom instructors. For example, the overall level of economic activity affects the number of recruiters and could easily be more influential than moving to a new building.

Similarly, the ranking of a particular school might not change if enough of its competitors also build new buildings. This is what has been happening across the country with the increased popularity of business education in general, and MBA programs in particular. So, even if the relative ranking of this business school did not change, it could be argued that failing to keep up with one's competitors would have resulted in a lower ranking rather than maintaining its relative position.

The overall pattern of results reported here supports Schneider's (1987) ASA model. That is, there was no long-lasting measurable effect of moving to new buildings because, for the most part, the people did not change.

The increase in teaching ratings during the first year in new buildings is consistent with the likely creation of positive affect. However, its temporary nature does not support the suggestion by Isen and Barron (1991) that long-lasting positive affect would result from physical changes. We think the best explanation is that there was a very positive, but temporary *contrast effect* for those who had experienced the old buildings before moving to the new ones. However, the contrast effect dissipated by the second year of occupancy. This is because none of the MBA students had seen the old buildings, and the faculty were in the second year of new offices, as well as the new MBA classroom.

The first author personally experienced a positive contrast effect during the first quarter he taught in the new buildings: I (Wanous) had been teaching a large undergraduate, required OB course about twice each year for over 10 years. My teaching rating for the first quarter after the undergraduate building opened was significantly higher than any rating prior to or after the move; it was a 4.6 on a 5-point scale. All of my other ratings fluctuated between 4.0 and 4.3. The 4.6 rating is clearly an outlier in the past 20 to 25 times I taught this class. It is probably no coincidence that it occurred the first time I taught in the new undergraduate classroom building.

Finally, as mentioned in our discussion of Study 1, there are important factors that ought to be affected by moving to new buildings, but which are not reflected in the *U.S. News* ranking method. For example, we think that it is reasonable to expect donations from alumni and corporations would increase as a result of new buildings.

Another local outcome that might result from moving is enhanced mission accomplishment facilitated by new buildings. For example, the research mission might be helped by facilities that enable faculty to conduct laboratory studies on those topics where this research method might be appropriate, for example, cognitive factors in decision making. Similarly, the teaching mission might be helped by facilities that permit greater use of teams in the learning process if breakout rooms for meetings are part of the new building.

These examples of research and teaching mission accomplishment are merely illustrations of the ways in which new buildings can have a very positive effect. It would be up to each school to assess the effects on these local measures of mission accomplishment because of the likely differences in mission definitions among business schools. With the exception of our school, where we had access to both recruiter visits and teaching ratings, we had to rely upon the best publicly available measure for making comparisons among different colleges nationwide.

REFERENCES

Baron, R. A. (1984). Reducing organizational conflict: An incompatible response approach. *Journal of Applied Psychology, 69,* 272–279.

Baron, R. A. (1994). The physical environment of work settings: Effects on task performance, interpersonal relations and job satisfaction. In B. M. Staw & L. L. Cummings (Eds.), *Research in organizational behavior* (Vol. 16, pp. 1–46). Greenwich, CT: JAI Press.

Borman, W. (1977). Consistency of rating accuracy and rating errors in judgment of human performance. *Organizational Behavior and Human Performance, 20,* 129–148.

Cooper, W. H., & Richardson, A. J. (1986). Unfair comparisons. *Journal of Applied Psychology, 71,* 179–184.

Cranton, P., & Smith, R. A. (1990). Reconsidering the unit of analysis: A model of student rating of instruction. *Journal of Educational Psychology, 82,* 207–212.

Hanges, P. J., Schneider, B., & Niles, K. (1990). Stability of performance: An interactionist perspective. *Journal of Applied Psychology, 75,* 658–667.

Isen, A. M., & Baron, R. A. (1991). Positive affect as a factor in organizational behavior. In L. L. Cummings & B. M. Staw (Eds.), *Research in organizational behavior* (Vol. 13, pp. 1–53). Greenwich, CT: JAI Press.

Macy, B. A., & Izumi, H. (1993). Organizational change, design, and work innovation: A meta-analysis of 131 North American field studies: 1961–1991. In R. W. Woodman & W. A. Pasmore (Eds.), *Research in organizational change and development* (Vol. 7, pp. 235–313). Oxford: Elsevier Science.

Mangan, K. S. (2002, June 7). The new 'arms race' in business-school buildings: Mammoth, expensive facilities are opening at many universities. *Chronicle of Higher Education*, 48.

Oldham, G. R., Cummings, A., & Zhou, J. (1995). The spatial configuration of organizations: A review of the literature and some new research directions. In G. R. Ferris (Ed.), *Research in personnel and human resources management* (Vol. 13, pp. 1–37). Greenwich, CT: JAI Press.

O'Reilly, C. A., III, & Pfeffer, J. (2000). *Hidden value*. Boston: Harvard Business School Press.

Scarpello, V., & Campbell, J. P. (1983). Job satisfaction: Are all the parts there? *Personnel Psychology, 36,* 577–600.

Schneider, B. (1987). The people make the place. *Personnel Psychology, 40,* 437–453.

Schneider, B., Goldstein, H. W., Smith, D. B. (1995). The people make the place: An update. *Personnel Psychology,* Vol. 48, No. 3, pp. 757–773.

Siegel, S. (1956). *Nonparametric statistics: For the behavioral sciences*. New York: McGraw-Hill.

Steele, F. I. (1973). *Physical settings and organization development*. Reading, MA: Addison-Wesley.

Sundstrom, E., & Sundstrom, M. G. (1986). *Work places: The psychology of the physical environment in offices and factories*. London: Cambridge University Press.

Wanous, J. P. (1980). *Organizational entry: Recruitment, selection, and socialization of newcomers*. Reading, MA: Addison-Wesley.

Wanous, J. P. (1992). *Organizational entry: Recruitment, selection, orientation, and socialization of newcomers* (2nd ed.). Reading, MA: Addison-Wesley.

Wanous, J. P., & Hudy, M. J. (2001). Single-item reliability: A replication and extension. *Organizational Research Methods, 4,* 361–375.

Wanous, J. P., Reichers, A. E., & Hudy, M. J. (1997). Overall job satisfaction: How good are single-item measures? *Journal of Applied Psychology, 82,* 247–252.

12

The People Still Make the Place

BENJAMIN SCHNEIDER

Valtera Corporation and University of Maryland (Emeritus)

EVOLUTION OF THE ASA MODEL

While seemingly straightforward, the conceptual and empirical issues surrounding the simultaneous study of personal and situational attributes are varied and daunting (cf. Walsh, Craik, & Price, 2000). My earliest research with Jack Bartlett (Schneider & Bartlett, 1968, 1970) was based on a conceptualization of person–environment (P–E) fit interacting with ability in the prediction of performance for insurance sales people. The framework proposed that ability would be reflected in performance when the environment fit sales agents' preferences and expectations. The hypothesis was that fit, not the environment and not people's preferences or expectations, moderated ability–performance relationships. Unfortunately, the data collected failed to support the hypothesis (Schneider, 1972, 1975).

At the time, many scholars were writing about the importance of person–environment fit in organizations (e.g., Lofquist & Dawis, 1969) or studying the implications of fit for understanding stress in the workplace (French, Rodgers, & Cobb, 1974), or higher-order need strength as a moderator of job characteristics–performance relationships (Hackman & Lawler, 1971). Given this general level of interest in the topic, it seemed appropriate to pursue additional efforts.

The second project was targeted on the straight interaction of person characteristics and organizational characteristics in predicting performance at work (Schneider, 1978a). The hypothesis was that ability itself interacted with the characteristics of the environment. Thus, in the first project described earlier, fit to the situation was conceptualized as the moderator of ability–performance relationships; here the situation itself was seen as the moderator. Again the data failed to substantiate the hypothesis.

A review of the literature after the failure (Schneider, 1978b) suggested a potential reason for the lack of significant findings in my work. As I examined this literature, it became clear to me that only in laboratory studies were significant interaction effects revealed. This suggested that labs can produce extremes of situations that might not characterize field settings. What is important here is the idea that only when there are extremes on one of the variables of interest is identification of statistical interactions likely (Schneider, 1978b).

This was a turning point for me in conceptualizing P–E fit and person–situation interaction and the relationship of these to other variables of interest. It was then that I discovered the then-burgeoning literature in personality on person–situation interaction (Endler & Magnusson, 1976; Magnusson & Endler, 1977; Pervin & Lewis, 1978). The interactionists argued that a combination of person and environment characteristics, usually a multiplicative combination, produced something different than would be expected from a simple linear or fit indicator of the two. The impetus for this interactionist vantage point was Mischel's (1968) attack on personality theory. This attack argued that situations, not persons, caused behavior. Interactionists retorted that maybe it is more than just the person, but it is certainly the person in interaction with the situation, not the situation alone, that is critical.

I began to wonder about how the person and the situation actually interacted in the everyday world and discovered in my readings that Pervin and Lewis (1978) called this everyday phenomenon by the name natural interaction. By natural interaction, Pervin and Lewis meant the natural byplay of persons with one another and other facets of the social and structural environment that produced the observed behavior. In further reading I happened on a wonderful paper by Bowers (1973) that demolished the extreme vantage taken by Mischel (1968); the paper is the basis of the attraction–selection–attrition (ASA) model because Bowers made two points in the paper that led me down the ASA road:

1. Research in laboratories showing the dominance of situations over traits does not reflect the real world because it fails to provide for the natural interaction of persons and situations.
2. A fundamental attribute of a true experiment, random assignment of participants to treatments, fails to permit the kind of self-selection into and out of situations that characterizes the ebb and flow of people in and out of settings. Bowers was suggesting that people, being not randomly assigned to organizations, choose themselves in and out of them, then behave in them, and thus perhaps determine them.

And this is how I arrived at my variation on Lewin's B = f(P, E) that E = f(P, B). My transposition means that environments are a function of the people behaving in them. Further, environments differ because they contain different kinds of people interacting in them.

I elaborated this idea about environments being a function of people behaving in them in a series of papers in the 1980s (Schneider, 1983a, 1983b), culminating in my presidential address to the Society for Industrial and Organizational Psychology (SIOP) in 1985 (see Schneider, 1987), where I outlined what has come to be called the attraction–selection–attrition (ASA) model of organizational functioning in a talk called "The People Make the Place."

THE ASA MODEL

The model provides a person-based conceptualization of why organizational environments look and feel the way they do. The model is based on Bowers's insight about nonrandom assignment of people to settings. The model leads to some straightforward and testable ideas:

1. People are differentially attracted to organizations such that they are attracted to organizations they believe they fit. People say to themselves implicitly or explicitly when job hunting that "I fit that place" or "I don't fit that place."
2. Through formal and informal selection practices, the people in settings also make choices; they choose to allow in (select) persons who they feel fit the setting. The more the setting restricts entry to it, the greater the fit of the person to the place. Indeed, a goal of formal selection procedures is to ensure that the range of person types in the setting is restricted to those who fit it.
3. People leave settings, voluntarily or involuntarily, if they do not fit well.

While these issues had been independently identified in numerous places, a consequence of them all occurring had not been identified: homogeneity. It is clear that if people are differentially attracted to settings, differentially selected by settings, and differentially leave settings, then those who remain in a setting will be similar to one another—not the same, but more similar to one another than they are similar to people in other organizations. They will have relatively similar personalities, interests, and values, and this hypothesis has come to be called the homogeneity hypothesis—that the ASA cycle yields homogeneity of personality within organizations. In Chapter 2 by Dickson, Resick, and Goldstein there is a nicely detailed review of the research literature on these propositions, including the homogeneity hypothesis, with sufficient support reported to warm the cockles (whatever those are) of my heart.

I also proposed an antecedent to the ASA cycle in organizations and a consequence of the homogeneity that the cycle causes. The antecedent concerned the role of the founder in largely determining the strategy, structure, and climate of the organization. Founders do this by operationalizing their personalities in the decisions they must make early on as the organization begins life. Schein (1992) and Aldrich (1999) have presented similar ideas. For example, Schein (1992, pp. 211–212) says:

> Founders not only choose the basic mission and environmental context in which the new group [organization] members will operate, but they choose the group members and bias the original responses that the group makes in its effort to succeed in its environment and integrate itself. Organizations do not form accidentally or informally.

Aldrich (1999, pp. 124–126) put the influence of the founder on homogeneity this way:

> When founders begin hiring they communicate information to potential recruits about the nature and mission of the firm.… Founders seem to focus on how to select others who resemble the early hires, or who will augment their skills. These practices increase the likelihood that early members will already be aware of the required routines and competencies.… Selection forces within emerging organizations tend to reduce variability, thus increasing their coherence by making them more homogeneous.

In short, by their actions, actions that emerge as ways of them implementing their personalities, founders have long-term consequences for the strategy, structure, and climate of the organizations they enact (see Schneider & Smith, 2004, for a review).

One final hypothesis I explicitly proposed (1983b, 1987) was that, due to the homogeneity that is an outcome of the ASA cycle, organizations would tend to fail in times of turbulence. The idea here is, as George Patton said, "If everyone is thinking the same thing then someone isn't thinking." That is, the proposal is that over time the people in a place come to look at and see the world in predictable ways and thus fail to see the necessity for change—and thus do not initiate the organizational changes necessary to adapt to the larger environmental changes.

A paper by Boone, Olffen, Witteloostuijn, and Brabander (2004) does an excellent job of explicating the issues. They did an archival study of 25 years of evidence from Dutch newspapers concerning "homosocial reproduction" in top management teams. Their hypothesis was that in times of crisis and environmental turmoil, such teams would diversify their membership as a coping strategy. What they found, however, is that top management teams close ranks rather than open themselves up to new input and insights. In a similar vein, Beckman, Burton, and O'Reilly (2007) found that diversity of experience and a history of prior affiliations in the industry in top management teams (TMTs) of start-ups in Silicon Valley were correlated with success of the firms in obtaining venture capital and eventually issuing an initial public offering of stock (IPO). Of considerable additional interest, they showed that founder exits when replaced by managers with diverse experiences also resulted in success. It is important to note that neither of these studies was of personality diversity and homogeneity, with the Boone et al. (2004) study focusing on demographics (age, history with the company, industry experience, and academic degree status) and the Beckman et al. (2007) study focusing on functional diversity and background affiliations of the TMT.

Another predicted consequence of the ASA cycle in organizations that I made in 1987 was that organizational change would be very difficult unless the people themselves in organizations were different people. That is, I claimed that organizational development (OD) and similar efforts were likely to be fruitless because they worked with existing people and those people would (1) be similar and (2) be comfortable and of a certain "sort," and very difficult if not impossible to change. The homogeneity of the personality of those in an organization undergoing change is still not mentioned as a cause of "resistance" in that literature (e.g., Burke, 2002), but that literature literally screams for such consideration. Consider the very interesting Chapter 11 by Wanous and Reichers, where everything changed but the people—and nothing changed.

In summary, there is good evidence for the basics of ASA theory—people are attracted, selected by, and stay with companies they fit. In addition, there is good conceptual and some empirical evidence for founder effects on organizations, and over the long term, evidence indicates that organizations come to take on the personality of their founders (Schneider & Smith, 2004). Finally, there are a few studies now of homogeneity in organizations, with one set of studies revealing that over time there comes to be homogeneity of personality and demographics in organizations, and the other set of studies indicating that homogeneity may not be useful for long-term organizational health—that, in times of crisis, organizations become more demographically homogeneous rather than diversify, and that when change is attempted, but with the same people, nothing changes.

ON DEMOGRAPHICS AND PERSONALITY

As Jackson and Chung note in Chapter 3, there are several studies that adopt the ASA framework but do so using demographics rather than personality. Pfeffer's (1983; see Williams & O'Reilly, 1998, for a review) proposal of a new field of study in organizational behavior—organizational demography—is the basis for that work. If one believes, as I do, in the zeitgeist leading to similar events and happenings, here is another case: Pfeffer's organizational demography proposals with regard to diversity and homogeneity were startlingly similar to my own with regard to personality. Over the years, evidence in support of these proposals based on demographics has also accumulated, and yet the two models have rarely been crossed in the same piece of research. That is, no study to my knowledge has simultaneously studied personality homogeneity/diversity and demographics homogeneity/diversity to explore their simultaneous and joint effects on outcomes of interest—like turnover or other indicators of organizational effectiveness. This is, of course, precisely what Chapter 3 recommends, and I would heartily agree because, as they note, research linking demographics and personality yield at best mixed results.

As Jackson and Chung also note, however, the issue of what is and is not a demographic variable is frequently slippery—just as what is and is not a personality variable. For example, in the Boone et al. (2004) and Beckman et al. (2007) studies, functional specialty was considered a demographic variable, yet there is considerable evidence to support the idea that functional specialization is related to vocational interests, which in turn are related to personality (Holland, 1997). In other words, it might be possible for some of the organizational demography scholars to code for more personality-related issues even when such measures were not administered. In a similar vein, personality researchers who are studying facets of the ASA model might have access to evidence like age and gender at a minimum, since those data are collected when personality tests are administered, and often there is additional demographics data in the form of level in the hierarchy in organizations and functional specialization. Projects like those suggested by Jackson and Chung are certainly overdue, always with the understanding that they are necessary because one cannot generalize from studies of demographics to what the personality effects might be, and vice versa (Tsui & Gutek, 1999).

BOUNDARY CONDITIONS ON ASA PROPOSITIONS

When the main effects for a theory or model have been established, it is time to seek the boundary conditions that might also be thought to play a role in the model. Sometimes boundary conditions are thought implicitly or explicitly to dominate the main effect, but this is rarely true. In short, demonstrating an interaction effect after the main effect has been accounted for is supplemental to the main effect and not a replacement for it.

In Chapter 4, Chatman, Wong and Joyce do something very interesting: They focus on what misfits do who do not leave. Of course ASA says misfits leave, so how could they focus on those who stay? Well, *leave* is a main effect of misfit, and there is always variability around that main effect, and the correlates of that variability we call the boundary conditions. Chatman et al. cite numerous studies to show there is a main effect also for the situation on behavior, but those studies miss the point of ASA, which focuses on fit; fit is the main effect in ASA work. Similarly, any reference to studies using personality data as a predictor either in favor of ASA or in denial of ASA misses the point, as it is the fit of the personality to the setting, not the personality itself, that is of interest in ASA. For example, Chatman (1991) reveals stronger effects for socialization tactics than for personality, but that is a main effect study not a fit study. On the other hand, Liao, Joshi, and Chuang (2004) support the hypothesis that lack of fit (dissimilarity) on both demographic variables and personality variables is related to deviant behavior in work teams. I must note that, while they did not hypothesize main effects for personality in deviant behavior, for both conscientiousness and agreeableness there were such main effects, with less conscientious and less agreeable people displaying more deviant behavior. It looks like both dissimilarity and main effects for some personality attributes can be useful.

Having said that, it is clear that situations also have an impact on people's behavior, and the more total the situation in terms of the demands made on people and the rewards given to people, the more constrained will be the behavior displayed there. I said in the 1987 paper, however, that people choose themselves into situations they fit, and where choice is available, only some people choose themselves into total situations like police and the military—and being a physician. Total institutions are also the locale for most studies of the effects of socialization (police, firefighters, the military). And is it not interesting that these are quite specifically the kinds of situations one must actively choose oneself into? I proposed in 1987 that people come to settings they have chosen themselves into "presocialized," and I continue to believe that. By this I mean, since people actively choose themselves into a setting based on perceived fit, it is not surprising that they become socialized readily. But it is a main effect, and there will be misfits, and it is definitely worthwhile studying the off-diagonals as well as the main effects.

My impression is that the most important unstudied boundary condition vis-à-vis ASA concerns the perception of choice that individuals feel they have or do not have. I submit the following proposition: The more people believe they have choice about where to go to work, the better will be the fit of people to the settings they join (Schneider, 2001). A corollary proposition is that the more choice organizations perceive they have about who they admit to the company, the more homogeneous will be the resultant new hires. In short, when people and organizations have choice, they maximize good fit—and homogeneity in organizations.

MULTILEVEL ISSUES AND THE ASA MODEL

Homogeneity From the Individual Level Up

Ployhart and Schmitt in Chapter 5 present the idea that it is not homogeneity or heterogeneity (deviance, variance) in individual differences that is positive or negative for units in organizations, but striking the balance between the two. That is, they argue that too much variability at the individual level in personality, for example, may be as bad as too much homogeneity, and the challenge is to balance the two to achieve both a feeling of being comfortable for members of the group and the tension due to variability that will generate ideas and innovation. I agree completely with this idea and would love to see research that explores where the balance point or points are and on which, for example, personality dimensions.

The evidence suggests, however, that organizations may not need to seek such balances. Thus, Ployhart, Weekley, and Baughman (2006) show that higher levels of some personality attributes at individual, job, and organizational levels of analyses are related to both satisfaction and performance at those different levels of analysis. They further show that for group levels of analysis, when there are higher levels of homogeneity (on emotional stability), the relationship between the group mean and performance at those levels is enhanced. So, homogeneity is a positive attribute at higher levels of analysis, which does not fit the ASA model prediction.

But their research was done on service workers, and the criterion was service performance. Their finding suggests that the ASA prediction that homogeneity impedes performance at group levels must be significantly modified, perhaps as a function of the outcome of interest. The homogeneity proposition might now say the following: When the group level outcome of interest is innovation, homogeneity (low variance, low deviance) in personality will negatively affect performance and group-level performance will be depressed.

Following Ployhart and Schmitt's multilevel frame of reference for ASA and staffing in general, we might also state a corollary homogeneity proposition as follows: When the outcome of interest is innovation, the relationship between relevant individual KSAOs and individual-level performance will be the same both in homogeneous and heterogeneous groups, but in the heterogeneous group, the average performance will be significantly higher. This proposition is shown pictorially in Figure 12.1. Note that this is not a moderator variable or boundary condition hypothesis, as it has to do only with intercept and not slope differences in the regression equation, an issue with which those of the validity generalization (VG) persuasion appear uninterested. That is, the VG literature showing no moderator effects for situations on individual predictor–criterion relationships should not be used to conclude that the situation has no effects on individual performance. So, in Figure 12.1, if one substitutes the labels "positive work climate" and "negative work climate" for the labels "heterogeneity in groups" and "homogeneity in groups," it is clear that there is an effect on individual performance, but not in the form of a moderator variable.

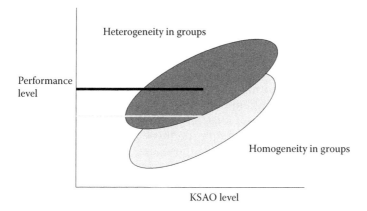

FIGURE 12.1. The proposed relationship between KSAOs and innovation performance at the individual level of analysis in both homogeneous and heterogeneous work groups where homogeneity and heterogeneity are with regard to the personality attributes within group.

Homogeneity From the Group Level Down

In Ployhart and Schmitt (Chapter 5) we see the homogeneity issue raised at different levels of analysis from the vantage point of individual differences—the traditional concern of personnel selection researchers. Contrast that approach with Chapter 10 by Nishii and Wright, which is concerned with including individual differences in the strategic management literature that formerly has been exclusively concerned with the organizational level of analysis. The juxtaposition of the two chapters is really quite wonderful because they approach the similar issue of variability but from two different research and practice traditions.

What is a bit disconcerting to me is that in both cases, the proposal is that homogeneity is good (Bradley, Brief, and Smith-Crowe in Chapter 9 and Bowen in Chapter 8 implicitly reach a similar conclusion, but more on them later). Thus, in Ployhart et al. (2006) it becomes clear that, at least for service workers, it is homogeneity of personality that relates to performance at different levels of analysis, and in Nishii and Wright the proposal is that homogeneity (this time of perceptions of human resources [HR] practices) is necessary for the HR practices–outcome relationship to be positive. Thus, following on the work of Bowen and Ostroff (2004), Nishii and Wright argue that homogeneity in the perception of HR practices works to corporate advantage when those HR practices are high in distinctiveness, consistency, and consensus.

The Nishii and Wright chapter is a tour de force in drilling down into the strategic human resources management literature in ways that (1) reveal the failure in that literature to entertain any individual differences whatsoever, and (2) detail ways that variability in the perceptions of HR practices can have a major moderating effect on the relationship between those HR practices and organizational performance. In a real sense, they introduce people in the form of individual differences in perceptions of HR practices into HR and show at least conceptually the importance of doing so.

Their chapter raised for me some very interesting questions I had not previously paid much attention to in my own writing. For example, are there personality attributes that are associated with individual differences in perceptions? For example, do those high on openness to experience see the world differently from those low on openness? When I asked myself that question, I deduced that the answer is "but of course." I did so based on clear evidence for this phenomenon with regard to emotional stability. Thus if one equates emotional stability (neuroticism) with positive and negative affectivity, it becomes clear that those higher on emotional stability are likely to see the world in more positive terms and be more upbeat, satisfied, and contented with that world. Ever since Joe Weitz (1952) showed that the telephone book is a more positive stimulus for some than for others, and that this positivity was related to job satisfaction, the research of Staw (e.g., 2004) and others (see Judge, 1992, for a review) has shown clearly these differences in perceptions.

I, of course, included perceptions in the original ASA model because perceptions of fit serve as a foundation for what follows in the model. What I had not done, and now must do, is consider more detailed issues with regard to perceptions and the role such perceptions play in the ASA model. In the next section I try to do this in a more comprehensive fashion facilitated by Chapter 6 by Newman, Hanges, Duan, and Ramesh, and Chapter 7 by Rentsch, Small, and Hanges.

ON THE ASA MODEL AND ORGANIZATIONAL CLIMATE

One of the delights of being an industrial–organizational (I–O) psychologist is the variety of issues on which you can work, all connected by the fact that they occur in the workplace—but all manner of behavior occurs in the workplace, so all is free game. I have worked on the following topics in detail: the ASA model with particular emphasis on personality and its role in organizations; organizational climate with a focus on the meaning of organizational practices for people there; and service quality, especially the relationship between service climate and customer satisfaction. What is the connection among these various topics?

People

People of similar sorts choose themselves in and out of organizations (ASA), people interact with one another and come to share perceptions of their workplace (climate), and employees and customers interact with one another and come to share their perceptions of the service relationship that ensues (strategic climate; Schneider, 1990). I propose that in all of these, similarity in people is a key to understanding the degree to which they will congregate together, see things similarly, and achieve a mutually reinforcing relationship.

Newman, Hanges, Duan, and Ramesh in Chapter 6 propose that networks are the foundation for climate perceptions in organizations and, further, that it is friendship networks based on demographic similarity that yield similarity in perceptions. As I and others (Bowen & Ostroff, 2004; Schneider, Salvaggio, & Subirats, 2002) have demonstrated, it is similarity in perceptions that yields the strong climates that relate climate means to outcomes. It is obvious to me that strong friendship networks are based not only on demographic similarity, but also on similarity in attitudes and opinions (Byrne, 1971; Festinger, 1954) and personality. In a very real sense, the friendship network is an ASA prediction when it is based on personality similarity. We can propose, for example, that people of similar personalities will form friendship networks and share common impressions of the settings in which they work, and these common perceptions are a function of numerous common experiences: common work, common out-of-work interests, common relationships with their leaders, similar socialization experiences, and so forth. To borrow from Rentsch, Small, and Hanges (Chapter 7), not all animals are cats, so not all animals see women as food, but cats will share common behaviors and impressions of women.

While Rentsch et al. seem to emphasize the latter issue, socialization, as causal in what they call similar (not shared or agreed on) climate perceptions, my thought, as noted earlier, is that people come to settings presocialized, that is, ready to be socialized to the setting due to their similar personal characteristics—it is not hard to socialize cats to be attackers. I would argue, for example, that police and firefighter organizations have the success they do in socializing their members (e.g., Van Maanen, 1975) because particular kinds of people choose to become police and firefighters. I would also predict that socialization of new recruits to the U.S. military has been far easier than it was in earlier times due to the fact that we now have an all-volunteer military with no draft to produce the variability that would yield difficulty in achieving uniform socialization.

In short, I propose that perceptions that are similar are a distal outcome of personality similarity, which in turn produces many common activities and experiences, and it is the actual and social sharing of activities and experiences that yields similarity in perceptions. We can thus also propose that similarity in personality yields common activities and experiences, not that similarity in personality causes similarity in perceptions. In other words, people do not just make up perceptions of their workplace out of their heads, but they have perceptions based on what actually happens to them, and it is what happens to them and around them that is related to their personalities. Just in case it is not clear, this is another variation on the formula $E = f(P, B)$; it is the kinds of people behaving in keeping with their own personal attributes that create the environments we observe and in which they behave.

Smith and I (Schneider & Smith, 2004) have indeed argued that personality is related to organizational climate (we used the term *culture*, but the same principle applies) because (1) founders of a particular personality enact specific organizational practices, (2) these practices attract particular kinds of personalities to the setting who further enact activities appropriate for them, and (3) the result is an organizational climate characterized by the type of personalities there. For example, accounting firms can be expected to be predominantly conscientious, advertising firms are more open to experience, sales firms are typified by emotional stability, and so forth. And within organizations, as Newman et al. and Rentsch et al. would find, sales people, advertising people, and accountants would tend to have their own friendship networks, their own specific variation on the organizational climate in which they work, and so forth. Holland (1997) showed this many years ago with regard to career interests, and there is evidence this will also apply to personality (Ployhart et al., 2006; Schaubroeck, Ganster, & Jones, 1998). Documentation of occupational subcultures in organizations has been known for many years (cf. Martin, 2002; Trice & Beyer, 1993), but while culture researchers attribute these subcultures to the occupation, Holland (1997) and I would attribute them to the personalities of the people who work in them. That is, the ASA model puts people and their personal attributes first.

A Methodological Note on Variance Within Organizations in Perceptions

A number of years ago I made a presentation called "Desperately Seeking Variance" at SIOP as part of a symposium on measuring climate. The essence of the paper was that sometimes we attempt to increase the variance in our measurements of phenomena, and sometimes we attempt to decrease variance in our measurements—and that since measurement is made by us, we can find variance or not find it where and when we want it. For decades, we attempted to reduce the within-group variance in our climate measures to legitimize within-group aggregation (Bliese, 2000), whatever the group. So, for organizational-level analyses, we wanted low within-organization variance and high between-group variance.

Even when we achieved low within-group and high between-group variance [through an F-test or ICC(1)], there was always accompanying within-group variance, identifiable when the measures focused on more specific or granular activities. When some researchers found within-group variability of this kind, it might have looked like climate was not an organizational phenomenon, but what it really showed is that variance always lurks if an attempt is made to measure it. It is only recently that climate researchers have sought this variance in climate perceptions and found it useful, as in the measurement of climate strength (Schneider et al., 2002). What Newman et al. show us is that this variance within is attributable to something itself that is measurable, friendship networks, and that the variance is not just error (something that Rentsch cleverly showed in her dissertation a number of years ago; Rentsch, 1990).

In summary, friendship networks in organizations yield shared climate perceptions that vary within organizations because people with similar personalities cluster together due to shared occupational/job personalities (Ployhart et al., 2006). The differences in perception are not directly attributable to personality, but to the situations those personalities create, and it is the perception of the different conditions or situations created that yields differences in climate perceptions.

A Conceptual Note on Cognition and Organizational Climate

Climate perceptions were not originally the foundation of climate research; climate was inferred based on the behavior of people in hypothetically different climates. So, for example, Lewin, Lippitt, and White (1939), who coined the term *social climates*, did not formally assess perceptions of the members of the boys' groups they studied, but inferred climate differences based on the differences in the behavior of boys who worked under different leadership styles. Emerging from the gestalt psychology tradition, climate referred to a pattern of behaviors that were predictable as an outcome of the situation created for members of groups led by different kinds of leaders. The pattern of behaviors was not all of the behaviors, but a sufficient number of important behaviors, such that a gestalt (whole) was apparent and to which meaning might be attached. But this approach was very labor intensive, and the notion of climate inferred perception, so climate assessment techniques were developed using survey methods such that by 1964 (Forehand & Gilmer, 1964) there was a sufficiently large literature to require a *Psychological Bulletin* review of it.

The key to the assessment of organizational (team) climate is the identification of a set of activities and experiences that captures the essence of the climate, not all activities and experiences. In much of what I have written in this section on climate, my focus has been on activities and experiences with meaning attached to those as an outcome. Rentsch et al. indicate that this approach to cognition in climate research is only one of three approaches. For example, meaning can be attached to objects (cat attaches meaning to woman as food), but in my way of thinking, this attaching meaning to objects is merely an application of meaning structures to previous activities and experiences. I address the issue of meaning in more detail later.

I was somewhat surprised that in neither the Hanges et al. nor the Rentsch et al. chapter were we introduced to the information processing literature (e.g., Lord & Foti, 1986) with which the authors are so familiar. This literature indicates (at least to me) that (1) people develop schemas over time and that (2) once developed, these schemas are highly resistant to change. In other words, if climate perceptions can be conceptualized as schema (all would agree this is no great conceptual leap), then it would be very difficult to change climate perceptions unless there were dramatic changes in activities and experiences over a relatively long period. And since the people in a setting share personal attributes and tend to see things similarly because they have created similar experiences, climate change, once again, requires different kinds of people because different kinds of activities and experiences only emerge from different kinds of people.

Summary

In retrospect, I did not do the work I should have done to make connections between my work on organizational climate and the ASA model, nor on the connections of the organizational climate research to more foundational issues regarding perceptions. While at a surface level I saw these connections, I did not do the scholarly work necessary to integrate them, and I am grateful to Hanges et al. and Rentsch et al. for showing how important cognition is to understanding climate perceptions. In the next section we will see that the ASA work and climate can be conceptually integrated against an important issue: the ethical (or "good") organization.

APPLICATIONS OF THE ASA MODEL AND CLIMATE THINKING

Another delight of I–O psychology (the first was the variety of issues on which one can work) is that as an academic, one can work on both more scholarly focused issues and issues that have relatively immediate salience for not only understanding behavior at work but for understanding organizational effectiveness. Further, one can even do work as a consultant to organizations to try to improve the way they function. I had the good fortune of doing all of these.

On the issue of organizational effectiveness, I have treated it both as a generic topic and as a strategic concept. By a generic topic I mean that within my writings on the ASA model I was not specific at all about what I meant by organizational effectiveness. In fact, the writings most often use terms like *organizational health* or *organizational demise*. The emphasis was then on survival in a global or generic sense, rather than with regard to specific outcomes. Conversely, in my work on service quality and service climate, a very specific organizational effectiveness outcome, customer satisfaction, has been the target of interest. In fact, as we will see later and as I noted earlier, I have not much integrated across the ASA and service climate work, but that certainly does not mean they should be kept on parallel rather than overlapping tracks.

And in some recent work I have tried preliminary integration (Salvaggio et al., in press), but more on that when I discuss Chapter 8 by Bowen.

For now I want to address Chapter 9 by Bradley, Brief, and Smith-Crowe, on the good organization. I want to use their chapter as a vehicle for introducing readers to the potential in both the ASA work and the climate work for focusing on specific outcomes of strategic interest to organizations. I want to show how the models and approaches can be used to effectively shed light on not only the people in organizations, but also what those people create for themselves and others.

The Good Organization: People and Environments

Bradley et al. present a thoughtful vantage point on what goodness is in organizations and how difficult it is to scale organizations as to goodness. The fact that it is difficult to scale organizations on goodness is not surprising, as we have difficulty scaling individuals on goodness—and performance of all kinds—as well. The difficulty emerges when one realizes that goodness, in organizations or in people, is not just in the outcomes achieved, but resides in the intentions, behavior, content of the displayed behavior, and principled reasoning (decisions) that lead to that behavior. This means that the goodness of a person or organization is defined as a process beginning with intentions and culminating in outcomes, and it is the entire process that is good, decent, or bad.

Further complicating issues is the point made by Bradley et al. that it is not just the people in an organization that make it bad, decent, or good, but the situation or context (strategy, structure, and culture) they create that is important. And from whence cometh these? From the organization's founder. By his or her decisions and behavior early in the life of the organization, attributions about the intentions of the founder become shared by members of the organization, setting in place a cycle of the process Bradley et al. say culminates in the goodness of the corporation. Of course, the prediction of goodness is not perfect, but probabilistic—as are all predictions—so there are no guarantees. Thus, as Bradley et al. outline, there are organizations that have a predominance of goodness yet still go bad due to circumstances.

And what might one of those circumstances be? One of those circumstances might be that, due to homogeneity, the organization becomes increasingly narrow in its focus and frames of reference and loses sight of what is required to remain good in the light of environmental change. Thus, the good corporation of the 1920s is not the good corporation of today because the definition of what is good has changed to include corporate social responsibility, "green," and providing for the health care of workers, issues that were not salient for the definition of goodness in the

1920s. The point is that intentions, behavior, decisions, and so forth, must be continually reevaluated and potentially renewed to maintain previous positions on any dimension of organizational consequence, including goodness. This means that while founders of successfully good organizations may have many admirable qualities and may create admirable organizations, the prediction would be that there can be too much of a good thing unless the good thing is constantly undergoing appropriate adaptation and change.

Based on this logic, I offer the following prediction: The longer an organization has been successful in how it functions and what it does, the more likely it is to fail. The implication is that organizations that fail to change and adapt and persist in what they do well that makes them successful, the more likely they are to fail in the future. Anyone who does not believe this prediction should carefully read Miller's (1990) book *The Icarus Paradox*. The Icarus metaphor is that the closer an organization comes to perfecting that which it does well (flying to the sun), the more likely the organization is to fail. Miller attributes this to time, but the ASA model attributes it to increasingly similar people working more and more diligently, getting everything that resulted in success perfected because that is who they are and what they do—and that is who is attracted to, selected by, and retained by organizations.

I have no doubt that organizations can also go from goodness to badness because of rotten apples slipping in, as Bradley et al. note. They also note, and I obviously agree, that the larger environment in which an organization functions can also have an effect. For example, Bradley et al. might predict that the astonishing bonuses earned by employees at Goldman-Sachs at the end of 2006 might stimulate people in other financial sector organizations to alter their intentions, behavior, and decisions such that they pay more attention to consequences and less to processes. In other words, academics are not likely to change from good to bad, but people at Morgan-Stanley are more likely to change than are academics (not that this is a prediction) because of the common membership and identity groups they share.

The Climate for Service

Bowen (Chapter 8) does a complete job of exposing readers to the world of services management and the various contributions to that field from marketing, operations management, and human resources/organizational behavior (HR/OB). I was lucky to stumble on services management early in my career (for the story of how this happened, see Schneider, 2000). I rather presciently deduced the thought that if one wished to understand the etiology of customer satisfaction, a good place to begin was with their experiences in dealing with organizations that served them. It was a short step to further deduce that if one wished to understand why customers had the experiences they had, a good place to start would be to ask employees who served them about the environment in which they worked. Voila, service climate.

The focus through more than 30 years of research on service climate has been on employee reports of the policies, practices, and procedures vis-à-vis service quality and the service behaviors that get rewarded, supported, and expected. In other words, I shifted the focus in employee surveys from what happens to employees to meet their own needs to what happens to and around employees that "tells" them to meet the needs of customers. To make a long story short, the evidence is now quite robust that employee reports about what they are told by the climate in which they work about the need to serve customers gets reflected in the customer satisfaction of those they serve (Dean, 2004; Schneider, Macey, & Young, 2006).

I was able for much of my career to have a split personality, at one and the same time devoting conceptual energies to the ASA model and to service climate without much integrating them. It is not that I saw them as separate, but that integrating across them for research purposes was very difficult. It was very difficult because of sample size requirements for quantitative research. Thus, to accomplish such research at the organizational or even unit level of analysis required large samples; unit- and organizational-level research is daunting, to say the least. This is especially true if the goal is to understand founder or employee effects on service climate or customer satisfaction as an outcome. There is anecdotal evidence for such founder and employee effects, with perhaps the two clearest cases being Walt Disney at the various theme parks and Herb Kelleher at Southwest Airlines.

Liao and Chuang (2004), however, accomplished the integration of the more individual personality issue and service climate studying multilevel influences on customer satisfaction in restaurants. They showed that the personality of waiters and waitresses as well as the service climate in which they worked jointly predicted customer satisfaction. In a more recent effort, again following the multilevel idea, but this time with a focus on the unit leader, Salvaggio et al. (in press) show that supermarket manager personality gets reflected in the service climate their subordinates experience. In this work, the personality of interest is core self-efficacy (Judge, Erez, Bono, & Thoresen, 2003), and results showed that employees in departments run by managers with more positive core self-efficacy reported a more positive service climate—and these effects for core self-efficacy were over and above those attributable to the various facets of the five factor model (FFM) of personality. We obviously require more work linking founder, leader, and employee personality to (1) the service climate such people create and (2) the customer satisfaction such personalities ultimately produce. As Ployhart and Schmitt (Chapter 5) noted, multilevel research is the way to do this.

CONCLUSION

Okay, you say, enough already. You have convinced me that the personality attributes of people in organizations have numerous multilevel effects that we have not much studied. Good. What I hope you understand from reading this book and my musings on the chapters is that you have to think simultaneously individual and organizational. The idea is not to abandon studies of individuals and their differences, but to ask how, in the natural world, individuals come to form collectivities with common attributes; study the individual and cross to the (unit and) organizational level. And then think about not only the positive correlates of the likely resulting homogeneity—like cooperation, cohesiveness, satisfaction, adjustment—but also the possible negative consequences for the collectivity—failure to sense when change is needed, persisting in doing what has worked in the past. I am absolutely convinced, as you can tell, that diversity of perspective is the key to long-term health for organizations, even given the almost uniform lack of findings in the present volume to support such a thought (see Boone et al., 2004, for an exception). Homogeneity may have its place at early stages in an organization's life and in social organizations, but in the later life of organizations that function in competitive business settings, diversity is necessary for survival. Why should it be different for organizations than for other living systems where diversity, for example, biodiversity, always wins?

There have been recent calls for more research on context (e.g., Johns, 2001; Rousseau & Fried, 2001) as a correlate of behavior in organizations. That is, of course, okay, but such pleas make it seem as if the context to be studied is somehow separate from the people in those contexts—that the context is separate from the people who inhabit them. If one follows ASA logic at all, this is a silly implicit conclusion, for without the people in them, organizations are not. It is the attributes of people in them that determine strategy, structure, and climate and make them the human systems they are; it is the human attributes that make them human systems and create the context some say we should study. How come no one wants scholars to report on and study the attributes of the people in organizations since they are the real context? After all, the people still make the place.

A PERSONAL NOTE

About a year after my colleagues at Maryland, Michele Gelfand, Paul Hanges, and Katherine Klein, held the festschrift for me (the basis for the present book), I awakened one night about 3:00 A.M., went to my computer, and sent them an e-mail expressing how meaningful the event had been for me. *Meaningful* does not quite capture the feelings of warmth, joy, pleasure, validation, and even wonder that I felt. It has been a wonderful ride, so *wonder* is the key term. I recently told friends in La Jolla about what

I was writing, and they looked at me with awe and said the following: "Wow, you mean they are doing this for you and you are still alive; how great." Indeed.

I am very proud of what I accomplished and the legacy I feel I carried on and left at Maryland. The legacy began not with me, but with Jack Bartlett, who is surely the father of the I–O program at Maryland. Jack opened up his mind, his extended bag of talents, his home, and his heart to the founding of the program, and all I did after he (and Irv Goldstein) brought me back was to continue his model. His model fits the ASA model to a T; he had strong values about people and their possibilities, which he demonstrated daily by involving his students in whatever he was doing, believed that he could attract like-minded souls (my good friend and colleague Irv Goldstein, for example) to perpetuate this high-involvement model, and believed in work spiced with levity and fun, and that anything was possible. The "anything was possible" turned into becoming one of the leading I–O psychology programs in the United States.

And we did over the years attract both wonderfully diverse faculty and students to the program. At various times during my tenure there we had Peter Dachler, Susan Jackson, Phil Bobko, David Schoorman, Rob Ployhart, and Ken Smith on the faculty; one can see the dedication we had to diversity in that gang. And the students? Too many to name here, but, to say the least, a diverse and interesting group (in terms of both demographics—gender and race—and personality). Near as I can tell, I directed on the order of 40 PhD dissertations, and every one of them was a thoroughly involving and rich immersion into the growth and development of a professional. I know I was demanding, an unforgiving nag (they would say a pain in the ass), unrelenting in my pushing of them to be the best they could be, and I delight to this day in their individual and collective accomplishments.

Before I quit I want to say something about my colleagues in the larger profession of I–O psychology. When students in the Maryland program would ask me what was best about I–O, my answer would always be the people in it. Special kinds of humans are attracted to, selected by, and stick with I–O in all of its guises (sounds like a theory to me). These special people are high on talent, low on arrogance, astonishingly hardworking for themselves and the Society for Industrial and Organizational Psychology, and joyful in the accomplishment of others. I thank my lucky stars almost every day that I stumbled on this field because the people in it have made it a great place to be.

And one last thought: my family. Those who have had the good fortune to meet and interact with and eat the wonderful food of Brenda quickly realize that she has been the source of inspiration and motivation for whatever I have accomplished. She pushed me to go to graduate school in the first place and then promoted going beyond the MBA to get the PhD. And she has supported me with good spirit and freedom to pursue this I–O thing and been by my side encouraging me in all that has followed.

Two of her major achievements, of course, are our son, Lee, and daughter, Rhody, who are two of the most interesting and lovable people I have had the good fortune to be with. On top of that, they have produced for us a troop of astonishingly beautiful and talented grandchildren—Boaz, Chloe, Cipora (CeCe), Gabriel, and Gillian. They all claim I squeeze them too hard and run when they see me coming—and I love it.

In final conclusion, I will borrow a line from Samuel Pepys: "And so to sleep."

ENDNOTE

1. For further insights into ASA, and staffing issues in general, as necessarily multilevel issues, see a summary of that work by Ployhart (2006).

REFERENCES

Aldrich, H. (1999). *Organizations evolving*. Thousand Oaks, CA: Sage.

Beckman, C. M., Burton, M. D., & O'Reilly, C. (2007). Early teams: The effects of team demography on VC financing and going public. *Journal of Business, 27*, 147–173.

Bliese, P. D. (2000). Within-group agreement, non-independence, and reliability: Implications for data aggregation and analysis. In K. J. Klein & S. W. J. Kozlowski (Eds.), *Multilevel theory, research, and methods in organizations: Foundations, extensions, and new directions* (pp. 349–381). San Francisco: Jossey-Bass.

Boone, C., Olffen, W. V., Witteloostuijn, A. V., & Brabander, B. D. (2004). The genesis of top management team diversity: Selective turnover among top management teams in Dutch newspaper publishing, 1970–1994. *Academy of Management Journal, 47*, 633–656.

Bowen, D. E., & Ostroff, C. (2004). Understanding HRM-firm performance linkages: The role of the "strength" of the HRM system. *Academy of Management Review, 29*, 203–221.

Bowers, K. S. (1973). Situationism in psychology: An analysis and critique. *Psychological Review, 80*, 307–336.

Burke, W. W. (2002). *Organization change: Theory and practice*. Thousand Oaks, CA: Sage.

Byrne, D. E. (1971). *The attraction paradigm*. New York: Academic Press.

Chatman, J. A. (1991). Matching people and organizations: Selection and socialization in public accounting firms. *Administrative Science Quarterly, 36*, 459.

Dean, A. M. (2004). Links between organisational and customer variables in service delivery: Evidence, contradictions, and challenges. *International Journal of Service Industry Management, 15*, 332–350.

Endler, N. S., & Magnusson, D. (Eds.). (1976). *Interactional psychology and personality*. New York: Hemisphere.

Festinger, L. (1954). A theory of social comparison process. *Human Relations, 7*, 117–140.

Forehand, G., & Gilmer, B. von H. (1964). Environmental variation in studies of organizational behavior. *Psychological Bulletin, 62*, 361–382.

French, J. R. P., Jr., Rodgers, W., & Cobb, S. (1974). Adjustment as person–environment fit. In G. V. Coelho, D. A. Hamburg, & J. E. Adams (Eds.), *Coping and adaptation* (pp. 316–333). New York: Basic Books.

Hackman, J. R., & Lawler, E. E., III. (1971). Employee reactions to job characteristics. *Journal of Applied Psychology, 55*, 259–286.

Holland, J. L. (1997). *Making vocational choices: A theory of careers* (3rd ed.). Odessa, FL: Psychological Assessment Resources.

Johns, G. (2001). In praise of context. *Journal of Organizational Behavior, 22*, 31–42.

Judge, T. A. (1992). The dispositional perspective in human resources research. In G. R. Ferris & K. M. Rowland (Eds.), *Research in personnel and human resources management* (Vol. 10, pp. 31–72). Greenwich, CT: JAI.

Judge, T. A., Erez, A., Bono, J. E., & Thoresen, C. J. (2003). The core self-evaluation scale: Development of a measure. *Personnel Psychology, 56*, 303–331.

Lewin, K., Lippitt, R., & White, R. K. (1939). Patterns of aggressive behavior in experimentally created "social climates." *Journal of Applied Psychology, 10*, 271–299.

Liao, H., & Chuang, A. (2004). A multilevel investigation of factors influencing employee service performance and customer outcomes. *Academy of Management Journal, 47*, 41–58.

Liao, H., Joshi, A., & Chuang, A. (2004). Sticking out like a sore thumb: Employee dissimilarity and deviance at work. *Personnel Psychology, 57*, 969–1000.

Lofquist, L. H., & Dawis, R. V. (1969). Adjustment to work. New York: Appleton-Century-Crofts.

Lord, R. G., & Foti, R. J. (1986). Schema theories, information processing, and organizational behavior, pp. 20–49. In H. P. Sims, Jr., & D. A. Gioia (Eds.), *The thinking organization*. San Francisco: Jossey-Bass.

Magnusson, D., & Endler, N. S. (Eds.). (1977). *Personality at the crossroads: Current issues in interactional psychology*. Hillsdale, NJ: Erlbaum.

Martin, J. (2002). *Organizational culture: Mapping the terrain*. Thousand Oaks, CA: Sage.

Miller, D. (1990). *The Icarus paradox: How exceptional companies bring about their own downfall*. New York: Harper Collins.

Mischel, W. (1968). *Personality and assessment*. New York: Wiley.

Pervin, L. A., & Lewis, M. (Eds.). (1978). *Perspectives in interactional psychology*. New York: Plenum.

Pfeffer, J. (1983). Organizational demography. In B. Staw & L. L. Cummings (Eds.), *Research in organizational behavior* (Vol. 5, pp. 299–357). Greenwich, CT: JAI Press.

Ployhart, R. E. (2006). Staffing in the 21st century: New challenges and strategic opportunities. *Journal of Management, 32*, 868–897.

Ployhart, R. E., Weekley, J. A., & Baughman, K. (2006). The structure and function of human capital mergence: A multilevel examination of the attraction–selection–attrition model. *Academy of Management Journal, 49*, 661–678.

Rentsch, J. R. (1990). Climate and culture: Interaction and qualitative differences in organizational meanings. *Journal of Applied Psychology, 75*, 668–681.

Rousseau, D. M., & Fried, Y. (2001). Location, location, location: Contextualizing organizational research. *Journal of Organizational Behavior, 22*, 1–13.

Salvaggio, A. N., Schneider, B., Nishii, L. H., Mayer, D. M., Ramesh, A., & Lyon, J. S. (in press). Manager personality, manager service quality orientation, and service climate: Test of a model. *Journal of Applied Psychology*.

Schaubroeck, J., Ganster, D. C., & Jones, J. R. (1998). Organization and occupation influences in the attraction–selection–attrition process. *Journal of Applied Psychology, 83*, 869–891.

Schein, E. H. (1992). *Organizational culture and leadership* (2nd ed.). San Francisco: Jossey-Bass.

Schneider, B. (1972). Individual preferences and organizational realities. *Journal of Applied Psychology, 56*, 211–217.

Schneider, B. (1975). Individual preferences and organizational realities revisited. *Journal of Applied Psychology, 60*, 459–465.

Schneider, B. (1978a). Person–situations selection: A review of some ability-situation interaction research. *Personnel Psychology, 31*, 281–297.

Schneider, B. (1978b). Implications of the conference: A personal view. *Personnel Psychology, 31*, 299–304.

Schneider, B. (1983a). Interactional psychology and organizational behavior. In L. L. Cummings & B. M. Staw (Eds.), *Research in organizational behavior* (Vol. 5, pp. 1–31). Greenwich, CT: JAI Press.

Schneider, B. (1983b). An interactionist perspective on organizational effectiveness. In K. S. Cameron & D. S. Whetten (Eds.), *Organizational effectiveness: A comparison of multiple models* (pp. 27–54). New York: Academic Press.

Schneider, B. (1987). The people make the place. *Personnel Psychology, 40*, 437–453.

Schneider, B. (1990). The climate for service: An application of the climate construct. In B. Schneider (Ed.), *Organizational climate and culture* (pp. 383–412). San Francisco: Jossey-Bass.

Schneider, B. (2000). Benjamin Schneider. In R. P. Fisk, S. J. Grove, & J. John (Eds.) *Services marketing self-portraits: Introspections, reflections, and glimpses from the experts* (pp. 173–188). Chicago: American Marketing Association.

Schneider, B. (2001). Fits about fit. *Applied Psychology: An International Review, 50*, 141–152.

Schneider, B., & Bartlett, C. J. (1968). Individual differences and organizational climate. I. The research plan and questionnaire development. *Personnel Psychology, 21*, 323–333.

Schneider, B., & Bartlett, C. J. (1970). Individual differences and organizational climate. II. Measurement of organizational climate by the multitrait-multirater approach. *Personnel Psychology, 23*, 493–512.

Schneider, B., Macey, W. H., & Young, S. A. (2006). The climate for service: A review of the construct with implications for achieving CLV goals. *Journal of Relationship Marketing, 5*, 111–132.

Schneider, B., Salvaggio, A. N., & Subirats, M. (2002). Climate strength: A new direction for climate research. *Journal of Applied Psychology, 87*, 220–229.

Schneider, B., & Smith, D. B. (2004). Personality and organizational culture. In B. Schneider & D. B. Smith (Eds.), *Personality and organizations* (pp. 347–370). Mahwah, NJ: Erlbaum.

Staw, B. M. (2004). The dispositional approach to job attitudes: An empirical and conceptual review. In B. Schneider & D. B. Smith (Eds.), *Personality and organizations* (pp. 163–192). Mahwah, NJ: Erlbaum.

Trice, H. M., & Beyer, J. M. (1993). *The cultures of work organizations*. Englewood Cliffs, NJ: Prentice Hall.

Tsui, A. S., & Gutek, B. A. (1999). *Demographic differences in organizations: Current research and future directions*. Lanham, MD: Lexington Books.

Van Maanen, J. (1975). Police organization: A longitudinal examination of job attitudes in an urban police department. *Administrative Science Quarterly, 20,* 207–228.

Walsh, W. B., Craik, K. H., & Price, R. H. (Eds.) (2000). *Person–environment psychology: New directions and perspectives* (2nd ed.). Mahwah, NJ: Erlbaum.

Weitz, J. (1952). A neglected concept in the study of job satisfaction. *Personnel Psychology, 5,* 201–205.

Williams, K. Y., & O'Reilly, C. A. (1998). Demography and diversity in organizations: A review of 40 years of research. In B. M. Staw & L. L. Cummings (Eds.), *Research in organizational behavior* (Vol. 20, pp. 77–140). Greenwich, CT: JAI Press.

Author Index

291

Subject Index

W

For Product Safety Concerns and Information please contact our EU
representative GPSR@taylorandfrancis.com Taylor & Francis Verlag GmbH,
Kaufingerstraße 24, 80331 München, Germany

Printed and bound by CPI Group (UK) Ltd, Croydon, CR0 4YY

08/05/2025

01864472-0001